Known Military Dead

During

The American Revolutionary War

1775 - 1783

Ex-Lieut. Clarence Stewart Peterson, M. A.

CLEARFIELD

Originally published
Baltimore, Maryland, 1959

Reprinted
Genealogical Publishing Co., Inc.
Baltimore, Maryland
1967

Reprinted for
Clearfield Company, Inc. by
Genealogical Publishing Co., Inc.
Baltimore, Maryland
1990, 1992, 1993, 1994, 1997, 1999, 2004

Library of Congress Catalogue Card Number 64-20411
International Standard Book Number: 0-8063-0275-5

Made in the United States of America

CLARENCE STEWART PETERSON

Baltimore, Maryland

Box 342

———

Author of:

Date 1959

F O R E W O R D

Gustavus Adolphus College
St. Peter, Minnesota

Those who fall in battle are often "nameless". On the battlefield
names are less important than numbers. It is different in homes and
families. Even the wardead must be recorded and reported by name.
Otherwise they could not be placed in the families and communities
from which they came, and who will grieve their passing.

The author has performed a service of love in making a thorough
study of those who died in the Spanish-American War and the Philippines
Insurrection 1896-1901 and compiling a complete and authentic list of
their names. He has already done a similar service for those who fell
in the War of 1812 in his "Known Military Dead During The War of 1812",
and those who fell in the Mexican War in his "Known Military Dead During
The Mexican War 1846-48".

A review of the "Acknowledgements" will give some indication of
the amount of research which has been involved in preparing this list of
names. On such thorough and detailed investigation does our assured
knowledge of the past rest. The "Introduction" further documents
the thoroughness of this investigation.

We are indebted to the Author for a growing list of significant
specialized studies which have made historical data accessible for
the more general student of history. The thoroughness of the research makes these studies completely reliable and extremely useful.

Edgar M. Carlson

President, Gustavus Adolphus College,

St. Peter, Minnesota

                    Maj. Gen. U. S. Grant, 3rd
                       College Hill
                       Clinton, N.Y.
                       October 31, 1957

Lieut. Clarence Stewart Peterson
P.O. Box 342,
Baltimore, Maryland

My dear Mr. Peterson:

          In general I can only say that such lists if accurate
and comprehensive, will doubtless be a great convenience to
many people looking up the public services of their forefathers,
and will save them the time and expense of a search through the
official records in the National Archives or Departmental
files.

                              Sincerely yours,

                              U. S. Grant, 3rd

(Author's note: Maj. Gen. U. S. Grant 3rd is the grandson of
the Union General U. S. Grant in the Civil War)

COMMONWEALTH OF PENNSYLVANIA
Governor's Office
Harrisburg
May 6, 1959

F O R E W O R D

It is fitting that Pennsylvanians should take a particular interest in a work
on the Known Military Dead During the American Revolutionary War, 1775-1783,
for the Commonwealth of Pennsylvania had a very important part in that
conflict, and a large proportion of those who died to create the nation were
sons of Pennsylvania.

William Penn and the early settlers of Pennsylvania came from beyond the
seas to establish a Commonwealth where they and their children might enjoy
the blessings of liberty and peace. Pennsylvania has always been peace-
loving, in keeping with the tradition handed down from her founders, and yet
her people have often fought to protect and maintain their free institutions.
They have realized that liberty must be fought for, even while they looked
forward to the ultimate triumph of the founders' ideals of peace.

Pennsylvania was third in population among the American colonies in 1776,
exceeded only by Virginia and Massachusetts. Ranking first in agriculture,
and beginning the development of important manufacturing industries,
Pennsylvania's adherence to the revolutionary cause was eagerly sought by
the leaders of New England and Virginia. Her capital, Philadelphia, the
greatest trading center of the colonies, became the meeting place of the
Continental Congress and the birthplace of the Declaration of Independence.

Many were the Revolutionary battles which took place on Pennsylvania soil,
Brandywine, Germantown, Whitemarsh, Paoli -- to name but a few. Many
Pennsylvanians fell here, as did men from other states; and many other
Pennsylvanians died in battles from Quebec to Georgia.

We shall never know exactly how many fought or exactly how many died. The
armed forces of Pennsylvania during the American Revolution were raised
according to many different plans as the occasion demanded, and as the ideas
of Congress and the General Assembly changed and developed. As a result, it
is well-nigh impossible to state the number of Pennsylvanians who served in
the Revolutionary War. By totaling all the available figures, with estimates
where records had been lost, the historian Egle once arrived at a hypothetical
total of 120,514 men from Pennsylvania in that war. Still more difficult is
the task of computing the number who died in the armed services in the
course of this struggle for freedom and independence. We are therefore
especially indebted to Mr. Peterson for his compilation of the Known Military
Dead During the American Revolutionary War, 1775-1783.

                                        DAVID L. LAWRENCE

May 4, 1959

STATE OF INDIANA
Executive Department
Indianapolis   4

June 1, 1959

Ex-Lieut, Clarence Stewart Peterson, M. A.,
Box 342,
Baltimore 3, Maryland

Dear Lieut. Peterson:

As the nineteenth star in the flag of our country,
Indiana was admitted into the Union in 1816.
Thus this sovereign state is old enough to have
buried within its borders numerous veterans of the
American Revolution, as well as some of the heroes
who fell in combat during that struggle. An outpost
of the Colony of Virginia, we too had our battles,
relatively important to the entire war but very
important in the winning on the frontier.

Therefore, Indiana is rightfully represented in
this collection of the known military dead, and all
those who cherish our country's historic beginnings
will welcome the results of your painstaking work.

                              Very truly yours,

                              Harold W. Handley

                              Governor of Indiana

HWH:vb

STATE OF NORTH CAROLINA
Executive Department
Raleigh
June 3, 1959

Mr. Clarence Stewart Peterson
Box 342
Baltimore 3, Maryland

Dear Mr. Peterson:

Thank you for informing me of your plans for
publishing your book on "Known Military Dead During
the American Revolutionary War 1775-1783."

Such a book should serve a most useful purpose
in providing needed information concerning the subject of
great historical importance.

With best wishes, I am

Sincerely,

Luther H. Hodges

LHH;rh

FOREWORD (continued)

EXECUTIVE DEPARTMENT

Annapolis, Maryland

May 5, 1955

Mr. Clarence Stewart Peterson
Baltimore 3, Maryland

Dear Mr. Peterson:

Following is brief foreword to your "Known Military Dead During the

American Revolutionary War of 1775-1783":

Research into statistics and the compiling of lists
are tedious tasks, but they are essential to the detail
and accuracy of history.

Orators and writers, both of prose and poetry, need,
at times, the statistics and the lists. They are valuable
for students and often necessary to the work of essayists.

Frequently such compilations are the important family
links that figure prominently in the settling of estates,
the obtaining of birth certificates, the location of lost
relatives, and many other occurrences in the lives of a
community, a State or a Nation.

It is fortunate, then, that the minds of some few
among us turn with determination and even with enjoyment
to that which most of us seek to avoid - the compiling of
the valuable and useful lists.

Clarence Stewart Peterson is such a compiler. This,
his latest work - "Known Military Dead During the War of
1775-1783" -- is a work that required very extensive research and time consuming inquiry. Like many of his earlier
productions it is a worthy and admirable addition to the
Nation's History.

Sincerely,

Theodore R. McKeldin

Governor

OFFICE OF THE GOVERNOR
State Capitol
Salem

Mark O. Hatfield   August 28, 1959
Governor

In this volume Clarence S. Peterson has made a real

contribution to history because he has taken on what must

have been an assignment of painful digging. With his

customary persistence he has brought from the past what may

be the only list of heroes during that eight-year period

of the Revolutionary War. Occasionally we are all too

quick to forget those who have given their all in battle

or otherwise during wartime service. We who are heirs of

the democracy these men fought and died for are the debtors

to Mr. Peterson for making their sacrifice known to the

generations yet unborn.

1

ACKNOWLEDGEMENT

In the preparation of "Known Military Dead During The American
Revolutionary War 1775-1783", special acknowledgement and thanks is due the
staffs in the National Archives, War Records Sections; the Chiefs of Military
History, Dept. of Defense; the staff of the Library of Congress, all of
Washington, D. C.

Special acknowledgement and thanks is also due the Adjutant Generals of
the United States and of the thirteen original states that fought the American
Revolutionary War; the state and local historical societies and libraries of
these thirteen states; the national and state officials of military parks
and monuments in these thirteen states; and all aid given by colonial and
patriotic organizations, public and private.

In this research, splendid assistance therein was given the author,
on personal visits, by the staffs of the Bridgeport, Connecticut Public
Library; New York Historical Society Reference Library; the New York Public
Library, and Columbia University Library, New York City; Newark City Library
and New Jersey State Historical Society Library, Newark, New Jersey; Phila-
delphia City Library and Penn. State Historical Society Library, Philadelphia,
Pa.; Delaware Archives, Wilmington, Delaware; Johns Hopkins University
Library, Peabody Library; the Maryland Historical Society Library, and the
Enoch Pratt Free Library, Baltimore, Maryland; the Richmond City Library and
the Virginia State Historical Society Library, Richmond, Virginia.

Bibliography

- Register To the Records Relating To Military Service - 1775-83. 1 vol.
- Roster of Connecticut Soldiers 1776-83. 1 vol.
- " " Delaware " 1776-83. 1 vol.
- " " Massachusetts " Crane's Reg. of Art. 1776-80. 1 vol.
- " " New Jersey Soldiers and Spencers and Forman's Reg. 1775-80. 1 vol.
- " " New York Soldiers and Livingston's and Malcolm's Reg.
      1776-83. 2 vol.
- " " North Carolina Soldiers 1776-83. 1 vol.
- " " Pennsylvania Soldiers 1776-81. 1 vol.
- " " Rhode Island " Hanssegger's German Reg. 1776-83. 1 vol.
- " " South Carolina Solders 1775-83. 1 vol.
- " " Colonel Hazen's 2nd Canadian Reg. and of Artifices 1776-83. 1 vol.
- " " Sheldon's & Moylan's Dragoons and Lee's Legion. 1 vol.
- Rolls of Officers of The Continental Army 1775-79. 1 vol.
- Register To Muster Rolls. 1775-82. 2 vols.
- Daughters of The American Revolution Lineage Book. 166 vols.
- Daughters of The American Revolution Yearbook. 1890-19.
- National Register of The Sons of The American Revolution
- Yearbook of The Society Composed of Descendants of The Men of The
      Revolution by Henry Hall.
- Director of The National Society of The Daughters of The American
      Revolution.
- Founding and Organization of The Daughters of The American Revolution.
      By Mrs. Flora A. Darling.
- History and Organization and Work of The National Society Daughters of
      The American Revolution.

2

- Sons of The American Revolution yearbooks from: Dist. of Columbia; New
  Jersey; Kentucky; Mass.; New York; Mich.; Missouri; Md.
- U. S. Pension Lists
- Navy Members of The Society of The Cincinnati - By Bryce Metcalf.
- Navy Files Revolutionary War In National Archives.
- Records of U. S. Land Bounty Grants To Revolutionary War Veterans
- Revolutionary Solders Buried In Indiana - By Margaret R. Waters
- Vt. Rev. War Rolls - By J. E. Goodrich.
- Rev. Soldiers Buried In Ill.   By Mrs. Harriet J. Walker.
- The Lebanon Conn. War Office 1891 S.A.R.
- Dunmore's War - By Thwaites & Kellogg - Pa.
- Hist. of Col. Edmund Phinney's 18th Cont. Reg. - N. Goold.
- Pa. S.A.R. - Fort Necessity and Shrines.
- Amer. Rev. Soldiers In Franklin Co; Pa. by V. S. Frederick.
- Hist. of Middlesex Co. N. J. By John Patrick Wall & H. E. Pickersgill
- S. Car. In The Revolution By Sara Ervin.
- Officers of The Continental Army Killed and Died In Service by Ray Alexander
- Orderly Books N.Y. 2nd & 4th Reg. 1778,1780,1783.
- List of Classes For Jan. 1781 Culpepper Co. Va.
- Watertown Mass. Soldiers In Colonial Wars and The American Revolution.
  By George F. Robinson
- Va. Inf. 6th Reg. 1776-78.
- Vital Records of Sandisfield, Mass. - Revolutionary Soldiers. By Eligur
  Yale Smith.
- Va. Inf. 6th Reg. Inf. 1776 Revolutionary War - By General Andrew Lewis.
- Revolutionary Soldiers Buried In Elkhart Co. Ind. - Mrs. F. C. Wherly.
- N.Y. - D.A.R. Pilgrimages To Graves of 126 Revolutionary Soldiers.
- Roster of Revolutionary Soldiers In Ga. By Mrs. Ettie T. McCall.
- N.C. - D.A.R. Roster of Soldiers From N. Car. In The Amer. Revolution.
- Martyrs Of The Revolution In British Prison Ships. By Geo. Taylor.
- Prisoners of War In Britain 1756-1815. Francis Abell.
- American Prisoners of The Revolution - Mrs. Danske Dainbridge
- Biographical Sketches of The Generals of The Continental Army Of The
  Revolution - By M. T. Leiter
- Orderly Book of Col. Wm. Henshaw of The Amer. Army 1775.
- Mutiny In January. By Carl C. Van Doren
- Supplies To Revolutionary Soldiers of Onandoga. By Wm. M. Beauchamp.
- Revolutionary War Records. By Gains M. Brumbaugh.
- U. S. Pay Dept. War Dept. Pierces Reg. - Reg. of Certificates - Issued,
  In D.A.R. 17th Report 1913-14.
- U. S. War Dept. - Letter From Secy. of War on Pensions - 672 p. 24 cm.
  16 Cong. 1st Less House Doc. #55
- Records of The Revolutionary War. By William Thos. R. Saffell.
- Rev. War Soldiers Buried In Clark Co. Ohio - O. Hist. Quart. Jan. 28
- Butler's Rangers, The Rev. War. By Benj. E. Cruikshank.
- Pulaski's Legion Roll - Md. Hist. Mag. Sept. 18
- Valley Forge Orderly Book of Gen. Geo. Weedon.
- Ala. Hist. Socy. Reprint ¼ 26.
- Hist. of Columbia County, N.Y. by Franklin Ellis.
- Pa. Mag. Vol 27. 1903
- Soldiers of Blair County, Penn. By Floyd G. Hoenstine.
- Pa. Archives Ser. #6
- Publications of Onondaga Hist. Assn. New York
- Soldiers of The Amer. Revolution, Chatanqua Co; New York
- Revolutionary Soldiers Buried In Cattaraugus Co; New York
- Memorial To Revolutionary Soldiers In Clinton, New York

- Revolutionary Soldiers of Summit Co. Ohio. By Mrs. M. W. Franz.
- History of Sevier Co. Ten. By Fred Matthews.
- Soldiers and Sailors of Lower St. George, Me. In The Revolution
    By F. B. Miller.
- Records of The Rev. Soldiers Buried In Mich. By D.A.R
- Soldiers and Sailors of The Revolutionary War Whose Graves Are Marked
    By the S.A.R.
- Roster of Graves or Monuments To Patriots of 1775-1783. By Com. S.A.R.
- Revolutionary Soldiers Buried In Ind. - 75. By D.A.R.
- Old #4 Chap. D.A.R. 1919-20 Charlestown, N. H.
- The Dist. of Columbia In The Revolution. By S. M. Ely - Col. Hist. Socy.'18
- N. Y. Hist. Socy. Collections 1914.
- Historical Memoranda - Mass. S.A.R. 1897-99-1901
- Kings Mountain Men - K. K. White.
- Revolutionary Soldiers In Ala. - Dept. of Archives & Hist.
- Register of Ancestors, Ga. - D.A.R.
- Revolutionary Soldiers Living In Ga. In 1827-28
- Pension Records of Revolutionary Soldiers Who Removed To Florida. By
    Jessie Robinson Fritot.
- Lee W. W. - Barkhamsted Men (Conn) In Various War 1775-1865.
- Rockwell, Geo. L. - Hist. of Ridgefield, Conn.
- Richter, V. W. - General Washingtons Body Guards.
- Coburn, Frank W. - The Battle of Apr. 19, 1775.
- Ohio Adj. Gen. Office - Soldiers of The American Revolution Buried in Ohio.
- Johnston, Henry P. - Yale and Her Honor Roll In The Revolution 1775-1783.
- Godfrey, Carlos E. - The Com. In Chiefs Guard In The Rev. War.
- Willis, George L. - Hist. of Shelby Co. Ky.
- Vermont Hist. Socy. Proceedings 1903-06.
- Muster Rolls of Pembroke Mass. During Revolutionary War.
- Official Records of Gov. Robt. Dinwiddie - Va. Hist. Socy, 1883
- Landers, Col. H. L. (F.A.) Yorktown, The Va. Campaign.
- Smith, Frank - History of Dedham, Mass.
- Newton, Wm. Monroe - Hist. of Barnard, Vt. With Genealogies.
- Doane, Gilbert Harry - Searching For Your Ancestors
- Rogers, Rev. Wm. - R. I. Historical Tracts #7.
- Vt. Hist. Socy. Proceedings 1861-2.
- Huguenots In Va., Collections Va. Hist. Socy. Vol V.
- Official Letters of Alex. Spotswood Lt. Gov. Vol I Va. Hist. Socy.
- Custer, Milo. - Soldiers of The Revolution Buried In McLean Co., Ill.
- Ray, Alex. Officers Of The Continental Army, Killed or Died In Service
- Maurer, Jean - Berks Co. Pa. Revolutionary Soldiers.
- Revolutionary Soldiers Receipts For Ga. Bounty Grants By Georgia.
- Hoyt, Max E. Index of Revolutionary War Pension Applications.
- Naval Records of The American Revolution 1775-1788.
- Hitman, Francis Bernard - Historical Register of Officers of The Continental
    Army April 1775 to Dec. 1783.
- Webster, Daniel - New England's Dead.
- Orderly Book and Journals Kept by Conn. Men In The Rev. War 1775-78.
- Conn. Men In The War of The Rev. 1812 etc.
- Hall, Charles S. Life & Letters of Maj. Gen. Samuel H. Parsons of
    Continental Army
- Hinman, Royal R. - Hist. Collection of Records Vol. VIII, XII - files of
    Conn. In Rev.
- Middlebrook, L.F. - Hist. of Maritime Conn. In The Rev.
- S.A.R. - Revolutionary Characters of New Haven.
- Peters, Samuel A. - A General Hist. of Conn. etc.

4

- The Public Records of The State of Conn.
- Rogers, Ernest Elias - Conn. Naval Office at New London In The Revolution.
- Conn. State Library - List of Rev. War Dead And About 25 Towns in card file.
- Pension Records. Conn. Rev. Solders. Draper Index 1917.
- Bellas, Henry H. - Hist.of Del. State Society Of The Cincinnati.
- Socy. of Cincinnati, Del - Unveiling of Monument.
- Rodney, Caesar - Letters.
- Whitely, William G. - Revolutionary Soldiers of Del.
- Ward , Christopher - The Delaware Continentals
- Delaware Archives Vol. I - III
- Georgia's Roster Of The Revolution Officers & Men,
- Revolutionary Records of The State of Ga. By Ga. Leg.
- Drayton, J. Memoirs of American Revolution
- Fleming, Berry - Autobiography of a Colony
- Ga. Journal of The House Assembly 1781-4 Rev. Rec. V. 3
- Moultrie, William - Memoirs of The American Revolution
- Vols. 6 & 3, 1771-82 Ga. Proceedings & Min. of Governor and Council 1754-82
- Minutes of Executive Council 1878-85.
- Steiner, B. C. - Muster Rolls & Other Records of Md. Troops In The Rev.
- Olson, Mrs. Luella Sinclair - List of 153 Soldiers From Md. Pensioners
- Steiner, B. C. - Western Maryland In The Revolution.
- Ward, Christopher - War Of The Revolution.
- Unpublished Revolutionary Records of Maryland Compiled By Margaret R.Hodges.
- McSherry, James - History of Maryland
- Field, Thomas Warren - Historic and Antiquarian Scenes In Brooklyn p.p. 81-88
- Memoirs of Late John Eager Howard.
- Guilford Battle Ground Co.
- Md. Loyalist Reg. Orderly Book Of The "Md. Loyalist Reg. In The Revolutionary
  War.
- Special Session - Centennial Com. Bull. 1926
- Dorsey, Ella Loraine - Smallwood's Immortals.
- Washington Irving's Life of Washington.
- Robt. Purviance - Balto. Town During Rev.
- Md. Council of Safety - Journal of Correspondence of Md. Council of Safety.
  Vol. 11, 12, 16, 21, 43, 45, 47, 48.
- U. S. War Dept. - Md. Pension Roll.
- Newman, Harry W. - Md. Rev. Records - Pension Claims, Bounty Land Application
- Dorsey, Ella Loraine, Smallwood's Immortals.
- Balch, Thomas - Papers On The Md. Line In The Rev.
- Smith, John S. - Memoir of Baron DeKalb p.p. 31-32.
- Gunby, Andrew A. - Col. Gunby Of The Md. Line.
- The Yorktown Sesqui Centennial.
- Chaplains & Clergy Of The Revolution
- Judson, L. C. - Logas & Heroes of The Amer. Revolution
- Generals Of The Continental Army Of The Rev.
- Green, F. M. - Heroes of The Amer. Revolution
- Revolutionary Soldiers in The Rev. Dept. of Archives
- Brumbaugh, Gains M. - Revolutionary Records of Md.
- Archives of Maryland - Vol. XVIII Muster Rolls and Other Records of Service
  of Maryland Troops In The American Revolution 1775-1783
- Mass. Soldiers and Sailors In The Rev. War By Secy. of Commonwealth
- Brown, Abram E. - Beneath Old Hearth-Stones.
- Goold, Nathan - Col. J. Scamman's 30 Reg. of Foot 1775
- Lincoln, Rufus - Papers of Capt. Rufus Lincoln.

- Martyn, Charles - Life of Artemus Ward.
- Taylor, Robt. J. - Western Mass. In The Revolution
- A. Memorial of The American Patriots Who Fell At Bunker Hill.
- Batchellor, A. S. - Misc. Rev. Documents of N. H.
- Hammond, I. W. - Rolls of N. H. Soldiers In The Rev. War.
- Kidder, Frederic - Hist. of 1st N. H. Reg. In The Rev. War.
- Upton, Richard F. - Revolutionary New Hampshire.
- Socy. of The Cincinnati, N. H.
- Bouton, Nathaniel - Documents. - Records of N. H. In the Rev. War. Vol 8 & 10
- N. H. State & Provincial Papers Vol. XIV - XVII. Rev. Doc. Vol. 30
                By I. W. Hammond & A. S. Batchellor
- D. A. R. - Rev. Soldiers Graves In Del. To Smithsonian 1944-46.
- Documents Relating To New Jersey Revolutionary Wer History.
- Official Register of New Jersey Officers & Men In The Revolutionary War.
- Furman, Moore Q. M. General - Letters.
- Kirkwood, Robert - Journal & Order Book.
- Sons Of The Amer. Revolution - Yearbook.
- Duer, Wm. Alexander - Life of Revolutionary War Maj. General
- Five Volumes - Documents Relating to Revolutionary History of New Jersey.
- New York In The Revolution Compiled By Comptroller E. C. Knight.
- Jones, Thomas - Hist. of New York During The Revolutionary War
- New York Public Papers of George Clinton
- Bliven, Bruce - Battle for Manhattan
- Johnston, Henry P. - Campaign of 1776 Around New York and Brooklyn
- Collections of The New York Historical Socy. Muster and Pay Rolls of The
                War Of The Revolution
- N. Y. State Archives Vol. I Dead Due Land In Military Tract
- Calendar of Historical Manuscripts Relating To The War of The Revolution.
- Cooke, Wm. D. (compiled) Rev. War Hist. of N. C. In 3 lectures
- Fitch, Wm. E. - Some Neglected Hist. of N. C. In The Rev. etc.
- Caruthers, Eli W. - Interesting Revolutionary Incidents.
- Gilmore, James R. - The Rear Guard of The Revolution.
- Connor, R. D. W. - Revolutionary Leaders of N. C.
- Daves, Edward G. - Md. & N. C. In 1780-81 Campaign
- Davis, Charles Lukens   Brief Hist. of North Carolina Troops In The
                Revolutionary War.
- Fanning, David - Account of Adventures In N. C.
- Narrative of Col. David Fanning.
- Murphy, Archibald Debow - Papers.
- General Joseph Graham - Papers of N. C. In The Rev. War.
- Moultrie, Wm. - Memoirs of The American Revolution Of North Carolina &
                South Carolina.
- Whitaker, Bessie Lewis - Provincial Council of Com. of Safety In N. C.
                Vol. 4 Hist. of Rev. p.p. 95-96
- State Records of N. C. - Vols. 9, 16, 17, p.p. 1002-1197 Index
- Stille, Charles J. - Maj. Gen. Anthony Wayne & Pa. Line In Cont. Army.
- Blan, Theodore Weber - Washington At Valley Forge.
- Shimwell, Lewis S. - Border Warfare In Pa. During Rev. War.
- Papers Relating To Pa. Navy 1775-1781.
- Memorandum Book of Com. and Council of Safety.
- Thomson, Charles - Pa. Papers Vol. 11.
- Wister Sarah - Journal.
- Persons Who Took Oath of Allegiance To Pa. 1776-94.
- Officers of Pa. In The Revolution 1776.
- Westcott, Thompson - Took Oaths of Allegiance 1777-89.

- Journals and Diaries of Revolution 1775-83.
- Pa. In The Revolutionary War 1775-83.
- Egle, Wm. H. - Muster Rolls of Navy, Etc. 1775-83
- Linn, John B. - Minutes of Pa. Bd. of War 1777
-   "   "   "   - Pa. In The Revolutionary War 1775-83
- Cowell, Benj. - Spirit of '76 In Rhode Island
- Revolutionary Correspondence 1775-1782- Letters By Governor
  Murray, Thomas H. - Irish Rhode Islanders In The Revolution
- Rider, Sidney S. - Attempt To Raise Regiment of Slaves in R. I.
- R. I. Revolutionary Correspondence 1775-1783.
- Smith, Joseph J. - Civil & Military History of R. I. 1647-1800
- David, Ebenezer - A R. I. Chaplain In The Revolutionary War.
- Brown, Tarleton - Memoirs of A Captain In The Revolutionary War.
- Salley, A. S. Jr. - Documents In S. C. In The Rev. War.
- Uhlendorf, Bernhard A. - Siege of Charleston - Letters
- Documents Relating To Hist. of S. C. In The Rev. War.
- Boddie, William W. - Marion's Men.
- James, W. D. - Life of Brig. Gen. Francis Marion.
- McCrady, Edward - Hist. of S. C. In the Rev.
- De Sanssure, W. G. - Names of Officers In S. C. Reg. In Rev.
- Draper, Lyman C. - King's Mountain and Its Heroes.
- Johnson, Joseph - Traditions and Reminiscences of The Revolution In the
  South.
- Jones, Charles C. - Sgt. William Jasper.
- Ramsay, David - History of Revolution In South Carolina.
- Sally, Alexander S. - Hist. of Orangeburg Co. S. C.
- Simms, Wm. G. - Hist. of S. C. From Discovery To State.
- Singer, Charles G. - S. C. Confederation.
- S. C. Com. of Navy Bd. - Journal of S. C. Navy 1776-80.
- Orderly Books of Capt. R. Gamble and Maj. W. Heath In 2nd and 3rd Va. Reg.
  Rev. War 1777-79.
- McAllister, Jos. T. - Index To Saffells List of Va. Soldiers In The Rev.
- Brumbaugh, Gains M. - Revolutionary War Records
- Va. State Lib. Dept. of Archives and History List of Revolutionary Soldiers
  of Va. 8th & 9th Annual Report.
- Gwathney, John H. - Historical Register of Va. In Rev.
- Burgess, Louis A. - Va. Soldiers of 1776.
- Orderly Book of Capt. Robert Gamble of 2 Va. Reg. Aug.-Nov. 1779
- Orderly Book of Maj. W. Heath of 3 Va. Reg. May-July 1777
- Va. State Lib. - List of Revolutionary Soldiers of Va.
- Stewart, Robert A. - History of Va. Navy In Revolution.
- S.A.R. Ky. Yearbook.
- Hart Freeman Hansford - Valley of Virginia In Revolution
- Wright, Marcus J. - Lafayettes Campaigns In Va. 1781.
- Campbell, Charles - History of Colony of Ancient Dominion of Va.
- Campbell, John W.   "   " Va. to 1781.
- McAllister, Joseph T. - Va. Militia In Revolutionary War.
- Nottingham, Stratton - Revolutionary Soldiers & Sailors from Nottingham
  County, Va.
- Nottingham   "   "   "   "   from Accomack Co.Va.
- Nottingham   "   "   "   "   "   Lancaster Co. Va.
- Eckenrode, H. J. - List of Revolutionary Soldiers of Va. - 8th, 9th Annual
  Reports, Va. State Library 1911 and 1912.

INTRODUCTION

No evidence is available that any previous attempt has ever been made publicly or privately to prepare a complete list of the known military dead during the American Revolutionary War 1775-1783. Such a list probably has been prepared, but if so, it appears to have been lost.

This list was never intended for publication and I planned to use this only for personal reference. But during this research in libraries and archives the suggestion was made to me repeatedly that this list of Known Military Dead During The American Revolutionary War 1775-1783 is of special value and should be published.

No complete list of the military dead of any war has ever been made. This is not a complete list. There are always the missing who were lost forever in every war. So the Americans have the Tomb To The Unknowns in the Arlington National Cemetery in Virginia. Some listed herein died after their military service in the Rev. War but during the war, some served several enlistments and in different organizations, one in twelve.

It is sincerely hoped, that in preparing this list of the Known Military Dead During The American Revolutionary War, some names have been rescued of those of long ago long since forgotten, and forever enshrined in the memories and souls of our ever grateful American people.

"History is but the life stories of us all. We meet and pass as ships that pass in the night with lights burning on port and starboard sides, but those who come after us may find a guide for the future pathway of life. Such a compass and chart have been left us by the Fathers of our Republic".

My search for military war dead began in 1939 before the outbreak of World War II. I found no list of military war dead for any of our six major wars or any of the minor ones. There are lists of those who died in the U. S. Navy and Marines in World War I. Since then lists of the known Military dead of World War II and the Korean War have been compiled Casualties given vary, 2000 are said to have died in British prisons in New York and 11,000 on one British prison ship alone, - the horrible Jersey.

The list of known military dead in the Revolutionary War was the most difficult to prepare of all four I have compiled on my spare time the past twenty years. This difficulty resulted from the destruction of government military records during a fire in Washington, D. C. November 8, 1800 and later by destruction and theft in 1814 when the British occupied and burned the National Capitol. There were also other causes of destruction. I have had to rely on private collections and on the state military records of the thirteen original states that fought the Revolutionary War, now found in the National archives, and the excellent yearbooks and Lineage Book of the Daughters of The American Revolution and similar material of the Sons of The American Revolution. The War Dept. in 1873, 1889, 1894, 1915 acquired records later deposited in the National Archives.

The following served as Adjutants Generals during the Revolutionary War: Maj. Gen. Horatio Gates June 17, 1775-June 5, 1776; Col. Joseph Reed June 5, 1776 - Jan. 22, 1777; Brig. Gen. Arthur St. Clair Jan. 22, 1777- Feb. 20, 1777; Brig. Gen. George Weedom Feb. 20, 1777 - Apr. 19, 1777; Col. Morgan

Connor Apr. 19, 1777 - June 18, 1777; Col. Timothy Pickering June 18, 1777-Jan. 5, 1778; Col. Alexander Scammel Jan. 5, 1778-Jan. 1, 1781; Brig. Gen. Edward Hand Jan. 8, 1781-Nov. 3, 1783; Maj. William North Nov. 5, 1783-Oct. 28, 1787.

In August 1941 I copyrighted a composite picture of the last surviving veterans of the three first major American Wars, according to the military records in the U. S. Adjutant General's office, which I had found in searching records for military dead in war time.

On this picture is Daniel Frederick Bakeman the last surviving veteran on record of the Revolutionary War. He died in Freedom,Cattarangus County, New York on April 5, 1869 aged 109 years, 5 months, 26 days. He is buried at Freedom, New York.

On this same picture copyrighted in 1941 is also Hiram Cronk the last surviving veteran on record of the War of 1812. Born April 29, 1800 and died May 13, 1905, aged 105 years, 14 days. Actually lived during three centuries. He is buried in Mount Victory Plot, Cypress Hills National Cemetery, Brooklyn, New York. Served as private in Captain Edmund Fullers Company, 157th Regiment (Westcots) New York Militia, Oct. 8 to Nov. 16, 1814. In 1955 my "Known Military Dead During War of 1812", was published.

The third on this composite picture dated 1941 that I prepared was Thomas Edgar Owen the last surviving veteran on record of the war with Mexico. He was born in Philadelphia, Pa; June 17, 1831, died September 3, 1929 at John Dickson Home, Washington, D. C.,aged 98 years, 2 months, 17 days and buried in the Congressional Cemetery, Wash., D. C. He served as apprentice on Frigates Experience, Pennsylvania, Potomac and Allegheny, Feb. 10, 1846 to Aug. 8, 1849.

In 1957 my " Known Military Dead During Mexican War 1846-48", was published.

In 1958 my "Known Military Dead During The Spanish American War and The Philippines Insurrection 1898-1901", was published.

During World War I it was my duty, privilege and honor to serve in the American Expeditionary Force 1917-1919. Since no lists existed back in 1939 of the known military dead in our nation's wars I then proceeded to prepare these four with a feeling of a sense of duty, honor and loyalty to my comrades in arms who lie buried on some foreign field, and at home, and have turned to dust that is forever American.

In listing the known military dead during the American Revolutionary War, I have simply given the veteran's name, date of death - usually the year, and the state given is, where those interested can perhaps most easily trace him, where he was born or the state organization in which he served or where he died and is buried. It would take several specially trained in research a number of years to give more fully in detail necessary information for genealogical and other reference purposes.

The D.A.R. and S.A.R. have done excellent in caring for graves of Revolutionary War Veterans.

It would be splendid if veterans of recent wars would aid in searching for and marking and caring for neglected graves of veterans of all our wars. Perhaps in days to come a grateful nation might erect a military memorial with the names of those who gave their lives in wartime and memorialize them till this nation shall be no more.

The official date given the American Revolutionary War is from April 19, 1775 to November 3, 1783 - about 8½ years. Early important dates are: Battles of Lexington & Concord April 19, 1775. Capture of Ticonderoga May 10, 1775; Mecklenburg, N. C. Declaration of Independence adopted May 20, 1775. Battle of Bunker Hill June 17, 1775; Capture of Montreal Nov. 13, 1775; Defeat at Quebec Dec. 21, 1775.

Historian General Martha L. Moody, N.S.D.A.R. in Vol. 51-1904 very well states: "Citizenship entails duties and responsibilities that must be met as well as the privileges which they enjoy - in this manner seeking to perpetuate the ideals for which the men of the American Revolution gave of their lives and fortunes."

Historian General Mary Cooley Bassett, N.S.D.A.R. Preface to Lineage Book, Vol. XL 1902 says most appropriately: "To glance through this catalogue of names, is to be reminded of pioneer days and blood, of lives keen to defend, ready to fight, fearless to risk, and to imitate. It is to recall men and women of kingly courtesy and queenly grace, of virile personal charm and force, worthy to be patterns for our own age and people.

"As we think of those for whom these names stand, seeking a new country, and finding themselves in a new environment that made for equality of being and of opportunity, we realize that there and then was the beginning of that real Democracy to which we are heirs.

"Shall we descendants of these patriots, be mere decadent parasites upon our noble inheritance, feeding upon glories won by men and women who counted life well lost in the pursuit of spiritual liberty? The laurel may not pass from brow to brow; it belongs only to the winner.

"As the past closes, the future opens. We need all the courage the past can give us; we need all the consecration it can inspire.

These thousand soldier patriots who offered life itself, today beckons us on, and nerve us modern patriots by their splendid cheer, the tenacity and simplicity of their faith, their inspired vision, and their perception of spiritual freedom, to meet the ever increasing number and complexity of the problems and conflicts of our day."

July 4th, 1959
Baltimore, Maryland

Songs of The American Revolution

Edward Arthur Dolph in his book of Soldier Songs "Sound Off" states that before the battle of Bunker Hill "the Americans frequently wrote ballads to express their ideas about tea and taxation. Ballads of the Burgoyne Campaign, and songs such as 'The Battle of the Kegs' and 'Mad Anthony Wayne' wore very popular".

British song tunes were borrowed for nearly all the Revolutionary War songs. Melodies from old English colonial tunes and British military songs were almost American native composers like Francis Hopkinson almost entirely lacking. American National music did not appear for many years. Musical instruments were lacking except for a few fifes and drums, in the American Army.

The British marched on Lexington to the tune of "Yankee Doodle" in April 1775. Verse without music were used to describe most of the battles of the Revolution.

When General Cornwallis surrendered at Yorkton the British band played "The World Turned Upside Down" and "Yankee Doodle" was played by the band of the Continental Army.

The origin of the tune "Yankee Doodle" is clouded in the mystery of the distant past. It may have been a Roman Church chant in the 12th century, an Irish air, a Welsh Jig, a Dutch harvest dance, a Hungarian folk-dance, or a Pyrenees folk tune. Dolph supports the following theory as to its origin! In 1758 during the French and Indian War, a British Army surgeon, Doctor Richard Shuckburgh, an American resident of nearly a lifetime, was encamped near Albany, N.Y. on the old Van Rensselaer estate with General Abercrombie. The ridiculous rustic appearance of the mobilizing provincials caused the humorist Doctor Shuckburgh to write and set to music the words of the song that has come down to us known as "Yankee Doodle". This original song was lost. The present version was perhaps composed in 1775 at Cambridge, Mass. at the Provincial Camp when General Washington was in command there.

Burl Ives in his song book mentions these Revolutionary War songs: "The Rifleman's Song at Bennington", "The Battle of Saratoga", "The Yankee Man Of War," "Johnny Has Gone For A Soldier", "How Happy The Soldier", "The Battle of The Kegs", "Sir Peter Parker," "Cornwallis Country Dance," My Days Have Been So Wondrous Free".

Edward A. Dolph mentions, among others, these songs from the days of Yankee Doodle and the Revolution: "Come Out, Ye Continentalers", "Come Swallow Your Bumpers, ye Tories," "Follow Washington," "Free America," "How Stands The Glass Around", "Mad Anthony Wayne", "Saratoga Song", "Sergeant Champe", "Swamp Fox," "Volunteer Boys".

"How Stands The Glass Around", was sung in 1759 in Quebec by General James Wolfe to his officers, and it was sung for nearly a century thereafter in the early American Wars. "Come Out, ye Continentals", was said to be a true soldier song and was still sung in the Mexican War. One of the most convivial songs of the American Revolution "the Volunteer Boys" was written by the Englishman Henry Archer who came here in 1773 and became a Continental Army Volunteer. "The Girl I Left Behind Me" was brought to America in the early days by the British Army before the American Army existed. Here it remained to become the Regimental song of the Seventh Infantry. It was a popular Civil War song. General Custer's Indian fighters in the Old Seventh Cavalry sang it on the western plains. At West Point every June at graduation at the last class assembly this tune is a part of the medley march played by the Academy band.

Known Military Dead During The American Revolutionary War 1775-1783

Abbet, Samuel	Pvt. 13 Mass	Died	3-23-78
Abbey, Samuel	Sgt. 2 N.Y.	"	8-5-80
Abel, Frederick	N.H.	"	12 -77
Abell, Robert	Mass	"	1-5-76
Abiel, Leonard	Chaplain Mass	"	78
Aborn, Moses	Pvt. Mass	"	8-17-77
Abbot, Benjamin	Pvt. 10 Mass	"	11-5-78
Abbot, John	N. H.	"	8-31-79
Abbot, Philip	N.H. Bunker Hill	Killed	6-17-75
Abbott, Daniel	Mass. Enlisted at 16 yrs.	Died	4-17-81
Abbott, George	Pvt. Mass	"	12-22-75
Abbott, George	Q. M. "	"	1775
Abbott, John	Pa.	Killed	1778 Ind
Abbott, Uriah P.	Pvt. 11 Mass	Died	11-16-78
Abbott, Waddington	Pvt. 1 S.C.	"	11-18-76
Abbott, William	Pvt. 2 N.Y.	"	3-8-81
Acey, Samuel	Pvt. 1 N.J.	"	4-20-77
Ackerman, Daniel	Pvt. 2 N.Y.	Killed	3-23-77
Ackerson, Benj.	Pvt. N.Y.	"	9-8-78
Adams, Abel	Pvt. Mass	Died	1-16-82
Adams, Amos	Chaplain Mass	"	1775
Adams, Andrew	Pvt. Mass	"	9-23-82
Adams, Daniel	Pvt. Pa	"	1777 Prison
Adams, David	Matross Mass	"	1783
Adams, Davis	Matross 13 Mass	"	7-13-78
Adams, Ebenezer	R.I.	"	8-1-82
Adams, Ezekiel	Mass	"	8-1-77
Adams, Iedediah	Pvt. 8 Mass	Killed	9-19-77
Adams, Isaac	N.H.	"	6-17-75
			Bunker Hill
Adams, Jacob	Pvt. Md.	Died	3-24-83
Adams, James	Mass	"	1775
Adams, James	Del	"	6-13-78
Adams, James	Lt. N.H.	"	3-11-81
Adams, Jesse	N.Y.	"	1781 Va.
Adams, John	Pvt. 1 SC	"	2-29-76
Adams, Jonathan	SC	"	1783
Adams, Joseph	Sgt. S.C.	"	6- 1781
Adams, Joseph	Sgt. Mass	"	1778
Adams, Joshua	Pvt. 7 Mass	"	10-12-77
Adams, Mitchell	2 S C	"	4- 83
Adams, Mathew	Sgt. Conn	"	1776
Adams, Moses	Sgt. Mass	"	1778
Adams, Nathan Jr.	Lt. Conn	"	1782
Adams, Nathan	Capt. 6 Del	"	3-27-76
Adams, Nathaniel	Conn	Killed	1781 Groton
Adams, Niper	Pvt. N C	Died	7-27-77
Adams, Moses	Sgt. 13 Mass	"	6-13-78
Adams, Palatiah	Pvt. 7 Mass	Killed	11-11-78
Adams, Paul	N.Y.	"	1777
			Stillwater
Adams, Peter	Mass.	Died	9-27-78
Adams, Robert	Capt. 6 Pa.	Killed	6-21-76

Adams, Samuel	Pvt. Conn.	Died	6-16-81
Adams, Saint	Pvt. 4 Mass.	Killed	5-31-77
Adams, Winborn	Lt. Col. Mass	"	8-18-77
Adams, Winburn	Lt. Col. N. H.	Died	9-19-77
Adams, Wm.	Pvt. 10 N.C.	"	5-28-83
Adams, Zebulon P.	Pvt. 15 Mass	"	2-1-78
Adamson, Jacob	Pvt. Md.	"	3-24-83
Adcock, Edmund	Pvt. 10 N.C.	"	6-7-83
Adcock, George	Pvt. 1.N.C.	"	8-21-78
Adkinson, Richard	Pvt. 10 N.C.	"	10-18-81
Adore, Mark	Pvt. Conn.	"	12-30-77
Adverson, John	Pvt. Mass	"	3-13-76
Agden, Moses	Ensign N.J.	Killed	
Aiken, James	Pvt. N.H.	Died	7-28-77
Aimont, Jean Francois	France	"	1781 Va.
Ainsworth, Nathan		"	1777 N.Y. Prison
Airs,	Surg. S.C.		1777
Aitkins	Sgt. N.J.	Killed	8- 1776 By Indians
Akerman, Benjamin	N.H.	Died	8-24-83
Albright, Philip	Pvt. 1 N.J.	"	12-17-76
Albee, Amariah	Pvt. 2 Mass.	"	9-26-77
Alcox, Daniel P.	Conn	"	8-12-77
Alden, Judah	Capt. Conn	"	8-22-77
Alden, Ichabod	Col. N.Y.	Killed	11-11-78 By Indians
Aldrich, Abraham	Pvt. 6 Mass.	Died	9-10-77
Aldrich, David	R. I.	"	10-30-80
Aldridge, Jacob	Pvt. N.Y.	"	
Aldridge, Solomon	Pvt. 7 Mass	"	12-12-77
Alerton, Jesse	Pvt. 1 N.J.	"	8-31-77
Allard, Andrew P.	Pvt. 15 Mass.	"	9-1-77
Allds, Isaac	Pvt. N.H.	"	1778
Allen, Augustus	Sgt. 13 Mass.	"	9-19-77
Allen, Charles	R.I.	"	9-23-83
Allen, David	Lt. Ky.	"	1783
Allen, David	Cpl. Va.	"	1779
Allen, David	Lt. Va.	"	1783 Prison
Allen, Eliphalet	Pvt. Mass	"	1783
Allen, Elisha	Sgt. Vt.	"	1780
Allen, Elijah	Pvt. 2 Mass	"	10-29-77
Allen, Enoch	Pvt. Can.	"	8-29-78
Allen, Heber	N.H.	"	1782
Allen, Ichabod	Col. Mass	Killed	11-11-78 By Indians
Allen, Jacob	Capt. 2 Mass.	"	9-19-77
Allen, Jacob	Lt. Mass	Died	77 Bemus Hgts.
Allen, James	Pvt. Conn	"	10-8-77
Allen, James P.	Pvt. 11 Mass	"	8-3-77
Allen, John	Mass	"	1782
Allen, John	Lt. 5 N.C.	"	9 -1780
Allen, Jonathan P	Pvt. 12 Mass	"	8-20-78
Allen, Jonathan	Lt. Mass	"	1780
Allen, Joseph Viall	R.I.	"	10-1-80

Name	Unit	Status	Date/Notes
Allen, Joseph	Mass.	Died	1781 Va.
Allen, Moses	Col. Ga.	"	2-8-79
Allen, Noah	Lt. R. I.	Killed	9-16-83
Allen, Noah	Ensign Conn.	Died	10-27-76
Allen, Oliver	N.Y.	"	1775
Allen, Samuel		"	2-16-80 English Prison
Allen, Thomas	Mass	Killed	6-17-75 Bunker Hill
Allen, Thomas	Lt. 3 N C	Died	8-26-80 Prison
Alexander, Morgan	Capt. Va.	"	1783
Alexander, William	Maj. Gen. N.Y.	"	1783
Alexander, Abraham	N.Y.	"	1775 Liconderoga
Alexander, Abraham	Mass	"	1776
Alexander, Abraham	N.Y.	"	1776
Alexander, Amos	Del	"	1780
Alexander, Amos	Md.	"	1780
Alexander, James	Pvt. 6 Mass	"	12-26-77
Alexander, Levy	Pvt. 6 N C	"	8 -77
Alexander, Morgan	Col. Va.	"	1782
Alexander, Seth	N.H.	"	1780
Alexander, Walter	Del.	"	1780
Alexander, William	Maj. Gen. N.J.	"	1-15-83
Alexander, William	Lt. 5 Md.	Killed	8-27-77
Alexander, Willin	Pvt. 2 N.C.	Died	3-14-78
Allen, Thomas P.	Pvt. Conn.	"	8-10-79
Allen, Thomas P.	Sgt. Va.	"	1780
Allen, William	Pvt. 1 Md.	"	9-3- 78
Allen, William	14 Mass.	"	1-31-78
Allen, Willin	Pvt. 2 N C	"	1-7-78
Allin, Samuel	Pvt. Conn	"	7-26-77
Allin, James	Pvt. 1 N.J.	"	1-26-77
Allison, Andrew	Pvt. NC	"	1779
Allison, Joseph	Pvt. 3 SC	"	9-25-79
Allison, Micah	Pvt. N.Y.	Killed	Ft. Montgomery
Allyn, Simeon		"	1781 Ft. Griswold
Almiquid, John P.	Pvt. 11 Mass	Died	3-23-78
Almond, Augustus	Navy	"	7-27-81 English Prison
Alsop, John	Pvt. Md	"	1783
Alsop, Joseph	Md	"	1778
Alwood, Richard	Pvt. 1 N.J.	"	4-4-78
Alwood, Lewis	Pvt. 1 N.J.	"	2-28-77
Amee, Moses	Pvt 18 Cont	"	11-3-76
Ames, Abraham P.	8 Mass	Killed	10-7-77
Ames, Alvin	Pvt. 2 Conn	Died	11-11-77
Ames, Ebenezer	Lt. Mass	"	1779
Ames, Isaac	Pvt. 5 Mass	"	2-1-78
Ames, John	Pvt. 7 N. C.	"	11-15-77
Ames, Sylvanus	Rev.Md.	"	1778
Ames, Sylvanus	Chaplain Mass	"	1778
Ames, Sylvanus	Chaplain Valley Forge	"	1778 Pa.

14.

Name	Unit	Status	Date	Place
Amidon, Samuel	Lt. Mass		1783	
Amiss, Levi	Seaman Va	''	1780	
Amos	Pvt.	''	5-28- 81	
Amsden, Jesse	Pvt. 13 Mass	''	1-9- 78	
Amsden, Joel	N.H.	''	5-25-75	
Amtong, Francis	Pvt. 2 N Y	''	6-13-77	
Anderson,	Maj. Md	Killed	3-15-81	Guilford C.H.
Anderson, Dana	Conn	''	1778	Wyo.
Anderson, Danl.	Pvt. Conn	Died	4-15-81	
Anderson, David P.	Pvt. 11 Mass	''	9-28-78	
Anderson, Ephraim	Capt. N.J.	''	1783	
Anderson, Ephraim	Adj. N.J.	''	12-7-75	
Anderson, Henry	Capt. S C	Killed	1781	By Tories
Anderson, Jones	Pvt. 5 N. C.	Died	11-14-77	
Anderson, James Sr.	Maj. 4 N C	''	6-12-78	
Anderson, Robert	N. J.	Killed	8-6-77	Oriskary
Anderson, Wilson	Cpl. 5 N C	Died	3-15-78	
Andiger, Mathien	France	''	1781	Va.
Andre, Millard	France	''	1781	Va.
Andreas, Ludwig	N.J.	''	4-9-82	
Andres, Jeremiah	Pvt. Conn	''	1782	
Andres, Martin	Pvt. Pa.		1783	
Andrew, Jeremiah	Cpl. 2 Md.	''	10-2-78	
Andrew, Seth	Mass	''	1781	Va.
Andrews, Amasa	Pvt. 5 Mass	''	8-28-77	
Andrews, Ebenezer P.	Conn.	''		
Andrews, Israel P.	Pvt. 8 Mass	''	5-27-78	
Andrews, John	Pvt	''	7-11-77	Conn
Andrews, Joseph	Lt. Mass	''	12-1-77	
Andrews, Joseph	Lt. ''	''	9-11-80	
Andrews, Samuel	Conn	''	1776	
Andrews, Samuel P.	''	''	2-15-77	
Andrews, Samuel	Pvt. 15 Mass	''	7-1- 78	
Andrews, William	Sgt. 8 Mass	''	10-17-77	
Andrus, Gideon	Pvt. 2 Reg.	''	1 - 81	
Andrus, Jeremiah	Mass	''	7-17- 82	
Anett, Jacob	Del	''	7- 78	
Angell, Samuel	R I	''	4-9- 83	
Anger, Robert	Pvt. 5 Mass	''	7-1-77	
Angevaise, Nicolas	France	''	1781	Va.
Angleir, Joseph	Pvt. 1 Md	''	3 9-77	
Angles, James	R I	Killed	12-31-75	Que.
Angline Cornelius	Pvt. N. C.	Died	7- 77	
Ankarloo, David	French Navy - Sweden	''	1780	
Ankeny, DeWalt	Md.	''	1781	
Anibel, William	Mass	''	1781	Va.
Anson, Thomas or Jonas	Pvt. 1 N J	''	11-24-77	
Anstey, John	Pvt. 2 Reg.	''	5-26-76	
Antoney, James	Pvt. 2 Mass	''	3-16-78	
Anthony, Francis P.	Pvt. 12 Mass	''	11-19-78	
Anthony, John	Pvt. S. C.	''	5- 1781	
Anthony, Jonathan P.	Pvt. 11 Mass	''	12-10-78	

Anthony, Joseph	Pvt. 9 Mass	Died	12-26-77
Antony, Richard P.	Pvt. 15 Mass	"	4-10-78
Appleton, Samuel	Mass	"	1780
Appley, Jacob	N.Y.	"	4-30-78
Arbuckle, Matthew	Capt. Va		
Archdale, Theodore	Del	"	1-7-78
Archer, Benjamin	N. H.	"	3-23-81
Archer, Joseph	Lt. Va.	"	12-14-82
Archer, Nat.	Pvt. Mass	"	4-26-76
Armstead, John	Col. Va.	"	1779
Armstrong, Capt.	N. C.	Killed	
Armstrong, Elias	Pvt. Conn	Died	5-1-78
Armstrong, Fran C	Pvt. 7 Mass	Killed	5-3-78
Armstrong, George	Sgt. Can.	Died	1- 78
Armstrong, John	Capt. S C	"	10-3-78
Armstrong, Mark	Capt. Md.	Killed	6-18- 81
Armstrong, Robert	Pvt. 1 N. J.	Died	1-3-77
Arnal, Peter	Pvt. 5 SC	"	6-24-77
Arnett, William	Lt. 5 Md	"	2- 79
Arnold, Abijah	Pvt. Conn	"	8-24- 77
Arnold, John	Pvt. 2 Reg	"	9-14-77
Arnold, Noyce	Lt. 15 Mass	Killed	8-29-78
Arnold, Oliver	R I	Died	10-22-78
Arnold, Thomas	Pvt. 3 Md	"	8-22-79
Arthur, Bartholomew	Pvt. Conn		1781
Arundell, Dohickey	Capt. Va. Art	Killed	7-8-76
			Chesapeake Bay
Asabel, Barnes	Pvt. Conn.	Died	9-7-77
Ashbo, Samuel	Conn	Killed	6-17-75
			Bunker Hill
Ashe, John	General N.C.	Died	10-24-81
Ashley, Daniel	N. H.	"	8-1-81
Ashley, James	Pvt. N.Y.	"	10-19-80
Ashley, Linton	Cpl. Mass	"	2-18-78
Ashley, Simeon P.	Pvt. 11 Mass	"	9-30-77
Ashman, James	Lt. N. J.	"	9-11-76
Ashmead, Samuel	Pa	"	1776
Ashton, Isaac	Lt. Pa	"	1777
Ashur, Church	Pvt. 2 Mass	"	3-4-78
Aston, Benoni	Pvt. 4 N Y	"	4-16-79
Atchinson, Jeremiah	Pvt. 1 Md	"	9-23-78
Atchison, John	Pvt. Conn	"	2-1-77
Aten, Henry	N C	"	1780
Atherton, A.	Pa	"	7-3-78
Atherton, Jabez	Pa	"	7-3-78
Atherton, Lemuel	Pvt. 4 Mass	"	3-9-78
Atkins, Every	Del	"	11-20-75
Atkins, Isaiah	Mass	"	1782
Atkins, Josiah	Pvt. Conn	"	1781
Atkins, Jno.	Pvt. 5 Md	"	4-15-78
Atkinson, Philip	Pvt. N.Y.	"	9-17-78
Atkinson, Thomas P.	9 Mass		2-28-77
Atkinson, Wm.	Pvt. Mass	"	9- 78
Atward, Benjamin	Pvt. 9 Mass	"	9-5- 78
Atwater, David	Dr.	Killed	4-28-77
			Denbury Raid

Atwell, Francis	Capt. Va	Died	1781
Atwell, Hezekiah	Pvt. Mass	"	10-1- 78
Atwood, Benjamin	Mass	"	9-5- 78
Anbirc, Solomon	11 Mass	"	10-4-78
Austin, Absalom	Pvt. 9 N C	"	3-7-78
Austin, Cyrenious	Conn	"	6-10-78
Austin, George	Conn.	"	1781
Austin, John	Ensign Conn	"	1777
Austin, Richard	Md	"	1780
Austin, Robt.	Pvt. 1 Md	"	5-10-80
Auten, Thomas	Pvt. N J		1781
Avarrett, Thomas	Sgt. 10 N. C.	"	11-28-78
Aven, James	Pvt. N.C.		1778
Averell, Nathaniel	Mass	"	1781
Avery, William	Mass	"	1777
Avery, Benajah	Conn	"	1777
Avery, Christopher	Pa	"	7-3- 78
Avery, Daniel	Pvt. Ky	"	9-6-81
Avery, Daniel	Ensign Conn.	Killed	1781 Ft. Griswold
Avery, Ebenezer	Col. Conn	Died	1780
Avery, Ebenezer	Lt. Conn	Killed	9-6-81 Ft. Griswold
Avery, Ebenezer II	Md	"	1781 Groton Heights
Avery, Edward	Pvt. Mass.	Died	5-5-77
Avery, Elihu	Conn.	"	1779
Avery, Elihu	Cpl. N.Y.	"	1779
Avery, George	Pvt. Conn.	"	1781
Avery, Jasper	Sgt. Conn.	Killed	1781 Ft. Griswold
Avery, John P.	Pvt. 9 Mass.	"	1781
Avery, Jonas	Pvt. Conn	"	1776
Avery, Jonas	N Y	"	1776
Avery, Nathan		"	1781 Ft. Griswold
Avery, Solomon	Conn	"	1781
Avery, William	Mass	Died	1777
Andrews, Joseph	Lt. 15 Mass	"	11-22-77
Ayer, Richard	Capt. Mass	"	1780
Ayer, Thomas	S C	"	1781
Ayers, Fredk.	Pvt. 6 Md.	Killed	8-16-80
Ayers, John	Pvt. 6 Mass	Died	8-20-77
Ayers, Jonathan	Pvt. 15 Mass	"	6-28-78
Ayers, Lott	Pvt. 9 Mass	"	10-30-77
Aylett, William	Com. Gen. Va.	"	1781
Aylett, William	Pvt. Pa	"	1781
Aylette, William	Pa.	"	1780
Ayres, John	N. J.	"	4-29-77
Ayres, Stephen	N. H.	"	6-17-75
Ayres, Stephen	Pvt. Mass	"	1782
Azariah, Leonard	Pvt. N. J.	"	6-17-75

Babb, James	Pvt. 12 Mass	Died	1-1-78
Babcock, Christopher A.	R I	"	1780
Babcock, Elijah	Capt. Conn	"	1778
Babcock, Henry	Col. Yale Conn.	"	10-7-80
Babcock, James	Lt. Col. R. I.	Killed	1781
Babcock, James	Lt. Col. R. I.	Died	10-6-81
Babcock, James	Lt. Col. Yale Conn	"	1781
Babcock, John Prentice	Conn	Killed	1781 Ft. Griswold
Babcock, Joshua	Dr. Yale Conn	Died	4-1-83
Babcock, Joshua	Maj. Gen. R. I.	"	1783
Babcock, Nathan	Mass	"	1777
Babcock, Oliver	Lt. Conn	"	1777
Babcock, William	Pvt. R. I.	"	9-1-78
Babit, Reuben	Pvt. 1 N. Y.	"	5-1-78
Bachilor, William	Pvt. 3 Md	"	1780
Bacon, Abijah	Pvt. 9 Mass	"	1-25-78
Bacon, Daniel	Pvt. N.Y.	"	1776
Bacon, Daniel	Pvt. Conn	"	1778
Bacon, David	Lt. R. I.	"	1777
Bacon, Edward	Pvt. Mass	"	1783
Bacon, James	Sgt. Conn	"	1780
Bacon, John	Lt. Mass	Killed	4-19-75 Tex.
Bacon, John	Sgt. Mass	Died	5-19-75
Bacon, Josiah	Sgt. Mass	"	6-17-75
Bacon, Josiah, Sr.	Mass	Killed	6-17-75 Bunker Hill
Bacon, Reuben	Mass	Died	1775
Bacon, Reuben	N. H.	Died	6-1775(Bunker
Bacon, Samuel	Mass	"	1781(Hill
Backingham, Wm.	Pvt. 10 N C	"	11-25-78
Bachus, John	Pvt. 1 N. Y.	Killed	7-23-79
Badcock, Benjamin	Cpl. 6 Mass	Died	9-1-77
Badcock, Joseph	Pvt. Conn	"	5-24-78
Badeen, Nathan	Pvt. 18 Cont. Reg.	"	5-23-76
Badge, John	Pvt. 7 Mass	Killed	5-30-78
Bagg, Daniel Jr.	1st Lt. Mass	Died	12-21-76
Bagley, Jonathan	Ens. Mass	"	1780
Bagage, Jean	France	"	1781 Va.
Bailey, Daniel	Pvt. 8 Mass	"	2-21-80
Bailey, Andrew	Pvt. N. H.	"	11-13-81
Bailey	Lt. S. C.	Killed	10-9-79 Savannah
Bailey, Ezekiel	Sgt. Conn.	"	1781 Ft. Griswold
Bailey, Philip	Pvt. Md	Died	2-20-83
Bailey, Joseph P.	Pvt. 11 Mass	"	7-10-78
Bailey, John	Pvt. 8 Mass	"	3-29-78
Bailey, James	Drum Md	"	8-1-82
Bailey, James	Sgt. Md.	"	4-27-81
Bailey, Richard	R I	"	1780
Bailey, Samuel	Lt. Mass	"	6-17-75
Bailey, Samuel Jr	Cpl. Conn	Killed	6 17-75 Bunker Hill
Bailey, Samuel Jr.	Mass	"	4-19-75

18.

Name	Rank/Location	Died/Killed	Date
Bailey, Samuel	Va.	Died	1781
Bailey, Timothy	Lt. Mass	"	1777
Baker, Andrew	N.Y.	Killed	9-6-81
Baker, Francis	Col. N. J.	Died	1-6-83
Baker, Herman	Conn.	"	1- 77
Baker, Henry	Sgt. 4 N.Y.	"	7-27-78
Baker, Henry	Sgt. N. J.	"	1780
Baker, Isaac	Pvt. Can.	"	4-10-77
Baker, James	Sgt. 6 Md.	"	1-25-78
Baker, James	Mass	"	1776
Baker, Jethro	Md.	"	1777
Baker, Jonathan	N. Y.	"	1-14-77
Baker, Joseph	Pvt. 1 Md.	"	1780
Baker, Michael Sr.	Pa.	"	1779
Baker, Nathan	Pvt. 5 Mass.	"	5-15-77
Baker, Remember Jr.	Capt. Conn.	"	8-22-75 Can.
Baker, Remember	Capt. Vt.	Killed	1775 Camden
Baker, Thomas	Navy	Died	7 21-81 Eng. Prison
Baker, William	Pvt. 1 Md.	"	1780
Bakehorn, Jeremiah	" 2 N.Y.	"	5-10-80
Balcom, Samuel	Mass.	"	1783
Baldridge, William	Navy	"	7-21-81 Eng. Prison
Baldwin, Ebenezer	Chaplain Yale Conn.	"	10-1-76
Baldwin, Isaac	Capt. N. H.	Killed	6-17-75 Bunker Hill
Baldwin, Israel	Lt. Conn.	Died	3-16-78
Baldwin, Caleb	N. J.	"	1781
Baldwin, Isaac	Capt. Mass	"	1775 Bunker Hill
Baldwin, Israel	Lt. Conn	"	1778 New Haven
Baldwin, John	Pvt. Conn.	Killed	7-5- 79
Baldwin, Lewis	N. J.	Died	1782
Baldwin, Noah	Conn.	"	1776
Baldwin, Zacha	Sgt. N. J.	Killed	9-11-77
Balfour,	Col. N. C.	"	3-12-82
Balfour, Andrew	Lt. Col. N. C.	Died	1783
Balfour, Andrew	Col. N. C.	"	3-10-82
Ball, Joseph	Va.	"	1779
Ball, Joseph	Pvt. 1 N. Y.	"	10-1-77
Ball, Reuben	Pvt. Conn.	Killed	10-11-80
Ball, Samuel	Capt. N. J.	"	6-7-80
Ball, Samuel	Conn.	Died	1780
Ball, Stephen	Surg. N. J.		1783
Ball, Thomond	Paymaster, Pa.	"	1779
Ballane, Elijah	Pvt. R. I.	"	5-15- 78
Ballon, Duty	Pvt. R. I.	"	12-29-83
Ballon, Seth	Pvt. N. H.	"	9-15-78
Ballard, Benj. R.	Pvt. 9 Mass.	"	1-20-79
Ballinger, Henry	N. C.	"	1776
Balton, William	Mass	"	1780
Baltwood, Solomon	Pvt. Mass	"	1777
Bancroft, Edmund	Lt. 12 Mass.	"	6-25- 77

Bandy, John	Pvt. 2 Md.	Died	1778
Banet, John	Pvt. 1 N. Y.	"	12-4- 82
Bangs, Elkanah	Pvt. N. J.	"	7- 77 Prison Ship
Bangs, Isaac	Lt. Mass	"	9-12-80
Bangs, Joshua	Mass	"	2-3-78
Banks, Charles	Pvt. 4 Md.	"	5-21-79
Banks, Ebenezer	Conn.	"	1777
Banks, Stephen	Pvt. 1 S. C.	"	11-4-76
Benita, Abraham	Pvt. Pa.	"	1783
Banta, Hendrick	N. J.	"	1778
Banta, Samuel	N. J.	"	1783
Ban, Charles	Pvt. 4 N. Y.	"	2-22-78
Barton, Robert	N. Y.	"	1781 Va.
Baptist, Francis	R. I.	"	9-7- 80
Barbadoes, Isaac	Pvt. 15 Mass	"	12-1-77
Barbaton, Joseph	Guillamme-France	"	1780 Va.
Barber, Daniel	Conn.	"	4-7-79
Barber, David	Ens. Conn.	Killed	12-25-77
Barber, Edward	S.C.	"	4-19-75
Barber, Ellick	Pvt. R. I.	Died	5-15-80
Barber, Elijah	Conn	"	1780
Barber, Francis	Lt. Col. 2 N.J.	Killed	1780
Barber, Francis	Adj. Gen. N.J.	"	2-11-83
Barber, Francis	Col.	Died	1-6-83
Barber, John	Pvt. N.Y.	"	10-26-76
Barber, Nathaniel	Conn.	"	1782
Barber, Nathaniel	Sgt. 11 Mass	"	6-3-78
Barber, Robert	Lt. Pa.	"	1782
Barchley, James	Pvt. Can	Killed	1-2-77
Barclay, John	Pvt. Conn	Died	12-25-78
Bardsley, Gershom	Pvt. Conn.	"	11-30-81
Bardun, Robt.	Pvt. 1 N.Y.	"	5-8-77
Bardwell, Jonathan	Capt. Mass	"	1780
Barey, Jean Francois	France	"	1781 Va
Barker, Ebenezer	Mass	"	1781
Parker, Francis	Lt. Col.	"	1783
Barker, Jesse	Pvt. 15 Mass	"	10-8-78
Barker, John	N. J.	"	12-13-77
Barker, Kendall	Mass	"	1776
Barker, Samuel	N. Y.	"	7-29-76
Barko, Wyllis	Pvt. 1 N.C.	"	11-1778
Barlow, Robt.	Pvt. 9 N. C.	"	3-12-78
Barnam, Lenos	Pvt. Conn.	"	10-17-81
Barnam, Thomas P.		"	8-17-78
Barnard, Joel	Pvt. Mass	"	8-15-75
Barnard, Jonas	Pvt. N. H.	"	6-17-75
Barnard, Samuel	Capt. Mass	"	1782
Barnard, Thomas	Cpl. Mass	"	3-14-75
Barnes, Joseph Dr.	Surg. N. H.	"	10-29-81
Barnes, Moses	Capt. Mass	"	3-2-81
Barnes, Stephen Jr.	Conn.	"	1777
Barnes, Thomas	Pvt. 15 Mass	"	12-15-77
Barnes, Thomas	Pvt. 7 Mass	"	1-2-78
Barnes, Thomas	Conn	"	1778
Barnett, Saml.	Sgt. S. C.	"	1781

Barnett, William	N.H.	Died	4-19-76
Barney, Wheaton	Mass.	"	1781
Barney, Elisha	Capt. Mass.	"	1781
Barns, Abraham	Pvt. Conn.	"	3-1--78
Barns, Daniel	Pvt. Conn.	"	3-30- 78
Barnum, Caleb	Chaplain Mass	"	8-26-76
Barnum, Zeanas	Capt. Conn	"	1781 Va.
Baron, Daniel	N.Y.	"	1776
Barr, Aaron	N. H.	Killed	6-17-75 First killed at Bunker Hill
Barr, Will	Pvt. S.C.	Died	7- 81
Barrell, Colburn	Pvt. Mass	"	1782
Barrett, Colburn	Pvt. 10 Mass	"	11-30-77
Barrett, Humphrey	Mass	"	1783
Barrett, James	Col. Mass	"	1779
Barrett, James	Mass	"	1779
Barrett, James	N.H.	"	1779
Barrett, James	Capt. Mass	"	1779
Barrett, John	N. H.	Killed	6-17-75 Bunker Hill
Barrett, John	Pvt. 1 N.Y.	Died	12-4-82
Barrett, John	N.Y.	"	1781 Va.
Barrett, P. Nathan	Pvt. 5 Mass	"	7-6-77
Barrett, Oliver	Pvt. 11 Mass	Killed	10-7-77 Still- water
Barrett, Zaccheno	Capt. Md		1781
Barron, John	Lt. Mass	"	4-19-75 Concord
Barron, Timothy	Capt. N.H.	Died	1781
Barron, William	Lt. N H	"	3-26-78 Va.
Barrows, Daniel	R. I.	"	1779
Barrows, Daniel	Mass	"	1779
Barrows, Isaac	Lt. Mass	"	1779
Barrows, John	7 Mass	"	6-2-82
Barrows, Samuel	Mass	"	1775
Barrows, John	Mass	"	11-30-82
Barruch, James	Pvt. 5 Md	"	11-18-78
Barry, Michael	Pvt. Md	"	4-12-77
Barry, James	Sgt. Pa		1781
Bartholomew, John	Pa	"	1782
Bartholomew, Joseph	Conn.	"	1781
Bartholomew, Josh	Capt. Pa	"	3-16-78
Bartlet, Noah	Pvt. Conn.	Killed	4-26-77
Bartlet, Mathew	Mass	Died	1775
Bartlet, John	N.H.	Killed	9- 77
Bartlett, Josiah	Conn.	Died	3-6-82
Bartlett, Jobadiah	Lt. Mass	"	1779
Bartlett, Samuel	Capt. Mass	"	1780
Barton, Elias	2 S. C.	"	7-26-77
Barton, James Jr.	7 Mass.	Killed	5-30-78
Bascom, Elisha	Pvt. Mass.	Died	9-18-76
Base, James	Pvt. 12 Mass	"	12-18-77
Bashford, Peter	Pvt.	"	6-12-79
Baskins, William	Pvt. Can	"	1-12-77

Bason, Cesar	N.H.	Killed	6-17-75 Bunker Hill
Bass, Josiah	Navy	Died	7-21-81 Eng. Prison
Bass, Reuben	Pvt.	"	11-1-77
Basset, Walter	Pvt. 1 N.Y.	"	1780
Bassett, Abraham	Conn	"	1776
Batchelder, Jonathan	Lt. Mass	Died	1776
Batchelder, Nathaniel	Pvt. N.H.	"	1777
Batchelor, Prince	Pvt. 12 Mass	"	2-10- 78
Bate, Jonathan	N.H.	Killed	6-17- 75 Bunker Hill
Bateman, Charles	Pvt. 12 Mass.	Died	2-18-79
Bateman, Jona	Pvt. 2 N.C.	"	4-8-78
Bateman, Nathan	Pvt. Md	Killed	6-18-81
Bates, Caleb	Sgt. 9 Mass	Killed	9-11-77
Bates, Jesse	Mass	Died	1783
Bates, John	Pvt. Conn	"	6-28-78
Bates, John	Pvt. 6 Md	"	4-1-78
Bates, Joshua	Pvt. 15 Mass	"	7-2-78
Bates, Micah	Mass	"	7-2-77
Bates, Moses	Pvt. Mass.	"	1-10-81
Bates, Nathaniel	Mass	"	3- 77
Bates, Nathaniel	N.H.	Killed	9-19-77
Bates, Oliver	Capt. Mass	Died	7-4-75
Bathrick, Timothy	Pvt. 12 Mass	"	4-21-78
Battelle, Ebenezer	Lt. Mass	"	1776
Battle, Ebenezer	Col. Mass	"	11-6-76
Battles, James	Mass	"	1781 Va
Batton, Hugh	Pvt. 5 Md	"	8- 79
Baxter, Andrew	N.C.	"	1781
Baxter, John	Pa.	"	3-15-77
Baxter, Jonathan	Mass	"	3-15-78
Baxter, Richard	Pvt. Conn	"	6-6-78
Baxter, Thomas	Pvt. Md	"	9-24-83
Baxter, Thomas	N.H.	"	12-31-77
Bay, Charles	Pvt. 3 Md.	Killed	10-4-78
Bayden, Darius	Mass	Died	1783
Bayles, Augustine	N.J.	Died	2-23-82
Bayles, Platt	N.J.	"	1777
Bayless, Platt	Maj. N.Y.	"	1778
Baylis, John	Cpl. N.Y.	"	1775
Baylor, George		"	1781 Va.
Beach, Bermas	Conn.	"	1776 Prison Ship
Beach, John	Drum Md	"	12-15-82
Beach, Thomas	Pvt. 3 Mass.	"	9-4-77
Beagle, Absalom	Cpl. 1 N.J.	"	5-13-78
Beake, John	Pvt. 14 Mass	"	1-1-78
Beal, Jno.	Pvt. 2 N C	"	5-16-78
Beal, Zachariah	Capt. N.H.	"	10-27-77
Beale, Gershom	Pvt. 5 Mass	"	5-30-77
Beale, Nicholas	Pvt. 15 Mass	"	10-24-77
Beall, (Bell) Peter	Md	"	1778
Beall, Samuel	Col Md	"	1778
Beall, Zachariah	Capt. N.H.	"	10-27-77

Name	Unit	Fate	Date
Beals, Nathaniel	Navy	Died	7-21-81 Eng. Prison
Beaman, David	Pvt. Mass	"	1782
Beard, James	Pvt. 2 SC	Killed	10-9-79
Beard, John		Died	1780 Va
Beard, William	Pvt. 3 Md	"	9-11-78
Bearfield, Stephen	Pvt. 4 N C	"	2-1-78
Bears, Spencer	Pvt. 9 Mass	"	9-10-80
Beasley, Larkin	Pvt. Va	Killed	7- 78
Beason, Charles	Pvt. Pa	Died	1777 Prison
Beatto, Joseph	Mass	"	1780
Beatty, John	Ens. S.C.	"	10-7-80 Kings Mt.
Beaton, James	Pvt. 7 Mass	"	6-27-77
Beattie, William	Capt. SC	Killed	4-25-81
Beatty, John	Sgt. 6 Pa	Died	7-11-76
Beatty, Thomas	Pvt. Va		2-15-77 Prison
Beatty, William	Capt. Md	Killed	4-25-81 Hobkirk Hill
Beaty, Robert	NC	"	1781
Beaver, Nicholas	Pvt. R I	Died	11-6-77
Beaver, John	Pvt. Pa	"	1777
Bebout, Peter	N.J.	"	1782
Beck, Alexander	Pvt. 5 Md	"	11- 79
Beck, Nicholas	Pvt. 2 Pa.	"	1776
Beckwith, Elisha	Conn	Killed	1776 White Plains
Beckwith, Harris	Pvt. Conn	Died	2-19-78
Bedel, Etienne	France	"	1781 Va.
Bedel, Jacques	France	"	1781 Va.
Bedell, Jacob	N. J.	"	1777
Bedwell, Wm.	Pvt. R. I.	"	6-1-78
Bedner, Christian K.	Pvt. 1 N.Y.	"	12-18-78
Beebo, Martin	N Y	"	5-18-83
Beebe, Timothy	9 Mass	"	10-25-77
Beebee, Jonathan P.	Pvt. Conn	"	8-1- 77
Beebre, Jeremiah	Pvt. Conn	"	4-26-82
Beecher, David	Capt. Conn.	"	1783
Beek, Nathaniel	2 S C	"	3-8-79
Beers, Nathan	Lt.	Killed	7-5-79 New Haven
Beesley, Jonathan	Capt. N J	Died	6- 78
Beglo, Moses	Pvt. 4 N J	"	10-4- 77
Beggs, Thomas	Pvt. Va		1779
Belch, Philip	Pvt. 5 N C	"	11-21- 77
Belcher, Jonathan	Pvt. Conn	"	1780
Belden, Thomas	Conn	"	5-22- 82
Bell, Benjn	Cpl. 2 N C	"	4-17-78
Bell, David	Capt. Va.	"	1780
Bell, Frederick	N.Y.	Killed	1778
Bell, Frederick M.	Capt. N H	Died	10-8- 77
Bell, Jabez	Cpl. N. J.	Killed	9-30-78
Bell, James	Conn.	Died	1-3-82
Bell, John	Pvt. 1 N Y	"	10-8-78
Bell, Jonathan	Capt. Conn.	"	1776
Bell, Peter	Capt. Md.	"	1778
* Bell, John	N H	"	1778

Name	Rank/State	Status	Date
Bellamy, Jonathan	Lt. Yale Conn	Died	1-4- 77
Bellamy, Silas	Pvt. 4 N. Y.	"	5-27-78
Bellanger	Lt. France	"	1781 Va
Belmear, Francis	Md	"	1782
Belote, William			1782 Va.
Bemaine, George	N. H.	Killed	10-28-76 White Plains
Bemand, Elisha	Pvt. 2 Conn.	Died	9-1-77
Bemis, Reuben	Mass		1779
Benajah, Carpenter	Capt. R. I.	Killed	8-27-76
Bencham, Hodges	Sgt. 8 N C	Died	3-30-78
Benedisk, Gershon	Pvt. Conn.	"	8 -77
Benedict, Amos	Adj. Yale Conn	"	2-18-77
Benedict, Daniel	N.Y.	"	1777 Prisoner
Benedict, Eleazer	Pvt. Conn	"	7-28-78
Benefield, Thomas	Pvt. 7 Mass	"	6-10-77
Bengess, Jonathan	Pvt. 12 Mass	"	3-3-78
Berham, Silas	Lt. 2 Conn.	Killed	12-7- 77
Benison, William	Maj. S. C.	"	2-24-82
Benjamin, Benjamin	Pvt. 2 Conn.	Died	3-30-78
Benjamin, Colt	Pvt. Mass	"	1781
Benjamin, John Jr.	Conn.	Killed	6-24-81
Benners, John	Pvt. 3 N. J.	Died	10-4-77
Bennet, David	Pvt. Conn.	"	1776 Prison
Bennet, George	Pvt. Md.	"	10-1-82
Bennet, Benjamin	Pvt. Conn	"	11- 78
Bennet, Benjamin Jr.	Pvt. N. Y.	Killed	1779
Bennet, Jas.	Pvt. 7 N C	Died	1-26-78
Bennet, Joshua	Pvt. 2 N. Y.	"	10-17-78
Bennet, Peter	Pvt. 8 Mass	"	5-15-78
Bennet, Samuel	Pvt. 5 Mass	"	2-11-78
Bennet, Toby	Pvt. Conn	"	4 78
Bennett, Azell	Pvt. R. I.	Killed	6-28-78
Bennett, Benjamin	N. Y.	"	1779 Mini-Sink
Bennett, David	Me	Died	1777
Bennett, Ebenezer	Mass.	"	11-10-78
Bennett, Giles	Del	"	1-8-80
Bennett, Jacob	Mass	"	11-26-79
Bennett, Jno.	Pvt. 5 Md	"	7-1-77
Bennett, Joseph P.	Pvt. 11 Mass	"	12-10-78
Bennett, Nathan	Conn	"	9-20-77
Bennett, Nathaniel	Pvt. 2 Conn	"	3-17-78
Bennett, Richard		"	1-17-77
Bennett, Thaddeus	Conn	"	1777
Bennit, George	Cpl. Md.	"	10-1-82
Benny, John	Pvt. 5 Md.	"	8- 78
Benson, Henry	Sgt. Mass	"	4-7-77
Benson, Jacob	N.H.	"	10-28-79
Benson, Wm.	Pvt. 2 N.Y.	"	10-9- 78
Benston, John	Pvt. 5 Md.	"	4-20-77
Bent, Timothy	Pvt. 5 Mass	"	1- 78
Bentley, Samuel	Pvt. 5 Md.	"	8-1- 78
Bentley, Wm.	Pvt. 4 N. Y.	"	7-25-77
Benton, Caleb	Pvt. Conn	"	12-26-81 Va.
Benton, Caleb	Sgt. Conn	"	1783

Name	Rank/Unit	Fate	Date	Place
Benton, Edom	Pvt. 10 N. C.	Died	11-7-78	
Benton, James	Pvt. 5 Md.	"	12-21-77	
Berger, Jacques	France	"	1781	Va.
Bernard, Castilio	Pvt. 10 Mass.	"	8- 1778	
Bernard, John	Pvt. 5 Md.	"	7-15-78	
Berry, Divan	Ens. Conn	"	1783	
Berry, Divan Jr.	Capt. N. Y.	"	1783	
Berry, James	Pvt. Can.	Killed	6-23-78	
Berry, John	Pvt. N H.	"	10-7-77	
Berry, Thomas	Capt. N. H.	Died	1779	
Berry, Zachariah	Pvt. Md.	"	3-6-84	
Besard, Jean-Marie	France	"	1781	Va.
Best, James	Pvt. 3 Md	"	10-27-78	
Bettes, Jonathan	Pvt. 3 Mass	"	3-17-77	
Bettibone, Jonathan Jr.	Conn.	"	1776	
Bettice, James	Pvt. Conn.		7-28-78	
Bettin, Adam	Capt. N. J.	"	1781	
Beauchamp, Fountain	Pvt. Md.	"	1782	
Bevens, Benjamin	Pvt. N. H.	"	6-1-79	
Bexley, Josh	Pvt. 10 N. C.	"	6-6-83	
Beze, Antoine	Cpl. France	"	1781	Va
Bickford, James P.	Pvt. 7 Mass	"	6-10-78	
Bickford, Thomas	Pvt. 18 Cont.	Killed	1-1-76	
Bicknell, Nathaniel	Pvt. Mass	Died	1775	
Bicknell, Thomas	S C	Killed	10-7-80	King's Mt.
Biddle, Nicholas	Capt. U S M Pa.	"	3-7-78	
Bidgood, Jonathan	Pvt. R. I.	Died	10-22-77	
Bidlock, James Jr.	Pa.	Killed	7-3-78	Wyo.
Bidot, Jean	France	Died	1781	Va.
Bidwell, Daniel Jr.	Conn.	"	10-8-76	
Bieber, Johannes	Pa.	"	1777	
Bigelow, John	Maj. Conn.	"	6-23-80	
Bigford, Jeremiah	Pa.	"	7-3-78	
Bigford, Samuel	Pa.	"	7-3-78	
Biggs, John	Pvt. N. C.	"	1778	
Biggs, John	Pvt. Md.	"	7-1-83	
Bigham, Jas.	Pvt. 2 N. Y.	"	2-20-77	
Billet, John	Pvt. R I	"	7-30-78	
Billings, Ceasar	Pvt. 7 Mass.	"	12-29-76	
Billings, John Jr.	Pvt. Conn.	Killed	9-6-81	Groton Pt.
Billings, Jonathan	Cpl. Mass.	Died	1783	
Billings, Nathan	Pvt. R. I.	"	2-14-78	
Billings, Peleg	Conn.	"	1779	
Billings, Roger	Conn.	"	1777	
Billings, Samuel	Pvt. Conn.	Killed	1781	
Billings, Samuel	Pvt. Pa.	Died	1777	Wyo.
Billings, Timothy Jr.	Mass	"	6-10-81	
Billings, William	7 Mass.	"	5-11-77	
Billings, William	Cpl. Mass	"	1783	
Billings, William Sr.	Lt. Mass	"	1783	
Billins, Peter	Pvt. Conn.	"	12-26-81	
Billingerm John	5 S C	"	6-5-78	
Biltzenberger, Fracois	Sgt. France	"	1781	Va.

Bingham, Bartholomeo	Pvt. 2 Conn.	Died	9- 77
Binney, Benjamin	Pvt. Mass.		1783
Bird, Benj.	Pvt. R. I.	Died	6-15-79
Bird, John	Pvt. Mass	"	1777
Birge, Jonathan	Capt. Conn	Killed	1776 White Plains
Birge, Roswell	Conn	Died	10-24-77
Bishop, David	Pvt. Conn	"	4-18-81
Bishop, Eben	Pvt. 4 N.Y.	"	6-17-78
Bishop, Elias	Pvt. R. I.	"	9-6- 77
Bishop, Enos	Pvt. N.H.	"	8-8-78
Bishop, Isaac	Pvt. 5 N.Y.	"	12-9- 76 Conn.
Bishop, John P.	Pvt. Conn	"	1-16- 78
Bishop, Nicholas	Capt. Conn	"	1780
Bishop, Nicholas	Pvt. Conn	"	1780
Bishop, Nicholas	Conn.	"	1780
Bishop, Vincent	Pvt. 3 N. J.	"	11-28-77
Bishop, Jephaniah Jr	Mass	"	8-11-81 S.S. Prison
Bissell, Elisha	Pvt. Conn.	"	1776
Bissell, Josiah	Conn	"	12-21-76
Bissell, Zebulon	Conn.	"	1776 Prison
Bissell, Zebulon	Conn.	"	1777
Bixby, David	Pa.	"	7-3- 78
Bixby, Elias	Pa.	"	7-3- 78
Bixby, Isaac	Pvt. 9 Mass	"	3-18- 78
Bixby, Thomas Jr.	Mass	"	1782
Blaas, Jacob	Pvt. 1 N.Y.	"	1- 79
Blachley, Daniel	Pvt. N.Y.	"	1781
Black, David	" 4 N.Y.	"	7-9-78
Black, Joseph	Pvt. 15 Mass	"	2-20- 79
Black, Nathaniel	Pvt. Conn.	"	5-10-77
Black, Richard	Pvt. 10 Mass	"	2-1-78
Black, Robert	Pvt. N. C.	"	1781
Black, Samuel	Lt. Va.	"	1782
Blackburn, Hugh	R. I.	Killed	12-31-75 Que.
Blackburn, William	Lt. Va.	"	10-7-80 King Mt.
Blackley, Enos	Pvt. 7 Mass.	"	11-11-78
Blackley, Stephen	Pvt. 2 Conn.	Died	4-5-78
Blackman, Joseph	Pvt. Conn.	Died	11-25-81
Blackman, Josiah	Mass	"	9-4- 76
Blackwell, Jacob	Col. N.Y.	"	1780
Blackwell, Joshua	Me	"	1782
Blackwell, Micah	Q. M. Mass	"	9-30-81
Blair, John	Lt. Va.	"	8-18-80
Blair, John	N.H.	"	3-9-80
Blair, John	Capt. Art	"	8-18-80 Camden
Blair, Joseph	Pvt. 6 Mass	"	9-1-78
Blaisdell, Jonathan	Pvt. Mass	"	1781
Blaisdell, Thomas	N. H.	"	1777
Blake, Christ	Pvt. 5 N.C.	"	4-30-78
Blake, Ezekiel	Mass	"	1775
Blakely, Joseph	Pvt. Conn	"	11-13-77
Blakeman, Zachariah	Pvt. Conn.	Killed	1779
Blakeslee, David	Pvt. Conn.	"	1781

26.

Blakeslee, James	Lt. Vt.	Killed	1782
Blakney, David	Pvt. Conn.	"	7-27- 82
Blamer, John	Cpl. 10 N. C.	"	6-13-83
Blanchard, Asa	Pvt. 12 Mass	"	11-5-77
Blanchard, Benj.	R. I.	"	2-3-82
Blanchard, Benjamin	Pvt. 12 Mass	"	3-9-78
Blanchard, Joseph	Pvt. 9 Mass	"	9-22-79
Bland, Richard	Va.	"	10-6-76
Blanden, Francis	Mass	"	1775
Blank, Cornl.	Pvt. 2 N.Y.	"	2-15-77
Blasdell, Henry	Pvt. 10 Mass	"	5-7-77
Bliss, Elisha	Pvt. 15 Mass	"	12-12-77
Bliss, Ephraim	Mass	"	1778
Bliss, Jehiel	Pv. 2 Conn	"	5-22-77
Bliss, Oliver	Pvt. 3 Mass	Killed	2-3-80
Bliss, William	Pvt. Mass	Died	1782
Bloany, James	Del	"	5-10-77
Blocker, John	Pvt. Conn	"	8-19-82
Blodgett, Roswell	Conn	"	5-23-81
Blodget, Silas	Pvt. Conn	"	5-1-82
Blood, Abraham	N.H.	Killed	6-17-75 Bunker Hill
Blood, Daniel	Pvt. N.H.	Died	11-28-78
Blood, Ebenezer	N. H.	Killed	6-17-75 Bunker Hill
Blood, Joseph	N. H.	"	6-17- 75 Bunker Hill
Blood, Josiah	N.Y.	Died	1776 Ticon- deroga
Blood, Nathaniel	Pvt. N. H.	"	1782
Blood, Nathan	Sgt. Mass	Killed	6-17-75 Bunker Hill
Blood, Robert	Pvt. 8 Mass	Died	11-1-77
Bloomer, Robert	Capt. N. Y.	"	1783
Blount, Jno.	Pvt. 6 N. C.	"	1-24-78
Bloxon, Charles	Va.	"	1777
Bloxon, Stewart	Va.	"	1783
Bloxtan, Sam	Del	"	8-26-77
Blunderwill, John	Pvt. 3 Md	"	1780
Blush, Elijah	Pvt. 12 Mass	"	3-28-78
Bly, Lot	Pvt. 7 Co. 14 Mass	"	3-1-78
Bly, Rouse	Sgt. Conn.	Killed	8-27-67 L.I.
Blyth, John	N.H.	"	6-17-75 Bunker Hill
Boardman, Daniel	Lt. Mass	Died	5-31-77
Boardman, Isaac	Corp. Can.	"	1 -79
Bodle, Samuel	Sgt. N.Y.	"	1780
Bodley, William	Maj. Pa.	"	1780
Bodo, Otto	Col. N.J.	"	1-20-82
Body, Robert	Pvt. 6 Md.	"	8-16-80
Bogart John	Pvt. N.Y.	"	1780
Boissand, Michel	France	"	1781 Va.
Boles, William	Pvt. 2 Md.	"	5-1- 80
Bollinger, Henry	Pvt. N. C.	"	1776
Bolton, Jon A	Pvt. 2 N.Y.	"	5-26-78

Bolton, William Jr.	Mass	Died	5-7-1780
Bolton, William	Pvt. 3 Md.	Killed	1780
Boltwood, Solomon	Mass.	Died	1777
Bombrey, Geo.	Pvt. 1 N.Y.	"	1-8- 78
Bomer, James	Col. N. C.	"	1782
Bonchi, Louis	Pvt. Can	"	1-25-78
Bond, Jacob	Md.	"	1780
Bond, Joseph	Sgt. 2 Conn	"	1-28-78
Bond, Thos.	Pvt. 9 N. C.	"	12-13-77
Bond, William	Col. Mass.	"	8-31-76
Bone, Jas.	Cpl. 2 N.C.	"	6-17-83
Boney, Simon	Pvt. 3 N.J.	"	11-26-78
Bonner, Henry	N.C.	"	1779
Bonney, Jacob	Pvt. N.H.	"	7-7-78
Bonney, Simeon	Me.	"	9- 81
Boodwine, Peter	Pvt. 1 N.J.	"	11-15-78
Booge, Ichabod	Pvt. 2 Conn	"	8-1-78
Boon, Hawkins	Capt. 6 Pa.	"	7-28-79
Boon, Joseph	Pvt. N.J.	"	1776 Can.
Boon, Richard	Pvt. 1 Md.	Killed	3-15-81
Boone, Richard	Pvt. Md.	Died	3-15-81
Boor, Michael	Pvt.Pa.	"	1778
Booten, Simeon P.	Pvt. Conn.	"	11-26-77
Booth, James	Capt. W. Va.	Killed	1778
Booth, Jeremiah	Pvt. Conn.	Died	7-4-81
Booth, John	N.Y.	"	1779
Booth, John	Pvt. 1 Md.	"	9-8-78
Booth, Prosper P.	Pvt. 2 Conn	"	9-15-77
Booth, Thomas	Pvt. Del.	"	8-22-80
Bootman, Joseph	Sgt. 1 Md.	"	2-7-77
Bostick, Josiah	Pvt. 15 Mass	"	1-20-77
Boston, John P.	Pvt. Conn	"	5-10-77
Boston, Junier	Pvt. 10 Mass	"	11-12-79
Boston, Nell	Pvt. Mass	"	1-12-78
Boston, Toby	Pvt. Conn	"	12-18-77
Bostridge, Tho	Del.	"	12-5-77
Bostwick, Geo.	Del.	"	3-30-79
Bostwick, Joel	Conn	"	4-11-77
Bosworth, Amos	Pvt. Mass	"	9-12-78
Boughton, Joseph	Capt. Conn	"	1778
Bouillot, Benoist	France	"	1781 Va
Boulden, Thomas	Capt. Md.	"	1783
Bouldin, Thomas	Col. Va.	"	5-3- 83
Bouldin, Thomas	Md.	"	1780
Bourdin, Nicolas	France	"	1781 Va
Bourne, John	Mass	"	9-11-78
Bourville, Joseph	Pvt. 9 Mass	"	4-19-78
Bowders, John	Pvt. S C	"	5- 81
Bowen, Alexander	Pvt. N.J.	"	9-11-77
Bowen, Elisha	Pvt. 9 Mass	"	9-1-79
Bowen, John	Navy	"	11-27-78 Va.
Bowen, John	Pvt. 1 N Y	"	2-16-77
Bowen, Joseph	Ens. R. I.	"	1779
Bowen, Reece	Lt. S. C.	Killed	10-7-80 King Mt.
Bowen, Robert	Pvt. Va.	Died	1779

Bowen, Stoddard	Pa.	Died	7-3-78
Bowen, Thomas	Mass.	"	1782
Bowers, George	Pvt. Md.	"	5-1-81
Bowers, John	Pvt. 4 Mass	"	7-1-77
Bowers, Randolph	3 S. C.	"	10-10-79
Bowers, Thomas	Pvt. 3 Md	"	9-12-78
Bowers, William	Pvt. 15 Mass	"	6-27-78
Bowker, Joshua	Pvt. Mass	"	12-25-77
Bowles, David	6 Va.	"	1778
Bowls, John	Engr. R. I.	"	1-1-80
Bowman, Ebenezer	Pvt. 10 Mass	"	4-20-77
Bowman, Joshua	Capt. S. C.	Killed	1780 N.C.
Bowman, Joshua	Pvt. 1 N.C.	"	3-30-80
Bowman, Joshua	Capt. N. C.	"	6-20-80
Bowman, Solomon	Lt. Mass	"	1778
Bownd, Rodnam P.	Pvt. 2 N.Y.	Died	3-9-79
Box, Caleb	Pvt. 12 Mass	"	3-3-78
Boyall, Peter	Cpl. Md.	"	1-15-82
Boyce, Alexander	Capt. 6 SC	Killed	10-9-79 Savannah
Boyce, Daniel	Sgt. Del	Died	1-14-79
Boyce, John	Pvt. 10 N. C.	"	7-25-82
Boyce, Seth	Pvt. 8 N.C.	"	10-5-77
Boyd, John	S.C.	"	10-7-80 KingsMt.
Boyd, John	Pvt. 10 N. C.	"	3-22-78
Boyd, John	Pa	"	7-3-78
Boyd, Robert	N.H.	"	1-9-77
Boyd, Thomas	Q. M. Pa.	"	1778
Boyd, Thomas	Lt. Pa.	"	9-13-79
Boyd, Thomas	Capt. N.Y.	"	1779
Boyd, William	Lt. 12 Pa.	Killed	9-11-77
Boyden, Peter	Pvt. Mass.	Died	7-28-77
Boyer, Peter	Cpl. Md.	"	1-15-82
Boyer, Thomas	Pvt. Md.	"	1778
Boyes, James	N.H.	"	8-10-79
Boyle, James	Pvt. 6 Md.	"	8-16-80
Boyle, William	Pvt. Va.	"	2-25-77 Prison
Boyles, Job	Pvt. 4 NY	"	12-12-77
Boyles, Thomas H.	Maj. Pa.	"	1779
Boynton, Jacob	N.H.	Killed	6-17-75 Bunker Hill
Boynton, James	N.H.	Died	6-17-75
Boynton, James	Pvt. Mass	Killed	1775
Bozworth, Joseph	Pvt. R. I.	Died	5-21-77
Bracher, Isaac	Pvt. 10 N.C.	"	9-18-82
Bracket, Anthony	Pvt. 10 Mass	"	1-1-78
Bracket, Samuel	Pvt. Mass	"	6- 78
Brackett, John	Capt. Mass	"	1775
Brackett, John	Capt. Me	"	1775
Bradbury, Sanders	N.H.	"	11-15-79
Bradford, Gamaliel	Mass.	"	4-24-78
Bradford, James	Conn.	"	9-16-78
Bradford, Peabody	Mass.	"	9-5-82
Bradford, Robert	Mass	"	8-12-82
Bradford, Samuel	Capt. Mass	"	2-17-77
Bradley, Aaaron	Fifer	Killed	7-5-79 New Haven

Bradley, Daniel	Pvt. 1 Mass	Died	11-11-77
Bradley, Ezekiel	Del	"	11-6-78
Bradley, Francis	N C	"	1780
Bradley, George	Cpl. Md	"	11-31-82
Bradley, James	Pvt. 5 Md.	"	5- 79
Bradley, Jerem	Pvt. 3 Mass	"	12-20-77
Bradley, John	Cpl. Va.	"	1780
Bradley, Joshua	Mass	"	1780
Bradley, Josiah	N.H.	"	5-2- 78
Bradley, Richard	N.C.	"	1782
Bradley, Zebulon	Pvt. Conn	"	1779
Bradshaw, Samuel	Pvt. 18 Cont.	"	8-1-76
Bradshaw, Samuel	Mass	"	8-1-76
Bradsher, Jno.	Pvt. 8 N. C.	"	2-28-78
Bradstreet, Samuel	Sgt. Mass	"	1777
Brady, John	Capt. Pa.	Killed	1779 By Ind
Brady, John	Pa.	"	5-11-79
Brady, John Sr.	Capt. Pa.	"	4-11-79
			Lewisburg
Brady, Francis	N.C.	"	11-14-80
Bragdon, Josiah	Lt. Mass	Died	4-30-78
Bragdon, Josiah	N.Y.	"	4-27-78
Bragdon, Joshua	Capt. Me.	"	1778
Bragg, Ariel	Mass	"	1780
Brainerd, Jeptha	N.Y.	"	1777 Prison
			Ship
Brains, Michl	Pvt. 10 N.C.	"	9-9-77
Braley, John	Pvt. 11 Mass.	"	8- 78
Braman, Sylvanus	Mass	"	82
Bramble, Levin	Pvt. Md.	"	7-13-81
Branan, Ruben	N.Y.	"	10-22-81
Branard, Ansel	Pvt. 15 Mass.	"	10-12-77
Brendon, Charles	Pvt. 2 Conn.	"	1-15-78
Brandt, John	Maj. Va.	"	1781
Brannon, William	Del.	"	12- 78
Brannon, Jese	Pvt. 10 N.C.	"	8-25-79
Brant, Robert	Pvt. 9 Mass.	"	5-1-77
Brasher, Abraham	N.J.	"	12-7-82
Brasher, Abraham	Col. N.Y.	"	1782
Braswell, William	N. C.	"	1781
Bratt, James	Pvt. 1 N.Y.	"	9-7-78
Bray, Chas.	Pvt. 1 N.Y.	"	10-21-78
Brazelton, John	N.C.	"	3-14-81
Breckenridge, James	Lt. Vt.	"	4-16-83
Breed, John	Capt. Conn	"	11-3-80
Brent, George	Va.	"	1779
Brent, John	Fifer Md.	"	5-14-81
Brent, John	Capt. Va.	"	1781
Bretton, Daniel	Pvt. Conn.	"	1783
Brevard, John	Lt. Conn	"	7-21-79
Brewer, Benj.	Pvt. 7 N. C.	"	8-25-77
Brewer, Benjn.	Pvt. 10 N. C.	"	8-1-78
Brewer, Benjamin	Drummer Conn.	"	3-28-78
Brewer, James	Dr. N.Y.	"	11-20-80

Brewer, John	Pvt. Md.	Died	7-17-82
Brewer, Joseph	Mass	"	1779
Brewer, Peter	N.H.	"	10-7-77
Brewer, Thomas	Pvt. Conn.	"	9-13-82
Brewster, Amos	Pvt. 2 Conn.	"	11- 77
Brewster, Amos	Pvt. N.Y.	"	1777
Brewster, Isaac	N.H.	"	4- 82
Briant, Joseph	Capt. Conn.	"	8-11-83
Brice, William	Capt. Md.	"	1783
Brice, William	Lt. N.Y.	"	17.78
Bridel, Adam	Pvt. Pa.	"	1777 Prison
Bridge, Amos	R.I.	Killed	12-31-75 Que.
Bridge, Matthew	Rev. Mass	Died	9.2-75
Brient, Stephen	Pvt. 12 Mass	"	3-15-78
Briggs, Eliphalet	N.H.	"	10-11-76
Briggs, Jedediah	Mass.	"	1776
Briggs, Nathaniel	Pvt. 12 Mass	"	9-2-77
Briggs, Seth	Mass.	"	1781
Briggs, Thomas	Mass.	"	1779
Brigham, Asa	Maj. N.H.	"	11-6-77
Brigham, Paul	Capt. Mass	"	6-4-77
Brigham, Timothy	Col. Mass	"	10-1-75
Brigham, Uriah	Pvt. Mass	"	10-22-82
Bright, David	Pvt. Pa.	"	1783
Bright, John	Pvt. 1 S.C.	"	2-4-76
Brimall, Joshua	Pvt. 7 Mass	"	11-28 77
Brinckerhoff, Derrick	Col. N.Y.	"	1780
Brindley, Michael	Pvt. 7 Md.	Killed	10-4-77 George-town
Britt, Arthur	Pvt. 10 N. C.	Died	10-28-78
Brittain, Nathan	Va.	"	1776
Brittin, William Jr.	Capt. N.J.	"	1783
Brock, Barrett	Pvt. N.C.	"	1781
Brock, Nathl.	Pvt. 4 N.Y.	"	8-30-78
Brocow, John	Lt. N.J.	Killed	1777
Broderick, James	Pvt. R. I.	Died	1-17-78
Broderick, Joseph	N. H.	"	6-17-75
Brokaw, John	Lt. N.J.	Killed	1777
Bromagen, William	Pvt. 5 Mass.	Died	4-10-78
Bromell, Peter	Pvt. 5 Md.	"	6-26-77
Brookfield, Jacob	N. J.	"	1-2-82
Brookhouse, Robert	Capt. at Sea	"	1779
Brookin, Thos.	Sgt. 10 N. C.	"	8-5-82
Brooks, Abijah	Mus. 2 Conn.	"	8-3-77
Brooks, Edward	Lt. Mass	"	1776
Brooks, Eliaham	Pvt. 7 Mass	"	7-1-78
Brooks, Ethural	Pvt. Conn.	Killed	10-7-77 Saratoga
Brooks, Joseph	Pvt. 9 Pa.	Died	1-23-80
Brooks, Josiah	Pvt. Mass	"	2-23-82
Brooks, Josiah	Pvt. N.H.	Killed	6-17-75 Bunker Hill
Brooks, Samuel	Capt. Conn.	Died	1781
Brosius, Abraham	Pa.	"	1777
Broughton, John	Conn	"	1777
Broughton, Joshua	Pvt. 2 Md.	"	12-31- 79

Name	Rank/Unit	Status	Date	Notes
Brown, Abraham	Capt. Mass	Died	1777	
Brown, Amos P.	Pvt. 11 Mass.	Killed	7-7- 77	
Brown, Ben	Conn.	Died	1783	
Brown, Benjamin	Pvt. 12 Mass	"	11-15-77	
Brown, Benjn.	Pvt. 7 N. C.	"	2- 78	
Brown, Caleb	Lt. Del.	"	1-29-80	
Brown, Christian	N.Y.		1783	
Brown, Collins	Pvt. 1 N.C.	"	4-14-78	
Brown, Daniel	2nd Lt. N.J.	"	11-9-76	
Brown, David	Pvt. 9 N. C.	Killed	10-4-77	
Brown, Elias	Pvt. R. I.	Died	9-6-77	
Brown, Elias	N.H.	"	1779	
Brown, Francis	Pvt. Mass	"	1778	
Brown, George	Pvt. Conn	"	6-28-78	
Brown, Henry	Pvt. 10 N.C.	"	8- 81	
Brown, Henry	Pvt. 4 N.J.	"	12- 77	
Brown, Israel	Pvt. R. I.	"	7-1-78	
Brown, Israel P. Stevens	Pvt. Conn	"	8-19-77	
Brown, Jacob	Pvt. 7 Mass	Killed	6-28-78	
Brown, Jacob	Capt. Mass	Died	1776	
Brown, James	Pvt. 2 N.Y.	"	8- 1778	
Brown, James	Pvt. 3 Md.	"	12-1778	
Brown, John	Capt. Conn	"	1776	
Brown, John	Capt. N.Y.	"	1776	
Brown, John	Col. N.Y.	Killed	1780	Mohawk Valley
Brown, John 4th	Pvt. Mass	Died	2-14-78	
Brown, John	Pvt. 1 N.J.	"	1- 1778	
Brown, John	Capt. Conn	"	1776	
Brown, John	S C	"	10-7- 80	King Mt.
Brown, John	3 N.Y.	"	9-3-76	
Brown, John	Pa.	"	7-3-78	
Brown, John	Mass	Killed	4-19-75	Tex.
Brown, John	N. Y.	"	10-19-80	By Ind.
Brown, John	Yale Conn.	Died	10-19-77	
Brown, John	Sgt. Mass	"	6-17-75	
Brown, John	Capt. Conn	"	1776	
Brown, John	Pvt. Can	Killed	6-28-78	
Brown, John	Col. Mass.	Died	10-19-80	
Brown, John	Col. Yale Conn	"	10-1780	
Brown, John	Maj. N.Y.	Killed	1780	By Ind.
Brown, Jonas	N.Y.	Died	1781	Va.
Brown, Jonathan	N.H.	"	1775	
Brown, Joseph	Pvt. 7 Mass.	Killed	8-29-79	
Brown, Matthew	Md.	Died	4-22-77	Pa.
Brown, Moses	N.H.	"	6-5- 80	
Brown, Moses	N.H.	Killed	10-7-77	
Brown, Nathan	Vt.	Died	1781	
Brown, Nathan	Pvt. Conn	"	11-16-77	
Brown, Parley	Pvt. N.Y.	Killed	1776	
Brown, Robert	Pvt. 8 Mass	"	4-1-77	
Brown, Samuel	Pvt. Va.	"	2-26-77	Prison
Brown, Samuel	3 N.J.	"	4-30-78	
Brown, Silas	Col. Mass	"	3-31-81	
Brown, Solomon	Pvt. Conn	"	11- 78	

Brown, Solomon	Pvt. 18 Cont.	Died	10-25-76
Brown, Stephen	Capt. Conn	"	11-16-77
Brown, Thomas	2 Md.	"	11- 4-79
Brown, Thomas	Pvt. 1 N.J.	"	1-15-77
Brown, Thomas	Cpl. Md.	Killed	9-8-81
Brown, Thomas	Pa.	Died	7-3-78
Brown, Thomas	N.J.	"	1781
Brown, William	Pvt. 2 Conn	Killed	12-7-77
Brown, William	Del.	Died	8-18-77
Brown, William	N.J.	"	1782
Brown, William	Pa.	"	1777
Brown, William	1 Md.	"	1780
Brown, William	12 Mass	"	3-15- 78
Brown, William	Pvt. 8 Mass	"	5-11-78
Browne, Abraham	Capt. Mass	"	1777
Browne, William	Pa.	Killed	1777 Brandy-wine
Brownell, Isaac	Conn.	Died	1775
Brownell, Jonathan	Lt. R. I.	"	1776
Brownlee, Alexander	Ens. Pa.	"	3-15-81
Brownlee, James	Capt. Pa.	"	3- 81
Brownlee, Robert Jr.	N.J.	"	11-30-81
Brownlee, Robert Jr.	Conn.	"	11-3-81
Brownlee, William	N.J.	"	9-13-76
Bruce, John	Sgt. N.H.		1779
Brucem Simon	Mass	"	3-20-76
Brumblum, Thomas	Pvt. 7 Mass	"	2-20-77
Brumley, William P.	Conn	"	9-18-79
Brunner, Casper	Pvt. Pa.	"	1783
Brunner, John	Md.	"	1776
Brunean,	Lt. S C	Killed	10-9- 79
Brunson, Hezekiah	Pvt. Conn	Died	7-25-77
Brunson, Matthew	Pvt. S C	"	1781
Bryan, Capt.	N C	Killed	3-12-82
Bryan, Daniel	Pvt. 3 Md.	Died	12-7-77
Bryan, James	Pvt. Md.	Killed	9-15-81
Bryan, John	N. C.	"	1780
Bryan, John	Pvt. 2 Md.		1778
Bryan, Math	Del		12-8-81
Bryan, William	Capt. Ky	Killed	1781 By Ind.
Bryan, William	Pvt. Ky.	Died	1780 " "
Bryan, William	Pvt. N. C	"	1780
Bryant, Abraham	Pvt. 10 Mass	"	3-1-78
Bryant, Daniel	Mass	"	3-9-79
Bryant, David	Capt. Mass	"	9-11-77
Bryant, John	Pvt. 10 Mass	"	7-2-77
Bryant, John	Pvt. 7 Mass	"	3- 79
Bryant, Micah	Mass	"	1-28-76
Bryant, Thomas	Pvt. 4 N.Y.	"	9-22-77
Bryant, William	Mus. 3 N. J.	"	9-5-77
Bryard, William	Pvt. 12 Mass	"	9-7-77
Bryer, Peter	N. H.	"	4-1-78
Bryley, Chas.	Pvt. 1 N. C	Killed	9-17-77
Buchanan, Andrew	Brig. Gen. Va.	Died	1780
Buchanan, John	Lt.	"	10-7-83

Bucher, John	Conrad Chap Pa	Died	1780
Buck, Aholiab	Capt. Conn	Killed	1778 Wyo.
Buck, Aboliab	Pa.	Died	7-3- 78
Buck, Benjamin	Pvt. Conn.	"	3-1-78
Buck, Enock	Pvt. 2 N. Y.	"	1-14-79
Buck, Henry	Pa.	"	7-3-78
Buck, Isaac	Que	"	1776
Buck, William	Pa.	"	7-3-78
Bucker, John Conrad	Chap. Pa.	"	1777
Buckhout, Wm.	Cpl. 2 N.Y.	"	1- 79
Buckland, Stephen	Capt. Conn.	"	1782
Buckman, Joel	Pvt. 9 Mass.	"	12-26-77
Budd, Barnabus	Surg. N.J.	"	9-12-77
Budd, Bern	N.J.	"	12-14-77
Budd, Berne	Surg. N.J.	"	1777
Budd, James	Pa.	"	7-3-78
Budd, Thomas	Capt. N.J.	Killed	1778
Budding, John P.	Pvt. 1 S C	Died	10-21-76
Bugbee, Abejuk	Pvt. R. I.	"	3-11-78
Bugg, Sherwood	Capt. S C	"	1781
Bull, Epaphras	Conn.	Killed	1781
Bull, Michl	Mus. 2 N C	Died	1- 79
Bull, Roger	Mass	"	1783
Bullard, Ephraim	Mass	"	3-13-79
Bullard, John	Pvt. 18 Cont	"	10-20-76
Bullard, Joseph	Pvt. 4 N. J.	"	2 12-78
Bulle, Jean Joseph	France	"	1781 Va.
Bullen, Nathan	Pvt. Can	"	2-28-82
Bullin, John	Pvt. 15 Mass	"	9-30-77
Bullion, Wm.	Pvt. 1 N.Y.	"	1-20- 77
Bullock, Amos	Pa.	"	7-3- 78
Bullock, Arch	Pvt. 1 N.Y.	"	6-1- 80
Bullock, Archibald	S C	"	1777
Bullock, Archibald	Gov. Ga.	"	1777
Bullock, James	Capt. Va.	"	1781
Bullock, Jesten	Pvt. 3 Md.	"	1780
Bulotph, Jonathan	Capt. Conn	"	1777
Bump, Abel	Pvt. R. I.	"	3-1-78
Buncombe, Edward	Col. 5 N. C.	"	10-4-77 Prison
Bunce, David	Pvt. Conn	"	10-13-77
Bunn, Levi	Pvt. 3 N.J.	"	5-26-79
Bunnel, Levy	Pvt. Conn	"	8-25-77
Bunner, Rudolph	Col. Pa.	Killed	6-28-78 Mon-Mouth
Bunson, Asa	Pvt. 2 Conn	Died	2-27 78
Buntin, Andrew	N. H.	Killed	10-28-76 White Plains
Buntin, Andrew	Capt. N.H.	Died	1776
Buntin, William	Pvt. 2 Can	"	12-18-77
Bunting, William B.	Ens. Va.	"	8-1- 77
Bunting, William B.	Lt. Va.	"	4-1-77
Bunton, Andrew	Capt. N. H.	Killed	1776 White Plains

Burbeck, Edward	Capt. Mass	Died	1782
Burbridge, John	Pvt. Va.	"	1782
Burch, Benjamin	Sgt. Md.	"	11-3- 83
Burch, Samuel	Pvt. 1 N.Y.	"	7-20-78
Burcham, John	Del	"	7-17-78
Burchan, William P.	Del	"	12-7-78
Burck, Justus	Mass	"	1781 Va
Burg, John	Pvt. 9 Mass	"	6-14-78
Burgan, Joshua	Pvt. 5 Md.	"	10-19-78
Burges, Isaac	Pvt. 1 N. C.	"	7-10-78
Burges, Joseph	Pvt. 6 N.C.	"	8-7-77
Burgess, Covill	Pvt. Mass	"	1780
Burgess, James	Pvt. 3 S. C.	Killed	10-9-79
Burgess, Joseph	Pvt. 4 Md.	Died	11-17-78
Burgess, Thomas	Pvt. 2 Md.	"	8-10-79
Burk, Jonathan	Lt. Vt.	"	1-16-76
Burke, Isaiah	Vt.	"	1-16-76
Burke, James	R. I.	"	7- 79
Burke, Simeon	R. I.	"	7- 79
Burke, Simeon	Vt.	"	4-15-81
Burke, William	Cpl. 6 Pa.	"	10- 76
Burlew, Thomas	Pvt. 1 N.J.	"	11-15-78
Burley, John	Lt. N. H.	"	11-18-76
Burnan, Joseph	Pvt. 8 Mass	"	9-26-77
Burnes, Zekiel	Pvt. 2 Md.	Killed	8-16-80
Burnet, Matthias	Pvt. N.J.	Died	8-16-80
Burnham, Abel	Pvt. 18 Cont.	"	10-5-76
Burnham, Obediah	Pvt. 7 Mass.	"	7-15-78
Burnham, Phineas	Conn.	"	12-22-76
Burnley, Joel Terrell	Va.	"	1781 Va.
Burns, Henry	Pvt. 1 N.Y.	"	6- 77
Burns, James	Pvt. Pa.	"	1777 Prison
Burns, John	2 Md.	"	3- 1780
Burns, Michael	Pvt. 5 Md.	"	11- 1799
Burnall, Amos	Pvt. Conn.	"	3-30-78
Burnett, Charles	Pvt. 5 Md.	"	7-17-78
Burnham, Samuel	Mass	"	1782
Burr, Daniel	Pvt. Conn	"	7-15-78
Burr, Ephraim	Pvt. Conn	"	1779
Burr, Zebulon	Pvt. 6 Mass	"	12-29-77
Burrett, Abijah	Pvt. Conn	"	3-9-77
Burridge, Simeon P.	Pvt. 11 Mass	"	3-7-78
Burridge, William	Pvt. Mass	"	1-12-78
Burris, George	Pvt. 3 Md.	"	1-2-78
Burris, William	Pvt. Md.	"	12-20-77
Burroughs, Edward	Conn	"	9-14-76
Burroughs, James	N. J.	"	12-27-76
Burrows, Hubbard	Capt. N.Y.	"	1776
Burrows, Ihbbard	Capt. Conn	Killed	1781 Ft. Griswold
Burrows, Hubbard Daniel	Capt. Conn		1781
Burrows, John	Pvt. Can	Died	12-20-76
Burs, David	Pvt. 1 N.Y.	"	8-19-77
Bursley, Joseph Jr.	Mass.	"	1778

Name	Rank/Unit	Status	Date	Location
Burson, James	Capt. Pa.	Died	1783	
Burt, Deen	Mass	"	1778	
Burt, John	Mass.	"	1781	Va.
Burt, Thomas	Pvt. 1 SC	"	12-6-76	
Burton, Benjamin	Del	"	11-15-83	
Burton, Joab	Pvt. Conn.	"	8-25-78	
Burton, Robert	Pvt. Conn	"	3-1-78	
Burve, Matth	Pvt.	Killed	6-28-78	
Bury, John	Mass	Died	1781	
Bus, John	Lt. S C	"	10-9-79	
Bush	Lt. S. C.	Killed	10-7-80	Savannah
Bush, Chany	Pvt 4 N C	Died	1-2-78	
Bush, John	Lt 2 S C	Killed	10-9-79	
Bush, John	Lt		1779	Va
Bush, Lewis	Maj Pa	Died	9-11-77	
Bush, Richard	2 Md	"	2-12-79	
Bushby, Hugh	Pvt 2 S C	"	7-24-76	
Buskirk, John	Lt Va	"	1781	
Bussey, Edward	Lt Md	"	1782	
Bussey, Ishmal	Pvt 18 Cont	"	10-11-76	
Butler, Lt		Killed	1780	
Butler, Aaron	Ens Conn	Died	11-12-77	
Butler, Benjamin	P Pvt 2 Conn	"	4-4-78	
Butler, Charles	Lt. Conn	"	1783	
Butler, Charles	Sgt. Conn	"	1782	
Butler, Daniel	Pvt 8 Mass	"	3-7-78	
Butler, Ephraim	Pvt 15 Mass	"	12-2-77	
Butler, Ezekiel	Conn	"	6-26-81	
Butler, Jacob	Pvt 1 Md	"	3-20-77	
Butler, James	Cpl 11 Pa	Killed	4-23-79	
Butler, James	Cpl 15 Mass	Died	7-1-78	
Butler, James	Capt 8 C	Killed	1781	By Ind.
Butler, James	SC	"	11-7-81	Clouds Creek
Butler, John	Pvt 8 Mass	Died	2-21-80	
Butler, Jonathan	Pvt Conn	"	9-1-77	
Butler, Lawrence	Pvt 10 N C	"	3-24-82	
Butolph, Jonathan	Conn	"	1777	
Butt, Edward	Pvt Md	"	3-15-81	
Butterfield, Peter	Cpl N H	"	1783	
Buttery, Thomas	Pvt 3 Md	Killed	8-16-80	
Button, Mathias	18 Cont	Died	10-19-76	
Button, William	Pvt R I	"	1-24-78	
Buys, Simon	Pvt N Y	"	1775	
Byard, William	Capt. Pa	"	8- 1777	
Byars, Joseph	Cpl 6 Pa	"	9-25-76	
Byles, Thomas L.	Maj. Pa.	"	2-1-79	
Byrd, John	Pvt. 9 Mass	"	7-30-78	
Byrne, Charles	Pvt. 2 Md	Killed	8-16-80	
Byrne, Christopher	Pvt. 1 S C	Died	9-2-76	
Byron, Michael	Pvt. 5 Md	"	9-12-77	
Buzzard, Leighton	Pvt. 3 Md	"	5-15-78	

C

Name	Rank/Unit	Status	Date	Location
Cabal, William	Pvt. 2 Conn	Died	2-21-78	
Cabbage, Coural	Pvt Va	"	1-7- 77	

36.

Name	Rank/Unit	Status	Date/Notes
Cable, Joseph	Pvt. 14 Mass	Died	7- 78 Prison
Cade, John	Pvt. N. J.	"	6-15-76
Cadge, Jube	Pvt. 4 Mass	"	8-1-77
Cadwell, Daniel	Lt. Mass	"	1777
Cadwell, Mathew Jr.	Mass	"	3-24-83
Cadwell, Russell	Pvt. Conn.	"	7-11-77
Cady, Curtiss	Pvt. N. H.	"	4-4-78
Cady, Isaac	Conn.	"	1777
Cady, Solomon	Conn.	"	1776
Caesar, Jonathan	Pvt. Mass	"	6-6-78
Caesar, Thomas	Pvt. N. J	"	4-30-78
Cahoner, John	Pvt. Mass	"	6-28-78
Cail, Amo	Pvt. 7 N C	"	12-7-77
Cain, Able	Pvt Mass	"	1781 Va
Cain, Able	Pvt 4 N.Y.	"	2-1779
Cain, Thomas	Pvt Mass	"	1780
Calagan, John	Pvt 4 N Y	"	3-1782
Calaghan, John	N Y	"	1781 Va
Calderwood, James	Capt. Va	Killed	9-11- 77
Calderwood, James	Chap. Va.	"	1781
Caleb, Green	Conn	Died	10-23 76
Calkin, Reuben	Lt. 2 Conn	"	12-2-77
Callahan, Daniel	Mass	Killed	6-17-75 Bunker Hill
Callaway, William	Col. Va.	Died	1778
Callum, Fredk	Pvt. 10 N C	"	1778
Calor, Joseph	R I	"	1-16-77
Calvert, John	Va	"	1783
Caldwell, James	Chap N J	"	2- 9-76
Caldwell, James	Chap N J	Killed	11-24-81
Caldwell, John	Pa	Died	7-3-78
Caldwell, John	N H	"	2-19-80
Caldwell, Paul	N H	Killed	6-17-75 Bunker Hill
Calhoun, Charles	Pvt. Pa	Died	11-20-76
Calhoun, George	Capt. 10 Pa	"	3-21-79
Calkins, Stephen	Pvt. Conn		1781
Callaway, Richard	Ky	Killed	1780 By Ind.
Callaway, Richard	Va	Died	1780
Callaway, Richard	Col Va	"	1780
Callendar, Robert	Pa		1777
Camedia, William	Pvt. Conn	"	6-25-80
Cameron, Daniel	Pvt. N. Y.	"	1781
Cammel, Daniel	Pvt. S C	"	1781
Camp, Israel	Capt. Conn	"	1778
Camp, John	Pvt. Mass	"	1777
Camp, Joseph	Pvt. N. J.	"	10-20-80
Camp, Phineas P.	Pvt. Mass	"	1-28-78
Cameron, Josiah	Pa	"	7-3-78
Campbell, Archibald	Capt S C	Killed	1-3-82
Campbell, George	N J	Died	6-16-77
Campbell, Henry	N H	"	10-1-82
Campbell, Isaac	Pa	"	7-3-78
Campbell, James	Pa	"	11-26-76
Campbell, James	Lt. N C	"	1779

Name	Rank/Unit	Fate	Date	Notes
Campbell, John	Capt. Va	Killed	2-26-76	Moores Creek
Campbell, Nichs	Pvt. 7 Md	Died	1- 1779	
Campbell, Richard	Col. Va.	Killed	9-8-81	S C
Campbell, Robell	Lt. N. Y	"	1777	Oriskany
Campbell, Robert	Lt. N Y	Died	1777	
Campbell, Samuel	Lt. Va.	"	1778	
Campbell, Solomon	Pvt. 10 NC	"	4-1778	
Campbell, Thomas	Pvt. Mass	"	9-4-80	
Campbell, Wm	Cpl 6 N C	"	2- 80	
Campbell, William	Brig. Gen. Va.	"	1782	
Campbell, William	Capt. Va	"	1781	
Campbell, William	N H	"	1-8-76	
Campble, Robert	Capt	Killed	10-4-79	
Campble, William	Sgt. 8 Pa	Died	2-24-77	
Campble, Wm.	Cpl. 7 Pa	"	2-20-77	
Campher, John	Pvt. Md.	Killed	9-8-81	
Cane, Hugh	Pvt. Md.	Died	3-19-81	
Canfield, Daniel	Pvt. Mass	"	3-22-78	
Canfield, David	Pvt. N. J.	Killed	12-16-76	
Canfield, Josiah Dr.	Conn	"	2-11-78	
Cannon, Benjm	Mus 3 N C	"	5-1-78	
Cannon, Jno.	Pvt. 10 N C	"	8-25-82	
Cannon, Moses	Pvt. N J	Died	1-26-78	
Canus, Pierre	France	"	1781	Va
Cansins, Peter	Pvt 3 Md	Killed	10-4-78	
Cappock, Simons	4 Md	Died	7-16-79	
Carbury, William	Pvt. Pa	"	1777	Prison
Card, Edward	Pvt. Mass	"	1780	At Sea
Card, Josh	Pvt. 8 N C	"	10-4-77	
Carey, Cabb	Mass	"	1783	
Carey, H. Andrew	Sgt. 3 N C	"	9- 1777	
Carey, Chambers	N H	Killed	6-17-75	Bunker Hill
Carey, Eleazer	Pvt. Pa.	Died	1777	
Carey, Jonathan	Mass	"	10-12-75	
Carey, Joseph	Pa	"	7-3-78	
Carey, Zenos	Pvt. 14 Mass	"	2-17-78	
Cargill, John	Pvt. 3 Mass	"	10-30-77	
Carleton, David	N H	Killed	6-17-75	Bunker Hill
Carlson, John	Pvt. S C	"	9- 1781	
Carlton, George	N H	"	6-17-75	Bunker Hill
Carlisle	S C	"	9-9-81	
Carll, Evans	Pvt 11 Mass	Died	1-16-78	
Carlton, Nehemiah	Pvt. 10 Mass	"	3-1-78	
Carmady, Jas.	Pvt. 5 N C	"	5-12-78	
Carmichael, Alexander	Lt. Pa.	Killed	9-11-77	
Carmichael, Daniel	Ens. Pa.		1778	
Carnant, Jacob	Pvt. Md.	Died	9-15-81	
Carnes, Edward	Maj. Mass	"	1782	
Carpent, Richard	Mass		1781	Prison SS Jersey
Carpenter, Amasa	Lt. Conn	"	10-19-76	
Carpenter, Andrew	Pvt. Conn	"	1778	
Carpenter, Benajah	Capt. R I	Killed	8-27-76	L I
Carpenter, Henry P	Pvt. Conn	Died	10-14-77	
Carpenter, John	Pvt. Mass	"	12-10-78	

Carpenter, Moses	N Y	Died	1779
Carpenter, Robert	Cpl 8 Mass	Killed	10-7-77
Carpenter, Thomas	Mass	Died	12-7-76
Carpenter, Thomas	Pvt Mass	"	1779
Carpenter, William	Pvt. Mass	"	11-13-77
Carpenter, Zachariah	Mass	"	1775
Carr, John	Pvt Md	"	2-25-83
Carr, MacCrest	Capt. Mass	"	1779
Carr, Stephen	Pvt. Md.	"	10-13-81
Carrell, Benj	Pvt 5 N C	"	8- 1777
Carrol, Charles	Pvt	"	4-17-78
Carroll, John	Pvt Md	"	1-13-82
Carroll, John	Pvt Mass	"	1781
Carrults, William	Pvt 15 Mass	"	5-17-78
Carson, John	Lt. Md	"	5-17-78
Carten, James	Pvt. 5 Mass	"	3 30-78
Carter, Asaph	Mass	"	12-23-76
Carter, C. M.	Pa.	"	7-3-78
Carter, Charles	Pvt. 12 Mass	"	6-26-78
Carter, Daniel	Pvt. 2 Conn	"	3-24-78
Carter, Daniel	Cpl. 10 N C	"	7- 78
Carter, Eleazer	Lt. Conn	"	1777
Carter, H'bbard	Pvt. 6 N C	"	4-11-78
Carter, James	Maj. Ga.	"	9-17-80
Carter, Jno.	Pvt. 10 N C	"	11-18-78
Carter, John	Pvt. Md	Killed	9-8- 81
Carter, John	2 SC	"	10-9-79
Carter, Joshua	Pvt. Conn.	Died	1780
Carter, Joshue P	Pvt. Mass	"	3-7-78
Carter, Justenian	Pvt. 3 Md	"	8-11-78
Carter, Wm.	Pvt. 7 N C	"	4- 17-78
Cartledge, John	1 SC	"	9-9-76
Cartmel, John	" 2 N J	"	12-6-77
Cartwrite, Thomas	Cpl Can	"	9-9-81
Carty, Darby	Del	"	8-12-77
Caruthers, John	Lt. 12 Pa.	Killed	10-4-77
Carver, Eleazer	Lt. Mass	Died	1778
Cary, Eleazer	Pvt. Pa.	"	1779
Cary, Nathaniel	Pvt. Conn	"	1776
Cary, William	Navy	"	7-21-81
Carver, Thomas	Pvt. 6 Mass	"	12-2-77
Case, Joseph Jr.	Mass	"	1782
Case, Joshua	Pvt. N. J.	"	1777
Case, Solomon	Pvt. Mass	"	9-13-77
Case, William	Pvt. 5 Mass	"	1-24-78
Case, William	Pvt. Va	"	3-15-77 Prison
Caseey, Edmond	7 Mass.	"	8-24-81
Casey, Benjamin	Capt. Va.	Killed	9-1-77
Casey, Charles	Pvt. 4 Mass	Died	1-11-77
Casidy, Jno.	Pvt. 6 N C	"	1-28-78
Cassody, John	Pvt. Va.	"	2-15-77 Prison
Cassidy, Andrew	Navy	"	7-21-81 Eng.Prison
Cassidy, Barney	Pvt. 3 Md.	Killed	8-16-80
Cassidy, Charles	Pvt. 13 Mass	Died	5-30-78

Cason, Hilly	Cpl. 10 N. C.	Died	8-12-82
Cason, Wm.	Pvt. 3 N C	"	3-5-78
Casteen, Wm.	Pvt. 10 N C	"	9-14-82
Castel, Bradley	Pvt. Mass	"	7-19-78
Caswell, Edward	Pvt Conn	"	4-27-78
Caswell, Joseph	Pvt. 5 Mass	"	11-8-77
Cata, William	Sgt. Md.	"	6-18-81
Catchings, Benjamin	Maj. Ga.	"	1781
Catel, Jean	France	"	1781
Catlin, Benjamin	Conn.	"	2-23-82
Caton, Patrick	R I	Killed	6-28-78
Cattell, Benjamin	Capt. S C	Died	1782
Cavalier, Francois	France	"	1781 Va.
Caves, John	Pvt. 5 Md.	"	11- 79
Cavey, Owen	Cpl. Md.	"	2-16-81
Cellars, John	Pvt. 13 Mass	"	5-31-78
Chabrier, Fleury	France	"	1781 Va.
Chace, Macheson	Pa.	"	1776
Chadburn, Joseph	4 SC	"	8-5-76
Chadwick, John	Pvt. Conn.	"	11- 77
Chadwick, John	Pvt. N. J.	"	1783
Chaffin, Francis	Cpl. 15 Mass.	"	3-1-78
Chaffin, Francis		"	1778
Chalfield, Caleb	Pvt. Mass.	"	9-11-78
Chamberlin, Chs.	Pvt. 2 N. C.	"	5-22-78
Chamberlain, Benjamin	Pvt. 8 Mass.	"	4-15-78
Chamberlain, Benjamin	Mass.	"	1778 Valley Forge
Chamberlain, Benjamin	N H	Killed	6-17-75 Bunker Hill
Chamberlain, James	Capt. Conn	Died	1782
Chamberlain, James	Md.	"	1782 Conn.
Chamberlain, John	N. J.	"	3-15-83
Chamberlain, Luth	Pvt. 1 Conn	"	10-9-77
Chamberlain, Nathaniel	Pvt. Mass	Killed	4-19-75
Chamberlain, William	Cpl. 9 Mass.	Died	10-4-77
Chamberlain, William	N Y	"	1777
Chamberlin, Lewis	Pvt. Pa.	Killed	1777
Chambers, John	Cpl. Pa.	Died	8-20-76
Chambers, Mathew Brown	Pvt. 5 Md.	"	12-9-77
Chambers, Philip	Pvt. 2 Mass	"	10-15-77
Chambers, William	N J	"	3-6-77
Chamois, Claude Denis	France	"	1781 Va.
Champion, Reuben	N.Y.	"	3-29-77 Ticonderoga
Champion, Reuben	Surg. Mass	"	1777
Champlin, Asa	R. I.	"	1778
Champlin, Christopher	R. I.	"	7-13-82
Champlin, George	Lt.	Killed	3-4-78
Champney, Noah	Pvt. 5 Mass	Died	2-4-78
Chandler, Benjamin	Vt.	Killed	8-16-77
Chandler, David	Mass.	Died	1776
Chandler, Jesse Zachariah	Pvt. Vt.	"	1777
Chandler, John	Me	"	1778
Chandler, Joseph	N. H.	Killed	6-17-75 Bunker Hill
Chandler, Samuel	Capt. Conn.	Died	9-8-81

40.

Chandler, Zebedee	Lt. Mass	Died	12-2-77
Chaney, John	Pvt. Mass.	"	12-31-77
Channell, Nicihl	Lt. N. J.	"	3- 1-78
Chapin, Benjamin	Va.	"	1781
Chapin, Gideon	Pvt. 2 Conn.	"	10-29-78
Chapin, Hiram	Pvt. N H	"	3-15-83
Chapin, John	Mass	"	1780
Chapin, Josiah	Pvt. 2 Mass	"	4-15-78
Chapin, Merick	Pvt. 4 Mass.	"	1-22-78
Chapin, William	Pvt. Mass	"	1777
Chaple, Jabez	Sgt.		
Chappell, Amos	Capt. Conn	"	1777
Chapman, Alpheus	Pvt. 5 Conn	"	12-15-77
Chapman, Elihn	Pvt. Mass	"	2-15-78
Chapman, Elisha	Pvt. 5 Conn	"	10-10-77
Chapman, Ezra	Ens. N Y	"	9-1-78
Chapman, Henry	Pvt. 1 Md	"	6- 77
Chapman, Gershom	Pvt. 14 Mass.	Killed	8-31-78
Chapman, Henly	Lt. 4 Md.	"	9-4-79
Chapman, Isaac		Died	1776 Ticon-deroga
Chapman, James	Maj. N Y	Killed	1776
Chapman, John	Pvt. Conn.	Died	7-10-77
Chapman, John	Capt. Conn	"	1781
Chapman, Phineas	Conn.	"	1782
Chapman, Phineas	N. Y.	"	1782
Chapman, Reuben	Conn.	"	1776
Chapman, Richard	Lt. Conn.	Killed	9-6-81
Chapman, Rufus	Corp. Can.	Died	10-12-81
Chappell, James	Va.	Killed	1781
Chappell, James	Va.	"	1781
Chappell, James	Va.	"	1781
Charet, Gilbert	Cpl. France	Died	1781 Va.
Charien, Peter	Pvt. Mass	"	1778
Charles, Aaron	R I	"	3-1- 78
Charles, Nicholas	Pvt. Conn	"	2-2-77
Charet, Gilbert	France	"	1781
Chase, Caleb	Pvt. 4 N Y	"	9-1779
Chase, Eliphalet	Pvt. 9 Mass.	"	10-20-77
Chase, Israel	Pvt. 15 Mass.	"	3-20-78
Chase, Jonathan	Pvt. Va.	"	1781
Chase, Josiah	N H	"	1782
Chase, Nathan	Conn.	Killed	1781
Chase, Nathan	Mass.	Died	1781
Chaseley, Peter	Pvt. 4 N Y.	"	1-18-77
Chasey, Stephen	Pvt. 4 N Y	"	11-30-77
Chatfield, Levi	Pvt. Conn.	"	1781
Chatfield, Oliver	Pvt. Mass	"	1778
Chatfield, Samuel	Pvt. 4 N Y	"	10-24-78
Chatillon, Jacques-Antoine	France	"	1781 Va.
Chauvin, Julien	Pvt. France	"	1781 Va.
Chavaillard, Thomas	France	"	1781 Va.
Cheeney, Richard	Pvt. Conn.	"	10-12-79
Cheeney, William	Pvt. Conn.	Killed	6-17-75 Bunker Hill

Cheeseman, Aaron	Pvt. R. I.	Died	3-31-78
Cheeseman, Jacob	Capt. 1 N Y	Killed	12-31-75 Que.
Cheevers, Nathan	Pvt. 10 Mass.	Died	5-24-78
Cheney, William	Pvt. Conn.	Killed	1775 Bunker Hill
Chenery, Thomas	Pvt. 5 Mass.	Died	5-11-78
Cheret, Andre	Pvt. France	"	1781 Va.
Cherry, Dan'l.	Pvt. 5 N. C.	"	10-18-77
Cherry, Pomp	Pvt. Conn.	"	9-4-77
Chesebrough, Charles	Q. M. Conn.	"	1780 SS
			Cromwell
Cheshire, John	Sgt. Md.	Killed	6-18-81
Chesire, John	Pvt. 7 Md.	"	6-18-81 At 96 yrs.
Chester, John	4 N. J.	"	1776
Chesterman, William	Cpl. S. C.	"	1779
Chetry, Alex'r.	Pvt. 4 N. C.	Died	5- 78
Chevalier, Joseph	France	"	1781 Va.
Chevalier, de Marin			
Jean Baptiste	Capt. Conn. France	"	1781 Va.
Chevalier, Paul	France	"	1781 Va.
Chew, Samuel	Capt.	Killed	3- 78
Chidsey, John	Conn.	Died	1783
Child, Abijah	Pvt. 3 Mass.	"	9-5-77
Child, Asa	Pvt. Mass	"	12-8-77
Child, Levi	Conn.	"	1776
Child, Thomas	Sgt. Conn.	"	7-19-82
Childs, Aaron	Pvt. 11 Mass.	"	6-7-78
Childs, Ebenezer, Jr.	N H	Killed	6-17-75 Bunker Hill
Childs, Lemuel	Mass.	Died	1782
Childs, John	Lt. N. Y.	"	1777
Childs, Moses	Pvt. Mass.	"	1776
Childs, Timothy	Capt. Mass.	"	1781
Chilson, John	Pvt. 14 Mass.	"	1-1-78
Chilton, John	Capt. Va.	Killed	9-11-77 Brandywine
Chilton, William	Sgt. 5 Md.	Died	11-4-77
Chinn, Samuel	Pvt. 1 Md.	"	9-17-78
Chipman, Jacob	Mass.	"	12-9-77
Chittenden, Cotton P.	Pvt. Conn.	"	8- 77
Chittenden, Ichabod	Pvt. 2 Conn	"	8- 77
Christian, Benjn	Pvt. 4 N Y	"	6-15-78
Christian, John	Pvt. 2 Md.	"	2-12-78
Christian, Peter	Pvt. 4 N Y	"	5-29-78
Christian, William	Capt. Tenn.	"	1779
Christot, Jacques	France	"	1781 Va.
Chronicle, William	Maj. N. C.	Killed	10-7-80 Kings Mt.
Chrysoy, Aaron	Cpl. 4 Mass.	Died	2-5-78
Chumard, Thomas	N. J.	"	1781 Va.
Chumbler, Daniel	2 S. C.	"	12-18-76
Chunn, Jonathan	Pvt. 4 Md.	"	3-6-77
Church, Joel	Pa.	"	7-3-78
Church, Lazarus	Pvt. 1 Conn	"	9-5-78
Church, Solomon	Pvt. 14 Mass.	"	6- 78
Church, Thomas	Pvt. 4 Mass.	"	8-2-77
Cicil, Bartin	Cpl. Md.	"	1-13-82
Cilley, John	Navy	"	7-21-81 Eng. Prison

42.

Name	Unit	Status	Date
Cilley, Prince	Pvt. 1 Conn.	Died	2-6-78
Citizen, Morris	Pvt. Md.	"	5-15-81
Civill, Willm.	1 Md.	"	6-15-83
Clagett, Henry	Md.	"	1777
Clagett, Henry	Pvt. Md.	"	1778
Clagett, John	Pvt. Md.	"	1781
Claiborne, Thomas	Md.	"	1777 Va.
Clancy, Michael	Pvt. 5 Md.	"	11-15-79
Clap, Abiel	Mass.	"	1780
Clap, John	Pvt. 2 Mass.	"	4-22-78
Clap, Jonathan	Maj. Mass.	"	1782
Clap, William	Pvt. 5 Mass.	"	10-31-78
Clapp, Abiel	Capt. Mass	"	1780
Clapp, Asabel	Mass.	"	1783
Clapp, Galen	Capt. Mass.	"	1776
Clapp, Galen	Mass.	"	2-23-76
Clapp, Jonathan	Maj. Mass.	"	1782
Clapp, William	Pvt. Mass.	"	1778
Clapsoddle, Augustiness	Maj. 77 N Y	"	1777
Clapsoddle, Enos	Maj. N. Y.	Killed	1777
Clark, Lt.	N C	"	1780
Clark, Abner	Pvt. 5 N C	Died	1-28-78
Clark, Andrew	N Y	"	1-8-77
Clark, Arthur	Navy	"	7-21-81 Eng.Prison
Clark, Daniel	N. J.	"	1778 Valley Forge
Clark, David	Sgt. Conn	"	1778
Clark, David	Pvt. Mass.	"	3-17-77
Clark, David	Lt. Conn.	Killed	1783
Clark, Elisha	Pvt. 5 Conn.	Died	8-26-77
Clark, Gad	Conn.	"	10-22-77
Clark, George	Pvt. 3 Md.	Killed	10-4-78
Clark, Greenleaf	Capt. N H	Died	1776
Clark, Hannaniah	11 Mass.	"	3-1-79
Clark, Henry	Mass.	"	1777
Clark, Hezakiah	Pvt. N. H.	"	12- 81
Clark, Jas.	Cpl. 4 N Y	"	10-3-77
Clark, James	Pvt. 2 Conn.	"	3-31-78
Clark, James	Navy	"	7-21-81 Eng.Prison
Clark, Joe	Lt. Col. N. Y.	"	1776
Clark, Joel	Lt. Col.	"	1776 Prison
Clark, John Jr.	Sgt. Mass.	"	1-3-82
Clark, John	4 S. C.	"	8-5-76
Clark, John	Pvt. Mass.	"	1-5-78
Clark, John	Md.	"	1779 Va.
Clark, John	Pvt. 14 Mass.	"	7-1-78
Clark, John	Pvt. 6 Mass.	"	7-9-77
Clark, John	Pvt. 6 Mass.	"	1781
Clark, Jonathan	Pvt. 14 Mass.	"	4-3-78
Clark, Joseph	Mass.	"	1783
Clark, Josiah	Pvt. N. H.	"	11-20-81
Clark, Martin	Pvt. R I	Killed	12-31-75
Clark, Richard	Pvt. Conn.	Died	6-1-78
Clark, Samuel	Pvt. Mass	"	6-10-77
Clark, Selvanus	Conn.	"	8-19-76

Clark, Thomas	Capt. N. J.	Died	3-30-80
Clark, William	Mass	"	3-29-76
Clark, William	Pvt. 13 Mass.	"	9-30-77
Clark, William	Pvt. 10 Mass.	"	10-2-77
Clark, Saul	Mass.	"	11-11-77
Clarke, Benjamin	3 S. C.	"	1-16-79
Clarke, Hezekiah	Conn.	"	1776
Clarke, John	Sgt. 5 Md.	"	1-17-78
Clarke, John	Sgt. 7 Md.	"	6- 79
Clarke, Joshua	1st Lt. Md.	"	1781
Clarke, Richard	Pvt. 7 Md.	"	12- 78
Clarke, Thomas	Pvt. 3 Md.	"	5-1- 79
Clarke, William Jr.	Lt. N. Y.	"	1779
Classen, Nathan	Pvt. 5 Mass.	"	5-30-77
Clayes, John Jr.	Mass	"	1777
Cleary, John	Q. M. Sgt. 7 Md.	"	7-20-77
Cleaves, Edmond	Pvt. 9 Mass.	"	10-8-77
Clegget, John	Pvt. Md.	"	4-25-81
Cleland, Jonas	Pvt. 1 Conn	"	6-18-78
Clemans, Martles	Pvt. 11 Mass.	"	9-30-78
Clement, Augustin	Capt. France	"	1781 Va.
Clements, Isaac	Pvt. N. H.	"	12-31-80
Clements, Thos. B.	Pvt. Md.	"	8-1-83
Clemmens, Tho	Del	"	4-11-82
Clemments, James	Pvt. 10 Mass.	"	9-20-77
Clemons, Benjamin	Pvt. 2 N. J.	"	4-4-78
Clerk, George	Va.	"	1-1-79
Cleveland, Benjamin	Pvt. 6 Mass.	"	5-10-77
Cleveland, Edward	Pvt. Mass.	Killed	1776
Cleveland, Simon	Pvt. 3 Mass.	Died	12-19-77
Cleveland, Jabez	Pvt. Conn.	Killed	1775 Bunker Hill
Cleveland, John	Pvt. 2 Conn.	Died	1- 78
Clift, James	Pvt. 5 Md.	"	5- 79
Clift, William	Mass.	"	2-10-78
Clifton, Rich'd	Pvt. 3 N. C.	"	2- 78
Cline, Jacob	Pvt. 4 N. Y.	"	5-31-77
Clintick, John	Pvt. N. J.	"	3-26-78
Clinton, Peter	Capt. S. C.	"	1780
Cloarel, Jean	France	"	1781 Va.
Clock, John	Conn	"	1- 82
Clogston, Paul	N. H.	"	6-17-75 Bunker Hill
Clore, Christian	Pvt. Md.	"	3-1-82
Close, Christian	Pvt. Md.	"	3-1-82
Close, Samuel	Sgt. Mass.	"	7-5-77
Clothier, John	Conn.	Killed	1777 In Battle
Clothyer, John	Pvt. 2 Conn.	"	11-14-77
Cloud, Abner,	Pvt. Pa.	Died	1783
Clough, Alexander	Lt. N. J.	"	12- 78
Clough, Alexander	Adj. N. J.	"	1776
Clough, Reuben	Pvt. 11 Mass.	"	10-1- 77
Clough, Samuel	N.H.	"	1778
Cloyes, Elijah	Capt. N. H.	"	1779
Cloward, Thomas	Pvt.	"	2-15-76
Coal, Ebenezer	Pvt. 2 Mass.	"	5-17-78

44

Name	Unit/Location	Status	Date/Location
Coal, Rosel	Corp. Can.	Died	4-12-77
Coalman, Saml.	Pvt. 3 Md.	Killed	10-4-78
Cobb, Ebenezer	Mass.	Died	11-10-82
Cobb, James	Pvt. 10 Mass.	"	8-19-78
Cobb, Kendel	Pvt. Md.	"	11-10-81
Cobb, Seth	Sgt. 14 Mass.	"	1-24-78
Cobb, Seth	Mass.	"	1-15-78
Cobb, Wm.	Pvt. 7 N. C.	"	1-26-78
Coble, Shadrock	Pvt. 5 N C	Killed	10-4-77
Coburn, Benjamin	N.H.	Died	1-21-87
Coburn, Daniel	Mass.	"	5-12-75
Coburn, Phineas	Mass.	"	9-8-75
Coburn, Rowlins	Pvt. N. H.	"	1780
Cochrane, William	Lt. Mass	"	1779
Cochren, John	Pvt. Md.	Killed	3-15-81
Cochran, James	Pvt. 1 Pa.	Died	10-20-76
Cochran, Jonathan	Pvt. N. H.	"	3-24-78
Cocks, Ichabod	Pvt. 6 Mass.	"	1-5-77
Cockendall, Elijah	Pvt. Md.	"	7-18-82
Cockey, Peter	Ens. 3 Md.	"	2- 79
Cockring, Patrick	Pvt. 11 Mass.	"	8-1-80
Cocq, Antoine	France	"	1781 Va.
Coe, Daniel	N. Y.	"	1782
Coe, Hezekiah	Pvt. 1 Md.	"	11-31-77
Coe, John	Md.	"	1782 N. Y.
Coe, Oliver	Conn.	"	12-31-75
Coffin, Enoch Jr.		"	1781
Coffin, Henry		"	1781
Coffin, Josiah		"	3- 78 S S Jersey
Coffrin, James	Pa	"	7-3-78
Coffrin, William	Pa.	"	7-3-78
Cogan, Patrick	Q. M. N H	"	8- 78
Coginee, John	Pvt. 9 Mass.	"	4-
Cogsdell, Joseph	Pvt. 2 Conn	"	8-1-78
Cogswell, Jonathan	Pvt. Mass	"	1782
Cogswell, Nathaniel		"	3-23-83
Cohoon, Reuben	Pvt. 4 Mass	"	7-25-78
Coin, William	Pvt. 2 N. J.	"	10-10-77
Coin, Michael	Pvt. 5 Md.	Killed	8-16-80
Coit, Solomon	Conn.	Died	8- 76
Colar, Andre	France	"	1781 Va.
Colbert, Rich'd	R I	Killed	12-31-75 Que
Colbourn, Thomas	N H	"	6-17-75 Bunker Hill
Colburn, Andrew	Lt. Col. N H	"	9-19-77
Colburn, Joseph	Mass.	Died	3-18-76
Colburn, Robert	Pvt. Mass.	"	1783
Colby, Eli	N. H.	"	8-16-77
Colby, Moses	N. H.	"	4-16-77
Colby, Powell	Pvt. Vt.	"	1780
Colby, Spencer	Pvt. 8 Mass.	"	9-17-77
Colby, Stephen	Pvt. N H	Killed	11-2-81
Colby, Zebulum	Pvt. N H	Died	10-7-79
Colcord, Samuel	N H	"	1-23-83
Coldrain, Titus	Pvt. 9 Mass.	"	3-20-78

Cole, Consider	Mass.	Died	9-29-75
Cole, Elkana	Pvt. 4 Mass	"	8-12-78
Cole, Ephraim	Drum 2 Mass.	"	4-19-78
Cole, Ephraim	Mass.	"	9-13-75
Cole, Isaiah	Pvt. 15 Mass.	"	12-14-77
Cole, J. B.	Sgt. 3 Md.	Killed	10-4-78
Cole, John	N H	"	6-17-75 Bunker Hil
Cole, Gideon	Pvt. Mass.	Died	6-1-79
Cole, Henry	Pvt. 4 N Y	"	10-18-77
Cole, Hezekiel	Pvt. 2 Mass.	"	9-23-77
Cole, John	Pvt. 2 Conn	"	6-10-78
Cole, John	Pvt. 2 Md.	"	3- 79
Cole, Michael	Pvt. Md.	"	8-16-81
Cole, Reuben	Pvt. Mass.	"	5-26-78
Cole, Robt.	Pvt. 1 N C	"	4-28-78
Cole, Samuel	Pa.	"	7-3-78
Cole, Thomas	Sgt. 6 Md.	"	4-2-78
Cole, Timothy	Pvt. Conn.	"	11-2-83
Cole, William	Pvt. N. J.	"	3-15-78
Cole, Zebulon	Del	"	9-16-78
Coleman, John	Pvt. N. J.	Killed	
Coleman, John	Lt. Va.	Died	1779
Coleman, Joseph	Lt. N. Y	"	1777
Coleman, Phineas	N H	"	8-15-83
Colihorn, Robt.	Pvt. 2 N C	"	5-16-78
Coller, Isaac	Pvt. Mass.	"	4-2-78
Collier, Isaac	Pvt. 3 S C	"	12-29-78
Collimore, Benja	Cpl. 11 Mass	"	10-23-77
Collins, Benjamin	Pvt. N H	"	7-22-78
Collins, Daniel	Pvt. 11 Mass.	"	12-7-77
Collins, Ephraim	Pvt. N H	"	1778
Collins, Jno	Pvt. 10 N C	"	3-26-83
Collins, John	Pvt. Pa	"	11-22-76
Collins, Richard	Pvt. N H	"	1778
Collins, Richard	Pvt. Pa	"	1782
Collins, Saml.	Mus. 2 N C	"	4-18-78
Collins, Thomas	N H	Killed	6-17-75 Bunker Hill
Collins, William	Pvt. 5 Md	Died	12-30-77
Colne, Andre	France	"	1781 Va.
Colson, Peter	Pvt. 13 Mass	"	9-2-78
Colt, Benjamin	Pvt Mass	"	1781
Colter, William	Pvt. 3 S C	"	8-1-78
Colton, Aaron	Cpl. Mass	"	1778
Colton, Moses	Mass	"	1777
Comstock, David	Pvt. Conn	"	1782
Comstock, James	Conn.	Killed	1781 Ft.Griswold
Comstock, John	Lt. Conn	"	1776
Comstock, Robert	Pa.	Died	7-3-78
Combs, Caleb	Pvt. 8 Mass	"	5-13-78
Comins, William	Sgt. N Y	"	1778
Conway, James	Lt. Va.	"	12-28-76
Conant, Ebenezer	Lt. Mass.	"	1783
Conant, Joshua	Mass.	"	1777
Conant, Josiah	Pvt. 5 Mass.	"	5-23-77
Conant, Peter	Mass.	"	1783
Conant, Roger	Surg. Conn	"	2-6-77

Conant, Samuel	Pvt. 2 Conn	Died	3-1-78
Conant, Timothy	Cpl. 6 Mass	"	4-15-77
Couch, Charles	Pvt. Md.	"	8-24-81
Couch, John	Pvt. N J	Killed	3-18-78
Condict, David	Lt. Col. N J	Died	1777
Condict, Ebenezer	N J	"	4-3-77
Condit, Daniel	N J	"	11-11-83
Condit, David	Lt Col N J	"	1777
Condit, Zenas	Pvt. N J	"	1776
Condon, David P.	Pvt. 4 N Y	"	6-19-80
Condrone, John	Pvt. 5 Md.	"	1-8-79
Cone, Elisha	Pvt. Conn.	"	1783
Cone, John Sr.	Pvt. Conn.	"	10-5-77
Cone, Joseph	Pvt.	"	1779 At Sea
Cone, Oliver	Pvt. Conn	"	1782
Cone, Rufus	Pvt. Conn	"	1776
Cone, Samuel	Pvt. 4 N Y	"	5-3-78
Cone, W.	Pvt. 2 N C	"	9-16-77
Coneck, James	N H	Killed	6-17-75 Bunker Hill
Conely, Larance	R I	Died	12-24-76
Coney, William	Fifer Va	"	1779
Congleton, William	4 Md	"	8- 78
Conger, David	Pvt N J	"	1778
Congo, Jack	Pvt. Mass	"	10-30-78
Conklin, Edward	N Y	"	1779 SS Eagle
Conklin, Joseph	Pvt. Pa.	"	1777 Prison
Conlon, Michael Matross	Pa	Killed	6-20-76
Conner, Daniel	Pvt. Can	Died	7-24-77
Conner, Edward	Pv. Can	"	12- 79
Conner, James	Pvt. Pa	"	10-24-76
Connet, Solomon	Pvt. 4 Mass	"	5-1-78
Connery, William	Pvt. 8 Mass	"	7-20-78
Connell, John	Pvt. 1 SC	"	8-24-78
Connor, Doshey	Pvt. 10 N C	"	6-14-83
Connor, Jacob	Pvt. 7 N C	"	2-6-78
Connor, Jno	Pvt. 10 N C	"	12- 78
Connor, John	Pvt 9 Mass	"	10-17-77
Connor, Morris	Pvt Navy	"	7-21-81 Eng Prison
Connor, Wm.	Pvt 7 N C	"	4-21-78
Connoway, Henry	Fifer N Y	"	4-16-78
Conomy, Cuff	Pvt. Conn	"	11-13-77
Conrad, John	Pvt. Pa	"	6-3-81
Contel, Guillaume	France	"	1781 Va
Converse, Joshua	Pvt.	Killed	6-17-75 Bunker Hill
Conway, James	Pvt. 2 Md	Died	2- 80
Conway, James	Lt. Va.	Killed	12-28-76
Cooch, Thomas Sr.	Del	Died	11-16-83
Cook, Isaac	Capt. Conn	"	1780
Coolbroth, James	Pvt. 9 Mass	"	9-30-78
Cooley, Abel	Pvt Mass	"	1778
Cooley, Azariah	Pvt. Mass	"	1778
Cooley, Luke	Capt. Conn	"	1-1-77
Cooley, Robert	Pvt. 1 Md	"	10-6-78
Coolidge, Jonas	Mass	"	1776
Coolidge, Joseph	Pvt. Mass	Killed	4-19-75 Tex

Name	Rank/Unit	Status	Date
Cooley, Abel	Lt. 4 Mass	Died	6-13-78 Valley Forge
Cooly, Gabl	Pvt. 10 N C	"	1780
Coombs, William	5 Md.	"	8-5-77
Coon, James	Lt. Conn.	Killed	9-6-80
Coone, Adam	Md	"	7-15-79
Cooney, Michael	R I	Died	1779
Cootey, Samuel	Cpl. 6 Mass	"	9-4-77
Cook, Abel	Pvt. 2 Conn	"	12-23-77
Cook, Andrew	Pvt. Pa.	"	1783
Cook, Ceaser	R I	"	4-30-78
Cook, Daniel	Mass	"	1779
Cook, Ephraim	Mass	"	11-14-75
Cook, Geo.	Lt. 10 N C	"	1778
Cook, Ichabood	Pvt. Conn.	"	8-16-77
Cook, Isaac	Capt. Conn.	"	1780
Cook, John	N Y	Killed	11- 77
Cook, John	N J	Died	3- 83
Cook, John	Maj. N J	Killed	10-13- 77
Cook, John	R I	Died	2-13-77
Cook, Jonathan	Del	"	10- 77
Cook, Pomp	Pvt. 6 Mass.	"	11-29-78
Cook, Stepn	Pvt. 2 N C	"	11-19-79
Cook, Uzial	Pvt. Conn.	"	8-5-78
Cook, Samuel	Mass.	Killed	4-19-75
Cooke, Daniel	Pvt. Mass	Died	1779
Cooke, Isaiah	Pvt. Conn.	"	9-23-78
Cooke, John	R I	"	8-20-78
Cooke, Moses	Pvt 5 Md	"	3-1-79
Cooke, Nicholas	R I	"	9-14-82
Cooke, William Jr.	N J	Killed	12-27-82
Cooks, George	Pvt. 3 S C	Died	4-1-78
Cooks, James	5 S C	"	9-26-77
Cooley, Azariah	Pvt. Mass		1778
Coolidge, Joseph	Pvt. Mass	Killed	1775
Cooper	Lt. R I	Died	1779
Cooper, Apollis	Lt. Va	Killed	9-11-77
Cooper, Charles	Pvt. 3 Md	Died	11-16-77
Cooper, Jno	Cpl. 4 N C	"	4-16-78
Cooper, Jno	Pvt. 7 N C	"	7-7-77
Cooper, John	Pvt. 2 Mass.	"	6-3-78
Cooper, John	Pvt. 2 N J	"	1-13-77
Cooper, John	Pvt. 4 N Y	"	2- 78
Cooper, Josiah	Pvt. 7 N C	"	11-29-77
Cooper, Sam'l	Lt.	Killed	12-31-75 Que.
Cooper, Stephen	Pvt. Mass	Died	4-2- 77
Cooper, Thomas	Mass	"	12-7-76
Cooper, Thomas	Pvt. Md	"	4-1-82
Cooper, William	Pvt. 5 Md	"	12-20-70
Cope, John	Pvt. 2 Md.	"	10-10-78
Copen, William	R I	"	9-1-78
Copes, Solomon	Va.	"	1-28-78
Coplin, Job	Pvt. 10 N C	"	3-7-82
Coray, Anson	Pa.	"	7-3-78

Name	Unit	Status	Date
Coray, Jenks	Pa	Died	7-3-78
Coray, Rufus	Pa	"	7-3-78
Corbin, Lemuel	Mass	"	1782
Corey, Ezra	Pvt. 6 Mass	"	5-9-77
Corless, Jesse	N H	Killed	6-17-75 Bunker Hill
Corncall, John	Sgt. 3 Mass	Died	10-8-77
Cornee, Spencer	Pvt. 6 Mass	"	2-3-80
Cornell, John	Del	Killed	1-20-81
Corning, Benjamin	Pvt. Mass	Died	1783 Jersey Prison Ship
Cornish, Daniel	Mass	"	1781 Va.
Cornish, John	Pvt. 2 Md.	"	1779
Cornish, Jonathan	Pvt. 6 Mass	"	12-5- 77
Cornish, Joseph	Pvt. Conn	"	8-24-77
Cornish, Joseph	Lt. Conn	"	1776
Cornish, Wm.	Pvt. 6 N C	"	2-27-78
Corps, John	Pvt. 8 Mass.	"	2-11-77
Corry, James	Ens. S C	"	10-7-80 Kings Mt.
Corss,	Pvt. Mass	"	1776
Cortright, Christopher	Pa.	"	7-3-78
Cortright, John	Pa	"	7-3-78
Cornwall, Jacob	Pvt. 8 Mass.	"	7-8-77
Cost, Francis	Md.	"	1782
Costail, Sidet	France	"	1781 Va
Costail, Vidal	France	"	1781 Va
Coste, Vidal	France	"	1781 Va
Costner, Jacob	Maj. N C	"	1-16-79
Cotanch, Jno	Pvt. 10 N C	"	1782
Cothren, William	Lt. Mass	"	1779
Cottle, Daniel	Navy	"	6-7-77 Eng.Prison
Cotton, Theophilus	Col. Mass	"	1782
Cotton, Thomas	Me	"	12-29-81
Couch, James	Pvt. Mass	"	9-4-77
Condict, Zenas	N. J	"	12-20-76
Coulter, James	Pvt. N Y	"	1782
Council, Arthur	Capt. 6 N C	"	1777
Courtis, William	Mass	"	1779
Courtois, Etienne	France	"	1781 Va
Cousins, Edwd	Pvt. 5 Md.	"	8-21-77
Coutel, Guillaume	France	"	1781 Va
Couzins, David	Pvt 15 Mass	"	1777
Covell, Henry	Conn.	Killed	9-7-81 By Indians
Covenhoven, Dominicus	Pvt. N J		1778
Covington, Wm.	Adj. 3 N C	Died	4-13-78
Cowan, Joseph	Pvt. Pa		1777
Cowden, William	Pvt. 15 Mass	"	10-21-77
Cowel, Daniel	Pvt. 14 Mass	"	3-7-78
Cowenhoven, Lukes	N J	"	12-26-77
Cowles, Samuel	Conn	"	7-9-77
Cowls, Israel	Mass	"	1782
Cox, Benjamin	Pvt. 10 Mass	"	3-1778
Cox, Francis, Jr.	Lt. Mass	"	1782
Cox, Nath	Del	"	11-10-78
Cox, Solomon	4 S C	"	7-20-78

49

Cox, Wm.	Pvt. 10 N C	Died	11- 78
Coy, Samuel	Pvt. Mass	"	4-6- 78
Coyle, Arthur	Pvt. Can.	"	1-18-77
Cracary, Uriah	Pvt. 2 Conn	"	4-22-79
Crafts, Joseph	Cpl. Conn	"	1777
Crafts, Joseph	Pvt. Pa.	"	7-8-76
Craig, Geo.	Pvt. 5 N C	"	11- 77
Craig, John	4 N Y	"	2-17-78
Craig, John	Pvt. 4 N Y	"	7-26-80
Craig, Samuel	Pa	Killed	1777 Ind.
Craig, William	Del	Died	12-1-81
Craige, Archd	Pvt. 6 N C	Killed	10-4-77
Cram, Asa	N H	Died	6-17-75
Cramer, Adam	Pvt. Conn	"	8-19-77
Cramer, Jacob	R I	"	2-24-77
Cramer, John	N Y	"	1783
Crammer, Peter	Me	"	1782
Crampton, Calvin	Pvt. Conn.	"	2-18-78
Crone, Caleb	Lt. N. J.	"	1782
Crane, Ezra	Pvt. Conn.	"	1781
Crane, Joseph	Lt. N J	"	1778
Crane, Stephen	N J	"	1780
Cranner, John	N J	Killed	1779
Cranston, Abner	Maj. Mass	Died	5-29- 77
Cranson, Eben	Pvt. 9 Mass	"	9-3-78
Cranston, Abner	Maj. Mass	Killed	5-29-77
Craton, Thos.	Pvt. 4 N Y	Died	8-5-77
Crane, Stephen	Mass	"	1778
Crane, Eleazer	Pa	"	1776
Crane, Elijah	Mass	"	1781
Crane, Jared	Pvt. 2 Conn	"	4-7-77
Crane, John	N J	"	5-22-83
Crane, Joseph	Lt. N J	"	6-7-78
Crane, Samuel	N. J.	"	9-13-77
Crane, Silas	Mass	"	1781
Crane, Thomas	Pvt. N J	"	4-4-82
Crawford,	Col. Ky	Killed	6-11-82 By Ind.
Crawford	Lt.	"	10-9-81
Crawford, Alex	Del	Died	8-25-78
Crawford, Hugh	Conn	"	10-13-76
Crawford, James	Pvt. N J	Killed	2-13-77
Crawford, John	Conn	Died	10-13-76
Crawford, Newton	Pvt. Mass	"	6-25-77
Crawford, Patrick	Pvt. S C	"	1783
Crawford, Robert	N H	"	9-22-78
Crawford, Samuel	Capt. N Y	"	11-18-77
Crawford, William	Lt. Col. Va.	"	1782
Crawford, William		Killed	1782 By Ind.
Crawford, William			1782
Cresap, Michael	Capt. Md.	Died	11- 75
Cresap, Michael	Capt. N Y	"	10-18-75 Wyo.
Cressey, Daniel	N H	"	1777
Crether, Jerek	Pvt. 7 N C	"	3-14-78
Crill, Martin	Pvt. 2 N J	"	1-15-77
Croane, Timothy	Pvt. 3 Md.	"	7-8-78
Crocker, Joseph	Pa.	"	7-3-78

Crocker, Samuel	Pa.	Died	7-3-78
Crockett, George	Pvt. 10 Mass	"	8-11-77
Crockett, Samuel	Va.	"	1783
Croft, John	3 Pa.	"	1777
Cromwell, Oliver	Pvt. 10 Mass.	"	5-2-78
Crook, Martin	Pvt. 5 Md	"	12-6-77
Crooks, William	Pa.	"	5- 78
Crosby, Jacob	N H	"	6-17-75 Bunker Hill
Crosby, John	Pvt. Md.	"	7-24-82
Crosby, John	Del	"	1-12-78
Crosby, Nathan	Pvt. 10 Mass	"	7-6-77
Crosby, Stephen	Capt. N Y	Killed	9-15-76
Crosley, William	Mass	Died	1783
Cross, Abial	N H	"	4-20-78
Cross, Asa	Pvt. 8 Mass	"	6-30-78
Crossman, John	Pvt. 2 Conn	"	4-14-78
Crouch, Arthur	Pvt 5 Md.	"	7-20-77
Croswell, Mark	Pvt. 1 Conn	"	11-24-78
Crowell, Jedel	Pvt. 4 Mass	"	10-25-78
Crowell, Joseph	Pvt. Mass	"	1-14-83
Crozer, Thomas	" 5 SC	Killed	10-9- 79
Crozier, John	Pvt. 5 Md.	Died	8-16-80
Cruger, Wm.	Pvt. 4 N Y	"	7-30-78
Cruise, William	Pvt. 5 SC	"	5-12-77
Cudjoe, Ham	Pvt. Conn	"	2-18-78
Cuff, Copeny	Pvt. Conn	"	1779
Cuffman, John	Pvt. 1 N Y	"	5-2-78
Cuffrey, Pomp	Pvt. 11 Mass	"	6-14-78
Culbertson, Joseph	Ens. 5 Pa.	Killed	6-21-76
Cullen, John	Pvt. 4 Md.	Died	11-28-78
Cullimane, Jerema	4 Md.	"	7-28-79
Cullomine, John	Pvt. 3 Md.	Killed	6-28-78
Cullum, Israel	Pvt. 4 N C	Died	7-7-77
Culver, Daniel	Capt. Vt.	"	1776
Culver, Levin	Pvt. Del	"	2-7-81
Culver, Solomon	Pvt. 12 Mass	"	3-12-78
Cummings, Benjn	Pvt. 5 N C	"	5-5-78
Cummings, Ebenezer	Pvt. N H	"	1778
Cummings, Matthew	Pvt. Conn.	Killed	6-17-75
Cummings, Ephrain	Pvt. 6 Mass	Died	8-10-77
Cummings, Jno	Pvt. 10 N C	"	10- 78
Cummins, John	Pvt. Va	"	1-27-77 Prison
Cumpton, Ignatius	Pvt. Md.	"	10-13-81
Cunningham, Andrew	Del	"	9-12-82
Cunningham, Nathaniel	Pvt. Mass	"	10-6-75
Cunningham, William	Pvt. Mass	"	6-23-79
Curdinet, Francis	France	"	1781 Va.
Curdon, Louis Victor	France	"	1781 Va.
Curry, Robert	Lt. Pa.	Killed	1780 By Ind.
Currypool, Richard	Del.	Died	7-20-81
Currie, Richard	Pvt. Pa.	"	1776
Currier, Edmund	Capt. Mass.	"	1778
Currier, Jonathan	Pvt. N H	"	1778
Curries, Richard	Pvt. Pa.	"	1776
Currill, John	Pvt. 1 Md.	"	2- 79

Curry, Robert	Lt. Pa.	Killed	1780
Curtis, Caleb	Conn.	"	2- 81
Curtis, Eleazer	Capt. Conn.	Died	1779
Curtis, Elijah	Conn.	"	9- 78
Curtis, Elnathan	Maj. Mass	"	1781
Curtis, James	Pvt. 9 Mass	"	6-26-77
Curtis, Jesse	Pvt. 14 Mass.	"	3-27-78
Curtis, John	Pvt. 2 Conn.	"	3-23-78
Curtis, John	Pvt. Mass.	"	1783
Curtis, Josiah	Pvt. Conn.	Killed	1777
Curtis, Samuel	Capt. Mass.	Died	1777
Curtis, Samuel	Ens. Navy	"	7-21-81 Eng.Prison
Curtis, Thomas	Pvt. Conn.	"	1776
Curtis, William	Maj. Mass.	"	1779
Curwell, Peter	Pvt. 3 Md.	Killed	8-16-80
Curwin, Silas	Pvt. 4 N Y	Died	10-24-77
Cuschip, Simon	Pvt. Mass.	"	3-9-77
Cushing, John	Pvt. 14 Mass	"	10-1-78
Cushing, Loaring	Pvt. 10 Mass.	"	10-23-78
Cushing, Loring	Pvt. Mass	"	1777
Cushing, Pero	Pvt. 9 Mass.	"	5-16-78
Cushing, Peter	Capt. Mass	"	1783
Cushing, Pyam	Capt. Mass	"	1777
Cushing, Samuel	R I	"	6-28-78
Cushman, Allerton	Sgt. Conn	"	1-24-77
Cushman, Isaac	Pvt. 9 Mass.	"	11-7-77
Cushman, Thomas	Mass	"	10-30-77
Cushoy, Benjam	Conn.	"	5-7-78
Custard, John	R I	"	6-17-77
Custer, John	R I	"	6-17-77
Custis, John Parke	Va.	"	1781 Va.
Cutler, Abijah	N J	"	1778
Cutler, David	Mass	"	1783
Cutler, Dea Wm	NJ	"	1780
Cutler, Gershon	Mass.	"	7-12-77
Cutler, John	Fifer 2 Conn.	"	11-15-77
Cutler, Nathan	Pvt. 5 Mass.	"	10-3-77
Cutler, Nathan	N H	"	3-6-78
Cutting, Jonas	Pvt. N H	"	1780
Cutting, Silas	Pvt. 5 Mass.	"	12-30-77
Cuyler, Henry	Capt. Ga.	"	1781
Cuzzars, Joseph	2 Mass.	Killed	8-8-77
Cypril, Child	Pvt. N H	Died	1778

D

Dada, William	Mass.		1776
Dade, Robin	Lt. Va.	Died	8- 76
Daggett, Arthur	Capt. Mass.	"	1775
Daggett, Bretherton	Maj. Mass.	"	1783
Daggett, Ebenezer	Ens. Yale Conn	"	11-20- 81 Va.
Daggett, Ebenezer	Ens. Md.	"	11-20-81
Daggett, Napthali	Conn.	"	1780 In Prison
Daggett, Nathan	Mass.	"	1778
Daggett, Philip	Conn.	"	1783

Name	Rank/Unit	Status	Date	Notes
Daggett, Samuel	Pvt. Mass.	Died	4-19-77	
Daily, Jno.	Sgt. 7 N C	"	12-15-77	
Daily, Thomas	Pvt. 2 Md.	"	10-27-79	
Dale, Amos	Mass	"	1781	
Dale, James	Pvt. Va.	"	1777	
Dallobee, James	Pvt. Conn.	"	10-2-78	
Dallas, Archibald	Capt. N J	Killed	1-28-79	
Dalley, Samuel	Pvt. Mass.	Died	2-1-77	
Dalton, Caleb	N H	Killed	6-17-75	Bunker Hill
Dalton, William	2 S C	"	10-9-79	
Damon, David	Mass	Died	1778	
Damon, Samuel	Pvt. 13 Mass.	"	7-26-78	
Danforth, James	Mass	"	1777	
Dana, Anderson	Pa	Killed	1778	Wyo.
Dana, Anderson	Md.	Died	1778	Conn.
Dane, John	Mass.	Killed	1777	
Dane, Samuel	Mass.	Died	1777	
Danigon, John	Pvt. 4 N J	"	1-31-78	
Daniel,	Col. N Y	"	1782	
Daniel, Jno.	Cpl. 5 N C	"	12-30-77	
Daniel, Josh	Mus. 7 N C	"	7- 77	
Daniels, David	Mass	"	5-21-76	
Daniels, David	Cpl. Mass.	"	7-11-76	
Daniels, John	R I	"	10-21-79	
Daniels, Joseph	Mass.	"	6-2-79	
Daray, Bertrand	France	"	1781	Va.
Darby, Nathaniel	Pvt. Mass.	"	9-28-78	
Darby, Andrew	Pvt. Mass.	"	1783	
Darland, Abraham	Pvt. 9 Pa.	"	12-7-79	
Darling, Bonner	Navy	"	7-21-81	Eng.Prison
Darling, Daniel	Pvt. Mass.	"	12-13-77	
Darling, Ezra	Pvt. 5 N Y	"	2-13-79	
Darling, Jabez	Pa.	"	7-3-78	
Darling, Thomas	Mass.	"	10-22-78	
Darnall, Isaac	Del	"	12-10-78	
Darrah, Henry	Capt. Pa.	"	6- 82	
Darrance, George	Lt. Col.	"	1782	Wyo.
Dashiell, Wm.	Surg. 2 Md.	"	12-5-80	
Daton, Samuel	Pvt. 3 N Y	"	9-16-77	
Daton, Samuel, Jr.	Pvt. N Y	"	11-1-77	
D'Ambert, Peter	Pvt. Pa.	"	1777	Prison
Daven, Joel	Pvt. N J	"	2-15-77	
Davenport, Bernard	Pvt. 12 Mass	"	6-20-78	
Davenport, Charles	Conn.	"	1779	
Davenport, Conrad	Pa.	"	7-3-78	
Davenport, Hezekiah	Lt. Conn	Killed	4-27-77	
Davenport, John		"	1781	Guilford C. H.
Davenport, John	Pvt. Mass.	Died	1776	
Davenport, Pomp	R I	"	3-24-80	
David, Ebenezer	Chap. R I	"	3-19-78	
David, Yves	France	"	1781	Va.
Davidson, Daniel	R I	Killed	12-31-75	Que.
Davidson, James	Pvt. N J	Died	1780	
Davidson, William Lee	General N C	Killed	2-1-81	

Name	Unit	Status	Date	Notes
Davies, Wm.	Drum Maj. R I	Died	6-23-80	
Davis	Capt. 11 Pa.	Killed	4-23-79	
Davis, Aaron	Col. Mass	Died	1777	
Davis, Caleb	N J	"	1783	
Davis, Conrod	N J	"	10-15-81	
Davis, David	Pvt. Mass.	"	3-7-78	
Davis, Ebenezer, Jr.	Pvt. Mass.	"	12-7-76	
Davis, Ezekiel	Pvt. N H	"	6-16-79	
Davis, Hezekiah	Conn.	"	1776	
Davis, Isaac	Capt. Mass.	Killed	4-19-75	Concord
Davis, Isaac	Capt. N H	Died	1776	
Davis, Jacob	Pvt. 5 N Y	"	9- 77	
Davis, Jno.	Pvt. 2 Md.	Killed	8-16-80	
Davis, Jno.	Pvt. 2 Md.	Died	12-16-78	
Davis, John	Pvt. Md.	"	8-12-82	
Davis, John	R I	"	8-15-78	
Davis, John	Pvt. Mass	"	1-15-77	
Davis, John	N H	Killed	6-17-75	Bunker Hill
Davis, John	Pvt. N H	Died	4-15-78	
Davis, Joseph	Capt. Pa.	Killed	4-23-79	
Davis, Joseph	Pvt. 3 N Y	Died	1- 79	
Davis, Joseph	Pvt. N H	"	8-13-79	
Davis, Joshua	Pvt. Navy	"	7-21-81	Eng.Prison
Davis, Matthew	Pvt. 9 Pa.	Killed	7-16-79	
Davis, Nathaniel	Pvt. N H	Died	9-18-83	
Davis, Peter	Pvt. Mass	"	4-26-78	
Davis, Peter	Lt. Vt.	"	1-2-81	
Davis, Richard	Pvt. 14 Mass	"	8-17-79	
Davis, Samuel	Pvt. Va.	"	2-15-77	Prison
Davis, Samuel	Pvt. Mass	"	3- 1-78	
Davis, Thomas	Pa.	"	1781	
Davis, Thos.	Pvt. 3 N Y	"	8- 1777	
Davis, William	Pvt. Md.	"	4-20-77	
Davis, William	Cpl. Md.	"	9-9-78	
Davis, William	Pvt. 12 Mass	"	10-28-78	
Davis, William	N C	"	1781	
Davis, William	Lt. Col N C	"	1780	
Devisson, John Andrew	Capt. Va.	"	1782	
Dawance, George	Col. Conn.	Killed	1778	
Dawes, Thomas	Lt. Col. Mass.	Died	1778	
Dawsey, Nicholas	2 S C	"	10-7-76	
Dawson, Samuel	Capt. 8 Pa.	"	9-3-79	
Dawson, Edward	Pvt. Pa.		1783	
Day, Francis	Cpl. 7 Md.	"	10-27-78	
Day, Gideon	Pvt. 7 Mass.	"	11-11-78	
Day, Isaac	Conn.	"	9-15-79	
Day, James	Conn.	"	12-25-82	
Day, Jno.	Pvt. 2 N C	"	1-14-78	
Day, Joseph	N Y	"	1775	
Day, Samuel	N J	"	3-25-77	
Dayly, James	Pvt. 2 Md.	"	12-29-77	
Dayton, David	N J	"	1777	
Dayton, Henry	Col. R I	"	4-5-82	
Dayton, Michael	Capt. Conn.	"	1776	
Dayton, Michael	Md.	"	1777	Conn.

Dayton, Solomon	12 Mass	Killed	7-8-77
Deacon, Pearce	Pvt. Md.	Died	11-1-82
Deake, Lemuel	Conn	"	4-15-80
Deal, Michl	Pvt. S C	"	5- 81
Deal, Reuben	Pvt. 2 N C	"	4-28-78
Deal, Wm.	Pvt. N C	"	3-5-78
Dean, Abiel	Mass	"	1781
Dean, Abijah	Mass	"	10-26-78
Dean, Absolum	2 S C	"	1-8-79
Dean, Bradley	Pvt. 5 N Y	"	4-28-77
Dean, Bradley	Pvt. Conn.	Killed	4- 77
Dean, Cutler	Pvt. 5 N Y	Died	10-4-77
Dean, Ebenezer	Pvt. 7 Mass	"	10-7-77
Dean, Israel	Mass	"	7-3-75
Dean, Jeremiah	Pvt. Conn.	"	8-28-79
Dean, John	Pvt. 6 Mass.	"	7-18-77
Dean, Philip	Pvt. Mass.	"	1780
Dean, Robt.	Pvt. 10 N C	"	11-11-82
Dean, Simon	Pvt. Mass.	"	11-15-77
Dean, Thomas	Pvt. 5 Md	"	7-15-78
Dean, Thomas	Capt. Mass	Killed	1780 Prisoner
Dean, Thomas	Mass	Died	1778
Deane, John	Pvt. Md	"	12-15-81
Dearborn, Thomas	N H	"	1778
Dearlove, James	Pvt. 3 Md.	Killed	8-22-78
Debago, Simon	R I	Died	4-30-78
Debow, William Matross	Pa.	"	11-24-76
DeBoge, Baron	Lt. Col. Poland	Killed	1778
DeCamp, John	N J	Died	1782
Decoster, Joseph	Pvt. 15 Mass	"	10-14-79
Decoune, Louis	Cpl. France	"	1781 Va.
Dedman, Robert	Sgt. Va.	Killed	1781
Deffnal, William	2 S C	Died	9-1-78
DeForest, David	Conn	"	6-2-83
Deford, John	Pvt. 5 Md.	"	10-10-79
DeHart, Jacob	Aid-de-Camp Pa	Killed	7-21-80
DeHart, Maurice	Maj. NJ	"	1781
Deichert, Warner	N Y	"	1780 By Ind.
Deitrick, Peter	Conn	Died	1780
Deitz, Johannes	N Y	Killed	1782 By Ind.
DeKalb, John	N Y	Died	1783
DeKalb, Baron	Brig. Gen. Ga.	"	8-16-83
De LaGrange Myndert	Lt. N Y	"	78
De La Loge Pierre Louis	Lt. France	"	1781 Va.
Delamater, Hendrick	N.Y.	"	1783
Delamater, Samuel	Pvt. N Y		1781
Deland, Benjamin	Mass	Killed	4-19-75
Delany, Cornelius	Sgt. 4 N J	Died	3- 78
Delance, Luther	Pvt. Conn	"	9-23-80
Delopet, Richard	Pvt. Pa.	"	1781
De la Rodierre	Col. France	"	1780
Delefraney, John B.	Pvt. 6 Md.	"	11-30-78
Deleider, Henry	R. I.	"	10-29-76
DeLuce, Francis	Pvt. Mass.	"	1780
Dely, John Wheelwright	Pvt. Can.	"	3-19-79

DeMarin, Jean-Baptiste	Capt. Com. France	Died	1781	Va.
Demick, Benjamin	Pvt. Mass	Died	3-17- 78	
Doming, Ephraim	Conn.	"	1783	
Demond, Moses	Pvt. 5 N Y	"	12-10-81	
Demott, Peter	Pvt. 3 N Y	"	1-9-78	
Dempsey, Squire	Pvt. 5 N C	"	5-17-78	
Denby, Richard	Pvt. Md	"	5-8-83	
Denerran, Mathew	Maj. Va.	"	1779	
Denhard, Thomas	R I	"	9-16-76	
Denico, Joseph	Pvt. 12 Mass	"	1-15-78	
Denis, Aaron	Ens. Mass.	"	1780	
Denis, Solomon	Cpl. Mass.	"	1777	
Denison, Daniel	Conn.	"	1778	
Denison, James	Capt. N Y	"	1778	
Dennett, David	N H	"	8-20-77	
Dennis, Abner	Pvt. 6 N C	"	9- 78	
Dennis, Adam	Pvt. Pa.	"	1777	Prison
Dennis, Hezekiah	Pvt. 5 N C	"	1-12-78	
Dennis, Jean	Pvt. Can	"	6-6-77	
Dennis, Robt.	Pvt. 9 N C	"	3-6-78	
Dennis, Wm.	Pvt. 10 N C	"	9- 79	
Dennison, Wetheril	Pvt. 6 Mass	"	7-20-77	
Demmit, Davis	Pvt. 11 Mass	"	1-20-78	
Denny, Edward	Pvt. 6 Pa.	Killed	6-10-76	Three Rivers
Denotter, George	Pvt. N Y	Died	1-1-77	
Denslow, Elijah	Pvt. Conn	"	1779	
Denslow, Joel P.	Pvt. Conn	"	7-1-78	
Denslow, Philander	Capt. Conn	"	1-2-78	
Denson, Isaac	Pvt. 5 Md.	"	5-22-78	
Denson, Wm.	Pvt. 9 N C	"	9-1-79	
Dent, John	Pvt. 2 Md.	"	1778	
Denton, D.	Pa.	"	7-3-78	
Deoran, James	Pvt. 5 Md.	"	12-23-77	
DeParis, Jacques	Cpl. France	"	1781	Va.
Depese, Jesse	Cpl. 2 N J	"	10-12-77	
Depew, John	Pvt. N Y	"	8- 78	
Derby, Thomas	N H	"	10-7-76	
Derby, Thomas	Mass	"	1776	White Pl.
DeSanssure, Louis	Lt. 3 S C	Killed	10-9-79	Savannah
DeSatur	Capt. France	Died	1781	Va.
Desilve, Joseph	Pvt. Mass	"	6-28-78	
DeSireuil, Jean Jarlan	Capt. France	"	1781	Va.
Desmont, Joseph	France	"	1781	Va.
DeStadesman, Jean	N Y	"	12- 80	
Determine, Nicolas	France	"	1781	Va.
DeTurck, John	Pvt. Pa.	"	1781	
Detrick, Peter	Ens. Pa.	"	5- 81	
Devaise, Joseph	France	"	1781	Va.
Devendorf, (Diefendorf) Henry	Capt. N Y	Killed	8-6-77	
Deveney, Peter	2 S C	Died	10-18-79	
Devillers, Gabriel	France	"	1781	Va.
Deviger, Daniel	Pvt. R I	Killed	12 31-75	Que
Dewall	Lt. Md.	"	9-9-81	

Dewees, William	Col. Pa.	Died	1782	
Dewey, Daniel	Mass.	"	4-1- 76	
Dewey, Elisha	Pvt. N Y	"	5-1-78	
Dewey, Enoch	Pvt. Mass.	"	1778	
Dewey, James	Pvt. Conn	"	10-12-78	
DeWitt, John	Lt. N Y	"	1781	
Dewit, Aaron	Pvt. N Y	"	2-18-77	
DeWoolf, Benoni	Pvt. Conn.	"	3-28-78	
Dexter, Darins	Pvt. Conn.	"	1-10-78	
Dexter, Gideon	Pvt. R I	"	3-1-78	
Dexter, John	Mass	"	5-3-83	
Deze, Andre	France	"	1781	Va
Diamond, Moses	N Y	"	1781	Va
Dias, Joseph	Pvt. Mass	"	1781	SS Prison
Dick, James	Pvt. Conn	"	3-9-78	
Dickenson, Israel	Pvt. Mass	"	11-5-77	
Dicker, Simeon	Pvt. N J	"	6-28-77	
Dickerson, Draper	2 S C	"	10-1-78	
Dickerson, John	Capt. N C	"	1783	
Dickerson, John	Pvt. 3 N Y	"	10-1-78	
Dickerson, Nathaniel	Pvt. Va		1778	
Dickerson, Peter	Capt. N J	"	5-10 80	
Dickey, Robert	N H	"	4-27-83	
Dickey, Benj.	Pvt. N. H.	"	9-19-77	
Dickinson, Ebenezer	Mass	"	1780	
Dickinson, Edmund B.	Maj. Va.	Killed	6-28-78	
Dickinson, Isaac	Pvt. Conn	Died	3-1-78	
Dickinson, Israel	Capt. Yale Conn	"	11-18-77	
Dickinson, Nathaniel	Sgt. Va.	"	1782	
Dickinson, (Dixon) Samuel	Pvt. 4 N J	"	11- 77	
Dickson, Richd.	Pvt. Md.	"	12-27-82	
Dickson, William	Pvt. 4 N J	"	6-30-78	
Dididiere, Nicolas	France	"	1781	Va
Diefendorf, Henry	Col. N Y	"	1777	
Dietz, Johannes	Pvt. N Y	"	1782	
Dietz, William	Capt. N Y	"	1782	
Dike, Jonathan	Pvt. 9 Mass	"	2-24-78	
Dilano, Nathan	Pvt. Mass	"	8-14-77	
Dill, George	Pvt. R I	"	2-20-77	
Dill, James	Lt. Pa.	Killed	9 11-77	
Dillon, James	Lt. 7 N C	"	9-8-81	
Dillon, John	Conn	"	6-17-75	Bunker Hill
Dillon, John	2 SC	Died	1-14-76	
Dittzer, Jean	France	"	1781	Va
Dimon, David	Lt. Col. Conn	Killed	9-17-77	
Dimon, John	Pvt. Conn	Died	1777	
Dimond, Moses	Pvt. Conn	"	10-2-78	
Dingle, Samuels	2 SC	"	1 13-77	
Dingman, Ande	Pvt. N Y	"	2 26-78	
Dinis, Joseph Tinier	France	"	1781	Va
Dinsmore, Samuel	Pvt 18 Cont.	"	4-15-76	
Dinwiddie, Hugh	Lt. Col. Pa.	"	1777	
Dique, Donnier, Francois	France	"	1781	Va.
Sisarm, Francis	Pvt. 1 N C	"	3-12-78	
Disheroon, Thos	Pvt. 7 Md	"	2 10-79	

Divine, James	Pvt. Pa	Died	7-3-78
Dixon, Henry	Capt. N C	"	7-17-82
Dixon, Henry	Pvt 6 N C	..	8- 77
Dixon, Henry	Pvt 3 N C	"	7-17-82
Dixon, Henry	Col. N C	"	1782
Dixon, Henry	Capt. N C	"	1779
Dixon, John	Pvt. Pa	"	1779
Dixon, Richard	Pvt. Md	"	12-27-82
Doane, Jonathan	Mass	"	1780
Doane, Samuel	Mass	"	8-25-78
Dobbins, Wm.	Cpl. 10 N C	"	6-28-83
Dobbs, William	Capt. NYC	"	1781
Dobbs, William	Conn.	"	1781
Dobel, John	Mass	"	4-8-78
Doblin. George	Pvt. NY	"	4-22-78
Dobon,	Capt N C	Killed	1778
Dobson,	Capt. NC	"	6-20-80
Dobson, Henry	Capt Md	"	9-8-81
Dobson, John	Pvt. Md	Died	1-31-76
Doby, John	Pvt. SC	Killed	1781
Dod, Caleb	Maj N J	"	1780
Dodd, Caleb	Maj. N J	Died	1780
Dodge James	Pvt. Conn	"	9-25-78
Dodge, James	N H	Killed	6-17 75
Dodge, Job	Pvt 15 Mass	Died	9-25-75
Dodge, Jonathan	Pvt Mass	"	5-12-78
Dodge, Nathan	Pvt Conn	"	5-20-78
Doggatt	Capt 6 SC	Killed	6-20-79
Dogget, Benj	Capt Va	Died	1780
Dogget, Richard	Capt Va	Killed	1780 SC
Doggett, Ichabod	Mass	Died	1781
Doharty, James	Capt SC	Killed	1781
Dole, Benjamin	N H	"	6-17-75
Dolph, Moses	Pa	Died	1779
Dolson, Jacob	N Y	"	1779
Domas, Lewis	2 SC	Killed	10-9-79
Dominick, Benj	Pvt Md	"	9-8-81
Domino, Jean	France	Died	1781 Va
Donaldson, Alexander	Pvt Pa	"	1783
Donally, Hugh	Pvt 10 N C	"	1-24-82
Donally, William	Pvt Va	"	1-10-77 Prison
Donnom, William	Capt 4 SC	Killed	10-9-77
Donnovan, Richard	Lt 6 Md	"	8-16-80
Donovan, Matthew	Maj 9 Va	Died	1777
Donovan, Patrick	Pvt Can	"	7-30-77
Donovan, Richard	Lt 6 Md	Killed	8-16-80 SC
Doodes, Joseph	Pvt N Y	Died	1-15-78
Door, Bowers	Navy	"	12-16-79 Eng Prison
Doolittle, Abraham	Lt Conn	"	1776
Doolittle, John	Pvt N H	"	10-7-77
Dorr, William	Pvt Can	"	2- 78
Dorchester, Caleb	Pvt 12 Mass	"	9-15-78
Dorman, Joseph	Conn	Killed	7-5-79

Name	Unit	Status	Date	Note
Dorman, Math	Del	Died	6-22-77	
Dorrance, George	Pvt. Pa.	"	1778	Wyo.
Dorrance, George	Lt. Col.	"	1778	"
Dorrington, John	Mass	"	10-15-83	
Dorrance, George	Pa	Died	7-3-78	
Dorsey, Levin	Md	Killed	1781	
Dorsey, William	Navy	Died	6-26 81	Eng Prison
Doty, Solomon	Pvt 14 Mass	"	4-6-78	
Doud, Giles	N Y	"	1776	
Doud, Giles	Capt Conn	"	1776	
Douge, Jas	Pvt 1 N C	"	5-3-78	
Dougherty, Edmund	Sgt. Md.	"	1-15-81	
Dougherty, John	Pvt. 4 N J	"	5-24-78	
Dougherty, Philip	Pvt Can	"	1-14-78	
Doughty, John	Cpl Mass	"	7-23-77	
Doughty, Jonathan	Pvt 12 Mass	"	1-30-78	
Doughty, William	N J	"	9-21-79	
Douglas, Charles	Pvt Pa	"	3-1-78	
Douglas, John	Va	"	1776	
Douglas, Moses	Pvt 1 N J	"	3-1-77	
Douglas, William	Col Conn	Killed	5-27-77	
Douglas, William	Mass	Died	1777	
Douglass, James	Pvt 2 Md	Killed	8-16-80	
Douglass, Vance	Pvt Mass	Died	9-19-77	
Dounel, Jobez	Pvt 11 Mass	"	11-6-78	
Dourian, Ezra P	Pvt Conn	"	10-2-81	
Dowdy, Geo	" 10 N C	"	4- 78	
Dowling, Lawrence	Pvt 1 N J	"	10- 77	
Dowling, William	Pvt SC	"	1783	
Downer, Ezra	Conn	"	1781	Va
Downey, Andrew	Pvt Can	"	10-6-78	
Downey, John Sr	Pvt Pa	"	6-3-81	
Downing, Abijah	Pvt Conn	"	12-13-80	
Downing, George	Pvt Pa	"	7-3-78	
Downs, Patt	Pvt 3 N Y	"	9-15-78	
Doyer, Peter	Pvt 2 Md	"	12-7-79	
Doyl, Thomas		Killed	6-17-75	
Doyle, Hugh	Pvt 4 N J	Died	3- 78	
Drake, Abraham	Lt Col Mass	"	1781	
Drake, Augustine	Conn	"	5-6-77	
Drake, Elijah	Mass	"	78	
Drake, Lemuel	Conn	"	4-15-80	
Drake, Samuel	N Y	"	6- 78	
Drake, Thomas	Lt Va	Killed	1-21-77	
Draper, Abijah	Maj Mass	Died	1780	
Draper, Joseph	Pvt Mass	"	1776	
Draper, Josiah	Pvt Mass	"	1777	
Draper, Richard	Pvt 15 Mass	"	1-31-79	
Draper, Roger	Pvt 5 N C	"	4-16-78	
Draper, William	Pvt 13 Mass	"	9-13-77	
Draper, William	Capt Mass	"	1776	
Dressor, John	Capt 15 Mass	"	6-29-78	
Drexler, David	R I	"	6-16-78	
Dring, Thomas	Capt 2 N C	"	9-11-77	

Name	Rank/Unit	Status	Date	
Druary, Zedekiah	N H	Died	8- 77	
Drudge, Thomas	Pvt Md	"	4-10-83	
Drummond, James	Lt Va	"	1783	
Drury, Elisha	Pvt Mass	"	2-22-82	
Drury, Nathan	Capt Mass	"	4-1-82	
Drury, Zedekiah	Pvt Mass		1777	
Dryar, Israel	Pvt 15 Mass	Killed	8-29-78	
Dryden, Nathaniel	Ens. SC	Died	10-7-80	King Mt.
Duball, Oliver	Pvt. 7 Mass	"	11-11-78	
Dubois, David	Capt SC	Killed	10-9-77	
Du Bois, Zachariah	Maj N Y	Died	1783	
Dubourg, Nicolas	France	"	1781	Va
Dudley, Daniel	Pvt 7 Mass	"	11-11-78	
Dudley, David	Conn	"	2-19-80	
Dudley, Roberts	Pvt Conn	"	1782	
Dudley, Samuel	N H	"	10-11-81	
Dudley, Timothy	Pvt N H	Killed	1778	
Duly, Oliver	Pvt 7 Mass	Died	12-6-77	
Dufut, Michel-Philippe	France	"	1781	Va
Duff, David		Killed	1780	Kings Mt.
Dugan, Edward	Pvt 6 Md	Died	9-10-78	
Duggin, Jesse	Pvt 5 N C	Killed	10-4-77	
Dugros, Luc	France	Died	1781	Va
Duhogue, John	Pvt Md	"	12-20-82	
Duke, Francis	Pvt. Conn	Killed	1777	
Duke, Sherard	Pvt 10 N C	Died	10- 81	
Dumb, Frederk	Pvt Conn	"	7-26-77	
Dumb, Frederk	Pvt 5 N Y	"	10-1-77	
Dumont, Denis	France	"	1781	Va
Dunbar, Alexander	Pvt N J	"	4-1-77	
Dunby, Richard	Pvt Md	"	5-8-83	
Dunham, Gershorn P	Pvt Conn	"	12-31-77	
Dunham, Silas	Lt Conn	Killed	12-7-77	
Dunigan, Jno	Pvt 4 N J	Died	1-31-78	
Dunkam, Abner	Pvt Can	"	3-8-78	
Dunlap, John	Pvt Pa	"	1777	
Dunlap, Richard	Pvt Pa	"	1781	
Dumnagan, John	Pvt Md	"	1-25-83	
Dunning, Jacob	Lt N Y	"	1781	
Dunnington, Francis	Pvt Md	"	4-23-83	
Dunster, Peter	Pvt 6 Md	Killed	9-16-80	
Dunton, John	Pvt 15 Mass	Died	3-29-78	
Dunwoody, Hugh	Pa	"	1777	
Dunbar, Alexander	Pvt 4 N J	"	4-1-77	
Duncan, Thomas	Pvt N H	"	11- 78	
Dunbar, Samuel	Mass	"	1783	
Dunlap, James	Pvt N Y	Killed	1777	
Dunlap, Jas.	Cpl. N Y	Died	10-3-79	
Dunlap, Richard	Capt. Pa	"	6-3-81	
Dunlap, Williams	Pvt N Y	"	1780	
Dunn, James	Pvt Va	"	1780	
Dunn, Jeffrey	Pvt 10 N C	"	1-12-79	
Dunn, Levi	Pvt Pa	"	7-3-78	
Dunn, Malachi	10 N C	"	12- 78	

Dunn, Peter	Capt Va	Killed	9-26-77
Dunn, Thomas	N Y	Died	1781
Dunn, William	Pvt 6 Mass	"	8-18-77
Durand, James	R I	"	10-17-77
Durant, Samuel	12 Mass	"	10-13-77
Durfee Daniel	Pvt Conn	"	9-2-82
Durfee, Ephram	Pvt Conn	"	12-27-77
Durfee, Joseph	Pvt Mass	"	1775
Durgan, Patrick	Pvt 5 Md	"	11-21-79
Durgin, Benjamin	N H	"	3-7- 78
Durkee, Asa	Cpl Conn	"	5-28-78
Durkee, Jeremiah	Pvt Mass	"	1775
Durkee, Jeremiah	Conn	"	1775
Durkee, John	Col Conn	"	1781
Durkee, John	Col Conn	"	5-30-82
Durkee, John	Col Conn	"	3-1-82 Bear Hill
Durkee, Robert	Pa	"	7-3-78
Dusenburgh, Philip	2 SC	"	8-21-78
Dutton, Joseph	Mass	"	5-1-75
Dutton, Thomas	Pvt Md	Killed	9-8-81
Duty, Mark	N H	Died	1783
Duvall, Edward	Capt 2 Md	Killed	8-16-80
Duvall, Peter	Pvt 9 Mass	Died	12-21-79
Duvall, William	Md		1777
Dveater, Jno	Pvt 2 Md	"	2-5-79
Dwight, Seth	Mass	"	11-19-76
Dwinels, Amos	Pvt 15 Mass	"	12-15-77
Dwire	Pvt N H	"	7-7-77
Dyckman, Abraham	Lt N Y	"	1782
Dyckman, Stephen	Pvt Conn	"	3-9- 77
Dye, Jonathan	Lt Va	Killed	9-11-77
Dyer, Benjamin	Pvt 15 Mass	Died	8-22-78
Dyer, Christopher	Lt Mass	"	10-31-77
Dyer, Christopher Jr	Lt R I	"	1777
Dyer, Joseph	Mass	"	9-4- 75
Dyer, Timothy	Pvt 9 Mass	"	7-27- 77
Dysart, Warner	N Y	Killed	1780
Dyke, Benjamin	Sgt. N H	Died	1777
Dykeman, Abraham	N Y	"	3-17-82
Dysart, James	N C	"	2-1-81
Dysart, William	N C	"	2 1-81

E

Eackman, Jacob	R I	Died	5-20-78
Eads, Henry	Pvt Md	"	1782
Eady, Thomas	Pvt Va	Killed	3-7-81
Eagan, Timothy P	11 Mass	Died	12-1-77
Eager, Uriah	Capt Mass	"	12-30 80
Eagles, Thomas	Pvt N J	"	8-8-83
Eagleston, Bennet	P Pvt Conn	"	1783
Eakin, Samuel	Chap Del	"	8-29-83
Eakin, Samuel	Chap. N J		1783
Ealn, William	Pvt Conn	"	7-23-77
Earl, Jesse	Pvt Conn	"	1780

Name	Rank/Unit	Status	Date	Note
Earl, Moses	Pvt 1 N J	Died	1- 78	
Earl, Timothy	Pvt 9 Mass	"	2-1- 79	
Early, Jeremiah	Col Va	"	1779	
Easeltyne, Richard	Maj N Y		1783	
Easte, Benjamin	Mass	Killed	6-17-75	Bunker Hill
Easter, David	Pvt 9 N C	Died	2-22-78	
Eastman, Caleb	N H	Killed	6-17-75	Bunker Hill
Eastman, John	Pvt N H	died	7-8- 77	
Eastman, Jonathan	Pvt N H	"	5-11-78	
Eastman, Joseph	Pvt N H	"	10-30-77	
Easton, Ebenezer	Conn	"	1776	
Eastwood, Amariah	Pvt 4 N J	"	3-5-77	
Easty, Benjamin	N H	Killed	6-17-75	
Eaton,	Maj Ga	"	5-21-81	Ga
Eaton, Epaphus	Pvt Conn	died	5-31-77	
Eaton, James	Pvt Mass	"	1777	
Eaton, Jeremiah	Mass	"	1780	
Eaton, John	N H	Killed	6-17-75	
Eaton, Jonathan	Pvt 9 Mass	Died	3-6-78	
Eaton, Joseph	Lt. Mass	"	7-2-79	
Eaton, Joshua	Mass	"	5-3-72	
Eaton, Joshua	Sgt 8 Mass	Killed	10-7 77	
Eaton, Joshua	Pvt 14 Mass	died	12-24-77	
Eaton, Pinkertham	Maj. 3 N C	Killed	6-5- 81	
Eaton, William	N C	Died	1780	
Ebenezer, Cox	Col N Y	"	1777	
Eberhard, Michael	Pvt Pa N Y	"	1783	
Ebey, George	Pvt Pa	Killed	1779	
Eccleston, John	Pvt Md	Died	1782	
Ecles, Thomas	Sgt. Mass	"	1783	
Eddy, Caleb	R I	"	5-31-78	
Eddy, Robbin	Pvt 14 Mass	"	7-29-77	
Eddy, Zacheriah Jr	Mass	"	6-9-77	
Eddy, Zecheus	Pvt 14 Mass	"	6-9-77	
Edes, Benjamin	Pvt 15 Mass	"	10-7-77	
Edes, Thomas	Sgt. Mass	"	1783	At Sea
Edgerly	Capt Md	Killed	9-9-81	
Edgerton, Daniel	Capt Vt	Died	6-24- 83	
Edgerton, Jonathan	Cpl Conn	"	6-1-78	
Edgerton, Sims	Pvt Conn	"	10-8-82	
Edings, Benjamin	Pvt SC	"	1780	
Edmiston, William	Capt	Killed	1780	Kings Mt
Edmon, Maurice	France	died	1781	Va
Edmonds, Elias	Lt Col Va	"	1781	
Edmondson, Andrew	Ens	Killed	10-7-80	Kings Mt.
Edmondson, Robert Sr	Lt. Va.	"	10-7-80	"
Edmondson, William	Capt Va	"	10-7-80	"
Edmunds, David	Lt S C	Died	1778	
Edmunds, Thomas	Capt. Va.	Killed	9-9- 81	
Edmundson	Capt SC	died	10-7-80	Kings Mt.
Edom, Maurice	France	"	1781	Va
Edson, Joseph	Capt Conn	"	10-2-77	
Edson, Robert	Cpl 1 N J	"	4-13-77	
Edward, David	4 N Y	"	3-16-78	

Edward, Denny	Pvt Pa	Died	6-19-76
Edward, James	R I	"	5-1-78
Edwards, Andrew	Pvt 13 Mass	"	12-28-76
Edwards, Dan	R I	"	7-24-77
Edwards, Isaac	2 S C	Killed	6-28-76
Edwards, Jno	Pvt 2 N C	Died	2-15-78
Edwards, Joseph	Capt N J	"	1782
Edwards, Wm	Pvt 6 Md	"	4-1-78
Eells, Waterman	Capt Mass	"	1777
Eggers, Elijah	Pvt 2 N Y	"	12-17-81
Eggleston, Joseph	Pvt. Conn	"	6-18-81
Egre, Paul	France	"	1781 Va
Fichelberger, George	Q M Pa	"	1780
Eichelberger, George	Md	"	1780 Pa
Eicholtz, Jacob	Pvt Pa	"	1776
Elbert, Samuel	Maj. Gen. Ga	"	11-2-80
Eldredge, Samuel	Mass	"	11-8-81
Eldredge, William	P Pvt Conn	"	1-12-82
Eldridge, Ceasar	R I	"	8-31-78
Eldridge, Daniel	Pvt Conn	"	1781
Eliot, Joseph	Mass	"	12 15-77
Eliot, Joseph	Mass	"	9-25-82
Elkins, Henry	Capt Mass	"	1782
Ellery, Nathaniel	Mass	"	1778
Elliot, Alexander	R I	Killed	12-31-75
Elliot, Joseph	Mass	Died	1 31-78
Elliot, John	Pvt N H	"	5-20-78
Elliot, Daniel	Pvt 11 Mass	"	1- 78
Elliott, Bernard	Lt Col 4 SC	"	10-25-78
Elliott, Joseph	Lt 1 SC	"	1778
Elliot, John	Pvt N H	"	10-7-77
Elliott, Joseph	Conn	"	1775
Elliott, Joseph	Capt. Mass	"	1775
Ellis, Jacob	Pvt 5 N Y	"	12-19-81 Va
Ellis, Joseph	N H	"	3-9-78
Ellis, Josiah	Pvt 15 Mass	"	5-17-77
Ellis, Paul	Capt 14 Mass	Killed	6-28-78
Ellis, Reuben	Pvt 5 Mass	Died	1-31-77
Ellis, William	Pvt Md	"	6-26-81
Ellison, Joseph	3 SC	"	9-25-79
Ellison, Richard	Pvt 7 Md	"	5-26-79
Ellison, Robert	Lt Md	"	1780
Ellison, Samuel	Pvt N J	"	1781
Ellsworth, Charles	Capt Mass	"	1780
Ellsworth, Charles	Capt Conn	"	1-4- 77
Elmer, Samuel	Lt. Conn	"	1777
Elmes, Jonathan	Pvt Mass	"	10-30-77
Elmore, John	Pvt N J	"	1-15-78
Elsworth, Riley	Pvt Can	"	3-5-80
Ely, Claude	France	"	1781 Va
Ely, Levi	Capt N Y	Killed	10-19-80
Ely, Phineas	Pvt Mass	Died	6-8-78
Emanuel, Primus	Pvt Mass	"	6-11-78
*Elliott, Joseph	Capt Mass	"	1775

63

Name	Rank/Unit	Fate	Date
Emerson, William	Rev. Mass	Died	1776
Emerson, Oliver	Cpl 9 Mass	"	7-7-78
Emery, Thomas	Pvt 4 N J	"	2- 78
Emery, William	Del	"	7-10-78
Emory, James	Pvt 7 Mass	Killed	10-8-77
Emory, Stephin	Pvt 2 N C	Died	10- 78
Empsen, Cornelius	Pvt Can	"	5-10-77
Ene, Martin	Ens. Conn	"	10-11-80
Engle, Bartel	Pvt Md	"	8-6-79
English, Benjamin	Capt N H	Killed	7-5-79
English, Benjamin	Ga	"	7-5-79
English, Dan'l	Pvt 5 Md	Died	1779
English, Dan'l	Pvt 5 Md	"	1-17-77
English, John	Pvt 4 N Y	"	5-1-78
English, Thomas	Navy	"	10-16-78
English, William	Pvt Can	"	3-15-77
Ennis, John	Navy	"	7-21-81
Eno, Martin	Ens Conn	Killed	10-11-80
Enoch, Ela	N H	"	1777
Ephram, Ebeneren	Pvt Mass	Died	1-4-77
Ephraim, Abel	Pvt 9 Mass	"	6-26-78
Epler, John	Lt Pa	"	1782
Eppes, Francis	Lt Col	"	10- 80
Eppes, Francis	Lt Col Va	Killed	8-27-76 L I
Epting, Adam F	Pvt S C	"	1780
Erickson, Moses	Pvt 1 N J	Died	8-1-78
Erle, William	Pvt Conn	"	7-23-77
Erskine, Robert	RRS N J	"	10-2-80
Erwin, John	Drum Maj 2 N Y	"	9-28-77
Esselstyn, Richard	Maj N Y	"	1783
Estabrook, Clancey	Conn	"	1776
Estell, John	Pvt N J	"	1780
Estill, James	Capt Ky	Killed	3-7-82 By Ind.
Estmioc, John	Pvt 7 N C	Died	8- 77
Etheridge, Jno	Pvt 6 Md	"	11-16-79
Ethridge, Dan'l	Cpl 8 N C	"	1-19-78
Evance, Thomas	2 SC	"	12-18-77
Evans, Andrew	Pvt 2 Mass	"	1778
Evans, Benja	Pvt 5 Md	"	10-31-79
Evans, Daniel	B K	Killed	4-19-75
Evans, David	Pvt 9 Mass	Died	6-5- 78
Evans, Henry	Pvt Conn	"	11-1-81
Evans, John	Pvt Va	Killed	11-12-71
Evans, John	Lt N H	Died	2-25-81
Evans, John	Pvt 2 N Y	"	9-24-77
Evans, Rowland	Pvt SC	Killed	1781
Evans, William	Pvt 2 Md	Died	5-16-78
Evans, Thomas	Pvt 6 N C	"	4-30-78
Evans, William	Pa	"	1783
Evarts, John	Pvt Conn	"	4-19-83
Evens, Daniel	Pvt N H	Killed	6-17-75 B. H.
Evens, Nathan	Pvt 9 Mass	Died	12-10-77
Everts, Jeremiah P	Pvt Conn	"	2-21-78
Everet, Jno	Pvt 1 N C	"	8- 78
Eveleigh, George	Lt 2 SC	"	12-18-77

Name	Rank/Unit	Status	Date	
Eveleth, William	Pvt 14 Mass	Died	10-6-79	
Everton, Wm	R I	Killed	10-22-77	
Everill, Ebenizer	Cpl Conn	Died	9-29-80	
Evins, Magon	Del	"	10-25-82	
Evins, Timothy	N H	"	6-17-75	B H
Ewing, James Sr	Pvt Pa	"	1782	
Ewing, John	Pvt Can	"	5-1-77	
Ewing, Nathaniel	Capt Md	"	1780	
Ewing, William	Pvt Pa	"	1781	
Eyers, Samuel	Pvt N H	"	2-17-80	
Eyre, John	Col. Pa.	"	1781	
Ezekiel, Angell	R I	"	1782	

F

Name	Rank/Unit	Status	Date	
Faddles, Jos	Pvt 10 N C	"	12-17-83	
Faey, Joseph	Ens. N H	Killed	9-19-77	
Fagg, Samuel	Pvt 11 Mass	Died	8-22-77	
Faills, Eben	N H	Killed	6-17-75	
Fairbanks, Abel	Pvt 14 Mass	Died	11-26-77	
Fairbank, Comeing	N H	Killed	6-17-75	
Fairbanks, David	Capt Mass	Died	4-19-76	
Fairbanks, Johns	Pvt 5 Md	"	8-15-80	
Fairbanks, Joshua	Lt Mass	"	7-15-83	
Fairbanks, Joshua	Pvt Mass	"	1781	
Fairbourn, William	Pvt Md	"	3-16-82	
Fairburne, Wm	Pvt Md	"	3-16-82	
Fairess, Hugh	Pa	"	12-20-77	
Fairman, Richard	Conn	"	9-22-75	
Fairservice, John	Pvt 6 Mass	"	11-30-80	
Fales, Jonathan	Mass	"	1780	
Fales, London	Pvt 14 Mass	"	7-15-78	
Fales, Moses Jr	Mass	"	1780	
Falls,	Capt SC	Killed	1780	
Falls, Gilbraith	Capt N C	Died	1780	
Fanning, Joshua	Lt Va	"	1778	
Fanning, Nathan P	Conn	"	4-12-78	
Farnham, Levi	Cpl. N Y	"	1776	
Fansett, Amovah	Lt N Y	"	6-17-75	
Fantz, Jacob	Pvt R I	"	2-10-77	
Farence, Owen	Pvt 3 Md	"	5-7-80	
Farewell, David	Pvt 3 Mass	"	10-28-77	
Faris, Joseph	Pvt 4 N J	"	8-16-77	
Farley, Joseph	N H	"	10-23-80	
Farmer, Nathaniel	Mass	"	1778	
Farnesworth, Samuel	Cpl 15 Mass	"	4-8-78	
Farnham, Levi	Cpl N Y	"	1776	S S Prison
Farnham, Stephen	Pvt 8 Mass	"	5-31-77	
Farnsworth, Abel	Mass	"	4-17-82	
Farnsworth, Abel	Mass	"	4-17-82	
Farnsworth, Nathl	Pvt Conn	"	4- 82	
Farnum, John	Pvt 8 Mass	"	5-7-78	
Farr, John	Pvt N J	Killed	3-24-82	
Farra, Noah	Pvt 2 Mass	Died	7-26-77	
Farrar, Samuel Sr	Mass	"	1783	

Farrell, James	Matross Pa	Killed	6-20-76
Farrell, Peter	Cpl Md	Died	6-18-81
Farrer, Samuel	Lt Mass	"	1783
Farrington, Eben	Pvt 1 Mass	"	4-8-78
Farris, William	Sgt 15 Mass	"	11-26-77
Farrow, Gershon	Pvt Mass	"	9- 78
Farrow, Rosanna	Water SC	"	1783
Farrow, Thos	Pvt 6 N C	"	2-8- 78
Farthing, Robt	Pvt 6 Md	"	5-27-78
Farwell, Joseph	N H	Killed	6-17-75
Fasset, Benjamin	Pvt Conn	Died	1780
Faulkner, William	Capt N J	"	4-25-76
Faunce, James	R I	"	1782
Fay, Benjamin	Mass	"	10-6-77
Fay, James	Pvt 15 Mass	"	5-4-78
Fay, James	N Y	"	1782
Fay, John	Vt	Killed	1777
Fay, Joseph	Ens. N H	Died	12-2-77
Fay, Josiah	Capt N Y	"	1776
Fay, Josiah	Mass	"	8-8-76
Fay, Steven	Capt Vt	"	5-17-81
Fay, Thomas	Sgt 11 Mass	"	5-3-78
Fayerweather, John	Lt Mass	"	1776
Faxon, Elisha	Mass	"	1776
Faxen, Thomas	Pvt. Pa		7-3-78
Fearall, John	Matross Md	"	1782
Felch, John	Capt Mass	"	10-28-76
Felder, John Henry	Capt SC	"	1779
Felder, Henry	Col Ga	"	1783
Felder, Henry	Capt Ga	Killed	1783
Felix, John	Pvt Conn	Died	11-31-78
Fellows, Amos	Capt Conn	"	1777
Fellows, Benja	Pvt 15 Mass	"	2-18-78
Fellows, David	Ens. Conn	Killed	12-10-79
Fellows, John	Pvt Conn	Died	6-15-78
Fellows, Samuel	Mass	"	1778
Felps, Garret	Pvt 2 N C	"	1-30-78
Felps, Moses	Pvt 2 Mass	"	3-17-78
Felt, George	Pvt 3 Mass	"	8-23-77
Fenn, Benjamin Jr	Lt. Conn	"	10-27-80
Fenn, Benjamin Sr	Conn	"	2-20-78
Fenn, Benjamin	Lt Col Conn	"	1778
Fennel, Edward	Pvt 7 Md	"	12- 79
Fenton, Elijah	Conn	"	1776
Fenton, Joshua	Pvt 7 N C	"	3-24-78
Fenton, Nathaniel	Pvt Conn	"	10-1-77
Fenton, Thomas	Sgt 6 Mass	"	1-17-78
Fenwick, William	Pvt 15 Mass	"	4-23-77
Ferguson, Patrick	Col SC	"	10-7-80 Kings Mt.
Ferree, Jacob	Pvt. Pa	"	1782
Ferris, Benjamin	N Y	"	1779
Ferris, James	Pvt N Y		1780
Ferrey, Claude-Pierre	France	"	1781 Va
Ferry, Samuel	Pvt 9 Mass	"	6-1-78

Name	Unit	Status	Date	Note
Ferrell, Wm	Pvt 10 N C	Killed	5-10-80	
Fessender, John	Pvt 7 Mass	Died	11-5-77	
Fibbs, Richard	Sgt N J	"	10-4-77	
Fielas, Philip	Pvt 2 N Y	"	8- 78	
Field, Daniel	Pvt 11 Mass	"	1-22-78	
Field, David	Pvt Conn	"	1778	
Field, Ezekiel H	Va	Killed	1782	By Ind.
Field, Henry	Lt Va	Died	1778	
Field, Joseph	Mass	"	1777	
Field, Michael	N H	"	6-28-78	
Field, Samuel	Conn	"	1783	
Fields, Jonathan	Pvt 12 Mass	"	1-17-78	
Fields, Timothy	Pvt 10 N C	"	9- 79	
Fielding, Lewis	Brig. Gen. Va.	"	1781	
Fielding, Lewis	Pvt. Va	"	12- 81	
Figgs, Charles	Del	"	1-4-79	
Fikes, Jos	Sgt 1 N C	"	1-4-78	
Filburt, Nathan	Pvt 11 Mass	"	1-15-78	
File, Philip	Pvt R I	"	3-5-77	
Filer, Roger	Pvt Conn	"	1778	
Filer, Thomas	Pvt N Y	Killed	1777	
Fillebrown, Isaac	Pvt 7 Mass	"	5-3-78	
Filts, Edward	Pvt 15 Mass	Died		
Finch, Benjamin	Pa	"	7-3-78	
Finch, Daniel	Pa	"	7-3-78	
Finch, Elisha	Pa	"	7-3-78	
Finch, John	Pa	Killed	1778	At Wyo.
Finch, John	Pa	Died	7-3-78	
Fincomb, Amos	N Y	"	1781	Va
Finesse, John	Pvt 2 Mass	"	9-9-78	
Finley, John	Md	"	1783	Pa
Finley, John	Maj. Pa.	"	1783	
Finney, Ezra	Pvt. Mass	"	1780	
Finney, John	Pvt 2 Mass	Killed	6-28-78	
Finney, Nelson	Sgt. Mass	Died	1-22-81	
Firis, James	SC	Killed	11- 81	
Firstraw, Anthony	1 SC	Died	3-24-77	
Fish, Aaron	R I	"	6-28-78	
Fish, Caleb	Pvt 2 N Y	"	3-30-79	
Fish, Cornelius	R I	Killed	6-23-80	
Fish, Ebenezer	Capt Mass	Died		
Fish, Elnathan	Mass	"	11-5-77	
Fish, Nathan	Pvt. Mass	"	1776	
Fisher, Balzer	Pvt R I	"	3-15-77	
Fisher, Benjamin	Mass	"	1777	
Fisher, Danl	Pvt 6 Md	"	9-11-77	
Fisher, Hendrick	N J	"	5-10-79	
Fisher, John	Pvt N J	"	7-1-78	
Fisher, John	Mass	"	2-10-77	
Fisher, Jonathan	Lt Mass	"	1777	
Fisher, Jonathan	N J	"	1777	
Fisher, Joseph	Pvt Md	"	11-20-82	
Fisher, Nathan Jr.	N Y	"	10-16-76	
Fisk, Amosa	Conn	Killed	6-17-75	
Fisk, John Willis	Conn		1776	

Name	Rank/State	Status	Date	Notes
Fisk, Peter	N H	Killed	6-17-75	
Fiske, Isaac Jr	Pvt Mass	Died	9-19-78	
Fist, John	1 SC	"	11-18-76	
Fitch, James	Conn	"	2-10-78	
Fitch, James P	Pvt Conn	Killed	6-28-78	
Fitchett, Cornelius	Pa	Died	7-3-78	
Fitten, Isaiah	Pvt SC	Killed	9- 81	
Fithian	Capt N J	"	10-8-77	
Fithian, Philip	Chaplain N J	"	10-4-76	
Fithian, Samuel	N J	Died	11-2-77	
Fitts, Daniel	Pvt Conn	"	1775	
Fitts, John	N H	"	1781	
Fitts, Nathan	Lt N H	"	1-29-81	
Fitz-Randolph James	N Y	"	1781	Prison
Fitzgerald, Jeremiah	Pvt Md	"	8-1-82	
Fitzgerald, Morris	Pvt 4 N J	"	11- 77	
Fitzpatrick, Bors	Pvt 6 Md	"	3-7-79	
Flagg, Abel	Pvt Mass	"	4-19-75	
Flagg, Ebenezer	Maj R I	Killed	5-14-81	
Flagby, John	N Y		1781	Va
Flanders, Jarvis	Mass	Died	1778	
Flegart, Archibald	Pvt R I	"	10-20-76	
Fleming, Capt		Killed	1-3- 77	
Fleming, Charles	Pvt Pa	Died	1777	Prison
Fleming, Charles	Lt Col Va	"	1778	
Fleming, James	Col Va	"	1778	
Fleming, William	Col Mass	Killed	8-31-78	
Flemming, Jno	Col 6 Md	Died	2-24-78	
Flemming, Jno	Col 1 Md	"	11-20-77	
Fletcher, Daniel	Maj Mass	"	1776	
Fletcher, James	Navy	"	1- 81	Eng Prison
Fletcher, Lawrence Dr.	Maj. 4 N Y	"	4-26-78	
Fletcher, Phineas	Pvt. N H	"	12-1-81	
Fletcher, Raymond	Pvt. 11 Mass	"	3-1-78	
Fletcher, Rich'd	Pvt 7 Md.	"	10-24-77	
Fletcher, Wm	Sgt. 10 N C	"	1-20-79	
Fling, Patrick	Pvt Conn	"	7-19-77	
Fling, Phil	Navy	"	7-21-81	Eng Prison
Flinn, John	Pvt 4 N J	"	2-8-77	
Flinn, Wm.	Pvt 10 N C	"	7-6-78	
Flint, Peter	1 SC	"	11-9-75	
Flint, Samuel	Capt. Mass	Killed	10-7-77	
Flint, Samuel	N Y	Died	1777	
Flint, William	Pvt Mass	Killed	4-19-75	
Flock, John	Sgt. N Y		1779	
Flock, Matthias	Pvt R I	"	10-4-77	
Flood, James	Pvt 1 Mass	Died	6-8-78	
Flood, Luke	Pvt 1-SC	Killed	6-28-76	
Flournoy, Samuel	Sgt. Va	Died	1780	
Flowers, Benjamin	Pvt Conn	"	1-1-78	
Flowers, Edward	Pvt Md	"	6-1-81	
Flowers, Philips	Pvt Ger.	Killed	10-4-77	
Flowmoy, Samuel	Sgt. Va.	Died	1780	
Floyd, John	Ky	Killed	1783	
Floyd, John	Col Ky	Died	1783	

Name	Unit	Status	Date	Note
Floyd, Saml	Pvt. 5 Md	Died	4-2-77	
Flury, Wm	Sgt. 5 N C	"	3-16-78	
Foard, John	Pvt. 5 Md	"	1-15-77	
Fobes, John	Mass	"	1783	
Fockel, Gottlieb	N C	"	12-17-78	
Foering, Christian Frederick	Rev. N. J.	"	3-29-79	
Fold, James	Pvt. 2 Mass	"	5-9-77	
Folks, Jos	Pvt. 10 N C	"	9-14-82	
Folks, James	Pvt. N C	"	1782	
Follett, Eliphalet	Vt.	Killed	1778	Wyo.
Follett, Eliphalet	Pa	Died	7-3-78	
Follett, Joseph	Pvt. Md.	"	7-25-82	
Folliot, Benjamin	Drum Md.	"	6-17-81	
Folliet, Joseph	Pvt. Md	"	7-25-82	
Fonda, Dana	N Y	"	1780	
Fonda, Donw	N Y	Killed	1780	By Ind.
Foot, Ebenezer	Pvt. Conn	Died	6-7-78	
Foote, Joseph	Pvt. Conn	"	1779	
Forbes, Absalom	Mass	"	1778	
Forbes, Arthur		Killed	1781	
Forbes, John	Capt. 2 SC	"	3-15-81	
Forbush, Robt	Pvt. 10 N C	Died	6-15-83	
Ford, Amos	Pvt Conn	"	2- 78	
Ford, Benjamin	Lt Col Md	Killed	4-35-81	
Ford, Boston	Pvt Conn	Died	10-35-77	
Ford, David	Mass	"	8-7-82	
Ford, James	Mass	"	1783	
Ford, Jacob Jr	N J	"	1779	
Ford, Jacob D	Col N J	"	1-19-77	
Ford, John	N C	Killed		
Ford, Roberts	Sgt. 4 Md	Died	4- 80	
Ford, Timothy	Pvt. 2 N Y	"	4- 78	
Ford, Tracy	Pvt. 7 Mass	"	10-7-77	
Forgtae, Ebenezer	Pvt. N H	"	11-14-77	
Forrester, Thos	Pvt. 6 N C	Killed	10-4-77	
Forster, John Jr	Pa	"	1780	
Fortune, Cato	Pvt. 12 Mass	Died	5-15-78	
Fortune, Jacob	Pvt. Conn	"	5-9-78	
Foss, Levi	Capt. 1 Mass	"	11-30-77	
Foss, Pelatiah	Pvt. 12 Mass	"	10-1-77	
Foster, Ebenezer	Pvt. 7 Mass	"	10-12-77	
Foster, Ebenezer	Ens. 14 Mass	Killed	10-19-77	
Foster, Ebenezer	Ens. Mass	Died	9-19-77	
Foster, Fletcher	Mass	"	11-28-77	
Foster, Isaac	Mass	"	12-27-81	
Foster, Job	Pvt Mass	"	1777	
Foster, Jack	R I	"	1-22-78	
Foster, James	Pvt Md	"	6-30-81	
Foster, James	Capt. Va	"	11-15-77	
Foster, John	Pvt. 2 Mass	"	6-15-78	
Foster, John	Mass	"	2-17-78	
Foster, John	Navy	"	6-7-77	Eng. Prison
Foster, John	N H	"	3-9-81	
Foster, Jonathan	Pvt R I	"	11-8- 81	
Foster, Joseph	Mass	"	1780	

Foster, Joshua	N H	Died	8- 1776
Foster, Obadiah	Pvt. Mass	"	7-25-80
Foster, Nash	Pvt. Mass	"	10-7-77
Foster, Samuel	Sgt. N Y	"	5-6-78
Foster, Stephen	N H	Killed	6-17-75
Foster, Timothy	Mass	Died	1775
Foster, William	Chap Pa		1780
Foster, Zephaniah P	Pvt. Conn	"	3-1- 78
Fosto, Antonia	Pvt. N H	"	7-7-77
Fountain, William	Pvt. 5 Md	"	10- 78
Fowler, Abraham	Conn	"	9-30-79
Fowler, James	Sgt. 6 Mass	"	9-29-77
Fowler, John Sr.	Conn	"	5-14-81
Fowler, John	Navy	"	1777 Prison
Fowler, Jonathan	Pvt. R I	"	6-19-77
Fowler, Jonathan	Pvt. Md	"	9- 83
Fowler, Philip	Cpl. Conn	Killed	6-17-75
Fowler, Richard	Pvt. N Y	"	1782
Fowler, Thomas	N Y	Died	12-21-76
Fowler, William	Ens N Y	"	2-27-82
Fowler, William	Ens Yale Conn	"	2-28-82
Fowler, Wm	Pvt. 9 N C	"	3-16-78
Fowles, James	N Y	"	1781 Va
Fox, Abraham	Pvt Mass	"	1777
Fox, Ansel	Pvt 1 Mass	"	12-25-78
Fox, Gideon P	Pvt Conn	"	9-11-77
Fox, Jabez	Capt. Conn	"	1780
Fox, Jonathan	N H	"	10-26-82
Fox, Joseph	Pvt Conn	"	10-4-78
Fox, Robert	Pvt Conn	Killed	12-7-77
Fox, Roger	Conn	"	6-17-75
Fox, Stephen	Pvt Conn	Died	4-7-78
Foy, Peter	S C	"	1782
Foye, John	Navy	"	10-16-78 Prison
Francis, Ebenezer	Capt N Y	Killed	1777
Francis, Ebenezer	Col Mass	"	7-7- 77
Francis, John P	Pvt. Conn	Died	2-22-79
Francis, Joseph	Pvt 15 Mass	"	9-24-77
Francisco, Thos	Pvt 9 N C	"	3-23-78
Francois, Antoine	France	"	1781 Va
Francois, Scholder		"	1781 Va
Frankford, Wm	Pvt N H	"	4-17-79
Franklin, Bark Joseph	3 SC	"	7-30-79
Franklin, Francis	Pvt. 3 Md		
Franklin, Jerusha H	Pa.	"	1781
Franklin, John	Pa.	"	7-3-78
Franklin, Peter	Pvt. 10 Mass	"	4-21-77
Fraser, John	S C	Killed	1779
Frederick, Thomas C	Pa	Died	1781
Free, Nero	Pvt. Conn	"	12-10-78
Free, Pomp	Pvt Conn	"	2-28-78
Free, Prince	Pvt Conn	"	1-7-78
Freeman, Barnabas	Pvt Mass	"	1781
Freeman, Edmund	Pvt Mass	"	7-22-82
Freeman, Elkanah	Cpl Mass	"	1778

Freeman, Gift	Pvt Conn	Died	12- 1780
Freeman, Guy P	Conn	"	12-18- 77
Freeman, Jonah	Pvt Conn	"	10-11-79
Freeman, Joseph	Cpl 3 Mass	"	10-31-78
Freeman, Kedar	R I	"	7-26-78
Freeman, Prince	Pvt Conn	"	4-5-78
Freege, Jesse	Sgt N J	"	7-3-78
French, Asa	Cpl Mass	"	9-11-78
French, Benjamin Jr	N H	Killed	10-29-76
French, Carlos (Charles)	Conn	Died	11-9-83
French, Ephraim	Pvt Mass	"	1780
French, Ezekiel	Pvt 11 Mass	"	1-29-78
French, John	Vt.	"	1781
French, Joseph	Col. N H	"	3-21-76
French, Joseph Jr	Mass	"	9-20-75
French, Nathaniel	Conn	"	11-3-81
French, Noah	Conn	"	1-7-81
French, Thomas	Cpl. Mass	"	10-30-77
French, William	N H	Killed	6-17-75
Frenier, John	Drum 5 N Y	Died	12-20-81
Freshwater, Thomas	Pvt 4 N J	"	3-16-77
Fricker, John	Cpl 2 Md	"	3-1-79
Frimier, John	N Y	"	1781 Va
Frink, Silus	Sgt Conn	"	2-8-78 Va
Frisbee, James	Mass	"	1779
Frisby, Abiel	Pvt. Conn	"	10-15-77
Frisby, Levi	Cpl. Conn	"	12-31-77
Fromee, John	Pvt. 5 Md	"	4-28-77
Frost, Abraham	Pvt. 7 Mass	"	9- 77
Frothingham, Thomas	Mass	"	1776
Fry, Abraham	N C	"	1778
Fry, Benjamin	Mass	"	1778
Fry, Henrich	N C	"	1775
Fryar, Josiah	Pvt 2 N C	"	6-18-78
Frye, James	Col Mass	"	1776
Frylsitz, Conrad	Pvt R I	"	1-5-77
Fugenot, Noel	France	"	1781 Va
Fulford, John	Mass	"	1780
Fulford, John	Maj Md	Killed	1781
Fullar, Samuel	Pvt. 3 Mass	"	2-3-80
Fuller, Abner	Pvt. Conn	Died	1776 Prison Ship
Fuller, Archelaus	Maj. Mass	"	1776
Fuller, Asa	Pvt. 14 Mass	"	9-15-79
Fuller, Amos	Pvt. 15 Mass	"	4-8-78
Fuller, David	Cpl. Mass	"	1781
Fuller, Ebenezer	Lt. Vt.	"	1777
Fuller, Edward	Mass	"	3-3-83
Fuller, Jabez	Pvt. 6. Mass	"	10-16-77
Fuller, Jedulhan	Mass	"	11-15-79
Fuller, Jeremiah	Pvt. 15 Mass	"	7-16-78
Fuller, Job	Pvt. Mass	"	1783
Fuller, Joshua	Sgt. Mass	"	8-23-77
Fuller, Nathan	7 Mass	"	2- 83

Fuller, Richard	Lt. 1 SC	Died	
Fuller, Stephen	Pa	Killed	7-3-78
Fuller, Thomas	Pa	Died	7-3-78
Fullerton, John	Pvt. 1 N Y	Killed	6-4-79
Fullerton, John	Capt. SC		1779
Fulton, Alexander	Pvt. 2 N Y	Died	12- 78
Furman, Wood	S C	"	1783
Furnan, Abraham	Pa	"	6-1-77
Fussell, Saml	Pvt 10 N C	"	4-5-79
Fyler, Roger	Conn	"	1778

G

Gable, Simeon	Ens N J	Died	8-8-77
Gage, Daniel	Capt N H	"	1775
Gage, Samuel	Pvt. 10 Mass	"	7-16-77
Gage, William	Mass	"	10-2-77
Gagnebey, Bernard	France	"	1781 Va
Gailard, Silas	Conn	"	9-16-75
Gaillard, Charles	Pvt S C	"	1780
Gailor, William P	Pvt 1 Conn	"	4-20-78
Gaines, Levi	Pvt. Conn	"	6-25-78
Gains, B. Pomp	Pvt. 3 Mass	Killed	7-22-77
Gale, Edward	Capt Md	Died	10- 79
Gale, Elijah	Pvt 4 Mass	"	6-1- 78
Gale, Geo	Pvt 10 N C	"	12- 79
Gale, Isaac	Sgt. Mass	"	1779
Gale, Jesse	Pvt. 4 Mass	"	3-24-80
Gallahue, Charles	Capt. Va	"	3-23-77
Gallahue, Charles	Capt. Va	"	5-24-77
Galley, Peter	Pvt. Pa	"	1782
Gallop, Thomas	Mass	"	1-24-78
Gallop, Thomas	Pvt 1 Conn	"	4-26-78
Gallup, George	Ens Conn	"	1781 Drowned
Gallup, Joseph	Conn	"	1778
Gallup, Thomas	Lt. N H	"	9-3-77
Golotet, Jean	France	"	1781 Va
Galtier, Jean	France	"	1781 Va
Gamble, Samuel	Pvt. SC	"	1780
Ganet, John	3 N Y	"	11- 77
Gantt, Dr. Thomas III	Md	"	1781
Gardner, Abraham	Col N Y	"	1782
Gardner, Amos	Pvt R I	"	2-16-78
Gardner, Isaac	Maj. Mass	Killed	4-19-75
Gardner, John P	Pvt Conn	Died	5-1-77
Gardner, John	Pvt Pa	Killed	1778
Gardner, Nichols	Pvt 14 Mass	Died	6-22-78
Gardner, Prince	" R I	"	10-20-80
Gardner, Simon	Mass	"	1781
Gardner, Simon	Mass	"	8-4-78
Gardner, Thomas	Pvt 14 Mass	"	9-15-77
Gardner, Thomas	Col SC	"	6-17-75
Gardiner, Benjamin	Pvt Mass	"	1778
Gardiner, John	Pa	Killed	1778 By Ind & Brit.
Gardiner, Othaniel	Lt. N Y		1777
Gardiner, Thomas	Col	Killed	6-17-75

Gare, Silas	Pa	Killed	1778 Wyo.
Garland, James	Capt. Va	Died	1781
Garland, James	Capt. N Y	Killed	1781
Garland, James	Pvt. 6 Md	Died	10-18-77
Garnes, Jeffrey	Pvt 7 N C	"	1-22-78
Garnet, William	Surg. Can	"	2-1-78
Garnsey, Oliver	Pvt. N H	"	1778
Garnsey, Robin	Pvt. Conn	"	2-18-78
Garrett, Enoch	" 5 Md	"	8-18-78
Garrett, John	Maj Pa	Killed	7-3-78 Wyo
Garrish, James	Pvt 13 Mass	Died	5-29-77
Garrison, Garret	N J	"	10-7-81
Garrison, Peter	Pvt N Y	Killed	1776
Garran, Charles Olney	Pvt	Died	4-1-78
Garver, Septimus	" Conn	"	6-12-77
Garvy, Matin	Pvt N C	"	3- 78
Gaskey, James	Pvt SC	Killed	10-9-79
Gaston, Robert	Lt SC	Died	10-9-79
Gaston,	SC	Killed	10-9-79
Gatchel, Abel Pvt	Mass	"	7-7-77
Gates, Benjamin	Pvt Mass	Died	7-9-78
Gates, Chester	Pvt Mass	"	2-28-78
Gates, Daniel	Pvt Mass	"	1-1-78
Gates, Ephraim	Pvt Mass	"	3-14-78
Gates, Silas	Conn	Killed	1781
Gates, Jonah	Pvt Conn	Died	2-9-78
Gatreen, John	Pvt Md	"	1-21-77
Ganthier, Francois	France	"	1781 Va
Gaurd, Jno	Pvt N C	"	3-23-78
Gausse, Philippe	France	"	1781 Va
Gantrow, Stephen	Pvt Mass	"	8-7-78
Garvin, Benjamin	Navy	"	7-21-81 Eng Prison
Gay, Fisher	Col Yale Conn	"	8-27-76
Gay, Simeon	Conn	"	2-22-77
Gaylord, Aaron	Capt. Pa	Killed	1778 Wyo
Gaylord, Aaron	Pa	Died	7-3-78
Gaylord, Charles	Conn	"	1777
Gaylord, Samuel	Conn	"	1778
Gaze, Daniel	N H	"	1775
Gear, Joseph	Capt Pa	"	1780
Geary, Josh	Pvt N C	"	8- 77
Geary, Richard	Pvt Md	"	
Gee, James	Capt	"	11-12-77
Geer, Regin	Pa	"	7-3-78
Gelwicks, Frederick	Md	"	1783 Pa
Genies, Joseph	France	"	1781 Va
George, Josiah	Mass	"	1778
George, Knouse	Pa	"	1782
George, William	Pvt Md	"	7-24-82
Gershom, Rice	Mass	"	1781
Gibbon, John		"	1777 SS Prison Jersey
Gibbs, Benjamin	Conn		1783
Gibbs, Micah	Pvt Mass	Killed	10-7-77
Gibson, John	Capt Md	Died	

Name	Rank/Unit	Status	Date
Gibson, John		Killed	1778
Gibson, John	N H	"	6-17-75
Gibson, Jona	Pvt Md	Died	
Gibson, Robt	Pvt N Y	"	5-10-78
Gibson, Thos	Ens 10 N C	"	1- 82
Gilbert, Elisha	Sgt Conn	"	1-6- 78
Gilbert, Jedidiah	Cpl 13 Mass	"	3-22-78
Gilbert, Jno	Pvt 10 N C	"	5-6-78
Gilbert, John	Capt Conn	Killed	7-5-79
Gilbert, Joseph	Col Mass	Died	1776
Gilbert, Joseph	N Y	"	1777
Gilbert, Michael	Pvt Conn	Killed	7-5-79
Gilbert, Samuel	Capt Mass	Died	1775
Gilbert, Thomas	Pvt 4 Mass	"	11-13-78
Gilchrist, John	Pvt 4 N Y	"	1-30-79
Giles, John	Pvt 2 Md	"	7-18-78
Giles, Thomas Sr	Mass	"	4-20-75
Gilhampton, Robert	Pvt 4 Md	"	10-1-81
Gill, Alex	Pvt 10 N C	"	6-18-83
Gill, Thomas	Pvt 3 SC	"	12-2-76
Gillam, Thomas	Pvt Md	"	1778
Gille, John	" 3 Mass	"	7-30-77
Gillespie, James	Pvt 4 N Y	"	2-11-80
Gillespie, James	Pvt N J	"	12-30-76
Gillett, Charles	Pvt Conn	"	1776
Gillett, Jonathan	Lt Conn	"	1779
Gillett, Ebenezer	Conn	"	4-8-76
Gillevay, James	Pvt 7 Mass	Killed	5-30- 78
Gilliam, John	Lt Va	Died	1776
Gillis,	Bugler N C	"	2-12-81
Gillson, Daniel	Sgt. 5 Mass	"	1-13-78
Gilman, Israel	Lt Col N H	"	2-20-77
Gilman, Nicholas	Adj N H	"	4-7-83
Gilman, Samuel	Capt N H	"	1778
Gilmer, David	Pvt Va	"	1-26-77
Gilmore, James	Pvt Mass	"	2-25-78
Gilson, Daniel	Sgt Mass	"	1778
Gilson, Eleazer	Pvt Mass	"	1777
Gilson, Samuel	Sgt Mass	"	1779
Ginnings, Geo.	Pvt 10 N C	"	1-7-83
Girand, Joseph	France	"	1781 Va
Gist, Nathaniel	Ens SC	"	10-7-80
Givens, Thomas	N C	"	5-10-80
Gladding, William G	Pvt Conn	"	12-13-83
Glanet, Louis	France	"	1781 Va
Glass, Robert	Pvt 2 N J	"	3-1- 77
Glass, Robert	2 Pa Killed	"	5-19- 80
Glanhan, Jereh	Pvt 5 N C	Died	4-21-78
Glazier, Levy	Pvt 1 Conn	"	6-16-77
Gleason, Andrew	Pvt Conn	"	9-9-80
Gleason, Isaac	Pvt Mass	"	1776
Gleason, Micajah	Capt Mass	Killed	1776
Glenny, William	Lt N Y	"	10-30-81
Glidden, John	Sgt. N H	Died	1781

Name	Unit	Status	Date	Note
Glover, Joseph	Col SC	Died	8-3-83	
Glover, Lewis	Navy	Died	7-21-81	Prison
Goalt, Benjamin	Pvt Mass	"	4-3-78	
Goddard, David	Capt 9 Mass	Killed	10-7-77	
Goddon, William	Pvt 1 N J	Died	10-28-78	
Godfrey, John	Pvt 12 Mass	"	4-25-79	
Godfrey, Nathan	Cpl Conn	"	1775	
Godfrey, Thomas	Pvt Can	Killed	8-22-77	
Godin, John	Del	Died	12-1-81	
Goff, William	Cpl Mass	"	9- 78	
Goffe, John	Col N H	"	1781	
Goffe, John	Mass	"	1781	
Goffe, John	N H	"	1781	
Goffe, William	Pvt N H	"	9-19-77	
Goforth, Preston	SC	"	10-7-80	
Goggin, Francis	Pvt Can	"	2- 78	
Gold, Abraham	Conn	Killed	1777	
Gold, Moses	Pvt N H	Died	1-10-78	
Golder, John	Pvt 2 N J	"	6-7-80	
Goldsmith, Ephraim	Capt	Killed	10- 76	
Gonos, James	Pvt 2 N J	Died	9-2-77	
Gonzalus, Joseph	N Y	"	4-1-82	
Goodale, Asa	Pvt N H	"	7-7-77	
Goodenough, Hopstel	Pvt 6 Mass	"	7-19-77	
Goodin, Christopher	Capt 5 N C	Killed	9-8-81	
Goodman	Capt N C	"	9-9-81	
Goodman, William	Pvt 2 N J	Died	3-4-78	
Goodrich, Aaron	Pvt Conn	"	12-22-77	
Goodrich, Caleb	Conn	"	1777	
Goggin, John	Lt Va	"	11- 77	
Gold, David	Pvt 7 N C	"	10- 78	
Gold, Nehemiah	Pvt N H	"	8-10-78	
Goldsborough, Henry	Pvt Md	"	6-17-81	
Goldthwait, Ebenezer	Conn	Killed	4-19-75	
Gonya, Antoine	France	Died	1781	Va
Good, Peter	Pvt Va	"	2-15-77	
Goodale, Thomas	Pvt 10 Mass	"	9-6-77	
Goodenow, Daniel	Pvt Mass	"	5-28-77	
Gooding, William	Pvt Mass	"	1776	
Goodman, William	Capt 4 N C	Killed	9-8-81	
Goodrich, Caleb	Lt Mass	Died	7-27-77	
Goodrich, David P	Pvt Conn	"	10-12-81	Va
Goodrich, Ezekial	Lt 8 Mass	Killed	10-7-77	
Goodrich, Gideon	Pvt Conn	"	7-5-79	
Goodrich, Nath'l	R I	"	12-31-75	Que
Goodrich, Wm	R I	"	12-31-75	"
Goodrich, William	Mass	Died	1-21-82	
Goodrich, William	Mass	"	1776	
Goodridge, Ezekiel	Mass	Killed	10-7-77	
Goodspeed, Ebenezer	Pvt Mass	Died	1779	
Goodspeed, Simeon	Pvt 14 Mass	"	1-28-78	
Goodwell, Samuel	Pvt 10 Mass	"	11-30-77	
Goodwin,	Capt N C	Killed	9-9-81	
Goodwin, John D	Pvt 11 Mass	Died	2-15-78	
* Godbolt, John	2 SC	Killed	10-9-79	

Goodwin, Nathaniel	Capt Conn	Killed	5-1-77
Goodwin, Nathan Sr	Conn	Died	5-18-77
Goodwyn, Dinwiddie	Lt Va	"	1777
Googins, John	Cpl 11 Mass	Killed	7-7-77
Gordon	Lt SC	"	9-9-81
Gordon, John	N H	Died	6-17-75
Gore, Asa	Pa	"	7-3-78
Gore, George	Pa	"	7-3-78
Gore, Obadiah	Pa	Killed	1779
Gore, Silas	Pa	"	7-3-78
Gorham, Ned P	Pvt Conn	Died	1-6-78
Gorrelier, Pierre-Nicolas	France	Died	1781 Va
Goslin, Ambrose	Pvt 2 N C	Died	9-1-77
Goss, Elihu	Pvt Mass	Died	7-6-78
Goss, Simeon	Pvt Conn	"	3-6-82
Gott, John	Mass	"	1775
Goud	Lt 4 Md	Killed	9-8-82
Gouge, Moses	Pvt 13 Mass	Died	9-23-77
Gould, Lt	Md	"	1777
Gould, Abraham	Col Conn	Killed	4-27-77
Gould, Aholiah	Pvt 6 Mass	Died	10-8-77
Gould, David	Surg Va	"	7-12-81
Gould, Jennings Albert	Va	"	4-25-77
Gould, John	Sgt R I	"	10-23-77
Gould, Thomas	N Y	"	1776
Gould, William	Mass	"	9-6-78
Gould, William	Mass	"	1781
Gours, Ansel	Pvt 14 Mass	"	12-3-77
Gove, Eleazer	N Y	"	10- 77
Grace, John	Pvt 5 Md	"	6-25-77
Graham, James	NC	"	1782
Grardy, James	Mass	"	1781
Granger, Aaron	Pvt Mass	"	1782
Granger, Daniel P	Pvt Conn	"	12-31-78
Granger, Daniel	Fifer 3 Mass	"	7-5-77
Granger, John	Capt Mass	"	1-21-83
Granger, John	Mass	"	1782
Granger, Phineas P	Pvt Conn	"	7-20-81
Crannis, James	Pvt Conn	"	8-10-78
Grant, Benjamin	Lt N H	"	1776
Grant, George	Capt 9 Pa	"	10-10-79
Grant, John	Pvt 10 N C	"	11-16-78
Grant, Peter	Pvt 10 Mass	"	1-26-78
Grant, Samuel	Sgt. Conn	"	4-23-77
Grant, William	Conn	"	1783
Grant, Wm	Pvt 6 N C	"	8- 77
Graves, Benjamin	Pvt N Y	Killed	1781
Graves, Joshua	N H	Died	1777
Graves, Josiah	Pvt 3 Mass	"	7-25-77
Graves, Moses	Pvt 5 Md	"	11- 78
Graves, Roswell	Sgt N Y	"	1776
Graves, Zadoc	Pvt 8 Mass	"	3-19-78
Gray, Benj	Pvt 4 N Y	"	7-5-78
Gray, Daniel	Pvt 8 Mass	"	8-5-78

Gray, Elijah	Pvt Conn	Died	2-26-78
Gray, Hugh	Lt Mass	"	8-3-77
Gray, James	Col Mass	"	8-25-82
Gray, James	Lt 2 SC	"	10-22-79
Gray, James	2 SC	Killed	10-9-79
Gray, John	Pvt SC	Drowned	7- 81
Gray, Jonathan	N H	Died	6-17-75
Gray, Joseph	Cpl 2 Md	"	2-28-78
Gray, Moses	Mass	"	9-11-75
Gray, Nathaniel	Conn	Killed	1777
Gray, Richard	Pvt 2 Md	Died	12-15-78
Gray, Thomas	Pvt 2 Md	"	10-15-82
Gray, Thomas	Pvt Can	Killed	9-4- 77
Gray, Uriah	Pvt 11 Mass	Died	10-16-77
Gray, William	Pvt N C	Killed	1780
Gray, William	Pvt N H	"	1780
Greathouse, Herman	Pa	"	1782 By Ind.
Greaton, John	Col Mass	Died	1783
Greaton, John	Pvt Mass	"	9-20-77
Greaves, John	Pvt Conn	"	5-22-80
Gregory, Charles Stewart	Sgt Va	Killed	12-26-76
Gregory, Jedidiah	N J	Died	1-7-83
Gregory, John	Lt Va	"	2-2-77
Gregory, Samuel	Pvt 6 Md	"	2-6-78
Gregory, Thomas	Pvt SC	"	5- 81
Gregory, William	Capt Va	"	1771
Green, Asabel	Pvt Conn	"	11-24-77
Green, Christopher	Col R I	"	5-14-81
Green, Cuthbert	Pvt 7 Md	"	2-17-78
Green, Daniel	R I	"	4-30-78
Green, David	Pa	"	6-22-76
Green, David	Col Mass	"	1781
Green, Ezra	Pvt Conn	"	2-12-78
Green, George	Capt N J	"	1777
Green, James	Pvt Mass	"	8-21-79
Green, James P	Pvt Conn	"	2-23-78
Green, Jarvis	Pvt N C	"	1782
Green, Jarvis	Pvt. Ky	Killed	8-19-82
Green, John	Pvt 5 N C	Died	8-20-77
Green, Lert	Pvt 4 N Y	"	4-1-78
Green, Lucas	Pvt N H	"	6-17-75
Green, Oliver	Sgt R I	"	1-22-78
Green, Samuel	Pvt Can	"	3-8-77
Green, Thomas	Pvt Conn	"	12-26-77
Green, Timothy	2 S C	Killed	10-9-79
Green, William (Guide to Gen. Washington	N J	Died	1777
Green, Wilson	Cpl 10 N C	"	4-18-78
Greene, Benjamin	Pvt 9 Mass	"	3-1-78
Greene, Christopher	Col R I	Killed	5-14-81
Greene, Jack	Pvt R I	"	1-19-82
Greene, Jarvis	Ky Killed	Killed	1782
Greene, Philip	N Y	Died	1782
Greene, Wm Cato	Pvt R I	Died	7-25-80

77

Greenleaf, Benjamin	Pvt Mass	Died	12-20-80
Greenleaf, Daniel	Surg Mass	"	1-18-77
Greenleaf, Henry	Pvt Mass	"	2-7-77
Greenough, William	Mass	"	1777
Greenwell, Jesse	Pvt 4 Md	"	2- 78
Greenwood, Milburn	Pvt 6 Md	"	7- 78
Grey	Lt. SC	Killed	10-7-80
Grey, Eben	Lt Mass	Died	6-19-77
Gridley, Elnathan	Conn	"	1781
Gridley, Hezekiah	Capt Conn	"	7-21-76
Gridley, Martin	Pvt Md	"	10-10-78
Grieg, Henry	Pvt 7 Md	"	10-3-78
Griffin, John	Conn	"	5-5-77
Griffin, John	Conn	"	10-18-77
Griffin, Corbin	Surg Va	"	1777
Griffin, Curtis	Del	"	9-16-78
Griffin, Jona	Pvt. N H	"	10-1-81
Griffin, Josh	Pvt. 1 N C	"	3-4-78
Griffith, David	N H	"	2-2-79
Griffith, James	Pvt Va	"	2-15-77
Griffith, Paul Lewis	Pvt 5 Md	"	12-7-77
Griffith, Richard	Pvt. 11 Mass	Killed	9-19-77
Griggs, Ichobod Jr	Sgt. N Y	Died	1776
Griggs, Ichobod Jr	Ens Conn	"	1776
Griggs, John	Pvt Mass	"	9-14-79
Griggs, Joseph	Pvt Mass	"	9-3-79
Griggs, Thomas	Cpl Mass	"	1782
Griggs, William	Pvt Va	"	1779
Grimes, Torrence	Sgt. Pa	"	6-3-81
Grimes, William	Capt. Va	Killed	8-1-77
Grinage, Jno	Pvt. 10 N C	Died	6-20-83
Grinder, Jno	Pvt. 10 N C	"	6-29-78
Grinnell, Malacia	Pvt. R. I.	"	1780
Grishill, Jno.	Pvt. 2 Md	"	1778
Griswell, Warren P	Pvt. Conn	"	1-24-78
Griswit, Thos.	4 N C	"	1- 78
Griswold, White	Pvt Conn	"	1777
Gro, Jas.	Pvt 10 N C	"	11-16-78
Groatis, Lewis	Pvt Mass	"	10-30-79
Grose, Jacob	Pvt	Killed	1780
Gross, Isaac	Pvt Mass	Died	1777
Gross, Paul	Pa	"	1783
Gross, Philip IV	Pvt Pa	Killed	11-7-78
Grossetete, Antoine	France	Died	1781 Va
Grosvenor, Amoss	Pvt 11 Conn	"	10-26-76
Grosvenor, William	Conn	"	7-23-81
Groten, John	Va	"	1783
Grove, Joseph	Pa	"	1782
Grover, Gideon	Mass	"	1776
Grover, Jacob	Pvt Conn	Killed	12-7-77
Groves, Benjamin Jr	Conn	"	1781
Gabiand, Benoist	France	Died	1781 Va
Guelin, Nicolas	France	"	1781 Va
Guernsey, Oliver	Pvt N H	"	1778
Guiboisean, Francois	France	"	1781 Va

Gingor, Jacob	Pvt Pa	Died	1777
Guild, James	Conn	"	9-15-77
Guillaume, Joseph	France	"	1781 Va
Guilleraux, Joseph	France	"	1781 Va
Guliker, John	Capt Mass	"	2-3-89
Gully, John	Pvt 5 Md	"	3-21-78
Guinmeys, John	N J	Killed	1-11-77
Gunn, Abel	Pvt 15 Mass	Died	5-9-78
Gunn, George	Sgt 9 Mass	"	10-16-78
Gunsalis, John	Pvt N Y	Killed	1777
Gunsley, Joseph	Can	Died	2-10-77
Gunter, Williams	2 SC	Killed	10-9-79
Gurley, Jonathan	Conn	Died	1778
Gurley, Simon	Pvt 2 N C	"	5-6-78
Gurney, Jno	Pvt 5 Md	"	1-2-78
Guthery, Archibald	Pvt Pa	"	1778
Gutrey, William	Del	Killed	9-8-81
Guttery, Hy	Pvt 10 NC	Died	10- 78
Gwinup, John	N J	"	1-15-77

H

Hacker, Caleb	R I	Killed	12-31-75 Que
Hacket, Stephen P	2 SC	Died	6-2-77
Hackman, Thomas	Pvt 11 Mass	"	4-27-77
Hadden, Thomas	Lt Col N J	"	1778
Hadden, Robert Jr	SC	"	1783
Haden, James	Pvt R I	"	10-24-77
Haden, Joseph	Pvt 11 Mass	"	10-20-77
Hadley, Jonathan	N H	Killed	6-17-75
Hadley, Samuel	Mass	"	4-19-75 Lex
Hadley, Thomas	Capt Mass	"	4-19-75 Lex
Hadley, Thomas	Can	"	1781
Hadley, Thomas	Capt N C	Died	1781
Hagan, Leonard	Pvt Md	"	12-17-82
Hagarthy, George	Sgt Md	Killed	3-15-81
Hagar, Joseph Jr	Mass	Died	1776
Hago, Joshua	Pvt 14 Mass	"	8-4-77
Hagens, Edmund	Surg N Y	"	1777
Hager, Jonathan	Md	"	11-6-75
Hagget, James	Pvt 10 Mass	"	3-6-78
Hagget, Thomas	Pvt 10 Mass	"	6-20-77
haggett, Charles	Fife 14 Mass	Died	6-3-78
Hailey, Michael	Pvt 6 Md	"	4-12-79
Haines, John	Pvt Md	"	2-3-83
Haines, Joseph	Pvt. 4 N Y	"	11-29-78
Hair, Dominick	2 SC	"	9-30-76
Hair, Jas	Pvt Md	"	7-6-82
Haislip, John B	Pvt 1 Md	"	9-11-82
Hakes, Jonathan	Conn	"	1779
Halbard, Beriah P	Pvt Conn	"	11-16-77
Halbert, James	Lt Mass	"	1783
Halbert, James	Lt Mass	"	1777
Hale	Col	"	1780 Prisoner

Name	Rank/Unit	Status	Date	
Hale, Benjamin	N H	Died	12-4-81	
Hale, Billy	Pvt Conn	"	9-7-83	
Hale, Brian	Mass	"	12-13-78	
Hale, Isaac	"	"	1778	
Hale, Jacob	Ens Mass	"	7-9-82	
Hale, Jonathan	Capt. Mass	"	3-7-76	
Hale, Nathan	Col N H	"	9-23-80	
Hale, Nathan	Capt. Conn	"	9-22-76	Hanged by British
Hale, Nathan	Mass	"	1776	
Hale, Stephen	Pvt 14 Mass	"	7-2-78	
Hall, Abner	Pvt Conn	"	8-22-82	
Hall, Aquila	Md	"	1779	
Hall, Brian	Lt Mass	"	1778	
Hall, Daniel	Pvt 14 Mass	"	1-30-78	
Hall, Delany	Pvt 3 N C	"	3-13-78	
Hall, Ebenezer	Pvt Conn	"	8-7-77	
Hall, Eber	Pvt Conn	"	1-26-82	
Hall, Elihu	Md	"	1781	
Hall, Frederick	Pvt 2 Md	"	1777	
Hall, Henry	Pvt 1 Conn	"	1-1-78	
Hall, Hiland	Conn	"	6-16-81	
Hall, Jobez	Capt Mass	"	1776	
Hall, Jack	Pvt. Conn	"	3-31-79	
Hall, Jackson	Pvt 3 N C	"	1-7-78	
Hall, James	Pvt N Y	"	1-16-80	
Hall, Jeremiah	Mass	"	1-24-76	
Hall, John	Pvt 5 Md	"	6-7-79	
Hall, John	Pvt 2 Md	"	1-24-79	
Hall, John	Conn	"	1777	
Hall, John	Capt Vt	"	1777	
Hall, Jonathan	Mass	"	9-8-76	
Hall, Josiah	1 SC	"	12-18-75	
Hall, Leonard	Pvt 14 Mass	"	8-29-78	
Hall, Luther	Pvt Mass	"	7- 79	
Hall, Martin	Pvt 10 Mass	"	12-9- 77	
Hall, Nathan	Pvt 10 NC	"	8-24-79	
Hall, Prince	Pvt 2 Mass	"	12-18-78	
Hall, Samuel	Pvt 18 Cont	"	12-31-76	
Hall, Samuel	Pvt Conn	Killed	6-28-78	
Hall, Samuel	Chap. Mass	Died	1776	
Hall, Simeon	Pvt Conn	"	4-28-77	
Hall, Stephen	Capt Conn	"	1783	
Hall, Tobias	Pvt 4 Md	"	3-2-78	
Halleron, James	Pvt 4 Md	"	12-16-82	
Hallock, William	Capt N Y	"	1782	
Hallosos, Samuel	Pvt Conn	"	1-30-78	
Halsey, Silas	Cpl	"	1777	
Halstead, Leml	Capt 10 NC	"	1-12-79	
Haman, Moses	Pvt Pa	"	11-7-77	
Hamilton, Alexander	Capt Pa	"	1781	
Hamilton, Alexander		Killed	1781	
Hamilton, John	Pvt 3 N J		10-8-77	
Hamilton, Robert	Sgt Va	Died	1777	
Hamilton, Samuel	Sgt Pa	"	7-11-76	

80

Hamilton, William	Pvt Pa	Died	9-1-76
Hamilton, Willie	SC	"	1780
Hamlin, Edward	N J	"	1783
Hamlin, Elijah	Pvt 10 Mass	"	4-12-78
Hamlin, Jabez	Capt Conn	"	9-20-76
Hammond, Amariah	Pa	Killed	1778 Wyo
Hammond, Benjamin	Me	Died	1777
Hammond, Benjamin	Lt Pa	Killed	2-20-78
Hammond, Daniel	Mass	Died	1777
Hammond, George	Capt Mass	"	1782
Hammond, George	Pvt Mass	"	1-14-82
Hammond, John	Capt Va	"	1781
Hammond, Judah	Pvt N C	"	8- 77
Hammond, Seth	Pvt Mass	"	2-6- 78
Hammond, Stephen	Mass	"	1781
Hammond, William	Pa	"	7-3-78
Harmon, Isaac	Pvt 10 N C	"	8-1-82
Hammon, Wm	Pvt 7 Md	"	5- 79
Hampton, Anthony	S C	Killed	1776
Hamston, William	Pvt Md	Died	1-31-83
Hancock, John	Pvt 8 Mass	"	7-30-78
Hancock, Torrey	Cpl Mass	"	1778
Hand, Cornelius	Pvt 2 N J	"	8-29-78
Handley, Charles	Pvt R I	"	5-1-80
Handy, George	Lt Md	"	1783
Handy, George	Capt Md	"	1782
Hanford, Jesse	Pvt Conn	"	1777
Hannah, Daniel	Pvt Pa	"	6-7-76
Hannah, Miles	Pvt 3 Md	Killed	10-4-77
Hanners, Henry	Cpl 10 NC	Died	8-3-78
Hansen, Henry	N Y	Killed	1780
Hanson, Ebenezer	Cpl N H	Died	1782
Hanson, Henry	Pvt 2 Mass	"	3-20-78
Hanson, Henry	Lt N Y	Killed	1780
Hanson, Henry	N Y	"	1780
Hanson, John	Md	Died	1783
Hanson, Peter	Lt Md	"	1776
Hanson, Samuel	Md	"	6-29-81
Hanteville, Joseph	France	"	1781
Hany, Abraham	Pvt 4 N Y	"	5-4-78
Hanyerry, (Indian Guide)	N Y	"	1779
Hapson Henry	Capt Va	"	1780
Hapgood, Shadrock	Pvt Mass	"	1782
Harbinson, Matthew	R I	Killed	12-31-75
Harden, Joseph	Pvt Mass	Died	1775
Harden, William	Navy	"	5-7-77 Prison
Hardin, Martin	Va	"	1780
Harding, Alsop	Mass	"	1781
Harding, Barney	Pvt Mass	"	11-3-77
Harding, Benjamin	Pa	"	6-30-78
Harding, Edwd	Pvt 5 Md	"	2-1-78
Harding, John	Lt Mass	"	8-10-82
Harding, Nehemiah	Capt Mass	"	5-18-79
Harding, Samuel	Capt Mass	"	1780

Name	Rank/Unit	Status	Date
Harding, Samuel	Pvt. 8 Mass	Died	6-2-78
Harding, Seth	Capt.	"	1781
Harding, Stukley	Pa	"	6-30-78
Hardison, Hardy	Q M Sgt. 7 N C	"	12-18-77
Hardison, Peter	Pvt. 13 Mass	"	7-1-78
Hardman, John	Lt 2 Md	"	8-31-80
Hardman, John	Capt. Md	Killed	9-1-80
Hardy, Aaron	N H	Died	12-26-75
Hardy, Nathaniel	Pvt N H	"	3-5-78
Hardy, Theophilus	R I	"	1778
Hare, Abraham	Pvt 6 Mass	"	4-28-77
Hare, James	Pvt Md	"	7-6-82
Hare, John	Pvt Md	"	5-27-81
Hargraves, Dennis	Pvt 1 Md	"	2-10-77
Harker, Nathan	Pvt 2 N J	"	11-20-78
Harkes, Joseph	Pvt Conn	"	3-25-78
Harkness, James	Pvt Mass	"	1779
Harley, Daniel	Pvt Pa	"	10-23-76
Harley, Jeremh	Pvt 4 Md	"	1-1-78
Harlow, Elijah	Pvt Mass	"	1778
Harlow, Lewis	Pvt 5 Mass	Killed	7-22-77
Harlow, William Jr	Mass	Died	12-23-80
Harman, David	Pvt Va	"	2-15-75
Harmond, Jno	Pvt 10 N C	"	9- 81
Harmonns, Dunond	N Y	"	1778
Harney, Jonathan	Lt 3 Del	Killed	3-27-76 L. I.
Harper, Joseph Jr.	Conn	Died	1782
Harper, Richard	Pvt 5 Md	"	8-8-78
Harper, William	Pvt 2 Md	"	1-9-79
Harper, William	2 SC	"	3-24-77
Harwell, Holland	Pvt 5 N C	"	8-28-77
Harridon, Paul	Pvt Conn	"	7-13-77
Harrington, Caleb	Mass	Killed	4-19-75
Harrington, Edward	Capt N Y	Died	9-23-76
Harrington, Edward	N Y	"	1776
Harrington, Jonathan Jr	Mass	Killed	4-19-75
Harris, Ceaser	Pvt R I	Died	7-30-80
Harris, Evans	4 N Y	"	3-4-78
Harris, Griffin	Pvt S C	Killed	5- 81
Harris, James	Sgt. S C	Died	1781
Harris, John	Pvt Conn	"	12-30-78
Harris, John	Mass	Killed	1779
Harris, John	Lt Conn	Died	12-7-77
Harris, Luke	Pvt 7 Mass	"	10-14-77
Harris, Michael	Pvt 4 N Y	"	2- 79
Harris, Nathaniel	Pvt Conn	"	11-15-79
Harris, Samuel	Pvt Mass	"	2-1-78
Harris, Samuel	Pvt 10 Mass	"	5-19-78
Harris, Selas	Pvt 3 NY	"	8-17-77
Harris, Silas	Pvt 2 Mass	"	1-15-78
Harris, Thomas	N J	"	4-27-83
Harris, Thomas	Pvt 12 Mass	"	5-2-78
Harris, Waller	Mus 2 N J	"	12-11-78
Harris, William	Capt Mass	"	1778

Harris, William	Mass	Died	8- 78
Harrison, George	3 SC	"	10-10-79
Harrison, Jas.	Sgt 7 N C	"	8- 77
Harrison, James	Lt Va	Killed	10-7-77
Harrison, Henry	Pvt 10 N C	Died	9-20-82
Harrison, John	Capt SC	"	1780
Harrison, Philip	Pvt 4 N Y	"	8-19-77
Harrison, Samuel	Pvt Md	"	8-2- 82
Harrison, Thomas	Pvt 3 Md	Killed	10-4-77
Harrison, William	Capt Md	Died	1777
Harriss, Richard	Pvt 4 Md	"	1780
Harrod, John	Pa	"	1781
Harry, Andrew	Pvt R I	"	6-1-80
Harry, Peter P	Pvt Conn	"	4-17-78
Hart, Conrad	N Y	Killed	4-30-78
Hart, Ebenezer	Conn	Died	6-18-81
Hart, Elias	Navy	"	1777
Hart, Elijah	Conn	"	8-3-72
Hart, Jonathan	Pvt N Y	"	1777
Hart, John	Col N H	"	10-30-77
Hart, John	N J	"	5-11-79
Hart, Jason	Pvt Conn	"	12-27-77
Hart, Nathaniel	Ky	Killed	1782
Hart, Nathaniel	Capt N C	Died	1782
Hart, Samuel	Pvt 13 Mass	"	10-21-78
Hart, Thomas	Pvt 2 Md	Killed	8-16-80
Hart, Thomas	Pvt 3 N C	Died	6- 78
Hartly, Jno	Pvt 10 N C	"	6-20-78
Hartshorn, John	Pvt 1 Conn	"	7-27-78
Harnell, John	Pvt N H	"	6-29-81
Harvey, Asabel	Pvt Conn	"	1783
Harvey, Bailie	Pvt 3 SC	"	10-11-79
Harvey, James	Pvt 6 Md	"	12-16-77
Harvey, John	Pvt Conn	"	75
Harvey, Nathan	Pvt 1 Conn	"	5-26-1778
Harvey; Samuel	Pvt Pa	"	1778
Harvey, Silas	Pa	"	7-3-78
Harwood, James	Pvt N H	"	1777
Harwood, Reuben	Pvt 9 Mass	"	6-15-78
Hasbrouck, Jonathan	Col N Y	"	1780
Haskell, Bozzilla	Pvt 11 Mass	"	8-31-77
Haskell, Cavenale	Pvt 13 Mass	"	5-20-77
Haskell, Elnathan	Mass	"	1783
Haskell, Nathan	Mass	"	1780
Haskell, Nathaniel	Pvt Mass	"	7-30-77
Haskell; William	Pvt 18 Cont	"	11-18-76
Haskell, William	Pvt 14 Mass	"	5-2- 77
Haslet, John	Col Del	Killed	1-3-77
Hastings, John	Pvt Conn	Died	10-17-81
Hastings, Walter	Mass	"	1782
Haskins, Ira	Pvt Conn	"	12-1-81
Hatch, Benjamin	Pa	"	7-3-78
Hatch, David	Me	"	1778

Hatch, Joseph	Navy	Died	6-7-77
Hatcher, Benjamin	Capt SC	"	1781
Hatcher, David	Pvt 10 N C	"	9- 79
Hatfield, John	Del	Killed	1-20-81
Hatfield, San'l	Pvt SC	"	6- 81
Hathaway, John	Pvt Mass	Died	1780
Hathaway, Jonathan	Mass	"	1783
Hathaway, Joseph	N J	"	8-7-76
Hathaway, Shadrock	Sgt N J	"	10-8-77
Hathaway, Simon	Pvt N J	"	1-18-77
Hatten, David	Pvt Md	"	3-9-83
Hauck, Nathaniel	Pvt N Y	"	10-29-81
Haughton, Job	Pvt 13 Mass	"	3-1-78
Hauser, George	N C	Killed	
Hauteville, Joseph	France	Died	1781
Haven, Asa	Pvt 4 Mass	"	5-1-77
Haven, Benajah	Pvt 11 Mass	"	4-12-77
Haven, David Jr	Capt Mass	Killed	10-8-77
Haven, Elias	Mass	Died	1782
Haven, Elias	Capt Mass	Killed	4-19-75
Haven, Joseph	Capt Mass	Died	2-27-76
Havens, George	Pvt N J	"	7-27-77
Haviland, Ebenezer	Surg N Y	"	6-28-81
Hawes, Ichabod	Pvt Mass	"	1777
Hawes, John	Pvt Md	"	2-2-83
Hawkes, Adam	Mass	"	10-20-79
Hawkes, Adam	Mass	"	1778
Hawkins, Isaac	N Y	"	1781
Hawkins, James	Pvt 5 Md	"	2- 79
Hawkins, Joshua	SC	"	
Hawkins, Lodoc	Pvt Conn	"	10-20-77
Hawkins, Moses	Capt Va	Killed	10-4-77
Hawley, Ezekiel	Sgt Conn	Died	1776
Hawley, William	Navy	"	7-9-81
Hay, Samuel	Lt Col Pa	"	1783
Hayes, David	Pvt Pa	"	10-24-76
Hayes, Josiah	Mass	"	4-19-75
Hayes, Wm	Pvt SC	"	8- 81
Haygood, James	7 Mass	"	12-5- 82
Haymond, Owen	Ens 6 Md	Killed	6-28-78
Hayne, Isaac	Col SC	"	1781
Haynes, Aaron	Capt N J	Died	1783
Haynes, Benjamin	Conn	"	1780
Haynes, Cornelius	1 SC	"	11-6-75
Haynes, John	Pvt Md	"	2-2-83
Haynes, Joshua	N H	Killed	6-17-75
Haynes, Josiah	Mass	"	4-19-75
Haynes, Luke	Pvt N J	Died	3-15-77
Haynes, Wm.	Pvt 1 N C	"	3-23-78
Hays, Chas	Pvt 1 N Y	Killed	4-7-80
Hays, Charles	Del	Died	12-23-77
Hays, John	Ens 3 N J	"	11-3-77
Hays, Thomas	Lt N J	"	1777

Hays, Vachel	Drum Md	Killed	9-8-81	
Hayward, James	Mass	"	4-19-75	
Hayward, James	Mass	Died	1781	
Hayward, Josiah	Mass	"	1783	
Hayward, Samuel	Sgt	"		Prison
Haywood, James	Mass	"	1775	
Haywood, Titus	Fifer 14 Mass	"	11-5-77	
Haywood, William	Col N C	"	1779	
Hazard, Jacob	Pvt R I	"	2-6-81	
Hazard, Jacob	Pvt R I	"	9-1-78	
Hazard, James	Pvt R I	"	6-1-78	
Hazard, Jason	Pvt Can	"	2-20-77	
Hazell, Philip	Pvt 2 Md	"	9-9-78	
Hazen, Thomas	Pvt Vt	"	1782	
Hazens, Edmund	Surg Me	"	1777	
Hazey, Abraham	Pvt 11 Mass	"	2-10-80	
Hazilton, Jere	Pvt N H	"	5-12-78	
Hazle, Thos	Pvt 2 N C	"	2-28-78	
Hazzard, Aethus	Del	"	9-10-82	
Heacock, Ebenezer	Pvt Conn	"	4-18-81	
Heady, Peter	R I	Killed	12-31-75	Que
Heaguea, Cornelius	Del	"	3-15-81	
Heald, John	3 Mass	Died	1775	
Heard, Thomas	Sgt 2 Mass	Killed	7-22-77	
Hearl, James	Pvt 2 Mass	Died	10-10-77	
Heath, Charles	Pvt 5 Md	"	8-18-78	
Heath, John	Lt Va	"	1783	
Heath, Moses	Pvt N H	"	1783	
Heath, Solomon	Sgt Mass	"	1779	
Hebb, Joseph	Pvt Md	"	1782	
Heber, Allen	Maj. Vt	"	1782	
Hector, Lot	Pvt 14 Mass	"	11-10-77	
Hedden, Joseph Jr	N J	"	9-27-80	
Heddon, Jon	Pvt N Y	Killed	3- 78	
Hedger, Joseph	Pvt N J	Died	8-14-78	
Hedges, Joseph	Md	"	1777	
Hegan, James	Pvt Can	"	8-1-78	
Heifferman, William	2 SC	"	12-16-76	
Helfenstein, Peter	Maj Va	"	7-7-76	
Helm, Thomas	Lt Va	"	1778	
Helmes, Job	Pvt N J	"	3- 79	
Heman, William	Pvt 9 Mass	"	10-10-77	
Hemenway, Isaac	Pvt 6 Mass	Killed	1-30-78	
Hemingway, Samuel	Sgt Conn	Died	10-25-77	
Henesee, Edward	Pvt Md	"	4-28-83	
Henderson, Joseph	3 Va	"	1778	
Henderson, Robert	Pvt 7 Mass	"	11-11-78	
Henderson, William	Sgt	"	2- 78	
Henderson, William P	1 SC	"	2-18-77	
Hendren, William	Pvt Va	"	1783	
Hendrick, John	Pvt Conn	"	1-16-82	

Hendricks	Capt	Killed	12-31-75 Que
Hendricks, Abraham	Pvt 2 N J	"	2-8-77
Hendricks, Thos	Pvt 10 N C	"	10- 78
Hendricks, William	Capt Pa	Killed	12-31-75
Hendrickson, David	Col N J	Died	1782
Hendrickson, Zephen	Pvt Can	Killed	1-2- 77
Hendron, William	Pvt Va	Died	1783
Hendry, James	N Y	"	4- 80
Henigar, Henry	Ens SC	"	10-7- 80
Henkle, John Justus	W Va	"	8- 78
Henley	Maj	Killed	9-24-76
Henley, David	Pvt 1 NY	Died	11-28-78
Henry, James	Pvt Pa	"	6-3-81
Henry, Jno	Pvt 4 N C	"	1- 78
Henry, Thomas	Pvt	Killed	9-7-79
Henry, William	N H	Died	11-7-83
Henshaw, Joshua	Pvt 13 Mass	"	5-7-78
Hepburn, Peter	Sgt Conn	"	5-27-80
Hepenstatt, Francis	Pvt Mass	"	1775
Herbert, William	Capt Va	"	1776
Herkimer,	Gen N Y	Killed	8-6-77
Herkimer, Hans Yost	Pvt N Y	Died	1775
Herkimer, Henry	Capt N Y	"	1779
Herman, Jean	France	"	1781 Va
Horn, Jno	Pvt 10 N C	"	2-20-82
Herod, James	Pvt N H	"	12-1-77
Herrick, Ebenezer	N H	Killed	6-17-75
Herrick, Henry	N H	Died	1780
Herrick, Henry	Col Mass	"	1780
Herrick, Israel	Me	"	9-14-82
Herrick, Israel	Pvt Mass	"	1782
Herriman, Williams	Pvt 9 Mass	"	6-27-77
Herring, Benjamin	Mass	"	1781 At Sea
Herrington, Ezek	Pvt Conn	"	1-17-78
Herrington, William	Mass	"	1781
Herrington, Robert	10 Mass	"	10-18-77
Herron, Andrew	2 SC	"	12-4- 75
Horsey, John	Mass	"	1777
Hersey, Peter	Pvt N H	"	1-20-78
Herster, Andrew	Pa	"	1776
Hervey, James	Pvt 4 Pa	"	8-10-76
Hetrick, Christian	Pa	Killed	10-6-81
Hewins, Joseph	Pvt Mass	Died	1783
Hewit, Dethis	Pa	"	7-3-78
Hext, Martin	1 SC	"	5-4-78
Heywood, John	Pvt Mass	"	4-21-77
Heywood, Jonathan	Mass	"	1776
Hezekiah, Beleh	N C	"	1775
Hibbard, Abel	Pvt 4 N Y	"	6-26-78
Hibbard, Joseph	Conn	Killed	6-17-75
Hibbard, Samuel	Pvt 7 Mass	Died	9-30-77
Hickerson, Joseph	Va	"	1777

Name	Rank/Unit	Fate	Date
Hickey, Barabos	Pvt N H	Died	4-14-78
Hickley, John	Pvt 11 Mass	"	9-22-77
Hickney, John	2 SC	Killed	6-28-76
Hickox, Bethnel	Pvt Conn	"	12-7-77
Hickox, Samuel	Conn	Died	9-9-78
Hicks, Henry	Pvt 6 N C	"	12- 77
Hicks, John	Pvt Conn	"	1-10-77
Hicks, John		Killed	4-19-75
Hicks, John Jr	Mass	"	4-19-75
Hicks, Levi	Pa	Died	7-3-78
Hicks, C Tubel	Sgt 9 N C	"	1-27-78
Hidden, Adoniran	Navy	"	7-9-81
Hide, James	Pvt 18 Cont	"	8-4-76
Hide, Theophilus	R I	Killed	12-31-75 Que
Hicth, George	Pvt 2 N J	Died	2-5-77
Higby, Elihu P	Pvt Conn	"	12-30-77
Higley, Josiah	Pvt Conn	"	1778
Higgins, Benj.	Mass	"	9-17-77
Higgins, Herman P	Pvt Conn	"	5-1-78
Higgins, Joseph	Mass	"	1781
Higgins, Peter	Pvt.	"	3-24-78
Higgins, John	Pvt Md	Killed	6-14-81
Higgins, John	Pvt 3 NY	Died	6-7-80
Higgins, John	Lt N Y	"	7-12-76
Higgins, Thos	Pvt 6 N C	"	3-27-78
Higgins, Thomas	N Y	"	1781
Higgins, William	Del	Killed	1-17-81
Higley, Josiah	Pvt Conn	Died	1778
Hilbert, Nathan	Pvt 10 Mass	"	1-15-78
Hildreth, Hosea	Mass	"	12-20-76
Hildreth, Simeon	N H	"	1776
Hill, Abner	Pvt 2 Md	"	1778
Hill, Abraham	Pvt Mass	"	3-9-76
Hill, Absolom	Del	"	12- 78
Hill, Amos	Va	"	1781
Hill, Asa	Cpl 6 Mass	Killed	7-22-77
Hill, Benjamin	N H	Died	9-17-76
Hill, Caleb	Mass	"	1778
Hill, Charles	Va	Killed	
Hill, Daniel	Pvt 11 Mass	Died	9-7-78
Hill, David	Sgt 8 Mass	"	9-2-78
Hill, Edward	Pvt 2 Md	"	12-2-78
Hill, George	Del	"	4-15-81
Hill, George	Pvt 12 Mass	"	7-13-80
Hill, Israel	Pvt 7 Mass	"	8-15-77
Hill, Jabez	Conn	"	1779
Hill, Job	Cpl 6 Mass	"	3-18-76
Hill, John	Sgt Mass 18 Cont	"	6-9-76
Hill, John	Pvt Conn	"	5-5-77
Hill, Joseph	Pvt 10 N C	"	8-15-79
Hill, Joshua	Pvt 4 N Y	"	7-21-77
Hill, Justus	Pvt Conn	"	12-15-77
Hill, Richard	Pvt 5 Mass	"	3-1- 83
Hill, Robert	Pvt Va	"	1783

Hill, Samuel	Cpl Conn	Killed	6-17-75
Hill, William	Pvt 4 N Y	"	2-3-80
Hill, Thomas	Pvt 2 N J	Died	5-1-77
Hill, Timothy	Conn	"	2-7-81
Hillary, John	Pvt Md	"	12-27-82
Hills, Ebenezer	Pvt Conn	"	2-20-78
Hills, Ezekiel	Lt N H	"	7-14-80
Hills, John	Capt Conn	"	1782
Hills, John	Pvt Conn	"	1777
Hills, Jonathan	Pvt Conn	"	1776
Hills, John	Capt Conn	"	1782
Hills, Parker	N H	Killed	6-17-75
Hills, Samuel	Pvt 9 Mass	Died	4-13-78
Hillyard, Stephen	Pvt 5 Mass	Killed	7-29-77
Hilton, William	Lt 6 N C	"	7-15-79
Hiltzenberger, Francois	Sgt France	Died	1781
Hinckley, Ebenezer	Lt Me	"	1776
Hindmore, Richd	Pvt 3 Md	"	2-11-77
Hinds, Ebenezer	Pvt 11 Mass	"	5-30-78
Hinds, Jonathan	N J	"	3-5-77
Hines, Thomas P	Del	Killed	10-4-77
Hines, William	Mass	Died	1781
Hines, William		"	1781 Que Prison
Hinkley, John	Capt Me	Killed	1779
Hinman, Titus	Pa	Died	7-3-78
Hinsdel, Robert	Pvt Mass	"	8-31-82
Hinton, Joseph	Mus 7 N C	"	10-10-77
Hipenstall, Francis	Pvt Mass	"	1778
Hissett, Moses	Pvt 5 N C	"	5-3-78
Hitchcock	Yale-Conn	"	1-13-77
Hitchcock, Amosa	Pvt 6 Mass	"	5-5-77
Hitchcock, Daniel	Col Yale-Conn	"	1-13-77
Hitchcock, Joseph	Pvt 3 Mass	"	9-25-78
Hitchcock, Thomas	Sgt Conn	"	2-14-78
Hite, Thomas	Lt Va	"	1779
Hix, James	Mass	"	1781
Hixson, Richard	Pvt Mass	"	1778
Hoar, Josiah	Capt Mass	"	1779
Hoard, John	V Va	"	1780
Hobard, Cyprian	Pa	"	7-3-78
Hobart, Daniel	Mass	Killed	10-28-76
Hobart, Isaac	N H	"	6-17-75
Hobart, John	Mass	Died	1-24-77
Hobart, Simon	N H	Killed	6-17-75
Hobbs, Isaac	Pvt 7 N C	Died	8- 77
Hobson, Humphrey Richard	Pvt Mass	"	1783
Hobson, Moses	Mass	"	1775
Hodge, John	Pvt 13 Mass	"	8-27-77
Hodge, William	Conn	"	1779
Hodges, Henry	Capt Mass	"	1778
Hodges, Loudon	Pvt 14 Mass	"	9-9-78
Hodibuck, Conrad	Pvt 2 Md	Killed	8-16-80
Hoffman, John	Pvt 6 Md	Died	3-31-78

Hogan, James	Brig Gen N C	Died	
Hogan, Joseph	Mass	"	1776
Hogancamp, John	Pvt	"	4-1-78
Hogun, James	Brig Gen	N C	1-4-81
Hoggatt, William		Killed	6-17-75
Hoggitt, William	N H	"	6-17-75
Hoisington, Joab	Col Vt	Died	1777
Hoins, Peter	Pvt Conn	"	12-28-78
Hoit, Levi	Pvt N H	"	12- 81
Holbrook, David	Lt Mass	"	3-26-82
Holbrook, Jonathan	Cpl Mass	"	1776
Holbrook, Josiah	Pvt 14 Mass	"	12-22-77
Holbrook, Luke	Lt Mass	"	11-3-75
Holbrook, Phineas	Pvt 2 Mass	"	9-27-80
Holcomb, Jedediah	Cpl N Y	"	1779
Holcomb, Matthew	Pvt Conn	"	3-21-78
Holcomb, Obed	Lt Conn	"	1779
Holcomb, Timothy	Lt Conn		1776
Holden, Frederick	Del	"	1-10-81
Holden, Richard	Pvt Mass	"	1777
Holden, Thomas	Pvt 7 Mass	"	11-11-78
Holden, Titley	Pvt 11 Mass	"	11-7-77
Holden, William Sr	Mass	"	1776
Hole, Jonathan	Capt N Y	"	1776
Hole, Nathan	Pvt 12 Mass	"	10-7-77
Holibert, John	Pvt Conn	"	2-26-80
Holie, Samuel	Cpl Can	"	9-1-80
Holman, Abraham	Pvt Mass	"	11- 82
Holman, Jacob	Pvt 2 Mass	"	3-15-78
Holmes, Lt	S C	Killed	9-9-81
Holmes, David	Dr R I	Died	1779
Holmes, David	Surg Conn	"	3-20-79
Holmes, Hezk	Pvt 2 NY	"	12- 78
Holmes, John	N H	"	1777
Holmes, John	N J	"	1780
Holmes, Jonathan	Capt N J	"	1777
Holmes, Samuel	Pvt Conn	"	3-4-78
Holland, Antiphas	Pvt 9 Mass	"	9-22-77
Holland, Jeffery	Pvt 11 Mass	"	8-19-78
Holland, Josiah	Pvt 5 N C	"	6-7-77
Holland, Thomas	Capt Del	Killed	10-4-77
Holley, John	Pvt 10 N C	Died	9-16-82
Holley, Joseph	Pvt 10 NC	"	9-1-78
Hollibert, John	Pvt Conn	"	2-26-80
Holliday, George	Pvt Can	Killed	7- 77
Holliday, Isaac	Pvt Md	"	1-30-83
Holliday, James	Lt Pa	"	9-11-77
Holliday, John	Vt	Died	10-22-82
Hollis, Pompey	Pvt Md	"	4-28-83
Hollis, William	Matross Pa	"	5-31-76
Holloway	Capt SC	"	
Holloway, Jno	Pvt 2 Md	"	1-10-78
Holloway, Jonathan	Pvt 14 Mass	Killed	6-9-77
Holloway, Nathan	Pvt 11 Mass	Died	7- 78

Name	Unit	Status	Date
Hollyday, John Sr	Pvt 6 Md	Killed	8-16-80
Hols, John	Pvt 4 Md	Died	11-8-78
Holston, Stephen	Pvt Va	"	1776
Holt, James	Lt Conn	"	5-11-77
Holt, James	Pvt 7 Mass	"	7-26-77
Holt, Jesse	N H	Killed	6-17-75
Holt, John Jr	Conn	"	1781
Holt, Thomas Jr	Mass	Died	11-21-76
Homer, Fortune	Pvt 13 Mass	"	4-18-77
Honba, Renny	France	"	1781 Va
Honey, Calvin	Pvt N H	"	12-15-81
Honeywel, Cyrus	Pvt Can	"	2- 78
Honore, Jean	Baptiste France	"	1781 Va
Hood, John	Pvt Md	"	3-15-81
Hood, John	Pvt Md	"	12-20-82
Hood, Wm	Pvt 1 N C	"	2-14-78
Hoofnagle, William	Pvt Pa	"	2-5-76
Hooke, James	Lt Va	"	1783
Hooker, Hart Thomas	Mass	"	1775
Hooker, John	Pvt 4 N Y	"	7-31-77
Hooker, Joseph	Capt Mass	"	1783
Hooker, Thomas Hart	Conn	"	1775
Hoole, Joseph	Pvt 2 Md	Killed	8-16-80
Hooper, Jeremh	Pvt 4 Md	Died	10-6-78
Hooper, John	Pvt Mass	Died	3-18-78
Hooper, Robert	Pvt Mass	"	1779
Hooper, Thomas	Cpl Mass	"	1777
Hoosman, John	Pvt N J	"	1-23-78
Hoover, Henry	Pvt 10 N C	"	11-2-78
Hope, John	Cpl 14 Mass	"	5-31-78
Hopes, Robert	Capt Pa	Killed	9-11-77
Hoping, Thomas	Pvt 10 Mass	Died	5-16-78
Hopkins, Benjamin	Lt N Y	Killed	9-6-80
Hopkins, James	Pa	Died	7-3-78
Hopkins, John	Pvt 7 Md	"	12-19-78
Hopkins, John	Pvt Conn	"	3- 9-77
Hopkins, Lark	Col Yale Conn	"	10-26-76
Hopkins, Richard	Pvt Md	"	7-7-78
Hopkins, Weigh	Capt N H	Killed	7-15-79
Hopkins, Weight	Conn	"	1779
Hopson, Henry	Capt Va	Died	1780
Horner, Robert	Pvt 3 Md	"	8-10-77
Horp, Reice	Pvt 4 Md	"	3-1-78
Horton, Azariah	N J	"	3-25-77
Horton, James	Pvt 1 N C	Died	6-3-78
Horton, Jonathan	Surg N J	"	3- 80
Horton, Thomas	Capt NJ	"	1778
Hoskell, Jonathan	Lt Conn	"	1779
Hoskins, Chas	Pvt 1 NY	"	13-17-77
Hoskins, John	Pvt 5 Mass	Killed	9-19-77
Hoskins, Robert	Del	Died	1-1-79
Hosmer, Abner	Mass	Killed	4-19-75
Hosmer, Alisha	Cpl Conn	Died	4-19-75
Hosmer, Amos	Lt Mass	"	11-11-82
*Homans, Ichabod	Pvt 3 N J	"	6-6-1777

Hosmer, Elisha	Conn	Died	1779
Hosmer, George	Cpl 1 NY	"	1-15-78
Hosmer, Jonathan	N Y	"	1777
Hosmer, Stephen	Capt Mass	"	1782
Hosmer, Stephen	Md	"	1782
Hoskins, Robert	Del	"	1-1- 79
Hosmer, Abner	Mass	Killed	4-19-75
Hosmer, Alisha	Cpl Conn	Died	4-19-75
Hosmer, Amos	Lt Mass	"	11-11-82
Hosmer, Elisha	Conn	"	1779
Hosmer, George	Cpl 1 N Y	"	1-15-78
Hosmer, Jonathan	N Y	"	1777
Hosmer, Stephen	Capt Mass	"	1782
Hosmer, Stephen	Md	"	1782
Hosmer, Stephen	Mass	"	1775
Hosmer, Jonathan	Mass	"	1777
Hotchkiss, Caleb	Conn	Killed	1779
Hotchkiss, Ezekiel	Sgt N H	"	7-5-79
Hotchkiss, Jason	Pvt Conn	Died	5-19-76
Hotchkiss, Jesse	Pvt Conn	"	1776
Hotchkiss, John	Pvt Conn	Killed	7-5-79
Hotchkiss, John	Col Conn	"	7-5-79
Hotchkiss, Wm	Pvt 2 N Y	Died	6- 78
Hough, Phineas	Pvt Conn	"	1776
Hough, Wade	Conn	"	9- 76
Houghton, Abiather, Sr	Mass	"	1-8-77
Houpillard, Jacques	France	"	1781
House, Eleazer	Conn	"	1-20-77
House, Peter	Pa	"	1780
Houston, William Churchill	Capt Pa	"	1782
Houston, William	Pvt Pa	"	1781
Hovey, Ebenezer	Pvt 6 Mass	"	8-18-77
Hovey, Samuel	Mass	"	2-9-76
How, Abner	Capt Mass	"	1776
How, John	Conn	"	1783
How, Samuel	Sgt 14 Mass	"	4-4-78
How, Nathan	Capt Mass	"	1781
Howard, Caleb	Mass	"	1783
Howard, Christopher	Pvt 2 N J	"	5- 77
Howard, Cornelius	Sgt	"	10-1-81
Howard, John	Pvt 2 Mass	"	5-20-78
Howard, John	Pvt 14 Mass	"	7-9-78
Howard, Nathaniel	Pa	"	7-3-78
Howard, Nehemiah	Va	"	4- 77
Howard, Peter	Pvt Md	"	2-4-83
Howard, Robert	Pvt R I	"	11-15-77
Howard, Thomas	Pvt 2 Md	"	1-10-78
Howard, D Vochel	Capt	"	3-15-78
Howard, William	Va	"	1781
Howard, William	N Y	Killed	1776
Howard, William	Conn	Died	1776
Howe, Abner	N H	"	1781
Howe, Abner	Capt Mass	"	12-20- 76
Howe, David	Pvt Mass	"	8-8- 77
Howe, Eleazer William	Yale-Conn	"	11- 76

Howe, Eleazer William	Sgt N Y	Died	1776
Howe, Jonas	N H	Killed	6-17-75
Howe, Nathan	Capt Mass	Died	1781
Howe, Quash	Pvt 2 Mass	"	2-1-78
Howe, Solomon	Surg Conn	"	6-10-78
Howel, Iehiel	Pvt 4 N Y	"	6-26-78
Howell, Jno	Pvt 10 N C	"	9-20-78
Howell, John	Pvt N J	"	1779
Howell, Lewis	Pvt 2 N J	"	6-5-78
Howell, Samuel	Pvt Md	"	1780
Howell, Vincent	Pvt Va	"	
Howes, Elisha	Pvt Mass	"	5-18-79
Howes, Joshua	Pvt N Y	"	1778
Hoyt, Amos	Pvt 2 N J	"	3-15-77
Hoyt, Sliphalet	Pvt 9 Mass	"	9-18-77
Hoyt, Thomas	N H	"	1778
Hoyt, Thomas	Pvt Mass	"	1778
Hoyt, Thomas	Lt N H	"	1779
Hubbard, Capt		"	12-31-75 Que
Hubbard, Burrows	Capt	Killed	1781
Hubbard, Charles	Pvt 2 Md	Died	1778
Hubbard, Daniel	Conn	"	1777
Hubbard, Daniel	Capt Mass	"	12-19-77
Hubbard, Daniel	Pvt Mass	"	12-19-77
Hubbard, James	Mass	"	1775
Hubbard, James	Capt Mass	"	1776
Hubbard, Jas	Sgt 2 N Y	"	5-31-77
Hubbard, John	Conn	"	3-25-81
Hubbard, Joshua	Cpl 4 N Y	"	10-16-80
Hubbard, Jewell	Pvt N J	Killed	10-4-77
Hubbard, Jonas	Capt Mass	"	1775
Hubbard, Moses	Sgt N Y	Died	3-17-83
Hubbard, Richard	Capt N H	"	12-26-82
Hubbard, Warburton	Pvt 5 N C	"	5-5-78
Hubbel, Cato	Pvt Mass	"	9- 78
Hubbell, John	Pvt Conn	"	1782
Hubbell, John	Lt Conn	"	1782
Hubor, Leonard	Pvt Pa	"	1777
Huber, Rudolph	Pvt Pa	"	1779
Hublers, Georges	Capt Pa	"	2-7-79
Huchings, John	Pvt 13 Mass	Died	5-17-78
Huckleberry	Ind	"	1782
Hudgens, Ridgwell	Navy	"	2-4-78
Hudler, Leml.	Pvt 10 N C	"	4-19-78
Hudley, Joseph	Pvt 10 N C	"	1-28-80
Hudson, Benjamin	Pvt N H	"	
Hudson, Ebenezer	Pvt 14 Mass	"	3-14-78
Hudson, Ezekl	Pvt 5 N C	"	4-8-78
Hudson, John	Del	"	9-7-77
Hudson, Thomas	Pvt 5 Mass	"	11-21-77
Huestom, William	Pvt Pa	"	1781
Huff, Robert	Pvt 3 N Y	"	5-2-78
Huger, Benjamin	Maj 5 SC	Killed	5-11-79
Huggins, John	N H	Died	12-16-81

Hughes, Christopher	Pa	Died	1777
Hughes, George	Fifer Pa	"	8-2-82
Hughes, Isaac	Lt Col Pa	"	1782
Hughes, Jacob	Pvt 5 Md	"	11-5-77
Hughes, Joseph	2 SC	Killed	10-9-79
Hughes, Samuel	Pvt Md	Died	3-15-81
Hughes, William	Pvt Md	"	12-6-82
Huguet, Louis	France	"	1781
Huick, Robert	Pvt 3 N J	"	11-1-77
Hull, Cuffe	Pvt 6 Mass	"	10-25-75
Hull, Giles	Sgt Conn	"	3-1-80
Hull, Isaac	Q M N J	"	1780
Hull, Jesse	Conn	"	1781
Hull, Johiel	N J	"	1781
Hull, Joseph	Capt Conn	"	9-24-75
Hull, Joseph	Conn	"	6-12-78
Hull, Joseph	P Pvt Conn	"	6-22-77
Hull, Moses	Pvt Conn	"	6-27-81
Hull, Nathaniel	N H	"	9-6-77
Hull, Samuel	N H	"	9-8-77
Hum, Daniel	Pvt 4 Md	Killed	4-8-79
Humberson, Lyon	Ens S C	Died	10-7-80
Hume, Alexander	Lt 2 SC	Killed	10-9-79
Humes, Robert	Pvt Mass	Died	2-4-82
Humiston, John	Pvt Can	"	7-29-78
Hummel, Frederick	Maj Pa	"	1779
Humphrey	Lt R I	"	
Humphrey, Charles	Pvt Conn	"	1779
Humphrey, Elihu	Maj Conn	"	1777
Humphrey, Jonas	Pvt 2 Mass	"	2-3-80
Humphrey, Oliver	Conn	"	10-13-76
Humphrey, Richard	Pvt 2 Mass	"	1-1-79
Humphrey, Williams	Pvt 6 Mass	"	1-8-78
Humphreys	Lt	Killed	12-31-75 Que
Humphreys, John	Lt	"	1775 Que
Humphries, John	Capt	"	12-31-75
Humprey, Elihu	Maj Conn	Died	2-25-77
Hungerford, Benjamin	Conn	"	9-4-75
Hungerford, John	Pvt Conn	"	9-15-77
Hungsford, Dan	Pvt 1 N Y	"	12-22-77
Hunnewell, Daniel	Pvt 8 Mass	"	7-7-78
Huns, Geo	2 Pa	"	8-6-76
Hunt, Charles	Pvt 4 Md	"	2-1-77
Hunt, Eben	Navy	"	6-7-77
Hunt, George	Pvt Mass 18 Cont	"	3-14-76
Hunt, John	Sgt 10 Mass	"	1-1-78
Hunt, John	Sgt 6 Mass	"	12-15-77
Hunt, John S	Pvt Md	"	12-3-81
Hunt, Jonathan	N C	"	1782
Hunt, Nathaniel	Mass	"	11-16-83
Hunt, Stephen	Capt Mass	"	1778
Hunter, James	2 SC	Killed	6-28-76
Hunter, John	3 SC	Died	9-15-77
Hunter, Joseph	Pvt 3 N J	"	1-29-78

Hunter, Robert	N H	Died	1778
Hunter, Robert	Pvt 12 Mass	"	9-10-78
Hunter, Robert	Cpl 7 Pa	"	2-20-77
Hunter, William	Pvt 2 Mass	"	9-19-77
Hunting, Eben	Mass	"	6-22-77
Huntington, David	N H	Killed	6-17-75
Huntoon, Hilton	N H	Died	6-26-78
Hunwell, Israel	Pvt Mass	"	7-5-77
Hurd, Joseph			1778
Hurd, Joseph	Capt Conn	"	2-11-78
Hurlburt, John	Pa	"	1782
Hurlbut, Enoch	Pa	"	1776
Hurlbut, Enoch	Dr. Pa.	"	6-17-82
Hurlbut, Rufus	Sgt Mass	"	1781
Hurlbut, Squire	Pvt Conn	"	10-1-77
Hurlbutt, Rufus	Conn	Killed	1781
Hurley, James	Lt N J	Died	1777
Hurley, Jno	Pvt 4 N C	"	7- 77
Hurley, Josiah	Pvt 5 Md	"	1778
Hurley, Martin	Ens N J	Killed	10-4-77
Hursin, Francois	France	Died	1781
Hurt, Wm	Pvt 6 N C	Killed	10-4-77
Hussey, John	N C	Died	2-7-81
Huston, Alexander	Lt Pa	"	9-11-77
Huston, Joseph	Pvt Pa	"	1783
Huston, Alexander	Capt Pa	Killed	9-11-77
Hutchins, John	Pa	Died	7-3-78
Hutchins, Joseph	Col Va	"	1776
Hutchinson, James	N H	Killed	6-17-75
Hutchinson, John	Pvt N H	Died	6-22-78
Hutchinson, Nathaniel	Mass	"	1780
Hutchinson, Samuel	Pvt	"	7-3-78
Hutson, Thomas	Col SC	"	5-4-89
Hyde, Asa	Pvt Conn	"	1-18-82
Hyde, Elisha	Pvt Mass	"	1779
Hyde, Joshua	Vt	"	1779
Hyde, Thaddeus	Mass	"	1783
Hyde, Walter	Capt Conn	"	9-18-76
Hyde, Walter	N Y	"	1776
Hyde, Zina	Conn	"	9-18-76
Hyle, Coenrat	Pa	Killed	5-10-80
Hylo, Conrad	Pvt 3 N Y	"	5-10-80
Hynes, Isaac	Pvt 4 Md	Died	11-10-78

I

Ide, David	Mass	Died	1778
Ide, Jacob	Capt Mass	"	6-2-77
Ide, Joseph	Lt Me	"	6-16-78
Ingalls, Abijah	Mass	"	1777
Ingalls, Ebenezer	Pvt N H	"	1779
Ingersoll, Simon	Lt Conn	"	1777
Ingles, William	Col Va	"	1782
Inglish, Joseph	Pvt 5 N C	"	12-17-77

Ingalls, Zebediah, Jr.	Pvt Conn	Died	1778
Ingals, Pelatiah	Drum. 11 Conn	"	11-11-76
Ingersol, Daniel	Pvt 12 Mass	"	6- 1778
Ingley, William	Del	"	2-23-78
Ingraham, Daniel	Pvt Conn	"	12-9-77
Ingraham, Elijah	Pvt 14 Mass	Killed	7-7-77
Inman, Elijah	Pa	Died	7-3-78
Inman, Elisha	Pvt 1 R I	"	6-1-78
Inman, Israel	Pa	"	7-3-78
Inman, S	Capt SC	Killed	10-7-80
Inman, Shadroch	Capt SC	"	In War
Inslee, John	Pvt N J	Died	In War
Irby, Anthony	Col Mass	"	1781
Irby, Joseph & 2 Sons	SC	Killed	1781
Ireland, David	Pvt 15 Mass	Died	10-29-77
Irwin, Henry	Col 5 N C	Killed	10-4-77
Irwin, Isaac	Pvt Pa	Died	1783
Irwin, Robert	Pvt Can	"	3-18-77
Isaac, Abraham	Pvt R I	"	5-19-78
Isbell, Chauncy	Pvt Conn	"	1777
Israel, Herrick	Me	"	1782
Iund, Francois	France	"	1781
Ives, Abraham	Conn	"	1776
Ives, Caesar	Pvt Conn	"	8-7- 77
Ives, Gideon	Pvt Conn	"	1777
Ives, Titus	Pvt Conn	"	9-2-77
Ivey, William	Capt Va	"	In War

J

Jackson, Daniel	Pvt 2 N J	Died	2-1-78
Jackson, Edward	Pvt 7 N C	"	4-30-79
Jackson, Enock	Pvt 2 Mass	"	2-1-77
Jackson, Ephraim	Lt Col Pa	"	1777
Jackson, Ephraim	Pvt 11 Mass	"	12-19-77
Jackson, Ephraim	Lt Col Mass	"	12-19-77
Jackson, Ephraim	Lt Col Mass	"	1-1-77
Jackson, Giles	Mass	"	1780
Jackson, Hugh	SC	"	1779
Jackson, Jeremiah	Pvt 2 N J	"	5-1-77
Jackson, John	Pvt SC	"	5- 81
Jackson, John	Pvt 4 Md	"	12-21-79
Jackson, Jonathan	Pvt Conn	"	4-13-81
Jackson, Josiah	Mass	"	1778
Jackson, Nathan	Pvt Conn	"	7-25-78
Jackson, Prince	Pvt 1 R I	"	6-11-78
Jackson, Robert	Pvt SC	"	1781
Jackson, Samuel	Pa	"	7-3-78
Jackson, Solomon	Pvt 10 Mass	"	8-6-77
Jackson, Thomas	Pvt 4 Md	"	6-1-77
Jackson, William	Capt N Y	"	1776
Jackson, William	Pvt 9 Mass	"	11-17-79
Jacob, Ellis	N Y	"	1781

Name	Unit	Status	Date
Jacob, Ford	N J	Died	1777
Jacob, Jennison	Pvt 7 Mass	Killed	5-30-78
Jacob, John	Pvt Can	Died	4-3-77
Jaccbs, Elisha	Pvt Mass	"	1779
Jacobs, Henry	Mass	Killed	4-19-75
Jacobs, John	N Y	Died	1781
Jacobs, Jophar	Pvt Conn	"	2-20-78
Jacobs, Joshua	Pvt 5 N C	"	9-11-77
Jacoby, Nicolas	France	"	1781
Jacox, Jeremiah	Pvt Mass	"	10-16-77
James, Jacob	Mass		1781
James, John	Pvt 7 Mass	"	11-15-77
James, Morderar	Sgt N Y	"	1-13-78
James, William	Lt 7 Del	Killed	4-17-79
James, William	Col Va	Died	1780
James, William	2 SC	Killed	10-9- 79
Jameson, John	Lt Pa	"	1782
Jameson, Robert	Pa	"	7-3-78
Jansean, John	Pvt Mass	Died	11-7-77
Jaques, Joseph	Pvt Mass	"	7-25-83
Jaquith, Jonathan	Mass	"	1778
Jarvis, Jno	Pvt 10 N C	"	11-29-82
Jarvis, Nathaniel	Cpl N Y	"	1778
Jasper, William	Q M Sgt SC	Killed	10-9-79
Jaubert, Jean	France	Died	1781
Jauncey, Joseph	Capt SC	"	1779
Jay, John	Pvt Can	"	3-1-78
Jedeciah, Holcomb	Pvt Conn	"	1779
Jeduthan, Alexander	Mass	Killed	6-17-75
David, Jeffers	Pvt N J	Died	5-10-77
Jeffery, Daniel	Pvt Mass	"	6-16-77
Jeffery, Shadrock	Pvt 14 Mass	"	7- 1778
Jefferys, David	Pvt N J	"	5-1-77
Jeffrey, Jno	Pvt 10 N C	"	8-15-79
Jeffrey, John	Pvt 14 Mass	"	5-30-78
Jeffs, James	Pvt Can	"	1-14-78
Jemmison, Robert	Pvt Mass 40 Cont	"	4-24-76
Jenches, Oliver	Lt R I	"	2-3-84
Jencks, Jeremiah	R I	"	79
Jenkins, Jonathan	N H	Killed	6-17-75
Jenkins, Lot	Pvt Mass	Died	1776
Jenkins, Nathaniel	Ens 2 N J	"	4-5-79
Jenkins, William	Pvt Conn	Killed	11-15-77
Jenks, Oliver Lee	Pvt 1 R I	Died	2-3-82
Jenks, Primus	Pvt R I	"	10-11-78
Jennens, Ephraim	Pvt N H	"	11-22-77
Jennings, Beriah	Pvt Mass	"	5-12-76
Jennings, Joseph	Pa	"	7-3-78
Jennings, Joseph	Mass	"	1781
Jennings, Simon Lee	Pvt R I	"	4-21-78
Jennings, William	Lt R I	Killed	5-25-78
Jennings, Wm	Pvt 10 N C	Died	10- 78
Jere, Joe	Pvt 14 Mass	"	5-28-77
Jerome, Jeribbabel	Conn	"	1783
Jerrell, Ezekiel	Pvt 5 N Y	Killed	10-11-77

Jesup, Nathaniel P	Pvt Conn	Killed	6-28-78
Jewell, Hubbard	Pa	"	1777
Jewett, Amos Jr	Mass	Died	1777
Jewett, George	Mass	"	1776
Jewett, Joseph	Capt Conn	Killed	1776
Jinney, Reuben	Mass	Died	1777
Jller, John	Pvt 3 N J	"	11- 77
Job, Moses	Pvt 14 Mass	"	12-6-77
John, Silas	Drum 4 N Y	"	2-15-78
Johns, Benjamin	Pvt 5 N Y	"	2-1-78
Johns, Benjamin	Pvt Conn	"	3-1-78
Johnson, Abner	Mass	"	1778
Johnson, Abm	Pvt 4 Md	"	9-26-78
Johnson, Amos	Sgt N Y	"	12-26-76
Johnson, Amos	Pvt Conn	"	1776
Johnson, Barent	Capt N Y	"	1782
Johnson, Brutus	Pvt 10 N C	"	2-15-78
Johnson, Davis	Pvt Conn	"	4-6-80
Johnson, Daniel	Chap Mass	"	9-23-77
Johnson, Daniel	S C	"	1783
Johnson, Daniel	Chap Md	"	1778
Johnson, Daniel	Pvt Mass	"	9-11-77
Johnson, David	Lt R I	Killed	11-22-80
Johnson, David	Conn	Died	8-14-77
Johnson, Edward	Mass	"	1779
Johnson, Eliphalet	Conn	"	1779
Johnson, Elisha	Pvt 2 Cont	"	9-14-77
Johnson, Francis	Lt SC	"	1782
Johnson, Henry	Pa	"	7-3-78
Johnson, Isaac	Pvt N J	"	10-4-77
Johnson, Jacob	Pvt N J	"	4-25-80
Johnson, James	Sgt Conn	"	1-1-78
Johnson, Joel	Conn	"	10-23-77
Johnson, John	Pvt N H	"	1776
Johnson, John	Mass	"	1775
Johnson, John	Pvt Md	"	1-15-81
Johnson, John	Pvt Conn	"	8-8-79
Johnson, John	Pvt 2 Mass	"	8-28-77
Johnson, John	Cpl Mass	"	7-26-76
Johnson, Joseph	Pvt Conn	"	12-10-81
Johnson, Lewis	Mass	"	1778
Johnson, Martin	Sgt N J	"	8-5-79
Johnson, Nathan Jr	Mass	"	10-14-75
Johnson, Nathaniel	Pvt Pa	"	1777
Johnson, Philip	Pvt N J	"	10-2-77
Johnson, Philip	Col N J	Killed	8-27-76
Johnson, Samuel	Surg Pa	Died	4-4-79
Johnson, Samuel	Pvt Can	Killed	9-4-77
Johnson, Solomon	Pvt 10 N C	Died	9-15-78
Johnson, Thos	Pvt 3 N C	"	5-20-78
Johnson, Thomas	Pvt Mass	"	10-28-76
Johnson, Timothy	Pvt Mass	"	9-19-76
Johnson, Uriah	Capt 4 NY	"	2-7-78

Johnson, Vincent	Pvt 4 Md	Died	9-11-77
Johnson, William	Pvt N J	"	3-28-78
Johnston, David	N C	Killed	In War
Johnston, David	Lt R I	Died	11-22-80
Johnston, Francis	Pvt Va	Killed	3- 81
Johnston, John	Maj N C	Died	1779
Johnston, John	Sgt Pa	"	1-7-76
Johnston, Jonas	Col SC	"	1779
Johnston, Jonas	N C	"	1779
Johnston, Joseph	Navy	"	7-23- 81
Johnston, Moses	Pvt 2 N Y	"	12-30-76
Johnston, Philip	Col N J	Killed	9-12-76
Johnston, Rich	Pvt Pa	Died	4-3-78
Johnston, William	Chap N Y	"	1783
Johnston, Wm Jas	Pvt Can	"	6-17-77
Jolley, Rich'd	Pvt 1 N Y	"	6-10-77
Jolivet, Francois	France	"	1781
Jolliffe, John	Lt N J	"	1777
Jolly, John	Lt SC	"	1781
Jolly, Thomas	Pvt 10 Mass	"	1-1-78
Jolly, William P	Pvt Conn	"	12-1-77
Jonathan, Clapp	Maj Mass	"	1782
Jones	Lt SC	Killed	In War
Jones	Pvt Pa	Died	6-3-81
Jones, Aaron	Pvt 2 Md	"	2-17-79
Jones, Abraham	Pvt 7 Mass	"	12-9-77
Jones, Absalom	Pvt Conn	"	7-20-79
Jones, Anthony	Pvt Mass	"	1782
Jones, James	Capt N C	"	1777
Jones, John	Maj Ga	Killed	6- 79
Jones, Brimson	Cpl 2 N C	Died	6- 78
Jones, Caleb	2 SC	"	7-29-76
Jones, Chas.	Pvt 5 N C	"	3-2-78
Jones, Daniel	Pvt Conn	"	7-30-78
Jones, David	Cpl Md	"	1-15-81
Jones, David	Pvt N J	"	3-30-78
Jones, Ebenezer	Mass	"	11-4-79
Jones, Ebenezer	Mass	"	1776
Jones, Ebenezer	N H	"	8-23-83
Jones, Edward	Pvt 5 Md	"	3-13-77
Jones, Eleazer	Pvt Conn	"	1-6-78
Jones, Elijah	Sgt Mass	"	1782
Jones, Ezekiel	Pvt 2 Mass	"	11-24-79
Jones, Gershom	Pvt N J	"	4-2- 78
Jones, Henry	Pvt 4 N J	"	2-2-77
Jones, Isaiah	Pvt Conn	"	4-1-81
Jones, Jacob	Mass	"	1781
Jones, Jacob	Navy	"	7-23-81
Jones, James	Capt N C	"	1777
Jones, James	Del	"	10-3- 83
Jones, James	Pvt 2 Md	"	3- 78
Jones, John	Maj Mass	"	1776
Jones, John	Maj	Killed	1779
Jones, John	Capt Mass	Died	1776

Jones, John	Pvt 5 N C	Killed	10-4-77
Jones, John	Pvt 10 N C	Died	10-15-78
Jones, John	Pvt 7 N C	"	9-12-78
Jones, John	Pvt 6 Mass	"	4-6-78
Jones, John	Pvt 4 N J	"	3-24-78
Jones, Jonathan	Col Pa	"	9-26-82
Jones, Joseph	Pvt Can	"	9-15-82
Jones, Lewis	Fife 3 Md	"	12- 79
Jones, Lemuel	Mass	"	1778
Jones, Lytleton	Pvt 5 N C	"	9-20-77
Jones, Matthew	Pvt 2 N J	"	3-20-77
Jones, Moses	Pvt Conn	Killed	1781
Jones, Nathaniel	Lost at Sea		1778
Jones, Nathaniel	Surg. Mass	Died	9-4-79
Jones, Richard	Va	Killed	1781
Jones, Samuel	Ens 2 N C	Died	7- 78
Jones, Sam'l	Pvt 6 N C	"	7- 78
Jones, Sam'l	Pvt 15 Mass	"	9-26-80
Jones, Thomas	Pvt 11 Mass	"	7-7-77
Jones, William	Pvt Va	Killed	1781
Jones, William	Pvt Can	Died	5-24-77
Jones, William	Pvt 7 Md	"	5- 79
Jones, William	Pvt N Y	"	1-8-77
Jones, William Sr	2 SC	"	7-1-76
Jones, Windsor	Pvt 12 Mass	"	6-8-78
Jordan, John	Pvt 7 N C	"	3-17-78
Jordan, John	Pvt 10 Mass	"	2-17-78
Jordan, Nathaniel	Lt Col Mass	"	1779
Jordan, Nath'l	Pvt 2 N C	"	1-24-78
Jordan, Ramund	Pvt 10 Mass	"	3- 78
Jordan, Robt	Pvt 5 N C	"	8-24-78
Jordan, Simon	Pvt Navy	"	7-23-81
Jordan, William	Pvt 3 Md	Killed	10-4-77
Jordan, William	Pvt Can	Died	3-16-78
Jose, Richard	Pvt 12 Mass	"	7-10-78
Joseph, Reuben	Pvt N Y	"	2-23-77
Josselyn, Abraham S	Mass	"	5-28-78
Jouett, Mathew	Capt Va	"	11-15-77
Joulin, Jean	France	"	1781
Jovler, Caesar	Pvt Conn	"	8-7-78
Joy, John	Pvt Conn	"	11- 77
Joyce, William 2	Pvt Md	Killed	9-8-81
Juches, Cato	Pvt 11 Mass	Died	9-23-78
Judd, Eman'l	Corp Can	"	4-19-78
Judkins, Joel	Pvt N H	Killed	10-7-71
Judkins, Jonathan	Pvt N H	Died	3-4-78
Judson, David	Chap Conn	"	9-24-76
Judy, William	Lt Md	"	1782
Juland, Israel	Pvt 2 N J	"	9-20-77
Julien, Claud	France	"	1781
June, James	Pvt Conn	"	9-5-77
June, Stephen	Cpl Conn	"	5-7-78
Justus, Burch	Mass	"	1781

Name	Unit	Fate	Date
Kain, Francis	Pvt 4 Pa	Died	10-24-76
Kalb, de Baron	Maj Gen	Killed	8-16-80
Kamble, Stephen	Pvt Md	Died	9-1-82
Kantsman, Nicholas	2 Pa	"	1776
Karr, John	N H	"	10-22-82
Katon, Patrick	Pvt R I	Killed	6-28-78
Kearney, Dennis	Del	Died	1-28-78
Kearney, James	Pvt Pa	"	1777
Keasby, Edward	N J	"	1779
Keator, James	Pvt 2 Mass	"	7-31-77
Keaton, Cornelius	Matross Pa	"	9-16-76
Keck, Harry	Pvt Pa	"	1782
Keech, Samuel	Pvt 1 Md	"	4-10-77
Keeler, Jane	Pvt 14 Mass	"	5-28-77
Keeler, Samuel	Lt Conn	"	1781
Keen, Josiah	Pvt Mass	"	10-9-78
Keenan, Michael	Navy	"	7-21-81
Keene, Ephraim	Pvt 14 Mass	"	3-11-78
Kees, James	Pvt Can	"	9-20-81
Keeter, Nenemk	Pvt 10 N C	"	9-6-82
Keisler, John	Pvt N J	Killed	3-26-77
Keith, David	Mass	Died	1779
Keith, Ephraim M	Mass	"	1783
Keith, Seth	Pvt Mass	"	1783
Keith, Simeon Jr	Mass	"	1-3-76
Kell, Michael	France	"	1781
Kelley, John	Pvt 12 Mass	"	2-15-78
Kelley, John	N H	"	4-27-83
Kelley, Jonathan	N H	"	1778
Kelley, Robert	Lt Mass	"	1783
Kellogg, Benjamin	Can	"	12-12-79
Kellogg, Daniel	Gen. Arnolds Orderly at Que.	"	1776
Kellogg, Noah	Capt. Conn	"	1777
Kellis, Peter	Pvt Conn	"	6-11-78
Kello, William	Sgt Md	Killed	3-15-81
Kellum, Jno	Pvt 10 N C	Died	6-28-83
Kelly, Christopher	Pvt 2 N Y	"	9-21-78
Kelly, Hugh	Pvt 3 Md	"	9-16-78
Kelly, James	Sgt 5 Md	"	5-16-77
Kelly, Jas	Pvt 6 N C	"	4-15-78
Kelly, James	Pvt 1 N J	"	7- 78
Kelly, John	Col Pa	"	1783
Kelly, John	Pvt 6 Md	"	4-24-77
Kelly, John	1 SC	"	12-28-75
Kelly, Jonas	Pvt 3 Mass	"	10-2-77
Kelly, Lawrence	R I	"	3- 77
Kelly, Moses	Pvt 12 Mass	Killed	9-19-77
Kelly, Patk	Pvt 8 N C	Died	11-26-77
Kelsey, John	Pvt 4 N J	"	4-26-77
Kelson, Thos	Pvt 2 N Y	"	6-14-78
Kelton, Lucas	Pvt 9 Mass	"	3-7-78

Kemble, Jacob	Pvt Pa	Died	9-11-77
Komp, David	N H	"	6-17-75
Kemp, Joseph	N H	Killed	6-17-75
Kemp, Phineas	Pvt 14 Mass	"	6-28-78
Kemp, William	Pvt N H	Died	9-6-77
Kendal, Parker	Mass	Died	1776
Kendall, Aaron	Mass	"	1779
Kendall, Isaac	Pvt Conn	"	1776
Kenedy, Caleb	Pvt Pa	"	1-18-76
Kennedy, Eriskine	SC	"	2-17-77
Kennedy, Hugh	Mass	"	10- 78
Kennedy, John	Pvt Conn	Killed	7-5- 79
Kennedy, John	Pvt Va	Died	1781
Kennedy, John	Conn	"	6-21-81
Kennedy, Matthew	N H	"	10- 76
Kennedy, Samuel	Surg Pa	Killed	6-28-78
Kennedy, William	Pvt 6 Md	Died	10-15-78
Kennington, Joseph	Navy	"	1777
Kennison, Reuben		Killed	4-19-75
Kennister, Winthrop	Pvt Can	Died	3-18-82
Kenney, Amos	Pvt N H	Killed	10-7-77
Kenney, Edmund	Pvt 18 Cont	Died	8-3-76
Kent, Ezra	Pvt Mass	"	1779
Kent, John	Pvt 13 Mass	"	6-1-78
Kent, Nathan	Pvt Conn	"	2-4-78
Kent, Thos	Pvt 10 N C	"	9- 79
Kenyon, Joseph	Sgt 1 R I	Killed	6-28-78
Kerbe, Paul	Q M Sgt Pa	Died	1778
Kerber, Paul	Q M U V	"	1778
Kerker, Frederick	Pvt 1 R I	"	2-11-78
Kerman, Barma	Pvt 1 Md	"	7-19-77
Kerrick, Joseph	Cpl Md	"	12-27-82
Ketcham, Solomon	N Y	"	9-21-81
Ketre, Elisha	Pvt 12 Mass	"	7-28-77
Ketslaugh, Jacob	Va	"	5-6-77
Kettelie, James	Pvt Mass	"	1778
Kettle, Jacob	Pvt Pa	"	1777
Kettell, James	Sgt Mass	"	1778
Kews, Wm	Pvt Md	"	12-6-82
Keyhole, Peter	Pvt Conn	Killed	9-1-78
Keys, Cyprian	Pvt 14 Mass	Died	1-18-78
Kibbe, Isaac	Ens Conn	"	1780
Kibbee, Anthony	Pvt Conn	"	10-14-80
Kibbee, Nathaniel	Pvt 6 Mass	"	12-28-77
Kibble, Matthias	Pvt 4 N Y	"	4-1- 77
Kiblinger, John	Pvt Mass	"	4-4-77
Kidder, Joseph	Pvt 7 Mass	"	10-31-77
Kidder, Samuel	Ens Mass	"	1778
Kidlinger, Michael	Va	"	1778
Kilburn, John	Lt Mass	"	9-14- 76
Killam, Thomas	Mass	"	1782
Killeby, William Tyler	Ens 2 N C	"	4-6-77
Killgore, Charles	Va	"	1783
Killick, Henry	1 SC	"	12-2-1776

Killigrew, William	2 SC	Died	12-18-75
Killson, John	Pvt 9 Mass	"	4-19-77
Killum, Serus P	Pvt Conn	"	6-29-78
Kimball, Benjamin	Capt N H	Killed	8-23-79
Kimball, Benjamin	Capt Mass	"	1781
Kimball, Charles P	Pvt Conn	Died	8-16-77
Kimball, Ephraim	Mass	"	1782
Kimball, Joshua	N H	"	4-8-80
Kimball,	Sargent N H	"	1780
Kimball, Ziba	Pvt N H	"	1781
Kimble, Josias	Pvt 4 Md	"	1-1-79
Kimmey, Curtis	Del	"	10-5-77
Kincade, Peter	Pvt Md	"	1-1-82
Kincaid, Peter	Surg Md	"	1- 82
Kincbarr, Dublin	Pvt 2 Mass	"	9-30-77
King	Lt SC	Killed	9-9-81
King, Aaron Jr	Pvt Mass	Died	10-4-82
King, Charles	R I	Killed	12-31-75 Que
King, Dan'l	Pvt 1 R I	Died	4-20-78
King, Ezekiel	Pvt Conn	"	9-19-77
King, Francis P	Pvt Conn	"	10-5- 77
King, George	Capt Mass	"	1777
King, George	N J	"	7-2- 80
King, George	Pvt Mass	"	1- 7-77
King, James	Capt 1 N C	"	1780
King, James	Music N C	"	9-13-77
King, James	Lt N C	"	12-1-77
King, Jas	Pvt 2 N C	"	6-2-78
King, Jas	Pvt 10 N C	"	9- 79
King, James	Capt SC	"	1780
King, John	3 SC	"	10-10-79
King, Joseph	Pvt R I	"	8-10-77
King, Nathaniel	Pvt Mass	"	3-15-78
King, Paul	Mass	"	1782
King, Paul	Lt N H	"	1782
King, Robert	Pvt Can	"	1-6-79
Kingham, Nathan	Pvt Mass	"	10- 76
Kinaman, Edward	Ens 2 Mass	Killed	9-26- 77
Kingman, William	N H	Died	1776
Kingsbury, Absolom	N H	"	1777
Kingsbury, Asa	Lt Mass	"	1775
Kingsbury, Jabez	Pvt Conn	Killed	11-14-77
Kingsbury, Joseph	Cpl Mass	Died	10-17-75
Kingsbury, Oliver	Pvt Conn	"	12-11-81
Kinsey, David	Pvt 2 Md	"	1778
Kinsey, Jonathan	Pvt 4 N J	"	11-11-77
Kinsey, Lanham	Cpl Md	"	12-20-82
Kinsley, James	Matross N J	"	1782
Kinsley, Silas	Ens Mass	"	1775
Kihhvem, Michael	4 SC	"	4- 1777
Kinnil, Joseph	Lt SC	Killed	10-9- 79
Kinnelly, Patrick	Fifer Can	Died	6-25-82
Kinny	Pvt		In War
Kinsley, James	Matross N J	Killed	3-22-82
Kinston, Reuben	Pvt Mass	Died	1775

Kipp, Peter	Pvt N Y	Died	1780
Kirby, Griffith	Del	"	6-12-78
Kirk, Joseph	Me	"	10- 75
Kirk, William	Pvt 1 R I	Killed	10-22-77
Kirkland, Nathaniel	Lt Conn	"	10-12-77
Kirkpatrick, James	Pvt SC	"	1779
Kitchen, Joseph	Pvt 1 N J	"	12-19-76
Kitely, Francis	Pvt Md	"	4-25-81
Kittle, James	Pvt 8 Mass	"	2-15-78
Kittridge, John	Pvt Mass	"	7-10-76
Kline, George	Pa	"	10-26-79
Kline, Michl	Pvt SC	Killed	11- 81
Klinesmith, Baltzer	Pa	"	7-14- 80
Knap, Bonton P	Pvt Conn	Died	12-5-77
Knap, George	Pvt 14 Mass	"	4-23-78
Knap, Shadroch	Pvt Mass	"	3-10-78
Knapp, Benjamin	3 N Y	Killed	5-10-80
Knapp, James	Pvt N Y	"	1779
Knapp, Nathan	Conn	Died	1- 82
Knapp, Samuel	N Y	Killed	1779
Kneeland, Jonathan	Pvt Conn	Died	1780
Kneeland, Jonathan	Mass	"	1779
Knight, David	Pvt Me	"	4-5-80
Knight, Joseph	Pvt Mass	"	1-11-82
Knight, Square P	Pvt Conn	"	8-.12-77
Kinskern, Johanes	Pvt N Y	"	1781
Knoc, John	Pvt Md	"	1782
Knock, Geo	Del	"	5- 1782
Knott, James	Pvt 2 Md	"	1788
Knott, Jeremh	Pvt Md	"	1778
Knott, Jesse	Pvt N H	"	7-18- 78
Knowles, James	Lt	Killed	1777 At Sea
Knowles, James	Lt Mass	Died	1776
Knowles, John	N H	"	3-26-77
Knowles, Joshua	Pvt Mass	"	1776
Knowlton, Amos	Sgt 11 Mass	"	6-30-78
Knowlton, John	Navy	"	1777
Knowlton, Rice	Mass	"	2-17-78
Knowlton, Thomas	Col Conn	Killed	9-16-76
Knowles, Thomas	Pvt 7 Mass	"	11-11-78
Knox, Samuel	Pvt N H	Died	8-4-78
Knox, James	Pvt 4 N J	"	4-24-77
Kolb, Abel	Col SC	Killed	4-28-81
Koler, Adam	V Va	Died	1783
Kuhn, Adam Simon	Surg Pa	"	1780
Kullem, Thomas	Pvt N J	"	6-6-78
Kuns, George	Pvt Pa	"	8-6-76
Kuyper, Hendricus	Capt N J	"	8-17-83
Kymon, William	N Y	"	1781

L

Labor, Abraham	Col Pa	Died	1777
Labor, Leonard	Pvt 2 Pa	"	1776
Lacen, Joseph	Pvt 4 N J	"	9-1-80

Lacey, William	Pvt Can	Died	8-31-82
Leckland, Joseph	Pvt Can	"	1-1/-78
Lacorent, Moses	Pvt 6 Mass	"	7-13-77
LaCoste, Jean	France	"	1781
La Croix, Jean	France	"	1781
Lacy, James	Lt 6 SC	"	12-20-78
Lafin, Jeangeri	France	"	1781
Laforce, Peter	2 SC	"	7-15-76
La Fosse, Antoine	France	"	1781
La Fountaine, Charles	Pvt 7 Mass	"	7-27-77
Lehnnum, Kirney	Cpl Md	"	12-20-82
Laine, Philippe	France	"	1781
Lajoye, Jean	France	"	1781
Leka, Isaac	Pvt 4 Mass	"	3-15-78
Laky, John	Sgt 4 N J	"	1- 78
Lamb, Isaac	Pvt 4 N Y	"	9-19-77
Lamb, Jacob	Pvt Conn	"	12-7-81
Lamb, Jacob	Pvt Conn	"	2-20-79
Lambard, Joseph	Del	"	11-16-77
Lamar, Marian	Maj Pa	Killed	9-21-77
Lamson, Jonas	Pvt 13 Mass	Died	12-28-78
Lamson, Samuel	Pvt 8 Mass	"	1-20-78
Lamson, William	Pvt 13 Mass	"	3-10-78
Lanakee, Samuel	Pvt N H	"	8-4-78
Land, Benj	Pvt N Y	"	8- 78
Landers, William	Pvt 3 Mass	"	3-18-78
Landsgrove, John	Pvt 2 N J	"	4-5-78
Lane, Caleb	Mass	"	2-10-83
Lane, Cornelius	Pvt N J	Killed	6-27-78
Lane, James	Pvt 2 N J	Died	3- 78
Lane, Joshua	Pvt 11 Mass	"	4-30-78
Langden, John	Pvt N H	"	2-27-80
Langdon, Samuel	Lt Conn	"	9-13-78
Langley, Davis	Pvt 3 N J	"	10-19-77
Langley, Joseph	Pvt 14 Mass	"	3-7-78
Langley, Peter	R I	"	7-7-81
Langlois, Jacques	France	"	1781
Langsborough, William	Pvt 12 Mass	"	4-28-78
Lanham, Kinsey	Pvt Md	"	12-20-82
Lappington, Joshua	Pvt 12 Mass	"	4-29-78
Larcom, Henry	Mass	"	1780
Laring, David	Mass	"	1781
Laring, Thomas	Mass	"	1781
Larham, John	Pvt 8 Mass	"	10-2-78
Larkin, Mathias	Pvt 15 Mass	"	4-1-78
Larned, Ebenezer	Maj. Conn	"	12- 79
Larsell, Joseph	Pvt Can	"	2-5-77
Larson, Jonathan	Mass	"	1778
Lasiter, Jacob	Lt 9 N C	"	3-16-78
Lasiter, Josiah	Pvt N C	"	9-15-78
Lassiter, Theodosius	3 SC	Killed	10-9-79
Lassley, John	N Y	Died	1783
Latham, Cary	Conn	"	9- 80
Latham, Cary	Pvt Conn	Killed	8-1-81

Latham, John	Pvt 4 N Y	Died	12-29-78
Lathrop, Ebenezer	Capt Conn	"	1781
Lathrop, Joseph P	Pvt Conn	"	5-31-78
Lattin, William	Pvt Can	"	3-1-77
Laughton, Ebenezer	N H	Killed	6-17-75
Laughton, Jeremiah	Mass	Died	8-11-75
Laurens, John	Col SC	Killed	8-25-82
Laurens, John	Lt Col DC	Died	8-27-81
Laurent, Daniel	France	"	1781
Lawry, Michael	N J	Killed	1777
Lavender, George	Pvt Va	Died	1778
Lavender, George Michael	Pvt Va	"	1775
Lavender, Jno	Fife 3 Md	"	2- 80
Lawler, James	Pvt 3 Md	"	2-12-77
Lawrence, Benjamin	Cpl Mass	"	8-26-75
Lawrence, Daniel	Pa	"	7-3-78
Lawrence, Jno	Pvt Md	"	8-5-77
Lawrence, John	N H	Killed	6-17-75
Lawrence, Joseph		"	1779 At Sea
Lawrence, Joseph	Ens	"	6-4-77
Lawrence, Levi	Pvt 1 Mass	Died	9-11-80
Lawrence, William	Pa	"	7-3-78
Lawrie, James	Capt N J	Killed	1777
Laws, George	Pvt Md	Died	1-22-81
Lawson, Richard	Pvt 1 N C	Killed	10-4-77
Layton, John	Pvt 5 Md	Died	10-19-78
Layton, William	Pvt N H	"	12- 81
Lazell, Daniel	Mass	"	1776
Leach, Caleb	Mass	"	1783
Leach, Giles	Pvt Mass	"	1780
Leach, Ieshurum	Pvt 14 Mass	"	9-28-77
Leach, Jabez	Pvt R I	"	5-10-78
Leach, Jonathan	Pvt 10 Mass	"	12-23-77
Leach, Joseph	Pvt 8 Mass	"	3-10-78
Leach, Simeon	Lt Mass	"	1777
League, Absolom	Lt 2 SC	"	12-15-77
Lealand, Caleb	Pvt Mass	"	8-25-80
Leanard, Eli	Pvt Conn	"	6- 78
Leaning, Aaron	N J	"	8-8-80
Lear, John	Pvt Va	"	1780
Lear, Tobias	Capt N H	"	11-6- 81
Learned, Ebenezer	Conn	"	1779
Learned, Jedediah	Mass	"	1780
Leary, Cornelius	N C	Killed	1782
Leavenworth, Ebenezer	Lt Conn	Died	1778
Leathercoat, John	Pvt Conn	"	4-3- 78
Leavitt, John	N H	"	5- -81
Le Baron, James	Cpl Mass	"	1780
Le Comte, Pierre	Sgt France	"	1781
Ledyard,	Col Conn	"	9-6- 81
Ledyard, Fanny	Nurse Conn	"	In War
Ledyard, Francis	Pa	"	7-3-78
Ledyard, William	Col Conn	Killed	1776
Ledyard, Youngs	Capt Conn	"	1781

Name	Rank/Unit	Fate	Date
Lee, Charles	Maj Gen Pa	Died	10-2-82
Lee, David	Sgt N J	"	1781
Lee, Hezekiah Jr	Conn	"	1777
Lee, John	Sgt Conn	"	5-23-78
Lee, John	Pa	Killed	1782
Lee, Joseph	Fife 3 Md	Died	12-5-78
Lee, Richard	Pvt 11 Mass	"	5-1-77
Lee, Samuel	Pvt N H	"	3-28-78
Lee, Thomas	Sgt 5 Md	"	12-28-76
Lee, William Jr	5 Conn	"	9-11-76
Lee, William	Pvt Md	"	9-15-81
Leech, Daniel	1 SC	"	2-26-76
Leech, William	Pvt 1 Pa	"	11-24-76
Leeds, Samuel Sr	Mass	"	1778
Leete, Simeon	Conn	"	6-19-81
Lefevre, Joseph	France	"	1781
Leffingwell, Daniel	Conn	"	1778
Lefit, Naphtbeli	Pvt 7 Mass	"	10-7-77
Leftwich, Augustine	Capt	"	1780
Leggett, John	N Y	"	1780
Legrass, Joseph	Pvt 13 Mass	"	3-9-78
Leigh, Lewis	Sgt 10 N C	"	7-17-82
Leighton, Gideon	Cpl N H	"	1776
Leinhart, Jacob	Pvt Pa	"	1777
Leisenring, John Conrad	Pa	"	8-14-81
Leitch, Andrew	Maj Va	Killed	9-28-76
Leitch, Andrew	N Y	"	1776
Leland, David	Sgt Mass	Died	2-25-82
Leland, Isaac	N H	"	9-3-77
Lemmy, Joseph	Lt 1 N C	"	7-7-76
Lemon, James	Lt Pa	Killed	9-11-77
Lenox, Samuel	Pvt 3 N Y	Died	2-28-77
Lent, Abram	Pvt N Y	"	8- 78
Lent, Hendk	Pvt N Y	"	7-10-78
Lent, Hercules	Pvt N Y	"	9-12-77
Lent, James	2 SC	"	5-12-77
Leonard,	Capt SC	Killed	11- 81
Leonard, Abiel	Chap Mass	Died	1778
Leonard, Chris	Pvt 2 N J	"	4-5-77
Leonard, Daniel	Pvt 14 Mass	"	6-20-78
Leonard, David	Col Mass	"	7-1-77
Leonard, Seth	Mass	"	8-30-75
Leonard, Valentine	Pvt N C	"	1781
Le Riche, Jacques	France	"	1781
Lersne, Augustin	France	"	1781
Leslie, William	N J	"	1777
Lessure, Stephen	Pvt 6 Mass	"	3-11-78
Lester, Wait	Conn	"	9-6-81
Letcher, William	Va	Killed	1781
Lethgo, Wm	Pvt 10 N C	Died	4-1-82
Letman, William	Pvt Md	"	9-8-81
Letman, William	Pvt 2 Md	Killed	1778
Levitt, Abijah	Cpl 14 Mass	Died	8-31-77
Lewes, James	Pvt 6 Md	"	12-15-77
Lewis, Andrew	Brig Gen Va	"	1781

Lewis, Andrew	Maj Va		1781
Lewis, Benjamin	N J	Died	1781
Lewis, Benjamin	1 Md	"	4-10-77
Lewis, Benjamin	Mass	"	1777
Lewis, Charles	Col Va	Killed	10-10-74
Lewis, Charles	Col Va	Died	2-9-79
Lewis, Charles	Lt Va	"	1779
Lewis, David	Del	"	3-23-78
Lewis, Edward	Pvt 9 N C	"	5- 79
Lewis, Elnathan	Mass	"	10-16-78
Lewis, Fielding	Brig. Gen. Va.	"	1781
Lewis, Fielding	Pvt Va	"	12-25-81
Lewis, John	Pvt 9 N C	Killed	10-4-77
Lewis, John	Mass	Died	1781
Lewis, Joseph	Pvt Can	"	4-17-77
Lewis, Joseph	Mass	"	1783
Lewis, Joseph	Conn	Killed	1781
Lewis, Micajah	Maj 4 N C	"	1781
Lewis, Mingo	Pvt Conn	"	3-31-78
Lewis, Nathaniel	Mass	"	1778
Lewis, Nathaniel	Pvt 7 Mass	"	10-20-77
Lewis, Nathaniel	Pvt Conn	"	1777
Lewis, Peter	Pvt 3 N Y	"	4-24-78
Lewis, Richard	Pvt 5 Md	"	2-1-80
Lewis, Robert	Capt Conn	Killed	3-22-77
Lewis, Robert	2 N C	Died	11-7-81
Lewis, Robert	N C	"	1783
Lewis, Thomas	Pvt 18 Cont	"	10-18-76
Lewis, William	Lt Va	Killed	11-14-79
Lewis, William	Del	Died	9-10-81
Lewis, William	Lt Va	"	1780
Lewis, William	Pvt 4 N J	"	11- 77
Libbey, Edmund	Pvt 10 Mass	"	6-5-78
Libbey, Luke	Pvt Mass	"	2-1-78
Liguot, Pierre	France	"	1781
Lillas, Patrick	Pvt 12 Mass	"	9-23-77
Lilley, Abner	Pvt Conn	"	1-16-82
Limerick, Patrick	Pvt SC	"	1781
Lincoln, Lott	Pvt 13 Mass	"	3-20-78
Lincoln, Samuel	Pvt 8 Mass	"	3-2-77
Lindsey, Ephraim	Sgt Mass	"	1778
Lindsey, Henry	Pvt Conn	"	7-23-78
Lines, Ralph Jr	Conn	"	12-21-76
Lingo, Thomas	Pvt 7 Md	"	8- 78
Linn, William	Ky	Killed	1780
Linenkin, Benjamin	Navy	Died	12-16-79
Lines, Ralph	Pvt Conn	"	12-21-76
Linsey, Harry	Pvt 5 N Y	"	8-20-78
Linsey, Stephen	Mass	"	1781
Lionnois, Jean	France	"	1781
Lippett, Prince	Pvt R I	"	5-1-78
Lipscomb, Reuben	Capt 3 Va	"	10-3-78
Liscomb, Nathaniel	Pvt 9 Mass	"	9-20-77
Litchfield, Elisha	Pvt 2 Cont	Killed	7-15-81
Litchfield, Esperama	Pvt 10 Mass	Died	5-1-78

Litchfield, Isaac	Pvt 1 Mass	Died	12-22-77
Little, Benjamin	Pvt N Y	"	2-16-77
Little, Eneas	Pvt 3 N J	"	9-11-77
Little, George	Pvt Conn	"	4-22-77
Little, John	Capt N Y	Killed	1779
Little, Samuel	Pvt N J	"	10-4-77
Little, William	Pvt Md	Died	8-1-83
Littlefield, Edmund	Pvt Mass	"	1783
Littlefield, Simon Ray	Lt	"	3-31-80
Livermore, Levi	Pvt 6 Mass	"	11-23-77
Livingston, Philip	Pa	"	5-12-78
Livingston, Robert	Cambridge NY	"	1781
Livingston, Wm	Pvt 6 N Y	"	2-20-78
Lobb, James	Pvt 1 R I	"	6-5-79
Lock, Francis	Capt N J	Killed	9-15-77
Lock, James	Pvt Conn	Died	7-4-78
Lock, James	Pa	"	7-3-78
Lock, Orson	Pvt N H	Killed	9-19-77
Lock, Wm	Pvt 6 N C	Died	5-22-78
Locke, Francis	Col SC	Killed	9-25-80
Locke, George	Lt NC	"	In War
Locke, Jacob	Pvt 5 Mass	Died	11-9- '77
Locke, Joseph	Maj Mass	"	1777
Lockhart, Daniel	2 SC	"	7-1-76
Locks, James	Pvt 5 N Y	"	8-11-78
Locksalt, John	Pvt 3 N Y	"	6-18-77
Lockwood, Timothy	Capt Conn	"	1782
Loclen, John W	Pvt 1 Md	"	3- 81
Logan, William	Pvt Pa	"	1781
Loker, Jonas	Surg Mass	Killed	1775
Lombard, Solomon	Judge Me	Died	1781
Lombard, Timothy	Pvt 14 Mass	"	1-6- 78
Lombs, John	Pvt 11 Mass	"	7-7- 77
Lonass, John	Pvt Md	"	10-2-82
London, Sampson	Pvt 8 Mass	"	11-16-78
Long, John	2 SC	"	7-1-76
Long, John	Pvt Pa	"	1783
Long, Jno	Pvt 7 NC	"	2-24-78
Longer, John	Pvt 10 Mass	Killed	10-7-77
Long, William	4 SC	Died	3-15-76
Looker, Jonas	N H	Killed	6-17-75
Loomis, James	Mass	Died	1778
Loomis, Moses	Pvt Conn	"	9-27-81
Looney, Peter	6 SC	"	9-24-76
Lorain, Henry	Sgt 4 N C	"	7-13-78
Lord, George	Pvt 8 Mass	"	10-8-77
Lord, John	Conn	Killed	6-17-75
Lord, Jonah	Pvt Can	Died	1-8-81
Lord, Philemon	Pvt Conn	"	1-20-79
Lord, Simeon	Pvt 13 Mass	"	5-31-78
Loring, David	Mass	"	1781
Lormier, Augustin	France	Died	1781
Loring, Thomas	Mass	"	1782
Lorum, Pomp	Pvt 7 Mass	"	2-15-78
Losey, Benjamin	Pvt 4 N J	"	4-1-78
Losey, Cornelius	N J	"	1783

Lott, Job	Pvt 5 NC	Died	6- 1777
Loud, Caleb	Mass	"	1782
Loud, Jacob	Pvt Mass	"	1-3- 79
Lounsberry, Rich P	Pvt Conn	"	9-2- 82
Love, Alexander	Pvt SC	"	1781
Love, Samuel	Pvt 6 Pa	"	8- 76
Loveday, John	Pvt Md	"	8- 83
Lovejoy, Abijah	Vt	"	12-29-76
Lovejoy, Asa	Pvt N H	Killed	1- 80
Lovejoy, Isaac	Mass	Died	12-3- 79
Lovejoy, John		Killed	10-17-78
Lovejoy, John	Pvt 11 Mass	Died	10-13-78
Lovejoy, Jonathan	N H	Killed	6-17-75
Loveless, Elisha	Pvt 1 Md	Died	1-16-79
Lovell, Ebenezer	Pvt 18 Cont	"	11-15-76
Lovell, Ichabod	Pvt N H	"	7- 77
Lovell, Jacob	Mass	"	1776
Lovell, Robert	Va	"	1778
Lovering, Samuel	Pvt Mass	"	1781
Lovett, Richard	Pvt Pa	"	7-9-76
Low, Jeremiah	N J	Killed	6-20-78
Low, Peter	Pvt N Y	Died	1778
Low, William	Pvt 5 N Y	"	8-25-78
Lowe, Conrad	Pa	"	7-3-78
Lowe, Jacob	Pa	"	7-3-78
Lowell, Ebenezer	Ens 1 Mass	Killed	8-7-78
Lower, Adam	Pvt 1 R I	Died	7- 77
Lowery, Thomas	N Y	"	1783
Lowring, Thomas	Pvt 7 Mass	"	12-21-77
Lowry, John	Pvt Can	"	8-18-78
Lowry, Paul	Pvt 3 NY	"	3-20-1777
Lowry, Michael	N J	Killed	1777
Lloyd, Clement	Sgt Conn	Died	4-28-77
Lloyd, James	Pvt Can	"	10-17-81
Lloyd, Thomas	Capt N C	"	80
Logenby, Charles	3 N C	"	8-26-78
Lucas	Capt 6 Md	Killed	In War
Lucas, Billing	Pvt 10 N C	Died	9-5-79
Lucas, Matw	Pvt 5 N C	Killed	10-4-77
Lucas, Thomas	Lt Pa	"	10-4-77
Lucas, William	Pvt Md	"	10-1-82
Luckett, F Ware	Cpl 1 Md	Died	4-16-78
Luddington, Isaac	N Y	"	1782
Luddington, Timothy	Pvt Conn	Killed	7-5-79
Ludlow, David	Pvt 3 Mass	"	9-19-77
Ludlow, William	Can	Died	2-18-77
Luff, Thomas	Pvt 3 Md	Killed	8-16-80
Lufkin, Caleb	Mass	Died	1776
Luke, Cooley	Capt Conn	"	1-1-77
Luke, Hitchcock	Capt Mass	Killed	1782
Lum, Matthew	N J	Died	5-21-77
Lumberly, Simon	Pvt 7 N C	"	2- 78
Lunney, Philip	Pvt N Y	"	10- 78
Lunt, Samuel	Pvt 4 Mass	"	3-1-79
Lurman, Samuel	Ens N H	"	7-7-77
Luscomb, William	Pvt Mass	"	3-24-78

Luscomb, William	Pvt Mass	Died	3-24-78
Lush, Adj	SC	Killed	9-9-81
Luskin, Julen	Pvt 7 Mass	Died	11-20-77
Lusten, Benjamin Jr	Lt Col NY	"	1779
Luten, Lemuel	Cpl 7 N C	"	9- 77
Luther, Stephen	Pvt R I	Killed	10-22-77
Luts, Jno	Pvt 9 N C	"	11-10-78
Lycount, Wm Francis	Pvt Can	Killed	1778
Lydstom, Andrew	12 Mass	Died	8-1-77
Lyles, Zachariah	Pvt Md	"	6-18-81
Lyman, David	Lt Mass	"	1778
Lyman, Elijah	Lt Mass	"	1783
Lyman, John	Mass	"	1783
Lyman, Josiah	Conn	"	9-5-76
Lyman, Noah	Mass	"	1-2-78
Lynch, Owen	N Y	"	1781
Lyne, Matthew	2 SC	"	10-15-76
Lyon, Amosa	Conn	"	10-12-76
Lyon, Asahel	Conn	Killed	6-17-75
Lyon, Jacob	Sgt 3 Md	Died	9-5-81
Lyon, Jacob	Pvt 18 Cont	"	4-15-76
Lyon, Joseph	Pvt N Y	"	12-23-76
Lyon, Samuel	Pvt 11 Mass	"	7-23-78
Lyon, Thomas	Pvt Conn	"	9-12-77
Lyon, Zebulon	Pvt 7 Mass	Killed	9-11-77
Lyons, Henry	N Y	Died	1780
Loring, Thomas	Mass	"	1781
Lorum, Pomp	Pvt 7 Mass	"	2-15-78
Losey, Benjamin	Pvt 4 N J	"	4-1-78
Losey, Cornelius	N J		1783
Lott, Job	Pvt 5 N C	"	6- 77
Loud, Caleb	Mass	"	1782
Loud, Jacob	Pvt Mass	"	1-3-79
Lounsberry, Rich P	Pvt Conn	"	9-2-82
Love, Alexander	Pvt SC	"	1781
Love, Samuel	Pvt 6 Pa	"	8- 76
Loveday, John	Pvt Md	"	8- 83
Lovejoy, Abijah	Vt	"	12-29-76
Lovejoy, Asa	Pvt N H	Killed	1- 80
Lovejoy, Isaac	Mass	Died	12-3-79
Lovejoy, John		Killed	10-17-78
Lovejoy,	Pvt 11 Mass	Died	10-13-78
Lovejoy, Jonathan	N H	Killed	6-17-75

M

MacCorkle, John	Ens Va	Killed	1781
Maccumber, Jeremiah	Pvt 1 R I	Died	8-14-77
MacFarlane, Andrew	Capt Pa	"	1777
Mack, Elisha	Mass	"	1783
Mack, John	Conn	"	1775
Mackall, Benjamin	Capt Md	"	1776
Mackeen, James	N H	"	2-26-76
Macomber, Ira	Pvt R I	"	8-15-77
MacPherson, John	Maj Del	Killed	12-31-75 Que

MacPherson, Joseph	Pvt N H	Died	1783
Macy, Tristram	Sailor SC	"	1781
Madbury, Hezekiah	Pvt R I	"	3-24-77
Madly, James Sr	Va	"	1783
Maddox, Notley	Pvt 3 Md	"	9-16-77
Maddox, Walter	Pvt 7 Md	Killed	6-28-78
Madden, James	R I	Died	4- 77
Magee, William	Ens Pa	Killed	9-20-77
Magruder, Minian Beall	Ga	Died	1780
Maguan, Francois	France	"	1781
Mahan, Charles	1 SC	"	6-29-76
Mahere, Philip	Pvt N H	"	6-5-78
Maher, James	Pvt 14 Mass	"	3-10-78
Mahoney, Michael	SC	"	10-7-80
Mahoney, Thomas	Pvt Md	"	8-28-81
Mahony, Thomas	Pvt Ma	"	4-3-81
Main, John	Pvt Mass	"	10-9-76
Main, John	Pvt Conn	"	6-30-78
Main, John	Pvt 18 Cont	"	10-9-76
Maison, Jean	France	"	1781
Major, John	Pvt 3 N J	"	4-28-77
Malnd, And W	Pvt 1 NY	"	1-7-77
Malcolm, Thomas	Pvt 5 Md	"	4-6-77
Mallory, Francis	Col Va	Killed	1781
Malvon, Tim	Navy	Died	7-23-81
Malelrus, William	2 SC	"	2-24-77
Mammosh, Joseph	Pvt 5 Mass	"	9-30-78
Manodet, Bernard	Cpl France	"	1781
Manari, William	Pvt 2 N J	"	2-16-77
Manemlin, Philibert	France	"	1781
Manchester, Stephen	Pvt Mass	"	1-15-78
Manning, Joseph	Pvt Conn	"	1776
Manring, Robert	Mass	"	1781
Mansfield, Stephen	Pvt 18 Cont	"	11-14-76
Mansfield, Timothy	Conn	"	1781
Mansfield, Timothy	Pvt	Killed	10-14-81
Maliborn, Solomon	Pvt 5 N C	Died	2-27-78
Manlove, Matthew	Capt Del	"	1777
Mann, Daniel	Sgt Mass	"	1775
Manning, Joseph	Conn	"	1776
Manning, Robert	Mass	"	1781
Manning, Samuel	Pvt Conn	Killed	10-15-81
Manning, Thaddeus	Pvt Conn	Died	8-18-80
Manning, William	Mass	"	1778
Mannal, John	N H	Killed	6-17-75
Manvill, Nicholas	Pa	Died	7-3-78
Manwaring, Chs.	Pvt 4 Md	"	6-30-78
Marane, Vincent	2 SC	Killed	10-9-78
Marble, Leomi	Pvt 14 Mass	Died	7-3-77
March, Ichobod	N H	Killed	6-17-75
March, John	Lt 8 Mass	Died	10-18-77
Marchant, John	Pvt 2 N C	"	4-20-78
Marchant, Silas	Pvt Mass	"	1777
Marcy, Moses	Col Mass	"	1777

Marcy, Stephen	Capt Conn	Died	12-4-76
Marcy, William	Mass	Killed	4-19-75
Mardrick, Elisha	Va	Died	1782
Mardin, James	Pvt 1 R I	"	4-1-77
Marine, William	Pvt 1 N J	"	In War
Marion, Gabriel Jr	Lt 2 SC	"	1781
Maris, George	Pvt Ga	"	1783
Maris, George	Pvt N C	"	1782
Marival, Francois Charles	France	"	1781
Marks, William	Pvt N J	"	5-5-77
Marlin, Robert	Pvt 3 N J	"	1-8-78
Marlin, Zedohiah	Pvt 2 N J	"	3-25-77
Marsh, Abner P	Pvt Conn	"	5-31-78
Marsh, Anthony	18 Cont	"	9-7-76
Marsh, Ephraim	N Y	"	1781
Marsh, John	Conn	"	1782
Marsh, Joshua	Sgt N J	Killed	9-25-81
Marsh, Thomas	Sgt 4 Md	Died	1-5-78
Marsh, Timothy	Conn	"	1776
Marshall, David	Lt Conn	"	12-13-76
Marshall, Elisha	Pvt Conn	"	5-1-78
Marshall, Emanuel	Pvt 1 N C	"	4-5-78
Marshall, Ezra	Pvt 4 Mass	"	5-22-78
Marshall, James	Pvt N J	"	8-19-77
Marshall, Job	Pa	"	7-3-78
Marshall, John	N H	"	1776
Martian, William	Lt N J	Died	5-31-77
Martin, Alexis	France	"	1781
Martin, David	Pvt Va	"	1777
Martin, Edward	Lt Mass	"	1782
Martin, Henry	Pvt 5 Md	"	2-14-77
Martin, Ignatius	Pvt 1 Md	"	8-27-77
Martin, James	Pvt 14 Mass	"	6-6-78
Martin, John	Ens Pa	Killed	1777
Martin, John	Lt SC	"	In War
Martin, John	Pvt R I	Died	11-1-77
Martin, John 2nd	Pvt Md	Killed	2-15-81
Martin, John	Pvt 6 Mass	"	10-1-77
Martin, John	Pvt Ger Reg	Died	10-6-77
Martin, Joseph	Pvt Pa	"	6-3-81
Martin, Joshua	Pvt 10 N C	"	1-31-82
Martin, Louis	France	"	1781
Martin, Nicholas	Pvt 2 N J	"	6-1-78
Martin, Peter	Lt Pa	Killed	9-11-77
Martin, Samuel	Sgt 1 R I	Died	9-11-77
Martin, Sylvanus	Capt Mass	"	1782
Martin, Thomas	Navy	"	1-18-81
Martin, William	Capt SC	Killed	In War
Martin, William	Cpl Md	Died	12-31-82
Martindale, Samuel	Md	"	1781
Martling, Isaac	Sgt N Y	"	1779
Marvin, Jesse	Pvt Conn	"	2-15-78
Mason, Caleb	Ens Md	Killed	8-16-80
Mason, Elisha	Mass	Died	1780

Name	Rank/Unit	Fate	Date
Mason, George	Pvt Pa	Died	1777
Mason, James	Sgt R I	"	12-24-80
Mason, John	Pvt Conn	"	5-1-80
Mason, John	Pvt 10 N C	"	11-24-78
Mason, Jonas	Pvt 1 Mass	"	3-9-78
Mason, Joseph	Pvt Conn	"	4-16-78
Mason, Thomas	N Y	"	1781
Mason, Warren	Pvt 1 R I	"	8-28-78
Mason, William	1 SC	"	12-18-75
Massey, Daniel Loas	Pvt Md	"	1779
Massey, Thos	Sgt 3 N C	"	3-12-78
Massey, William	Pvt 6 Md	Killed	10-4-77
Mataran, Adam	Pvt Ger Reg	Died	11-15-78
Mather, Elihu P	Pvt Conn	"	12-17-78
Mather, John G	Conn	"	11-7-77
Mather, Joseph	Conn	"	1- 82
Mather, Moses	Chap Conn	"	1-7- 82
Mathews, Daniel	Pvt 14 Mass	"	9-23-77
Mathews, Elijah	N J	"	9-12-79
Mathews, James	Pvt 7 Md	"	10-7-78
Mathews, John	Pvt 2 N J	"	2-16-77
Mathews, Rowld	Pvt SC	"	5- 81
Matthews, Aaron	Sgt Mass	"	1778
Matthews, Elijah	N J	Killed	1779
Matthews, Elisha	Pvt 14 Mass	Died	6-26-78
Matthews, Henry	Capt Can	"	1-25-81
Matthews, Peter	Pvt Conn	"	4-5-78
Matthews, Robert	1 SC	"	6-26-76
Matthews, Robert	Sgt SC	Killed	11-1-79
Matthews, Robert	2 SC	"	10-9-79
Matthews, Thomas	Pvt N H	Died	3-16-81
Matthewson, Angus	Pvt 4 N Y	"	12-21-78
Matthewson, Josephs	Pvt 1 R I	Killed	8-28-78
Matthewson, New	Pa	Died	7-3-78
Mattison, Sam'l	Cpl 3 N Y	Killed	6-25-77
Mattock, Dan'l	Pvt 4 N Y	Died	12-21-78
Mattock, Samuel	Lt N J	"	1777
Mattocks	Capt SC	Died	10-7-80
Mattocks, Charles	Capt NC	Killed	10-7-80
Mattocks, John	Capt N C	Killed	10-7-80
Mattocks, Turner	Del	Died	1781
Matrose, James Kinsley	N J	"	3-3-82
May, Deacon Caleb	Conn	"	6-11-79
May, Ebenezer	Pvt 7 Mass	"	5-10-77
May, Ezra	Col Mass	"	1-11-78
May, John	Mass	"	6-9-83
May, John	Pvt Pa	"	1777
May, John	Pvt Conn	"	3-25-78
May, Major	Cpl 9 N C	"	11-27-77
Maybank, Joseph	Maj SC	"	1783
Mayo, Joseph	Sgt Mass	Killed	1776
Mayo, Thomas	R I	Died	1778
May, William	Pvt Can	"	5-28-78
Maybin, William	SC	"	1780

Maynard, Daniel	Pvt Mass	Died	4-6-83
Maynard, Micah	Pvt Mass	"	3-19-78
Maynard, Moses	Pvt Mass	"	3-26-82
Maynard, Nathaniel	Ens Mass	"	1-15-79
Maynard, Samuel	N Y	"	5-10-76
Maynard, Samuel	Mass	"	1776
Maynard, William	Capt Mass	"	1779
Mayo, Daniel	Pvt Conn	"	5-17-78
Mayo, John	Lt Mass	"	3-4-76
Mayo, Thomas	Mass	"	1776
Mayo, Thomas	Mass	"	1778
Maure, Leon	Cpl France	"	1781
Man, Abraham	Pvt N J	"	12- 77
Maverick, Samuel	Pvt Mass	"	3-5-70
Maxsell, Nath'l	N J	"	5-7-78
Maxwek, Gabriel	2 SC	"	In War
Maxwell, Daniel	Pvt 18 Cont	"	3-2-76
Maxwell, John	Sgt 6 Md	"	5-5-79
Maxwell, Richd	Pvt 4 Md	"	10-23-78
McAden, Hugh	Chap N C	"	1-20-81
McAdoo	N C	Killed	In War
McAllester, Matt	Pvt N J	Died	5-15-77
McAllister, Benjamin	Pvt N H	"	3-7-78
McAllister, Jas	Pvt 5 N C	"	3-7-78
McAtlee, Joseph	Pvt Md	"	8- 83
McBritian, William	Pvt N H	"	7-15-77
McCadden, William	Pvt 14 Mass	"	2-12-79
McCalister, Joseph	Pvt Md	"	3-24-83
McCall, James	Pvt Pa	"	1781
McCall, James	Col SC	"	1782
McCall, James	Col Ga	"	1782
McCann, John	Pvt 6 N C	Killed	10-4-77
McCann, Tho	Del	Died	4-10-80
McCargan, David	N Y	"	12-30-76
McCarroll, John	Pvt Pa	"	1777
McCarter, James	Mass	"	1781
McCarter, John	N J	"	10-14-77
McCarthy, Daniel	Pvt 3 Mass	Killed	9-19-77
McCarty, Nathaniel	N Y	Died	8-29-79
McCarty, Danl	Pvt 4 Md	"	6-17-77
McCarty, James	Pvt 3 Mass	"	4-15-77
McCarty, John	Pvt Mass	"	4-23-78
McCastelin, John	Pvt 18 Cont	"	12-26-76
McCaul, William	Pvt N J	Died	3-29-78
McCaulley, Nathaniel	Lt N H	Killed	8-31-79
McCausland, John	Pvt Pa	Died	1778
McCausland, William	Maj Pa	"	1781
McCawl, Wm	1 R I	"	4-4-82
McUlan, Dennis	Pvt Can	"	2-10-77
McClary, Andrew	Maj N H	Killed	6-17-75
McClean, Tho	Del	Died	12- 77
McClean, Thomas	2 SC	"	5-30-76
McCleary, David	N H	"	8-16-77
McClelan	Lt Pa	"	1776

McClelland, John	Lt Col O	Died	1782
McClelland, John	Pa	"	1775
McClintock, Alex	Lt Pa	Killed	9-11-77
McClintock, Nathaniel	Maj N H	"	1780
McCloskey, Charles	2 SC	Died	10-7-76
McCloughry, John	Lt N Y	"	1781
McClure, Alexander	Pvt Can	"	10-25-77
McClure, John	Pvt SC	"	8-18-80
McClure, John	Capt SC	Killed	1780
McClure, William	Surg SC	Died	1781
McCobb, Aaron	Pvt 6 Mass	"	3-1-78
McCollester, Daniel	Va	"	1778
McCollester, Joseph	Pvt Md	"	3-24-83
McCrillis, William	Pvt N H	"	1775
McClung, William	Pa	Killed	1779
McClure, John	Capt SC	Died	1780
McConneken, Jno	Pvt 2 Md	"	7-1-78
McCord, Mark	Cpl Pa		1781
McCorkle, John	Ens	Killed	1781
McCorkle, Samuel	Ens N C	Died	8-12-77
McCormick, George	Pvt Pa	Died	1777
McCoy, James	Pvt 6 Md	"	12-17-78
McCoy, John Sr	Mass	"	1776
McCoy, John	Pvt 5 N C	"	3-10-78
McCrah, William	Pvt N J	"	5-15-76
McCracken, Hugh	Pvt SC	Killed	6- 81
McCracken, William	Lt O	Died	11-4-82
McCrea, Samuel	Pvt 6 Pa	"	10-19-76
McCrillis, William	N H	"	6-17-75
McCrory, Thomas	Capt Md	"	1778
McCue, John	Del	"	9-2-77
McCue, Patrick	Del	"	11-6-78
McCullam, Patt	Pvt 7 Pa	"	3-15-77
McCuller, Joseph	Sgt 7 N C	"	4-3-78
McCullough, Thomas	Lt N C	Killed	1780
McCurdy, Archibald	N H	Died	11-4-77
McCurdy, James	N H	"	7-19-76
McCurdy, John	Pvt SC	Killed	1781
McDade, Charles	Pvt N J	Died	5-21-76
McDaniel, James	2 SC	Killed	6-28-76
McDavid, Henry	Pvt 1 N Y	Died	10-29-78
McDaniel	Capt Pa	"	6-3-81
McDaniel, Elisha	Cpl 3 Md	"	12-12-77
McDaniel, John	5 SC	"	3-6-77
McDaniel,John	Pvt 2 Mass	"	3-20-77
McDaniels, John	Va	"	1778
McDonald, Adams	Capt 1 SC	"	1778
McDonald, Angus	Lt Col Va	"	1778
McDonald, Archabald	7 Pa	"	1-5-77
McDonald, John	Pvt N J	"	4-6-77
McDonald, Jona	Pvt 10 NC	"	2-20-78
McDonald, William	Pvt 1 Pa	"	6-8-76
McDonald, Wm	Pvt 2 N J	"	3-1-77
McDonald, Wm	Sgt 5 Pa	Killed	9-11-77
McDougal, John	Pvt 2 N J	Died	2-8-77

Name	Rank/Unit	Status	Date
McDowell, John	Ens Pa	Died	1779
McDowell, John	Pvt Pa	"	1777
McDowell, John P	Del	"	4-12-78
McDowell, Joseph	N C	"	1775
McDugle, Jno	Pvt 2 Md	"	7-1-78
McEntire, Robt	Pvt SC	Killed	12- 81
McEwens, John	Sgt 4 N Y	Died	2-6-78
McFarland, Andrew	Me	"	1780
McFarland, Andrew	Lt Pa	"	1777
McFarland, Andrew	Capt 3 N J	"	2-2-77
McFarland, George	Ens N J	"	In War
McFarland, James	Pvt Mass 18 Cont	Killed	10-13-76
McFarlane, Elisha	Pvt 14 Mass	Died	11-29-77
McFarlane, Jas	Pvt 4 Pa	"	1-3-79
McFarlane, Robert	Del	"	2- 79
McFoshin, Caleb	Pvt 10 N C	"	11-4-78
McGaw, Nichs	Pvt 5 Md	"	2-17-77
McGee, William	Ens Pa	"	9-20-77
McGill, Samuel	Pvt SC	"	1781
McGillegan, Bar	Pvt 7 Pa	"	3-20-77
McGilvreay, William	N H	"	1783
McGinnes, John	Pvt N H	"	6-17-78
McGloughlin, George	Capt N J	"	In War
McGlochlin, John	Pvt Md	"	3-1-81
McGower, Michael	Pvt Md	"	9-8-81
McGown, Samuel	Pvt 7 Pa	"	1-5-77
McGratto, Daniel	N H	Killed	6-17-75
McGraw, John	Pvt 8 Mass	Died	6-10-75
McGraw, John	Pvt 2 Md	"	10-18-78
McGraw, Moses	Pvt Navy	"	7-23-81
McGraw, Stephen	Pvt Md	"	3-19-81
McGregor, James	N H	"	6-1-76
McGrew, Wm	Pvt SC	Killed	5- 81
McGuire, Phileman	Pvt 4 Md	Died	4-4-77
McGuire, Silas	Pvt 2 N C	"	7-1-78
McHaffe, Benj	Pvt Md	Killed	6-18-81
McHandy, Thomas	Pvt Md	Died	8-28-82
McHard, Joseph	Pvt Mass	"	12-17-79
McIntire, Alexr	Pvt 3 Md	"	6- 78
McIntire, Robert	Pa	"	7-3-78
McIntire, Robert	Drummer Pa	"	11-1-76
McIntosh, Archibald	N H	Killed	6-17-75
McIntosh, John	Pvt 5 Md	Died	9-30-78
McIver, Charles	SC	"	11-14-79
McKabe, Joshua	Pvt 7 N C	"	2- 78
McKaque, Wm	Pvt Pa	"	1777
McKaragham, William	Pa	"	7-3-78
McKay, Alexander	Fife 1 Md	"	7-14-77
McKay, James	2 SC	"	5-6-76
McKay, John	Pvt 10 N C	Killed	9-8-81
McKean, Robert	Maj N Y	"	1781
McKenny, Humphrey	Pvt Mass	Died	1779
McKeen, James	N H	"	2-26-76
McKee, Michael	Pvt 5 N Y	"	10-4-77

Name	Rank/Unit	Status	Date
McKendrick, Robert	Pvt 3 N J	Died	5-8-78
McKenny, James	Pvt 6 Md	"	10-25-78
McKenny, Timothy	Pvt N J	Killed	6-7-80
McKensey, Wm.	Pvt 1 Md	Died	4-20-77
McKindly, Wm.	Pvt 6 Md	Killed	8-16-80
McKinley, John	Ky	"	1782
McKinley, John	Capt Va	Died	1782
McKinley, John	Lt	Killed	1782
McKinney, James	Pvt Pa	Died	1777
McKinney, James	N Y	"	1781
McKinsey, John	Pvt 5 Md	"	10-29-77
McKnight, Benjamin	Pvt Va	"	2-15-77
McKnight, Daniel	Pvt Pa	"	1777
McKown, Patrick	Me	"	1779
McLain, Jacob	Pvt Ger. Reg	"	12-28-76
McLain, Robert Anthony	Pa	"	9-27-77
McLamar, Timothy	Pvt Md	Killed	6-18-81
McLane, Alexander	Navy	Died	7-23-81
McLannen, Alex	Pvt 12 Mass	"	5-15-78
McLaughlin, Alexr	Pvt 10 N C	"	10-1-82
McLean	N C	Killed	In War
McLellan, Alexander	Me	Died	1779
McLellan, Alexander	Capt Mass	"	10-4-79
McLemmy, Joseph	Lt N C	"	7- 76
McLoon, Josiah	Pvt N H	"	12- 81
McLowry, Alexander	Ens Conn	"	10-11-80
McLucas, Joshua	Pvt 12 Mass	"	11- 78
McLure, John	Capt SC	"	1780
McManners, James	Pvt 18 Cont	"	10-19-76
McManis, Barney	Pvt 7 Md	"	8-13-80
McMaster, John	Mass	"	1780
McMeyers, Andrew	Capt N J	Killed	10-4-77
McMicheal, William	Lt N J	"	1776
McMires, Andrew	Capt N J	"	10-4-77
McMorrow, Michael	Pvt 14 Mass		12- 78
McMullon, Chas.	Pvt 7 Pa	Died	1-8-77
McMullen, John	Pvt SC	Killed	9-8-81
McNab, Charles	Conn	Died	11-1-80
McNail, Alexander	Conn	"	7-23-83
McNames, Chas.	Pvt 1 NY	"	5-17-79
McNeal, Daniel	N H	"	3-11-82
McNeal, Hector	Col N C	Killed	9-12-81
McNeil, Archibald	Ky	"	3-19-77
McNeil, George	Pvt 7 Mass	"	5-3-78
McNeil, William	Pa	Died	1781
McNeill, John	Sailor	Killed	6-12-75
McNelos, Connolly	Pvt Can	Died	2-3-77
McPherson	Can	Killed	12-31-75 Que
McPherson	Aid deCamp R I	Died	In War
McPherson, A	Cpl 3 Md	"	12- 77
McPherson, John	Aid-de-Camp	Killed	12-31-75 Que
McPherson, Joseph	Pvt N H	Died	1783
McQuillin, Walter	Pvt 10 N C	"	12-1-81

Name	Rank/Unit	Status	Date
McRory, Thos.	Capt 9 N C	Died	11-2-1777
McSwaine, John	Pvt. Va	"	2-15-1777 Prison
McVay, Jno.	Pvt. 10 N C	"	9-6-1782
McWaters, Saml	Pvt. SC	"	4- 1781
McWay, Sailo	Pvt. 14 Mass	"	6-30-1778
McWilliams, Samuel	Del	"	10-12-1780
Meacham, John	Pvt 3 Mass	"	11-26-1778
Meacham, William	Capt Mass	Killed	6-17-1775
Mead, Ezra	Vt	Died	1781
Mead, Stephen	Pvt N J	Killed	7-2-1779
Mead, Sylvanus	Lt Conn	Died	1780
Meadbury, Hezekiah	Ens R I	"	3-24-1777
Meakens	Pvt Conn	"	1-9-1779
Means, Samuel	Pa	"	1780
Mebane, Robert	Lt Col 7 N C	"	10- 1781
Medbury, Hezekiah	Ens R I	Killed	5-17-1777
Meeker, Daniel	Pvt Conn	Died	1-6-1778
Meeker, Jacob	Pvt Can	"	1-4-1778
Meeker, Stephen	Pvt Conn	"	2-1-1778
Meeleman, A.	Pa	"	7-3-1778
Megginson, Wm.	Lt. Va.	"	In War
Meggs, Silvanus P.	Pvt. Conn	"	3-24-1778
Meigs, Bezai	Pvt. 2 Mass	"	4-9-1778
Meigs, Jehiel	Capt Conn	"	3-25-1780
Meigs, Jehial Jr	Capt Conn	"	12-27-1776
Meigs, Phineas	Conn	"	5-19-1782
Melchor, Joseph	Pvt. 10 Mass	"	10-7-1777
Mellen, Thomas	Lt Mass	"	1782
Mellone, William	Pvt 6 Md	Killed	8-16-1780
Melles, William	Pvt 5 Md	Died	2-29-1778
Mellet, Wentworth	Pvt 5 Mass	"	3-1-1780
Melona, Mathew P.	Pvt Conn	Killed	8-29-1778
Meloy, Thomas	Pvt 1 Mass	Died	2-27-1778
Melvin, John	N H	Killed	6-17-1775
Memory, Daniel	N H	"	6-17-1775
Menager, Louis	France	Died	1781
Menchen, Humphrey	Pvt Md	"	7-15-1781
Mendom, Robert	Va	"	3- 1777
Mercer, Hugh	Brig.Gen.N.J	Killed	1-16-1777
Mercer, Hugh	Maj. Scotland	Died	1-10-1777
Mercey, Ccto	Pvt N H	"	5-27-1778
Merchant, Benjamin	5 SC	"	3-6-1777
Mercier, Andoche	France	"	1781
Meredith, Huziah	Del	"	9-29-1778
Mereo, Prince	Pvt 9 Mass	"	6-3-1778
Merkot, George	France	"	1781
Merolds, Asha	Pvt Conn	"	9-4-1777
Merriam, Ebenezer	Pvt 9 Mass	"	4-1-1778
Nerruanm Nathan	Pvt Mass	"	11-11-1782
Merrill, Enoch	Mass	"	1778
Merrill, Joshua	Capt Mass	"	1782
Merrit, Peter	Cpl Conn	"	2-4-1778
Merritt, Joel	Pvt 10 N C	"	11-4-1778
Merritt, Peter	Pvt. Conn		1777
Merry, Josephs	Pvt 1 R I	"	2-13-1782
Mershon, Aaron	N J	Killed	1776
Mershon, Andrew	Pvt	"	8-27-1776
Merwick, Spencer	R I	"	12-31-1775

118

Mery, Antoine	France	Died	1781
Meson, John	Pvt Conn	"	4-7-1778
Messenger, Benoni	Mass	"	9-20-1777
Messenger, Gideon	Pvt Mass	"	9-20-1779
Messer, Abiel	Conn	Killed	1776
Messey, Joseph	Pvt 10 NC	Died	6-22-1783
Messick, Charles	Pvt Md	"	10-22-1783
Metcalf, John	Pvt 1 Md	"	7-15-1778
Metcalf, Jonathan	Mass	"	9-22-1778
Metcalf, Ozias	Pvt Mass	"	11-29-1777
Metcalf, Solomon	Pvt 5 Mass	"	10-19-1777
Mexico, Abm	Cpl 2 N C	"	6-20-1778
Meyers, Andrew W	Capt 1 N J	"	10-4-1777
Meyers, George	Pvt Md	"	1783
Meynema, Benj.	Pvt 4 N Y	"	4-30-1779
Mezick, Jacob	Lt 8 N C	"	12-11-1777
Michael, Nicholas	Pvt Pa	"	6-3-1781
Michell, John	Pvt Va	Killed	7-18-1781
Mickell, James	Pvt 1 R I	Died	7-15-1778
Mickolls, John	SC	"	1780
Middle, John	Pvt 7 Mass	"	3-9-1778
Middlebrook, Ephraim	Lt Conn	Killed	4-27-1777
Middleton, Thomas	Pvt 14 Mass	Died	7-27-1778
Miers, Christopher	Pvt Md	"	10-13-1781
Miers, John		"	3-20-1780
Mignon, Henry	Pvt Conn	"	9-5-1782
Mike, Joseph	Pvt	"	5-24-1778
Milbin, John	SC	Killed	1- 1781
Miles, Benjamin	Mass	Died	1776
Miles, Geo.	Pvt R I	"	4-30-1778
Miles, Reuben P	Pvt Conn	"	6-18-1778
Miles, Simeon	Pvt R I	"	12-31-1777
Milford	Pvt N J	"	In War
Millard, Andrew	Pa	"	7-3-1778
Millard, Elias	Pvt 1 R I	"	12-30-1777
Millard, Thomas	Pvt 4 Md	"	4-12-1777
Millaway, Joseph	Del	"	1778
Miller, David	Md	"	1778
Miller, David	Cpl 1 N Y	"	5-27-1778
Miller, David	W Va	"	3- 1782
Miller, Elijah Adj	N Y	"	8-21-1776
Miller, Garret	Capt N Y	"	1778
Miller, Hance	Del	"	3-29-1779
Miller, Heinrich	N C	"	12-15-1778
Miller, Henry	R I	Killed	12-31-1775
Miller, Jacob	Md		1779
Miller, Jacob	Pvt Pa	Died	1777
Miller, Jacob	Del	"	1778
Miller, Jacob	Pvt Pa	Killed	1782
Miller, James	N J	"	4-19-1775
Miller, James	Mass	"	4-19-1775
Miller, James	Sgt 8 Mass	Died	10-25-1775
Miller, James Henry	SC	Killed	In War
Miller, John	Pvt Can	Died	2-28-1777

Name	Unit	Fate	Date
Miller, John	Del	Died	10-13-1780
Miller, John	N Y	"	12-22-1776
Miller, John	Capt Pa	Killed	11-16-1776
Miller, John	Dr Del	Died	2-28-1777
Miller, John	Cpl 7 N C	"	3-4- 1778
Miller, John	Pvt Pa	"	1783
Miller, Joseph	Pvt Ger. Reg "		1-5-1777
Miller, Moses	N J	"	1778
Miller, Peter	Pvt Pa	"	1778
Miller, Thomas	Cpl N Y	"	1780
Miller, Samuel	Capt Pa	"	7-8-1778
Millert, Michael	France	"	1781
Millica, Abraham	Pvt 1 N J	"	2-1-1778
Milligan, Hicajah Allen	Pvt R I	"	3-18-1778
Milliken, James	N H	Killed	6-17-1775
Millington, Samuel	Pvt Conn	"	12-7-1777
Mills, Amos	Mass	"	4-19-1775
Mills, Edward	Pvt 5 Md	Died	8-15-1778
Mills, Elisha	Sgt Mass	Killed	4-19-1775
Mills, Elisha	Pvt 3 Mass	Died	9- 1777
Mills, Lewis	Conn	"	4-4-1782
Mills, Lewis	Lt Conn	"	1777
Mills, Nehemiah	Pvt 3 Mass	"	9- 1777
Mills, Timothy	N J	"	1777
Mills, Timothy	Pvt N Y	"	1781
Mills, Williams	Pvt Va	"	1783
Millet, Thomas	Pvt 8 Mass	"	10-18-1777
Millett, John	Pvt N H	"	12- 1779
Milvin, John	SC	Killed	11- 1781
Minard, Thomas	Conn	Died	9-6-1781
Miner, Joshua	Mass	"	1776
Miner, Joshua	Pvt Conn	"	1776
Miner, Thomas	Conn	Killed	1781
Minor, Jonathan	Pvt Conn	Died	4-28-1777
Minor, Moses	Pvt 1 N Y	"	6- 1777
Minor, Joseph	Mass	"	6-17-1775
Minott, Joseph	N H	Killed	6-17-1775
Mins, Asabel	Sgt N H	Died	6-17-1775
Minthorn, Philip	Sgt N J	"	1780
Minthorne, William	N J	Killed	10-7-1781
Mirick, James	Capt Mass	Died	1778
Mitchell, Benjamin	Pvt Mass	"	1-28-1778
Mitchell, Cornelius	2 SC	"	7-21-1777
Mitchell, George	Pvt Conn	"	10-26-1777
Mitchell, James	Pvt SC	"	9- 1781
Mitchell, Robert	Pvt Can	"	11-20-1782
Mitchell, Saml	Pvt 4 N Y	"	10-7-1781
Mitchell, Thomas	Maj Mass	"	7-1-1776
Mitchell, William	N H	Killed	6-17-1775
Mitchell, Zachariah	SC	Died	1-25-1777
Mitop, James	Pvt 3 N J	"	1-28-1778
Mix, Eli P	Pvt. Conn	Killed	7-15-1779
Mix, Lemus	Pvt Conn	Died	12-1-1781

Mix, Timothy	Lt N Y	Died	1778
Mobley, Edward Sr	SC	"	1782
Modlin, Ezekl	Pvt 10 N C	"	4-20-1778
Moger, Abijah P	Pvt Conn	"	3-25-1778
Moho, John	Pvt 7 Mass	"	1-1-1778
Moland, James	Pvt 6 Md	Killed	1777
Moline, Jean-Baptiste	France	Died	1781
Molton, Caesar	Mass	"	1781
Monroe, Edmund	Q M Capt Mass	Killed	6-28-1778
Monroe, Edmund		"	1778
Monroe, George	Mass	"	1778
Monroe, Zedediah	Mass	"	4-19-1775
Monroe, Robert	Ens Mass	Killed	4-19-1775
Montague	Pvt Va	Died	1778
Montague, Caleb	Md	"	1782
Montague, Caleb	Sgt Mass	"	1782
Montague, Caleb	Capt Mass	"	1782
Montague, David	Mass	"	1781
Montague, Thomas	Pvt Va	"	1779
Monard, Nicolas	France	"	1781
Monckton, Henry	Lt Col N J	"	6-28-1778
Mongin, Jean Baptiste	France	"	1781
Monk, Jonathan	Pvt SC	"	1781
Monson, Robert	1 SC	"	1-15-1776
Montail, John	Pvt 4 Mass	"	1-1-1777
Montel, Liberal	France	"	1781
Montford, Joseph	N C	"	3-25-1776
Montgomery, Hugh	N C		1779
Montgomery, Hugh	Del		1780
Montgomery, John	N Y	"	1782
Montgomery, Richard	Maj Gen N Y	Killed	2-31-1776 Que.
Montgomery, William	Ky	"	1781
Moody, John	Pvt N Y	Died	1776
Moody, Levi	Pvt Md	"	10-15-1782
Moody, Nathaniel	Pvt 8 Mass	Killed	9-19-1777
Moon, Abel	Pvt 10 Mass	Died	4-1-1777
Moon, Jacob	Lt N C	"	1781
Moor, Anthony	Pvt Conn	"	2-26-1778
Moor, Edward	Pvt Conn	"	5-11-1778
Moor, James	Pvt Ger Reg	"	12-24-1776
Moor, Robert	Col N H	"	10-25-1778
Moore	Lt Md	Killed	In War
Moore, Abm	Pvt 1 NY	Died	1-31-1777
Moore, Andrew	Pvt 7 Md	"	3-15-1781
Moore, Andrew	Lt Conn	"	1776 Que
Moore, Benjamin	Pvt 1 Mass	"	2-15-1778
Moore, Cuffee	Pvt 10 NC	"	8-17-1779
Moore, Daniel	Conn	"	3-27-1783
Moore, David	Pvt Mass	"	4-22-1776
Moore, Francis	Maj Ga	"	8-20-1782
Moore, George	N C	"	1778
Moore, Isaac	Capt 10 N C	"	7-10-1778
Moore, Jacob	Pvt 5 N C	"	4-28-1778
Moore, James	Brig. Gen NC	"	1-15-1777
Moore, James	Pvt Pa	"	1776

Moore, James	Pvt R I	Died	1779
Moore, John	2 SC	"	7-4-1776
Moore, John	Cpl 3 Pa	"	9- 1776
Moore, John	Pvt Pa	"	1779
Moore, John	Cpl 6 Pa	"	9- 1776
Moore, John	Pvt 3 N J	"	3-3-1777
Moore, John	R I	Killed	12-31-1775 Que
Moore, Joseph	Lt Conn	Died	1776
Moore, Josiah	Conn	"	1776
Moore, Kitt	Pvt Conn	"	8-9-1777
Moore, Lemuel	Pvt 5 N C	"	4-26-1778
Moore, Maurice Jr	Lt N C	Killed	1-18-1776
Moore, Ralph	Pvt 2 N C	Died	12-20-1778
Moore, Samuel	N H	"	1776
Moore, Willard	Maj Mass	Killed	6-7-1775
Moore, Zedekiah	Ens Md	Died	1- 1783
Moore, Thaddeus	Sgt 9 Mass	Killed	10-7-1777
Hooren, Benj.	Pvt Md	Died	2-2-1782
Moors, Simeon	Mass	"	1781
Horan, Benj	Pvt Md	"	2-2-1782
Moran, Patrick	2 SC	"	6-16-1776
Moredock, William	Pvt Va	"	2-15-1777
Morehead, Charles	Capt Va	"	1783
Morehouse, Thomas	Pvt Conn	Killed	12-7-1777
Moreton, Joshua	Pvt 4 Md	Died	7- 1779
Morey, Daniel	Mass	"	1783
Morey, James	Sgt 4 Mass	"	10-11-1777
Morey, Joseph	Pvt Conn	"	9-1-1777
Morgan, Able	Pvt 7 Pa	"	1-8-1777
Morgan, Christopher	Ens Conn	"	1781
Morgan, David	Capt Pa	"	1780
Morgan, Jereh	Pvt 3 Md	"	10-14-1778
Morgan, John	Mass	"	12- 1776
Morgan, John	Ens Va	Killed	1775 Que
Morgan, John	Pvt 18 Cont	Died	12- 1776
Morgan, John	Capt Pa	"	1782
Morgan, John	Pvt 12 Mass	"	11- 1778
Morgan, Johnson	Pvt 1 Md	"	7-25-1778
Morgan, Joshua	Pvt Conn	"	5-21-1778
Morgan, Nicholas	N Y	"	12-9-1782
Morgan, Phineas	Mass	"	5-26-1779
Morgan, Richard	Pvt 10 N C	"	9-23-1778
Morgan, Richd	Pvt 3 Md	"	10- 1778
Morgan, Thomas	Pvt 5 Md	"	11-1-1778
Morgan, William	Conn.	"	4-11-1777
Morrell, John	Pvt 14 Mass	"	1- 1779
Morrill, Ezekiel	N H	"	1783
Morrill, Henry	Col. Mass	"	1778
Morris Anthony	Capt N J	"	1-3-1777
Morris, Benjamin	Ens Pa	Killed	9-11-1777
Morris, Edmund	Pvt 5 Mass	Died	12-8-1777
Morris, Isaac	Pvt Mass	"	1778
Morris, James	Pvt 14 Mass	"	7-1-1778
Morris, James	Pvt 4 Mass	"	7-1-1777

Morris, Joseph	Maj N J	Died	1778
Morris, Joseph	Pvt Va	"	1778
Morris, Lewis Jr	N Y	"	1779
Morris, Michl	Pvt 3 Md	"	1-25-1778
Morris, Shadh	Pvt 5 N C	"	10-5-1777
Morris, Joseph	Maj 4 N J	"	1-7-1778
Morris, Joseph	Pvt Va	"	1778
Morris, Joseph	Maj N J	Killed	1-3-1777
Morris, Joseph	Lt N J	Died	1-5-1778
Morris, Joseph	Maj N. J	Died	1776
Morris, Joseph	Maj N J	"	12- 1775
Morrisett, Henry	Pvt 7 N C	"	3-28-1778
Morrison, Andrew	Va	"	1777
Morrison, George	Pvt 7 Md	"	4-4-1777
Morrison, John	Pvt 7 Mass	"	11-3-1779
Morrison, John	Pvt 8 Mass	Died	3-23-1777
Morrison, John	Pvt 2 N J	Killed	4-5-1778
Morrison, Thomas	N C	Died	1781
Morriss, John	R I	Killed	12-31-1775
Morrow, John	Pvt SC	"	1780
Morrow, Robert	Pvt Md	Died	1782
Morse, Caleb	N H	"	4-19-1775
Morse, Farrell	Pvt 6 N C	"	3-13-1778
Morse, Jacob	Pvt 4 Mass	"	7-27-1777
Morse, John Jr	Pvt Mass	"	8-29-1782
Morse, Joseph	Pvt 9 Mass	"	9-19-1777
Morse, Joseph	Md	"	1779
Morse, Joseph	Pvt Mass	"	12-16-1779
Morse, Mark	Mass	"	1783
Morse, Nathaniel	Sgt Vt	"	1781
Morse, Nathan	Pvt Mass	"	1783
Morse, Obadiah	Mass	"	1776
Morse, Pomp	Pvt Conn	"	4-10-1778
Morse, Thomas	Capt N H	"	1-7-1783
Morsell, John	Pvt 5 Md	"	8-10-1777
Morton, Jas	Pvt 4 Md	"	2-18-1777
Morton, John	Pa	"	1777
Morton, Samuel	Pvt 14 Mass	"	9-12-1777
Mortworth, Ingrahart	R I	Killed	12-31-1775 Que
Moseley, John	Mass	Died	9-1-1780
Moser, Cruise	Pvt 2 Md	Killed	8-16-1780
Moses, Daniel	Pvt Conn	Died	9-8-1776
Moses, David	Pvt 12 Mass	"	4- 1778
Moses, Henry	Pvt SC	"	7- 1781
Moses, Jacob	2 Pvt Md	"	3-15-1781
Moses, Moses	Pvt 7 Mass	"	12-31-1777
Moses, Sylvanus	N H	"	1-18-1782
Moses, Thomas	Pvt 18 Cont	"	7-23-1776
Mosier, John	Pvt Conn	"	7-10-1779
Moshier, William	Mass	"	1781
Mosley, John	Col Mass	"	9-1-1780
Moss, Elihu	Lt Conn	"	1778
Moss, Hugh	Maj Va	"	1780
Moss, Hugh	Pa	"	1780

Moss, Peter	Pvt Conn	Died	11-24-1778
Moss, Richard	Pvt 1 Mass	"	4-11-1778
Mossman, William	2 SC	"	9-2-1777
Mott, Charles	Capt SC	Killed	10-9-1779
Mott, Eliker	Mus. Conn	Died	7-20-1777
Motte, Charles	Maj SC	Killed	10-9-1779
Moul, Christoffel	Pvt N Y	Died	1783
Moulins, Antoine	France	"	1781
Moulton, Ebenezer	Mass	"	1783
Moulton, Gotham	Brig Gen Me	"	1777
Moulton, Jeremiah	Mass	"	1777
Moulton, Jothan	Brig Gen Va	"	5-12-1777
Moulton, Nathan	Pvt N H	"	6-2-1778
Moultrie, Thomas	Capt 2 SC	Killed	5- 1780
Movenhouse, Samuel	Pvt. N J	Died	4-12-1777
Moxley, Joseph	Pvt Conn	Killed	1781
Moxley, Joseph	N Y	Died	1781
Moyason, M William	3 Mass	"	8-4-1777
Moyer, Jacob	N Y	"	1777
Mudd, Martin	Sgt 1 Md	"	9-24-1778
Mugford, James	Capt Mass	Killed	5-19-1776
Muirhead, William	N J	Died	9-23-1776
Muirson, Heathcote	R I	"	7-27-1781
Mulford, David	N J	Killed	1777
Mulford, David	Col N Y	Died	1778
Mulford, Joseph	Pvt N J	"	3-21-1778
Mulatto, Dick P	Pvt Conn	"	5-31-1778
Muldroh, Robert	Pvt 6 Md	"	10-19-1778
Mull, Christian	Pvt Pa	"	1777
Mullen, Mich'l	Pvt 10 N C	"	12-8-1782
Muller, Nicolas	France	"	1781
Mullen, Dennes	Cpl Can	"	7-12-1777
Mumford, Augustus	Maj R I	Killed	8-27-1775
Mumford, Eben	Pvt 1 R I	Died	9-1-1780
Mumford, James	Sgt 4 N J	"	In War
Muncy, John	Lt N Y	Killed	1777
Mundin, Joseph	Pvt 10 N C	Died	12-20-1777
Munger, Elnathan	Pvt 4 Mass	"	10-5-1777
Munger, Aaron	Pvt Mass	"	11-2-1777
Munger, Wait	Pvt Conn	Killed	1777
Munn, Lewis	Pvt 4 Mass	Died	1-25-1778
Munro, Edmund	Q M N J	Killed	1778
Munro, George	N J	"	1778
Munroe, Abraham	Pvt 8 Mass	Died	3-11-1778
Munroe, Edmund	Capt 14 Mass	Killed	6-28-1778
Munroe, George	Pvt Mass	"	6-28-1778
Munroe, Zedediah	Pvt Mass	"	4-19-1775
Munroe, Joseph	Pvt Conn	Died	2-19-1778
Munroe, Josiah	Conn	"	1778
Munroe, Roberts	Ens Mass	Killed	4-19-1775
Munsell, Joel	Conn	Died	11-23-1777
Munsell, Jonathan	Conn	"	8-30-1780
Munson, T Moses	Pvt 2 Mass	"	5-12-1777
Munson, Peter	Mus Conn	"	6-12-1777

124

Munson, William	Pvt Conn	Died	4-1-1731
Murks, William	Pvt 3 N J	"	5-5-1777
Murphey, James	Pvt 2 Md	"	7-20-1778
Murphy, Cornelius	Pvt Can	"	1-14-1777
Murphy, Edmond	Pvt Conn	"	4-1-1777
Murphy, Henderson	Pvt Pa	"	6-3-1781
Murphy, Jas	Pvt 10 N C	"	10- 1781
Murphy, James	Pvt 2 Md	"	6-1-1778
Murphy, John	5 SC	"	12-29-1776
Murphy, John	Pa	"	7-3-1778
Murphy, Luke	Pvt Pa	"	1777
Murphy, Patrick	Pvt Va	"	2-15-1777
Murphy, Philip	Pvt 2 N J	Killed	4-5-1778
Murphy, Thos	Pvt Md	Died	1-28-1783
Murphy, Thos	Pvt 5 N C	"	2-3-1778
Murray, John	Pvt 4 Mass	"	7-1-1777
Murray, Joseph	Pvt N J	Killed	6-8-1780
Murray, Michael	Pvt 14 Mass	Died	6-28-1778
Murry, Solomon	Pvt Conn	"	8-11-1777
Murdock, Benjamin	Cpl N Y		1776
Murdock, Jesse	Pvt 2 Mass	"	10-31-1777
Mushaw, John	Pvt 10 N C	"	10-23-1778
Musquey, Anthony	1 SC	"	1-13-1780
Nutting, William	Cpl Conn	"	1776
Muzzy, Isaac	Mass	Killed	4-19-1775
Muzzy, James	Pvt 5 Mass	Died	6-20-1777
Myers, George	Md	"	1783
Nygatt, Austin		"	1776
Nygatt, Thomas	Pvt Conn	"	9-23-1782
Myhan, Wm	Pvt 10 N C	"	7-18-1778
Myres, Caspar	Pvt Va	"	2-16-1777
Nandain, Arnold Sr	Del	"	1782
Naramore, Samuel	Mass	"	12-4-1777
Naret, Nicolas	France	"	1781
Nash, Barnard	Pvt 1 Md	"	3-17-1777
Nash, Francis	Pvt 5 N C	"	3-1-1778
Nash, Francis	Brig Gen N C	Killed	10-4-1777
Nash, Francis	Lt Col Pa	"	1777
Nash, Isaac	Mass	"	8-17-1777
Nash, Jacob	Pvt	"	7-1-1779
Nash, John	SC	Died	2-12-1776
Nash, Noah	Mass	"	1775
Nash, Thomas	Pvt Mass	"	6-17-1778
Nason, Reuben	Pvt 18 Cont	"	9-30-1776
Nathan, Blood		"	In War
Neabit, Gotliep	Enc N C	"	12-11-1777
Neagle, William	Pvt 1 Md	"	2-4-1777
Neal, Andrew	Col N C	Killed	In War
Neale, Thomas	Pvt MD	Died	3-15-1781
Neble, Georges	France	"	1781
Nedson, John	Pvt Conn	"	4-25-1778
Needham, Anthony	Capt Mass	"	1783
Needham, Anthony	Conn	"	1783
Needham, Nathaniel	Pvt N H	"	1-2-1779

Name	Unit	Status	Date
Neele, William	Pvt SC	Died	5- -1781
Neeveling, Jacob	Pvt Pa	Killed	1777
Negro, Prince	Pvt Conn	Died	10-7-1777
Negro, Ned P	Pvt Conn	"	7-15-1778
Nehemiah, Frank	R I	"	12-23-1777
Neil, Christopher	SC	"	10-3-1776
Neil, Daniel	Capt N J	Killed	1-3-1777
Neil, Thomas	Col SC	"	1780
Neile, Samuel	Pvt Can	Died	4-17-1777
Neilson, Alexander	Del	"	1782
Neilson, Richard	Pvt Md	"	3-15-1781
Nelson, Arthur	Pvt 10 N C	"	10-24-1778
Nelson, Benjamin	Pvt 5 Mass	"	10- 1778
Nelson, Francis	Pvt 5 Mass	"	9-21-1777
Nelson, John	Pvt N Y	"	1777
Nelson, John	Pvt 1 N Y	"	1-22-1777
Nelson, Jonathan	Pvt Mass	"	9-12-1777
Nelson, Nehemiah	Pvt Mass	"	1782
Nelson, Samuel	N H	Killed	6-17-1775
Nelson, William	Lt Va	Died	12-4-1776
Nelson, William	Pvt 12 Mass	"	1-19-1778
Nelson, William	Pvt 5 N C	"	8-15-1778
Nenan, Nehemiah	Md	"	1781
New, Pierre	France	"	1781
Necomb, Simon	Conn	"	1776
Newell, Abra	Pvt 15 Mass	"	2- 1778
Newell, Samuel	Pvt 14 Mass	"	6-10-1778
Newell, William	Sgt 7 Md	Killed	10-4-1777
Newhall, Allen	Pvt Mass	Died	9-27-1781
Newhall, Ezra	Pvt Mass	"	3-2-1777
Newhouse, Anthony	Va	"	1780
Newman, Hugh	Sgt SC	Killed	10-9-1779
Newman, John	Mass	Died	12-17-1775
Newport, Daniel	Pvt 12 Mass	"	6-19-1778
Newport, James	Pvt 13 Mass	Killed	7-6-1777
Newsom, Aaron	Pvt 10 N C	Died	10-30-1778
Newton, Alvan	Mass	"	1778
Newton, Cyrus	Cpl Conn	"	9-21- 77
Newton, Edw'd	Pvt 10 N C	"	6-25-1783
Newton, Francis	Mass	"	4-18-1781
Newton or Tuton, Joseph	Pvt 7 Md	"	8-1-1777
Newton, Joseph	Pvt 5 Mass	"	1-25-1779
Newton, Solomon	Mass	"	1781
Newman, Solomon	Pvt 13 Mass	"	3-25-1777
Neyle, Philip	Lt 1 SC	Killed	5- 1780
Nettleton, Holan	Pvt Conn	Died	5-9-1777
Nettleton, William	Pvt Conn	"	1-7-1778
Neven, Edme	Cpl France	"	1781
Nevens, Phineas	N H	Killed	6-17-1775
Nevin, Ino	Sgt SC	Died	3-2-1778
Nevin, James P	SC	"	4- 1783
Nevin, William	SC	"	12-2- 1786
Neye, Jabez	Pvt 13 Mass	"	5-16-1778
Nicholas, Robert Carter	Va	"	1780

N

Name	Rank/Unit	Status	Date
Nicholas, Sam'l	Sgt 2 N C	Died	7-22-1777
Nicholls, Bristol	Pvt Conn	"	10-19-1777
Nichols, Abel	Sgt Mass	"	9-12-1778
Nichols, Daniel	Mass	"	6-11-1780
Nichols, Gorshorn	Pvt Conn	"	7-31-1779
Nichols, John	SC	Killed	1780
Nichols, Samuel	Capt Mass	Died	1781
Nichols, Samuel Jr	Mass	"	1781
Nicholson, Anthy	Pvt 4 Md	"	2- 1779
Nicholson, Geo.	Pvt Md	"	9-16-1779
Nick, Henry	Pvt R I	Killed	10-4-1777
Nickerson, Mark	Pvt 11 Mass	Died	8-24-1778
Nickles, Archibald	Pvt Can	"	1-12-1777
Nicols, Bethel P	Pvt Conn	Killed	7-11-1779
Niel, Jno	Pvt 3 N C	Died	11- 1777
Nightingale, Daniel	Pvt 7 Mass	"	5-8-1777
Niles, David	N Y	"	10-28-1776
Niles, David	Conn	Killed	1776
Niles, Joseph	Pvt 1 Mass	Died	4-14-1778
Nims, Asabel	Sgt N H	Killed	6-17-1775
Nixon, John	Pvt Va	Died	2-18-1777
Nixon, John	Lt Col SC	Killed	1781
Nixon, Robt	Pvt 5 Md	Died	1-14-1778
Nixon, Zachens	12 Mass	"	5-18-1777
Nixon, John	Pvt Pa	"	1777
Noble, Ashbel	Pvt 4 Mass	"	8-15-1777
Noble, David Sr	Pvt N Y	"	8-5-1776
Noble, Luke	Pvt Mass	"	1780
Noble, Martin	Pvt 2 Md	"	8-16-1780
Noble, Nathan	Pvt N Y	Killed	1777
Noble, Nathan	Me		1777
Noble, Simeon	Pvt 12 Mass	Died	7- 1778
Noble, Thomas	Pvt	Killed	In War
Nocake, Joseph	Pvt R I	Died	9-1- 1778
Noel, Jean	France	"	1781
Noland, Patrick	Pvt Md	"	9-1-1782
Noland, Patrick	Pvt 4 Md	"	8-29-1780
Nolloy, Dixon	Pvt 8 N C	"	1-10-1778
Nolly, Laurent	France	"	1781
Noonan, John	Navy	"	7-21-1781
Nooning, Wm	Pvt 4 N C	"	6-2-1778
Norcross, Daniel	Pvt Mass	"	1782
Normanton, William	Pvt 3 N J	"	3-2-1777
Norris, Cornelius	R I	Killed	12-31-1775 Que
Norris, John	Pvt Md	Died	1781
Norris, Philip	Pvt 4 Md	"	10-31-1778
Norris, Thomas	Pvt 3 N J	"	2-26-1779
Norris, William	Pvt 15 Mass	"	10-20-1777
Norris, William	Pvt SC	"	1781
Northrup, Abijah	Pvt Conn	"	10- 1779
Northrup, Amos	Lt Conn	"	3-19-1779
Northrup, Gamaliel	Lt Conn	"	1782
Norton, George	Pvt Conn	"	1777

N

Norton, George	Pvt NJ	Died	1777
Norton, George	Pvt Mass	"	12-26-1776
Norton, Henry	N Y	"	1781
Norton, Jacob	Mus 1 N C	"	7-28-1778
Norton, Job	Conn	"	1778
Norton, Robert	Pvt 5 Mass	"	5-10-1777
Norton, Robert	Pvt Mass		1783
Norton, William	Mus 1 N C	"	9- 1778
Norton, William	Pvt 4 N C	"	6-2-1778
Norwich, Martin	Mass	"	7-15-1778
Norwood, Peter	Pvt 8 Mass	"	7-30-1778
Noyelles, de Joh	N Y	"	1775
Noyes, Daniel	Mass	"	1781
Noyes, Thomas	Capt N H	"	7-30-1779
Noyce, Timo'y	Sgt R I	"	1-24-1778
Noyes, Wodleigh	Lt Mass	"	10-27-1777
Nuckolls, John	Pvt Va	Killed	1780
Nutter, Rober	Del	Died	2-5-1779
Nutting, Ephraim	Pvt Mass	"	1779
Nutting, John	Pvt 7 Mass	"	12-25-1777
Nutting, Robert	Pvt 4 Mass	"	10-23-1777
Nutting, Thomas	Pvt 7 Mass	"	12-1-1777
Nutting, William	Mass	"	1776
Nye, Isaac	Pvt 7 Mass	"	11-20-1777

O

Obannion, Thomas	Va	Died	In War
Ober, Benjamin	Capt Mass	"	1780 At Sea
O'Brien, Mark	Pvt	"	12-2-1776
O'Brien, John H	R I	"	4-22-1783
O'Bryan, John	Pvt 1 Md	"	4-25-1781
O'Caine, Dennis	Pvt	"	8-5-1776
O'Chout, Peter	Pvt 5 N Y	"	9-2-1777
O'Connell, Wm	Pvt 3 Md	"	1-24-1778
O'Daniel, Manuel	Pvt Conn	"	3-12-1777
Odin, Robt	Pvt 7 N C	"	12-25-1777
O'Donovan, Richard	SC	Killed	8-16-1778
Ogden, David	N J	Died	4-16-1777
Ogden, Edward	Pvt Pa	"	1777
Ogden, John	Pvt 9 Mass	"	8-13-1778
Ogden, Joseph	Pa	"	7-3-1777
Ogden, Moses	N J	"	6-7-1780
O'Hara, Joseph	Pvt 3 N J	"	11- 1778
O'Hara, William	Fifer 5 Md	"	11-22-1777
O'Key, John	Pvt 1 R I	"	9-3-1782
Olcott, Elisha	Conn	"	8-17-1776
Olcutt, B James	Pvt Conn	"	2- 28-1778
Oldham, Capt	Va	Killed	9-9-1781
Olds, Abner	Pvt 6 Mass	Died	4-29-1777
Olds, Ezekiel	Pvt Mass	"	1777
Olds, Zebulon	Pvt 1 Mass	"	3-20-1778
Clephant, Thomas	Pvt 5 Md	"	4-23-1778
Oliver, Olds	Pvt Conn	"	1781

O

Oliver, William	Cpl SC	Killed	10-9-1779
Olmstead, Israel	Pvt Conn	Died	1781
Olmstead, Jeremiah	Pvt Conn	"	2-18-1779
Olmstead, Justus	Pvt Conn	"	9-1-1782
Olmstead, Silas	Pvt Pa	"	1782
Olmstead, Silas	Pvt	"	1777
Olmsted, Jered	Pvt Conn	"	1779
Olmsted, Stephen	Conn	"	1778
Omsby, Tho	Pvt 1 R I	"	7-1-1778
Onderdonk, Abraham	N Y	Killed	1776
O'Neal, Daniel	Pvt 3 N J	Died	9-14-1777
O'Neal, William	Pvt Va	"	1778
O'Neil, James	Del	"	12-1-1782
Onissimus, John	Pvt 1 Mass	"	2-13-1778
Oquier, Louis	Pvt SC	"	1780
Oram, John	Pvt 3 N C	"	3-11-1778
Oram, Samuel	Pvt Md	"	9-1-1781
Orboeton, John	Pvt 14 Mass	"	6-28-1778
Organ, Thomas	Pa	"	1781
Orkengude, Erasmus	France	"	1781
Ormes, Jonathan	Pvt Conn	"	12-4-1777
Ormsby, Nathanl	Pvt 6 Mass	"	10-25-1777
Orr, Chas	Pvt 1 N C	"	1-20-1778
Orrick, Nicholas	Pvt Va	"	2-1-1781
Osborn, Alexander	N C	"	1776
Osborn, Danl	Pvt Conn	"	9-16-1777
Osborn, Ephraim	Pa	"	1779
Osborn, Ephraim	Mass	"	3-12-1779
Osborn, Ezekiel	Pvt Conn	"	1779
Osborn, John	Pvt 1 N J	"	11-5-1777
Osborn, William	Sgt 3 Md	"	1-24-1778
Osborne, Alexander	N C	"	7-11-1776
Osborne, Ephraim	Sgt Mass	"	1779
Osbourne, Absalom	Pvt 1 N J	"	2-17-1778
Osburn, Jonathan	Pvt 11 Mass	"	10-15-1779
Osgood, Jeremiah	Pvt Conn	Killed	4-20-1778
Osgood, John	Mass	Died	1775
Otis, Asher	Pvt 14 Mass	"	6-10-1778
Otis, David	Pvt Conn	"	1783
Otis, James	Mass	"	1783
Otis, James	Mass	"	1778
Otis, John	Pa	"	7-3-1778
Otis, Solomon	Mass	"	1780
Otto, Bodo Surg	Col N J	"	1782
Over, Thomas	Pvt 13 Mass	"	5-7-1778
Ovid, Scipio	Pvt 6 Mass	"	8-25-1777
Overton, Jno	Pvt 10 N C	"	9-9-1782
Overton, Joab	Cpl 7 N C	"	4-29-1779
Ovice, Eleazer	Pvt Conn	"	11-21-1778
Owen,	Capt SC	Killed	11- 1781
Owen, David	Pvt 6 N C	Died	4-28- 78
Owen, Omery	Pvt 3 N C	"	1- 1778
Owens, David	Pvt 13 Mass	"	4-1- 1778

129

		O		
Owens, John	Pvt 3 Md	Died	12- 1778
Owens, John	Pvt 5 N C	"	2-2-1778
Owens, Thos	Pvt 3 N Y	Killed	8-4-1777
Ozanne, Pierre	France	Died	1781

		P		
Pabst, Christian	France	Died	1781
Pack, James	Pvt 6 Md	"	10-4-1778
Packard, Marlborough	Pvt Mass	"	1781
Packer, William	Pa	"	7-3-1778
Paddleford, John	Dr Yale Conn	"	1779
Paddleford, Jonathan	N H	"	7-13-1783
Paddock, Elisha	Pvt 14 Mass	"	9-15-1777
Padelford, John	Mass	"	1779
Padrick, John	Pvt 2 N Y	"	6-20-1777
Page, Benjamin	N H	"	12-16-1782
Page, Jabez	N H	"	5-4-1782
Page, John	Rev N H	"	1-29-1782
Page, John	Pvt Mass	"	1782
Page, John	Lt Va	"	1780
Page, Jonathan	Pvt 7 Mass	"	6-10-1777
Page, Hathaniel	Mass	"	1779
Page, Timothy	Pvt Conn	"	4-17-1778
Pain, or Payne John	Capt N J	"	10-15-1781
Pain, John	Lt N J	Killed	9-25-1781
Paine, Benjamin	Conn	Died	1782
Paine, Daniel Jr	Conn	"	4-9-1777
Paine, Jerem	Pvt 1 Md	"	8-2-1777
Paine, Jonathan	Mass	"	1-3-1778
Paine, Nathaniel	Pvt 5 Mass	"	8-15-1778
Painter, Deliverance	Pvt	"	1781 At Sea
Painter, Elisha	Maj.	"	1-13-1781
Painter, George	Pvt Pa	"	1780
Palfrey, William	Mass	"	1777
Palfrey, William	Gen Mass	"	1780
Palis, Paul	France	"	1781
Palmier, Michel Joseph	Capt Ill	"	1780
Palmer, Abel	Pa	"	7-3-1778
Palmer, Allen	Pvt 1 R I	"	1-1-1779
Palmer, David	Conn	Killed	9-6-1781
Palmer, Elijah	Pvt Conn	Died	3-1-1778
Palmer, Henry	Pvt Pa	Killed	In War
Palmer, Jacob	Pvt 4 Md	Died	11- 1780
Palmer, James	Mass	Killed	10-28-1778
Palmer, John	Ens Conn	Died	9-18-1777
Palmer, Thomas	Pvt 2 Mass	"	10-4-1777
Palmeter, Joseph	Pvt 2 N Y	"	6-6-1778
Palmore, Joseph	Pvt 10 N C	"	7-13-1778
Pangborn, Limis	Pvt N J	Killed	12-30-1781
Pangman, Noah	Pvt 2 Mass	Died	1-12-1777
Paniolet, Jean	France	"	1781
Papelard, Jacques	Francois-France	"	1781
Paramore, Jas	Pvt 10 N C	"	10-20-1778
Parcel, Nicholas	N J	"	1780

130

P

Parcell, Thomas	Pvt N J	Died	1778
Pardee, Ebenezer	Pvt Conn	Killed	1776
Pardee, Isaac	Pvt	"	7-5-1779
Parfoot, Thomas	Pvt 5 Md	Died	4-2-1777
Paris, Claude Francois	France	"	1781
Paris, Gabriel	France	"	1781
Park, Aaron	Pvt 9 Mass	"	8-29-1777
Park, Andrew	Mass	"	7-6-1775
Park, Hezekiah	N Y	"	1776
Park, John	Pvt 11 Mass	"	10-1778
Park, John	Lt Pa	"	1780
Parke, Hezekiah	Cpl Conn	"	1778
Parke, James	Pvt 1 R I	"	11-27-1779
Parke, John	Lt Pa	Killed	1780
Parke, Silas	Pa	Died	7-3-1778
Parker, Abel	Pvt 11 Mass	"	11-8-1778
Parker, Benj	Pvt 9 Mass	"	8-14-1777
Parker, Bowen	Pvt SC	"	11-14-1777
Parker, Daniel	Pvt SC	"	1781
Parker, Ebenezer	Mass	"	1783
Parker, Eldad	Pvt Mass	"	7-5-1779
Parker, Fortune	Pvt Navy	"	7-21-1781
Parker, Henry	Pvt Pa	"	1777
Parker, James	Pa	"	1783
Parker, James	Pvt 10 Mass	"	9-23-1778
Parker, John	Pvt N J	"	3-4-1781
Parker, John	Pvt SC	"	11-25-1779
Parker, John	Mass	"	1778
Parker, John	Pvt 7 Mass	Killed	10-7-1777
Parker, John	Mass	"	1775
Parker, John		Died	9-7-1775
Parker, John	Mass	"	1783
Parker, James	Capt Mass	Killed	1775
Parker, John	Capt Md	Died	1775
Parker, John	Mass	"	9-17-1775
Parker, Jonas	Mass	Killed	4-19-1775
Parker, Jonathan	Me	Died	9-16-1775
Parker, Jonathan	Mass	Killed	4-19-1775
Parker, Joseph Sr	Mass	Died	1779
Parker, Kendal	Mass	"	1776
Parker, Killery	Pvt 10 NC	"	11-3-1779
Parker, Michael	Sgt N Y	"	1779
Parker, Moses	Lt Col Conn	Killed	6-17-1775
Parker, Nathaniel	Cpl Mass	"	6-17-1775
Parker, Richard	8 Va	Died	4-24-1780
Parker, Robert	N H	Killed	6-17-1775
Parker, Samuel Franklin	Maj N J	Died	1779
Parker, Thomas	Mass	"	4-9-1783
Parker, Timothy	Conn	"	1781
Parker, Walter	Pvt N Y	"	10-12-1777
Parkerson, James	Lt N C	"	In War
Parkhurst, Hugh	Mass	Killed	6-6-1776
Parkins, Abraham	Pvt 2 Mass	Died	3-20-1778
Parkinson, James	Lt 2 N C	"	3-26-1778
Parkinson, Jos.	Lt N C	"	3-26-1778

Parks, Andrew	Pvt 5 Mass	Died	11-1-1777
Parks, Sam'l	Pvt 7 N C	"	11-27-1777
Parmelee, Amos	Pvt Conn	"	1779
Parmelee, Daniel	Capt Conn	"	6-25-1780
Parmelee, Jeremiah	Ens Conn	"	1778
Parmelie, Jeremiah	Capt Conn	"	3-24-1778
Parmelie, Josiah	Capt Conn	"	3-24-1778
Parmenter, Jacob	Mass	"	1776
Parmenter, James	Mass	"	1781
Parmer, David	Pvt 6 Mass	"	10-5-1777
Parmeter, Amaziah	Pvt 2 Mass	"	10-29-1777
Parr, Kediah Aronson	N J	"	8-24-1771
Parriott, Is	Pvt 3 Md	"	8-4-1777
Parrott, George	Pvt Md	"	1779
Parsons, Gould	Pvt 11 Mass	"	11-11-1777
Parsons, Josiah	Lt Me	"	1780
Parsons, Oliver	Pvt Conn	"	7-2-1777
Parsons, John	Sgt 4 N Y	"	9-22-1777
Parsons, John	Pvt 6 Md	Killed	8-16-1778
Parsons, William	N H	"	6-17-1775
Partree, Emanuel	Pvt 4 N C	Died	10-4-1777
Partridge, Arthur	Pvt 5 Mass	"	9-31-1777
Partridge, Benjamin	Mass	"	9-16-1776
Partridge, Peter	Pvt 6 Mass	"	2-19-1778
Partridge, Samuel	N H	"	1776
Parvin, Benjamin	Cpl 2 N J	"	5-8-1777
Passage, George	Pvt N Y	Killed	1778
Passage, Henry	N Y	"	1778
Passell, Nicholas	Pvt N J	"	6-7-1780
Patch, Samuel	Pvt 9 Mass	Died	6-15-1778
Patch, Simon	Mass	"	1775
Patchen, Azar	Pvt Conn	"	8-16-1781
Patchen, Josiah	Conn		1781
Patchin, David	Pvt Conn	"	11-22-1781
Patrick, McGalls	Pvt Pa	"	4-1-1776
Patrick, Samuel	Pvt N J	"	1780
Patrick, William	Capt 7 Mass	"	5-20-1778
Pattee, Seth	Cpl N H	"	1780
Patten, John	Lt N H	"	6-20-1776
Patten, Nathaniel	Pvt Mass	"	1780
Patten, Samuel	Pvt Conn	"	11-15-1777
Patten, James	N H	Killed	6-17-1775
Patterson, Arthur	SC	Died	10-7-1780
Patterson, David	Pvt 10 Mass	"	11-9-1777
Patterson, Samuel	Pvt 2 N J	"	4-22-1777
Patterson, William	N C	"	10-7-1780
Patterson, William	Navy	"	7-21-1781
Patton, William	Lt Pa	Killed	10-4-1777
Paul, Stephen	Pvt 5 N C	Died	9-17-1777
Paul, William	Pvt 5 Md	"	4-12-1777
Paul, William	Pvt Conn	"	4-15-1778
Paulard Jean-Baptiste	France	"	1781
Paulint, Antoine	Capt Mass	"	1781
Paulson, John	Del	"	1782
Pawling, Levi	Col N Y	"	1782

Paybody, Benjamin	Pvt SC	Killed	10-9-1779
Payne, John	Capt N J	Died	10-15-1781
Payne, Josiah	Tenn	"	1782
Payne, William	Capt Va	"	1782
Peabody, John	Mass	"	7-29-1780
Peabody, Nathaniel	Mass	"	8-17-1778
Peabody, Seth	Pvt 7 Mass	"	9- 1777
Peabody, Stephen	Col N H	"	9-19-1782
Peacock, Adjoyjak	N J	Killed	1777
Peacock, Josiah	Pvt SC	Died	5-10-1779
Peacock, Thomas	Pvt Md	Killed	9-8-1781
Pearse, Abraham	Pvt R I	Died	9-1-1778
Pearson, Ebenezer	Mass	"	1779
Pearson, Ephraim	Pvt Conn	"	1776
Pease, Mathew	Pvt 7 Mass	"	11-20-1777
Pease, Samuel	Pvt Mass	"	5-30-1778
Pease, Uriah	Pvt Conn	"	11-14-1777
Pechin, Christopher	Pa	"	10-26-1779
Peck-Abel	Pa	"	1778
Peck, Calvin	Pvt 14 Mass	"	10-10-1778
Peck, Constant	Lt N J	"	4-9-1776
Peck, William	Mass	"	1776
Peck, Harmanus	Pvt N Y	"	1781
Peck, Hezekiah	Mass	"	10-4-1775
Peck, Ichabod	Lt Col R I	"	1776
Peck, James	Pvt Pa	"	11-18-1780
Peck, Jesse	Conn	"	1777
Peck, Jesse	N Y	"	1777 Prison
Peck, Moses	N J	"	1783
Peck, Nathaniel	Conn	"	1777
Peck, Tetus	Lt Conn	"	1776
Peck, Sylvester	Pvt 14 Mass	"	10-31-1778
Peck, William	Pvt Can	"	10-22-1781
Pecke, Ichabod	Pvt 1 R I	"	1-30-1778
Pecker, James	Surg Mass	"	1778
Pedrick, John	Pvt N Y	"	1777
Peebles	Capt Pa	"	9-2-1776
Peebles, Robert	Mass	"	1778
Peebles, William	N Y	"	1776
Peebles, William	Capt Pa	"	1776
Peek, Hermans	N Y	"	1781
Peers, Edmund	N H	Killed	6-17-1775
Peet, Abel	Pvt Conn	Died	4-30-1777
Pegon, Samuel	Pvt 7 Mass	"	1-31-1778
Peirce, Benjamin	Mass	"	1775
Peirson, Charles	France	"	1784
Peirce, David	Ens Mass	"	3-9-1779
Pelitier, Jacques	France	"	1781
Peltingill, Benjamin	Pvt N H	"	12-3-1779
Peltingill, Samuel	N Y	Killed	1777
Pemberton, Henry	Pvt Pa	Died	10-2-1776
Pemel, Jno	Pvt 4 N C	"	11- 1777
Pencil, Henry	Pa	"	7-2-1778
Pendar, John	Pvt Md	"	11-10-1781

P

Name	Rank/Unit	Status	Date
Pendell, Peleg	Pvt 2 Mass	Died	7-5-1777
Pendel, Tobias	Pvt Conn	"	5-10-1778
Pendleton, Joshua	Pvt Conn	"	1-6-1778
Pendleton, John	Pvt SC	"	5- 1781
Pendergast, Thomas	N H	"	5-20-1781
Pane, Jesse	Pvt Mass	"	8-5-1775
Pengra, George	Pvt Vt	"	1775
Penick, Thomas	Pvt 2 N J	"	8-8-1777
Peninger, Christopher	Pvt Va	"	2-15-1777
Penn, John	Pvt 4 Md	"	12-10-1777
Pennel	Maj Conn	"	10-19-1775
Penniman, Silas	Mass	"	5-12-1777
Penniman, William	Mass	"	1780
Pennington, John	Pvt 2 Md	"	9- 1778
Penny, Aaron	Pvt Conn	Killed	10-1-1777
Penny, Philaster	Pvt Conn	Died	6-28-1778
Perkins, Abijah	Conn	"	8-31-1778
Perkins, Abin	Pvt 9 N C	"	3-5-1778
Perkins, Brown	Pvt Mass	"	1778
Perkins, Elanthan	Conn	Killed	9-6-1781
Perkins, Elisha	Conn	"	9-6-1781
Perkins, Jacob	Mass	Died	1-11-1777
Perkins, James	Lt N H	"	1776
Perkins, Jesse	Pvt Conn	"	9-21-1782
Perkins, John	Ens 18 Cont	"	4-18-1776
Perkins, John	Pvt Pa	Killed	1778
Perkins, Luke	Conn	Died	9-6-1781
Perkins, Moses	N Y	"	1777
Perkins, Moses	Mass	"	7-21-1776
Perkins, Thomas		"	7-21-1781 Prison
Perkins, Stephens	Pvt 12 Mass	"	11- 1778
Perlee, Peter	N J	"	4-18-1781
Perley, Francis	Sgt Mass	"	3-4-1780
Perley, John	Mass	"	1778
Perrin, Charles	Pvt 12 Mass	"	4-6-1778
Perry	Capt SC	Killed	7-7-1781
Perry, Anthony	Mass	Died	1781
Perry, Cuff	Pvt 14 Mass	"	3-24-1778
Perry, Ezra	Pvt Mass	"	1783
Perry, Ganset	Pvt 1 R I	"	9-1-1778
Perry, Henry	Pvt R I	"	5-1-1777
Perry, James	Pvt Mass	"	9-12-1779
Perry, Jonathan	Pvt Mass	"	1783
Perry, Samuel	Pvt Mass	"	2-14-1781
Perry, William	Md	"	1783
Perry, William	Ens Mass	"	10-10-1777
Perry, William	Pvt 14 Mass	"	10-14-1777
Perry, Wm	Pvt 6 N C	"	3-13-1778
Perwiggin, Solomon	Pvt Conn	"	3-20-1778
Peter, Jack	N C	"	1780
Peters, Benj	Pvt 1 R I	Killed	10-23-1777
Peters, Joseph	Pvt 2 Md	Died	7-18-1778
Peters, Joseph	Pvt Conn	"	In War

P

Name	Rank/Unit	Status	Date
Peters, Simon	Pvt 9 Mass	Died	12-27-1778
Peters, Thomas	Pvt Conn	"	9-1-1779
Petrie, Dedrick Marcus	Lt NY	Killed	8-6-1777
Pettebone, Noah Jr	Pa	Died	7-3-1778
Pettee, Ebenezer	Mass	"	1783
Pettengill, Andrew	Lt N H	"	1777
Petterson, Perry John	Pvt R I	"	4-8-1778
Pettibone, Jonathan	Capt N Y	"	1776
Pettibone, Jonathan Jr	Pvt Conn	"	9-26-1776
Pettibone, Jonathan	Col Conn	"	1776
Pettibone, Samuel	Conn	"	12-25-1776
Pettingall, Samuel	Capt	Killed	1777
Pettingil, Samuel	Capt N Y	Died	1777
Pettingill, Andrew	N H	"	1777
Pettingill, Cutting	Pvt 9 Mass	"	3-1-1778
Pettingill, David	Pvt Mass	"	1778
Petty, Pettit	Capt N C	Killed	In War
Petyjohn, Thos	Cpl 10 N C	Died	1-19-1779
Peyton, Henry	Col Md	"	1781
Peyton, George	Ens Va	"	12-15-1776
Peyton, Robert	Lt Va	Killed	9-11-1777
Pfeifer, Frederick	Pa	Died	7-11-1777
Pharaoh, Abiah	Pvt Conn	"	5-15-1778
Phelps, Amos	Pvt Conn	"	1777
Phelps, Benja	Pvt Md 1	"	10-27-1778
Phelps, Edward	Pvt Mass	"	1-16-1776
Phelps, Elisha	N. Y	"	1776
Phelps, Elisha	Conn	"	7-14-1776
Phelps, Ezekiel	Lt Conn	"	1781
Phelps, Ezra	Pvt Conn	"	4-2-1778
Phelps, Ichabod	Sgt Conn	"	1776
Phelps, Isaac	Conn	"	1777
Phelps, Nathaniel	Pvt Conn	"	1781
Phelps, Noah	Ens Conn	"	3-16-1778
Phelps, Robert	Sgt Mass	Killed	6-17-1775
Phifer, John	N C	Died	1778
Philip, Arnold	R I	"	4-19-1783
Philip, William	Sgt 6 Md	"	2-15-1778
Philip, Wm	Pvt 10 N C	"	6-6-1783
Phillippi, John	Sgt Pa	"	1781
Philips, Abraham	Pvt 6 Md	"	8-9-1777
Philips, Amasa	Pvt 2 Mass	"	6-18-1778
Philips, Andrew	Pvt 4 N J	"	10- 1777
Philips, Daniel	Pvt 4 Mass	"	1-25-1778
Philips, George	Pvt Md	"	4-15-1781
Philips, James	Ens SC	"	10-7-1780
Philips, Noah	Ens Conn	"	3-16-1778
Philips, Samuel	Ens Va	Killed	1782
Philips, Toney	Pvt 1 R I	Died	2-22-1783
Philips, Wm	Pvt R I	"	5- 1778
Philips, William	Pvt SC	"	9-6- 1779
Philips, Zacha	Pvt 10 N C	"	1-16-1783
Phillips, Ayre	Pvt Conn	"	1775
Phillips, Geo	Pvt 1 Md	"	3- 1781

P

Name	Rank/Unit		Date
Phillips, Isaac	Pvt 14 Mass	Died	4-12-1778
Phillips, Jon	Pvt 4 N Y	"	12-14-1779
Phillips, Noah	Ens Conn	Killed	3-16-1778
Phillips, Samuel	Pvt 14 Mass	Died	4-20-1778
Phillips, Shuball	Pvt Conn	"	12-9-1777
Phillips, William	Sgt 6 Md	"	2-15-1778
Phineas, Sargent	Cpl Mass	"	1776
Phinney, Eli	Mass	"	3-3-1777
Phinney, John Sr.	Me	"	12-29-1780
Piatt, Daniel	Maj N J	"	4-16-1780
Pickard, Samuel	Mass	"	1778
Pickens, John	Mass	"	2- 1779
Pickens, Joseph W. W.	Capt SC	"	6- 1781
Pickering, John	Pvt Md	Killed	6-18-1781
Picot, John	N Y	Died	1-13-1777
Pidgin, Moses	Mass	Killed	6-17-1775
Pierce, Benjamin	Capt Conn	Died	1782
Pierce, Benjamin	Pvt Mass	Killed	4-19-1775
Pierce, Benjamin	Mass	Died	5-9-1781
Pierce, Ebenezer	Pvt Vt	Killed	1777
Pierce, Hardy	Pvt 10 N C	Died	10- 1778
Pierce, Hardy	Lt Mass	"	9-12-1781
Pierce, John	Pa	"	7-3-1778
Pierce, Moses	Mass	"	1777
Pierce, Nathan	Capt N H	"	1776
Pierce, Samuel	Lt Conn	"	10-1-1776
Pierce, Solomon	Pvt 14 Mass	"	10-11-1777
Pierce, Theaps	Pvt 5 N C	"	5-21-1778
Pierce, Thos	Pvt 2 N C	"	1-2-1778
Pierce, Thos	Pvt 5 N C	"	10- 1778
Pierce, Timothy	Lt Pa	Killed	7-3-1778
Pierce, William	Pvt N C	Died	1779
Pierre, Beher	France	"	1781
Pierre, Gilles	France	"	1781
Pierson, Charles	France	"	1781
Pierson, Ephraim	Pvt Ga	"	1776
Pierson, John Child	Cpl 11 Pa	"	11-2-1777
Pigeon, Moses	Mass	Killed	6-17-1775
Pike, Benjamin	Capt 6 N C	Died	10-11-1777
Pike, John	Pvt N J	Killed	2-5-1779
Pike, Simeon	Pvt Mass	Died	1775
Pike, Simeon	N H	Killed	6-17-1775
Piles, James	Va	Died	1778
Pillsbury, Caleb	Capt Mass	"	1778
Pindall, Nicks	Pvt 1 Md	"	7-31-1779
Pinegar, Edmund	Cpl R I	"	1782
Pinney, Abraham	Capt Conn	"	9-12- 80
Pinney, Benjamin	Capt Conn	"	11-25-1777
Pinnox, Isaac	Pvt 6 Md	"	3- 1779
Pipkin, Wm.	Pvt 10 N C	"	8-9- 1782
Pisgusk, Henry	Pvt 1 R I	"	1-23-1778
Pitcher, Ezra	Pvt 1 Mass	"	6- 1778
Pitman, John	Pvt 3 N Y	"	6-9- 1780

P

Pitt, John	Surg Va	Died	1779
Pithpen, Prince	Pvt	"	1-15-1780
Pitts, Spencer	Pvt SC	"	8-12-1776
Plains, Jordan	Pvt Conn	"	4-30-1778
Plant, Timothy	Pvt Conn	"	1777
Platt, Bayles	Maj N J	"	1777
Plimpton, Daniel	Lt Col Mass	"	1777
Plumb, Amariah	Pvt Conn	"	3-1-1778
Plume, Isaac	Ens N J	"	1779
Plummer, Davis	Pvt N H	"	7-26-1778
Poague, William	Ky	Killed	1778
Pock, Frederick	Pvt 1 R I	Died	9-28-1777
Pocknot, Hosea	Pvt 14 Mass	"	3-28-1778
Pognet, Daniel	Pvt 12 Mass	"	2-9-1778
Poguet, Joseph	Pvt 6 Mass	"	11-15-1777
Poheague, Josias	Conn	"	1781
Polch, William	6 Pa	"	9-22-1776
Polk, Thomas	Lt N C	Killed	9-8-1781
Polk, William	Lt SC	"	9-8-1781
Pollard, Asa	N H	"	6-17-1775
Pollard, Benjamin	Lt Mass	Died	1777
Pollard Kinsey	Pvt 2 Md	"	1778
Pollard, Wm	Pvt 1 R I	"	2-19-1778
Polley, Joseph	Mass	"	1776
Polly, William	Mass	Killed	4-19-1775
Polston, Emanuel	Pvt 4 Md	Died	7-30-1778
Pomp 'A Negro)	Conn	Killed	7-6-1779
Pomp, Peter	N H	Died	3-15-1778
Pomp, Richard	R I	"	5-13-1778
Pompy, David	Pvt Conn	"	4-23-1778
Pompy, John	Pvt Conn	"	5-1-1778
Pomeroy, Joseph	Pvt 3 Pa	Killed	9-23-1779
Pomeroy, Oliver	Lt Conn	Died	1776
Pomeroy, Seth	Brig Gen Mass	"	2-19-1777
Pomeroy, William P	Pvt Conn	"	2-23-1778
Pond, John	Pvt Conn	"	4-1-1777
Pond, John	Pvt Conn	"	3-29-1777
Pond, John	Lt N Y	"	10-26-1776
Pond, P	Corp Can	"	10-28-1778
Pond, Timothy	Pvt Conn	"	1780
Pond, Stephen	Mass	"	1776
Poneague, Josias	Conn	"	1781
Pool, Francis	Mass	Killed	6-17-1775
Poole, Eleazar Flogg	Lt Mass	Died	1776
Poole, Jacob	Lt Mass	"	6-13-1776
Poole, John	Pvt Can	Killed	9-4-1777
Poor, Enoch	Brig Gen N J	Died	9-8-1780
Poor, Moses	N H	Killed	6-17-1775
Poor, Nicholas	Navy	Died	7-21-1781
Poor, Peter	N H	Killed	6- 1775
Popens, John	Pvt 12 Mass	Died	7-16-1777
Popham, Francis	Matross Md	Killed	7- 1781
Porter, Aaron	Pvt Conn	Died	9-23-1778
Porter, Abner	N J	"	In War

P

137

Name	Unit	Fate	Date
Porter, Asabel	Mass	Killed	4-19-1775
Porter, Ⅱ Eleazer	Pvt 12 Mass	Died	2-22-1778
Porter, Jacob	Pvt Mass	"	10-26-1778
Porter, Jonathan	Mass	"	4-17-1782
Porter, Wm	Pvt 1 N C	"	3-5-1778
Porter, William	Pvt Conn	"	1778
Portress, Jno	Pvt 3 N C	"	5-1- 1778
Porterfield, Dennis	Capt 5 N C	Killed	9-8-1781
Porterfield, Charles	Col Va	"	8-16-1780
Porterfield, Charles	Lt Col N J	Died	1782
Post, Jeremiah	Capt N H	"	8-16-1777
Post, Peter	Lt N Y	"	1782
Pothress, William	Lt Va	"	1783
Polster, Peter	Pvt 5 Md	"	4-6-1777
Potter, Asa	Pvt 1 R I	Killed	10-22-1777
Potter, Benjamin	Pvt Mass	Died	2-26-1783
Potter, Isaac	Pvt 2 N Y	"	3-20-1778
Potter, Joel	Lt Conn	"	1778
Potter, Saml	Pvt 8 N C	"	9- 1777
Potter, Saml	Sgt 1 R I	"	10-1-1777
Potterfield	Capt N C	Killed	9-9-1781
Potts, William	Pvt N J	Died	1783
Potwine, John	Pvt Conn	"	8-21-1775
Powell, James	Pvt Md	"	1777
Powell, James	Pvt 5 Md	"	8-15-1778
Powell, John	Cpl 7 Md	Killed	10-4-1777
Powell, Miles	Lt Col Mass	Died	1781
Powell, Moses	Pvt 6 Pa	Killed	9-6-1776
Powell, Peter	Pvt 2 N J	Died	12-30-1779
Powell, Stephen	Pvt 10 N C	"	5-18-1783
Powell, Thomas	Lt Va	"	1782
Powers, David	Pvt 2 N C	"	5-3-1778
Powers, Eliot	Pvt N H	"	1783
Powers, Jonathan	Mass	"	1775
Powers, Stephen	Mass	"	1775
Powers, Stephen	Surg Mass	"	1780
Powers, Stephen	N H	"	1775
Pratt, Benjamin	Pvt 9 Mass	"	3-4-1778
Pratt, Daniel	Pvt 13 Mass	"	6-9-1778
Pratt, Ebenezer	Cpl Mass	"	10-26-1778
Pratt, Edward	N H	"	4-27-1781
Pratt, Ephraim	Mass	"	1776
Pratt, Ephraim	N Y	"	1776
Pratt, Jno	Cpl 5 Md	"	11-27-1777
Pratt, Jonathan	N Y	"	8-30-1776
Pratt, Micah	Pvt 12 Mass	"	1-20-1779
Pratt, Nehemiah	Mass	"	8-7-1778
Pratt, Reuben	Conn	"	1783
Pratt, Rufus	Vt	"	9-19-1777
Pratt, Solomon	Mass	"	1776
Pratt, Timothy	Pvt 11 Mass	Killed	7-7-1777
Pratt, William	Pvt N H	Died	12-20-1777

P

Prebble, Abraham	Pvt 10 Mass	Died	6-21-1778
Preble, David	Pvt 1 Mass	"	7-15-1779
Prentice, John	Lt Conn	"	1780
Prescott, Aaron	Pvt SC	"	1-21-1777
Prescott, Aaron	SC	"	1781
Prescott, Aaron	Pvt 4 N C	"	11-4-1777
Prescott, Benj	Sgt N H	Killed	6-17-1775
Prescott, Charles	Pvt 4 N C	Died	8-15-1777
Prescott, James	Mass	"	1780
Prescott, Thos	Pvt 10 N C	"	3-20-1778
Preston, And	Pvt 2 Md	"	7-4-1779
Preston, Isaac	Col N J	"	1777
Preston, William	Col N C	"	1783
Preston, William	N C	Killed	1783
Price, Benj A	Pvt 3 N Y	Died	8-10-1777
Price, Isaac	Pvt Va	"	2-5-1777
Price, John	Lt Pa	"	1780
Price, Micajah	Pvt 7 N C	"	11-15-1777
Price, Thomas	Pvt 6 Md	"	8-18-1778
Price, Samuel	Pvt N J	"	In War
Price, William	Pvt N C	"	1779
Prichad, William	W Va	"	1777
Pridgion, Thos	Cpl 8 N C	"	10- 1778
Priest, Gabriel	Mass	"	1781
Prindell, Enos P	Pvt Conn	"	10- 1778
Prince, James Jr	Pvt Mass	"	1775
Prince, Thomas	Mass	"	10-17-1783
Prince, Tukry	Pvt Conn	"	2- 1779
Prince, William	Pvt 3 Pa	"	11-25-1777
Prince, Jethro	Pvt 7 Mass	"	9-25-1777
Prime, Ebenezer	Rev N Y	"	10-2-1779
Prime, Ebenezer	Chap Mass	"	8-2-1779
Primier, John	N Y	"	1781
Prior, William	Pvt Md	"	2-15- 1781
Pritchard, James	Pvt 2 Md	"	7-18-1778
Pritchard, Jese	Sgt 6 N C	"	2- 1778
Pritchard, Jabez	Lt Conn	"	1777
Pritchard, Sam	Cpl 4 Md	"	3-10- 1777
Pritchard, Thos	Pvt 2 N Y	"	3-24- 1778
Proctor, Charles	Pvt 1 Md	"	11-3-1778
Proctor, James	N Y	"	1776
Proctor, James	Pvt N H	"	1776
Proctor, James	Pvt 6 Mass	"	3- 1777
Proctor, James		"	7-21-1781 Prison
Proctor, John	Del	"	8-5-1778
Proctor, Jonas	Pvt Mass	"	11-6-1783
Proctor, Walter	Pvt 1 Md	"	3-10-1779
Pronty, Isaac	Pvt Mass	"	In War
Pron, Joseph	France	"	1781
Proux, Pierre	France	"	1781
Provot, Charles	France	"	1781
Pruddin, Moses	Lt N J	"	1-11-1777
Puffer, Lazarus	Pvt Conn	"	1-15-1778
Puffer, Phineas	Mass	"	1781

Pugh, Willis	Ens Va	Died	5-1-1777
Pugh, Willis	Ens Va	"	1782
Pulaski, Casimir	Count Poland	Killed	10-9-1779
Pullam, Wm	Pvt SC	Died	5- 1781
Pulsifer, Benjamin	Pvt 9 Mass	"	5- 1778
Pulsifer, Ebenezer		"	1781 Prison
Purdy, Abraham	N Y	"	4-17-1778
Purdy, Jonathan	N Y	"	1783
Purnall, Thomas	Navy	"	7-21-1781
Putnam	Pvt Mass	Killed	1775
Putnam, Aaron	N Y	"	1780
Putnam, Ephraim	Vt	Died	1777
Putnam, Henry	Mass	Killed	4-19-1775
Putnam, Lodiwick	N Y	Died	5-21-1780
Putnam, Porley	Mass	Killed	4-19-1775
Pyam, Cushing	Capt Mass	Died	1776

		Q	
Qitten, Peter	Pvt R I	Died	3-10-1777
Gvocke, James	Pvt R I	"	3-5- 1778
Guockenbush, John	Pvt 1 NY	"	5-23-1777
Quameny, Charles P	Conn	"	3-1- 1778
Quarles, John	Lt Va	"	9- 1780
Quay, James	Pvt 4 Md	Killed	7-16-1779
Queenault, Paul	Capt Del	Died	12-1-1782
Querry, Samuel	Lt 2 SC	"	7-12-1779
Quicksill, John	Capt N J	"	1783
Quigg, Henry	Pvt 3 N J	"	10-4-1777
Quiggins, Henry	Pvt 3 Md	"	8-16-1777
Quiggle, Christian	Pvt N Y	"	1782
Quigley, Christian	Pvt Pa	"	1782
Quigley, James	Pa	"	1782
Quimby, Andrew	Pvt N H	"	1783
Quincy, Josiah Jr	Mass	"	1775

		R	
Raab, Carl	Lt French Navy	Killed	9-5-1781
Rabb, William	Pvt N C	"	10-7-1780
Radcliffe, William	Capt SC	"	11-7-1781
Radly, William	Pvt 2 N J	Died	11-24-1777
Raidy, Edmd	Pvt 6 Md	"	2-9-1777
Ralpalje, John	Pvt N Y	"	1783
Ralph, John	Pvt 1 N C	"	4-4-1778
Rammage, Alexander	Sgt N C	"	3-19-1779
Ramage, Alexr	Cpl 9 N C	"	3-19-1779
Ramage, Thos	Pvt 10 N C	"	10-15-1781
Ramage, Thomas	Pvt 1 N C	"	10-15-1781
Ramsay, Daziell	Pvt N C	"	10-7- 1781
Ramsay, John	Surg Pa	"	1776
Ramsay, Mills	Pvt 7 N C	"	1-2-1778
Ramsdale, Amos	Mass	"	2-9-1781
Ramsdell, Abednago	Pvt Mass	"	4-19-1775
Ramsdell, Nehemiah	Pvt Mass	"	11- 1782
Ramsey, John	Surg Pa	"	11-4-1776

Name	Rank/Unit	Status	Date
Ranier, Ichabod	3 N Y	Died	6-8-1778
Randolph, James	Fitz Pvt NY	"	1781
Rankin, Jonathan	Pvt N H	"	3-28-1778
Ranside, Andrew	Pvt Md	"	1782
Ransom, Samuel	Capt Md	Killed	7-3-1778
Ranstead, John	N H	"	1777
Ranaal, Moses	Pvt 6 Mass	Died	10-15-1777
Randall, Moses	Pvt 3 N Y	"	7-22-1778
Randle, Harry	Pvt 3 N Y	"	10-16-1781
Rahdolph, James	Fitz N Y	"	1781
Randolph, Malachia	F Pvt N J	"	1776
Raphel	Lt 4 SC	"	10- 1777
Rasko, Tekal	Cpl 1 N C	"	2-24-1778
Ratley, John	Pvt 3 N C	"	7-30-1778
Ravelia, Lewis	Pvt 1 NY	"	1- 1779
Ravertz, John	Pvt	"	7- 1777
Rawlins, Benjamin	Cpl N H	"	1777
Rawlings, Stephen	W Va	"	1783
Rewson, Thomas	Pvt Mess	"	1776
Raymond, Jonathan	Pvt Mass	"	1783
Raynsford, Richard	Conn	"	9-16-1775
Ray, Samuel	Pvt 1 Md	"	3-10-1780
Ray, Stephen	Pvt 7 N C	"	3-31-1778
Ray, Thomas	N C	"	1781
Ray, William	Sgt 5 Md	"	3-11-1778
Raymond, John	Mass	Killed	4-19-1775
Raymond, Nathaniel	Sgt Conn	Died	1779
Raymond, Newport	Pvt Conn	"	6-15-1777
Raymond, Sig	Pvt Conn	"	8-1-1777
Raymond, Solomon	Pvt Conn	"	4-9-1778
Raymond, William	Mass	"	1780
Rayne, William	Pvt 6 Md	"	9-27-1778
Rebbinder, Baron	Lt French Navy	Killed	4-12-1782
Read, Benjamin	Pvt R I	Died	1775
Read, Clement	Lt Va	"	8- 1781
Read, Isaac	Col Va	"	1781
Read, Oliver	Lt Mass	"	1780
Read, Samuel	N H	"	4-24-1783
Reamond, Job	12 Mass	"	2-5-1777
Reeson, Jacob	Pvt 6 Md	"	1-29-1779
Reddick, James	Del	"	12-4-1779
Redlon, Ebenezer	N Y	"	1777
Redner, George	Music 7 NC	"	11-4-1777
Redpith, John	Lt 4 N C	"	10-13-1777
Reed, Asahel	Mass	Killed	4-19-1775
Reed, Benjamin	Vt	"	6-17-1775
Reed, Benjamin	Lt 6 Mass	Died	9-19-1777
Reed, Calvin	Pvt 4 Mass	"	7-17-1777
Reed, Isaac	Col 4 Va	"	9- 1778
Reed, James	Pvt 3 Md	"	6- 1778
Reed, Jeremiah P	Pvt Conn	"	1-2-1778
Reed, John Jr	Mass	"	1780
Reed, Joseph	Sgt 1 N C	"	8-7-1777

Reed, Joshua	Mass	Died	1779
Reed, Michael	Pvt Pa	"	1782
Reed, William	Capt Mass	"	3-29-1778
Reed, William	Mass	"	1-13-1782
Reed, Simeon	Pvt 4 Mass	"	4-15-1778
Reed, Simeon	Vt	"	1783
Reeve, Isaac	N J	"	1778
Reeves, James	Pvt N J	"	12-30-1777
Reeves, John	Pvt 6 Md	"	3-16-1778
Regan, Basil	Pvt 4 Pa	"	6-21-1776
Reid, David	Capt N C	Killed	In War
Reily, Basil	R I	Died	1- 1779
Reily, James	Pvt Md	"	1-17-1781
Reily, John	Pvt 5 Md	"	9-2-1779
Reily, Patk	Pvt 5 Md	"	3-12-1777
Reimck, Christian	Surg 1 Pa	Killed	9-21-1777
Reinick, Christopher	Surg Pa	Died	9-21-1778
Remick, Benjamin IV	Md	"	1782
Remick, Samuel	Pvt 8 Mass	Died	3-21-1778
Remont, Charles	France	"	1781
Rennals, William	Pvt Conn	"	9-19-1778
Renne, Coral	Pvt 3 NY	"	5-16-1778
Rennet, Jonas	R I	"	10-15-1780
Rereside, Andrew	Pvt Md	"	12-16-1782
Retmire, Hend	Pvt 2 NJ	"	5-23-1777
Reveley, Christian	Sgt R I	"	9- 1777
Reyley, Daniel	Pvt 2 Pa	"	6-1-1776
Reynolds, Charles	Sgt Md	"	7-15-1781
Reynolds, Charles	Pvt 14 Mass	"	3-27-1778
Reynolds, James	Pvt N J	"	4-22-1777
Reynolds, John	Capt Md	"	1779
Reynolds, Jonathan	Pvt Can	"	2- 1778
Reynolds, Richard	Fifer 3Md	"	12-10- 1778
Reynolds, William	Pvt 10 NC	"	11-28- 1782
Reynolds, William	Pvt		
Reywood, Henry	Pvt 2 NJ	"	1-28-1777
Rhea, Joseph	Chap Md	"	1777
Rhodes, John	Lt Del	"	10-26-1780
Rice, Gershorn	Mass	"	1781
Rice, Joel	Pvt 8 Mass	"	9-1- 1777
Rice, John	Capt Mass 18 Cont	Died	5-18-1776
Rice, Jonas	Cpl Mass		1776
Rice, Jonathan	Pvt Mass	"	1780
Rice, Josher P	Pvt Conn	"	10-15-1777
Rice, Peter P	Pvt Conn	Killed	12-7-1777
Rice, Peter	Pvt Mass	Died	9-17-1780
Rice, Samuel	Pvt Mass	"	1782
Rice, Solomon	N Y	"	1776
Rice, Solomon	Pvt Conn	"	1776
Rice, Thomas	Sgt 1 NC	"	9-5-1777
Rice, William	Mass	"	1780
Rice, Aquila	"	"	12-13-1782
Rice, Jacob	Pvt SC	"	1780
Rice, Nath'l	Pvt Conn	Killed	7-11-1779
Richards	Sgt N J	"	9-11-1777
Richards, Abijah	Pvt 14 Mass	Died	4- 1779

Richards, Dick	Pvt 1 Conn	Died	7-21-1777	
Richards, Elisha	Pa	Killed	7-3-1778	
Richards, Humphrey	Mass	Died	5-28-1783	
Richards, Iram	Pvt 9 Mass	"	5-30-1778	
Richares, James	Pvt Mass	"	1778	
Richards, John	Mass	"	1781	
Richards, Samuels	Sgt 2 N J	"	9-11-1777	
Richards, Stephen	Pvt Conn	"	2-1-1778	
Richardson, Ezekiel	Mass	"	8-10-1781	
Richardson, Henchman	Mass	"	10-21-1775	
Richardson, Jacob	Cpl Mass	"	1780	
Richardson, John	Pvt Va	"	1776	
Richardson, Josiah	Pvt 8 Mass	"	1-25-1778	
Richardson, Kinsman	Pvt Mass	"	7-6-1778	
Richardson, Leonard	Pvt 6 Mass	"	9- 1777	
Richardson, Moses	Mass	Killed	4-19-1775	
Richardson, Nathaniel	Pvt N H	Died	6-24-1777	
Richardson, Richard	Gen SC	"	1781	
Richart, Jacob	Pvt R I	"	3-15-1777	
Richey, Jeremiah	Pvt 5 NY	Killed	4-16-1781	
Richmond, John	Navy	Died	7-21-1781	
Ricker, Abm	Capt 2 NY	"	2-16-1778	
Rickets, Reason	Cpl 1 NC	"	11-25-1779	
Riddle, Charles	Pvt Md	"	6-15-1781	
Rider, Daniel	Pvt Conn	"	2-2-1782	
Rider, Isaac	Pvt Mass	"	1776	
Riegel, Benjamin	Pvt Pa	"	1778	
Riely, Barney	Pvt 7 Md	Killed	8-22-1777	
Riemer, Geo. John	Pvt 1 NY	Died	12-16-1777	
Riford, Joseph	Pvt	"	1777	Prison
Riger, Peter	Pvt 2 NJ	"	7-15-1780	
Riggs, John	Pvt 1 Conn	"	5-20-1777	
Riggs, Peter	Pvt Mass	"	3-23-1776	
Riggs, Wheeler	Pvt Mass	Killed	8-7-1779	
Right, Timothy	2 SC	Died	2-12-1776	
Riker, Abraham	Lt NY	Killed	5-7-1780	
Riley, John	Pvt N J	Died	1778	
Riley, Lewis	Pvt 1 NY	"	12-2-1777	
Riley, Walter	Pvt 7 Md	Killed	10-4-1777	
Rinehart, Matthias	Mus 3 N J	Died	3-17-1778	
Rines, Thomas	Navy	"	6-7-1777	
Ring, Daniel	Mass	"	1782	
Ring, Jas Sr	Pvt 2 NC	"	12-1-1777	
Ring, James	Mus 2 NC	"	9-13-1777	
Ringer, John	Pvt R I	"	3- 1778	
Riotte, Pierre	Cpl France	"	1781	
Ripley, Charles	Lt	"	1778	Prison
Ripley, Hezekiah	Lt Mass	"	8-30-1778	
Ripley, Peter	Mass	"	1780	
Ripton, John	Pa	"	1781	
Rising, Aaron	Vt	"	1781	
Risse, Matthias	Pvt 2 N J	"	3-30-	
Ritchie	Capt SC	"	In War	
Riter, Daniel	Pvt N H	"	9-1-1779	

143

Rivers, Joseph	Pvt 1 NY	Died	3-25-1777
Roach, David	Pvt Pa	"	10-12-1776
Roach, William	Lt Ga	Killed	1780
Robb, William	N C	"	10-7-1780
Robbins, Benjamin	Pvt 13 Mass	Died	5-20-1778
Robbins, Daniel	Pvt 14 Mass	"	7-4-1777
Robbins, David	Mass	Killed	6-17-1775
Robbins, David	Sgt Conn	Died	1776
Robbins, Jacob	Lt Mass	"	11-25-1778
Robbins, Oliver	Me	"	4-11-1781
Robbins, Rufus	Mass	"	1776
Robbins, Samuel		"	11-20-1781 at Sea
Robbins, William	Pvt Mass	"	9-3-1775
Roberson, David	Pvt Conn	"	3-1-1779
Roberson, Samuel P	Pvt Conn	"	6-9- 1778
Roberts, Benjamin	Capt Va	"	1782
Roberts, Elias	Conn	"	1778
Roberts, Elias	Pa	"	7-3-1778
Roberts, Ephraim	Pvt Conn	"	1777
Roberts, Horatio	Pvt Md	"	3-1-1781
Roberts, Isaiah	Pvt. Conn	"	8-7-1778
Roberts, James	Pvt 6 Mass	"	4-28-1777
Roberts, Joel	Conn	"	1780
Roberts, John	Pvt Can	"	2-12-1782
Roberts, Jonathan Jr	Conn	"	7-7-1780
Roberts, Jonathan	Lt N Y	"	1775
Roberts, Josiah	Pvt 5 N Y	"	8-4-1778
Roberts, Kinchin	Pvt 3 N C	"	3-10-1778
Roberts, Moses	Capt Mass	"	2-11-1780
Roberts, Owen	Col 4 SC	Killed	6-20-1779
Roberts, Richd	Pvt Md	Died	8- 1778
Roberts, Thomas	Pvt	"	12-20-1777
Roberts, Samuel	Mus 1 NC	"	4-3-1778
Roberts, Thomas	Pvt Can	"	12-17-1777
Roberts, Thomas	Pvt Mass	"	5-25-1782
Roberts, Thomas	Pvt Pa	"	7-23-1776
Roberts, Winchin	Pvt N C	"	3-10-1778
Robertson, Edward	Sgt 6 NC	"	5-8-1772
Robertson, Henry	Drummer	"	2-6-1778
Robertson, James	Pvt Conn	"	3-31-1778
Robey, Joseph	Pvt 1 Md	"	9-25-1780
Robichon, Ferdinand	France	"	1781
Robins, Jacob	Mass	"	1-25-1778
Robins, John	Pvt 14 Mass	"	3-8-1778
Robins, John Purnell	Maj Md	"	1780
Robins, Joseph	Pvt Conn	"	3-25-1778
Robins, Joseph	Pvt Conn	"	5-31-1778
Robins, Thomas	Pvt N J	"	3-14-1779
Robins, Tim	Pvt 4 Mass	"	9-29-1778
Robinson, Abner	Pvt 14 Mass	Killed	9-19-1777
Robinson, Charles	Pvt Can	Died	8-10-1781
Robinson, David	Pvt 2 N J	"	3-1-1777
Robinson, Eben'r	Dr Conn	"	7- 1779

Robinson, Gain	Pvt Mass	Died	1778
Robinson, George	Pvt Mass 18 Cont	"	8-28-1776
Robinson, Lemuel	Col Mass	"	7-20-1776
Robinson, Jacob	Ens Mass	"	7-7-1778
Robinson, Jas	Pvt 3 NY	"	6-16-1778
Robinson, Jed	Pvt 2 N J	"	3-1-1777
Robinson, John	Md	"	In War
Robinson, John	Matross NC	"	2-12-1778
Robinson, John	Cpl 13 Mass	"	11-26-1777
Robinson, John	Pvt Conn	Killed	7-11-1779
Robinson, John	Pvt 1 NY	Died	1-24-1778
Robinson, Joseph	Cpl Mass	"	3-1-1777
Robinson, Reuben	Pvt 3 NC	"	9-4-1777
Robinson, William	Conn	Killed	6-17-1775
Robinson, Zophar	Pvt Conn	Died	3-3-1782
Roby, William	Mass	Killed	1776
Roche, Jean	France	Died	1781
Roche, Thomas	Pvt 5 Md	"	7-30-1777
Rockett, George	Pvt 1 NC	"	1779
Rockwot, Enos	Pa	"	7-3-1778
Rockwell, Danl	Sgt 1 Conn	"	5-4-1777
Rockwell, Joseph	Capt Conn	"	1778
Rockwell, Joseph	Pvt 6 Mass	"	10-6-1778
Rode, London	Pvt 9 Mass	"	12-9-1777
Rodges, Andrew	Lt Pa	"	1782
Rodgers, Arthur	Pvt 1 NC	"	10-22-1778
Rodgers, James	Ens 2 NJ	Killed	8-24-1780
Rodgers, Joseph	Pvt SC	Died	1781
Rodgers, Nathl	Pvt SC	Killed	1781
Rodman, Robert	Pvt 2 NJ	Died	5-14-1777
Rodney, Caesar	Del	"	1783
Roe, John Sr	N Y	"	1782
Roebuck, William	Va	"	1781
Rogers, Filer	Conn	"	1778
Rogers, Andrew	Lt Pa	"	1782
Rogers, Alex	Q M S SC	"	8- 1781
Rogers, Asahel	Pvt Conn	"	4-6-1778
Rogers, Daniel	Pvt N H	"	7-20-1777
Rogers, Ebenezar	Pvt Conn	Killed	6-28-1778
Rogers, Enoch	Pvt 4 Mass	Died	8-18-1777
Rogers, Ezekiel	Conn	"	1781
Rogers, Isaiah P	Pvt Conn	"	9- 1777
Rogers, Jas.	Pvt 3 NY	Killed	7-3-1777
Rogers, John	N H	Died	11-13-1776
Rogers, John	Lt Mass	"	11-13-1776
Rogers, Joseph	Pvt Conn	"	7-14-1779
Rogers, Lemuel	Pvt Conn	"	3-25-1778
Rogers, Nathnl	Pvt 4 Mass	"	3-31-1778
Rogers, Patrick	Lt 1 NC	"	4-19-1778
Rogers, Richard	Pvt N H	Killed	9-19-1777
Rogers, Samuel	Lt Mass	Died	1781
Rogers, Samuel	Pvt NY	"	1779
Rogers, Samuel	Capt Mass	"	1777
Rogers, Thomas		"	1776

		Died	1776
Rogers, Thomas		Died	1776
Rogers, Thomas	Mass	"	10-11-1776
Rogers, William	Pvt NY	"	1775
Rogers, William	Pvt 10 NC	"	8-29-1782
Rogers, William	Capt	"	1779 At Sea
Roland, Ellis	Pvt 9 Mass	Killed	8-3-1777
Rollo, John Norton	Conn	Died	3-20-1777
Rominck, Joseph	Pvt R I	"	5-20-1778
Rooser, Hory	Cpl 2 NY	"	2-16-1778
Roadman, Peleck	Pvt 9 Mass	"	6-2-1778
Roosevelt, Jacobus	Capt NY	Killed	1776
Root, Azariah	Lt Col Mass	Died	1777
Root, Elisha	Lt Conn	"	9- 1776
Root, Martin	Pvt 9 Mass	"	6-1-1777
Root, Samuel	Pvt Conn	"	1782
Roper, James	Pvt 2 N J	Killed	2-23-1777
Ropes, Benjamin	Lt Mass	Died	1778
Rosbrugh, John	Rev N J	"	1-2-1777
Rose, Elijah	Conn	"	11- 1776
Rose, John	Dr Conn	"	10-3-1783
Rose, Jonathan	Pvt 4 Mass	"	2-20-1778
Rose, Russell	Pa	"	1780
Rose, Thomas	Pvt Can	Killed	1-2-1777
Rosebrugh, James	Chap Pa	Died	1777
Roseburgh, John	Chap Pa	Killed	1777
Rosencrance, Daniel	Capt NY	Died	1782
Rosencrants, James	Pvt Pa	"	1777 Prison
Rosengrants, Peter	Pvt N J	"	7-17-1778
Ross, Pvt	Pa	"	6-3-1781
Ross, Pvt	N J	"	11-22-1776
Ross, Benjamin	Conn	Killed	6-17-1775
Ross, Daniel	2 SC	Died	3-26-1778
Ross, Eliakin	Cpl N J	Killed	7-2- 1779
Ross, Enoch	Pvt 14 Mass	Died	3-29-1778
Ross, Francis	Maj N C	"	3-31-1779
Ross, James	Ranger Pa	"	1780
Ross, Jeremiah	Pa	"	7-3-1778
Ross, John	1 SC	"	4-7-1777
Ross, Perrin	Lt Conn	Killed	1778
Ross, Timothy	Pa	Died	7-3-1778
Rossburgh, John	Chap NJ	Killed	1776
Rossiquol, Francois-Joseph	France	Died	1781
Rossiter, Elnathan	Mass	"	12-9-1780
Rossman, Simeon	Pvt 14 Mass	Killed	9-19-1777
Roster, Thomas	Pvt 5 Md	Died	4-30-1777
Roswell, Fitch	N Y	"	12-17-1782
Rouffe, Gottfried	Sgt France	"	1781
Rough, Peter	Pvt 4 N C	"	3-15-1778
Roundy, Asael	Pvt N H	"	1-17-1778
Roundy, Luke	Ens 9 Mass	"	10-20-1777
Rountree, Thomas	Pvt Va	"	1781
Roussel, Jean Baptiste	France	"	1781
Rowell, Elias	Pvt 8 Mass	"	3-1-1778
Rowland, Evans	Pvt SC	"	In War
Rowland, William	Pvt 9 NC	"	3-11-1778

Rowlandson, Wilson	Pvt Conn	Killed	6-17-1775
Rowlings, Jacob	Pvt Can	Died	2-25-1777
Roy, John	Pvt 2 N J	"	8-31-1777
Roy, John	N J	"	1780
Roy, William	Pvt 5 Md	"	4-7-1778
Royal, Jacob	Pvt 14 Mass	"	3-1-1779
Royal, James	Cpl 1 NC	"	3-6-1778
Royal, Samuel	Pvt 14 Mass	"	3-29-1778
Royall, Joseph	Pvt N C	"	1778
Royals, Joseph	Lt 1 N C	"	3-6-1778
Royce, Amos	Pvt N H	"	5-5-1778
Royce, Joel	Pvt N H	"	1782
Royce, Jotham	Pvt Conn	"	12-1-1781
Roys, Joel	Mass	"	9-4-1782
Rudolph, May John	Md	"	1782
Rudrick, Emanuel	Pvt Conn	"	1-26-1778
Rueff, Johannes	Pvt N Y	"	1779
Ruggles, Edward	Pvt Mass	"	1778
Ruggles, Nathan	Mass	"	1776
Ruggles, Samuel	Conn	"	1778
Rugles, Edward	Mass	"	1778
Ruland, Jehiel	3 N Y	"	4-16-1779
Rule, William	Pvt Pa	"	1782
Rullins, William	N Y	"	1781
Rumble, John	Pvt 14 Mass	"	3-3-1778
Rumer, Cornelius	Cpl L NC	"	4-29-1778
Rumph, Jacob	Capt SC	"	1778
Rumsey, Charles	Col Md	"	1780
Runell, John	Pvt N H	"	2-1-1778
Runnells, Owen	Pvt 18 Cont	"	2-29-1776
Rush, Conrad	Pvt	"	2-15-1777 Prison
Rush, George	Cpl N J	"	1782
Russel, James Jr	Mass	"	1781
Russel, John	Pvt 1 NC	"	9-20-1781
Russel, Urias	Pvt NC	"	10-7-1781
Russell, Aaron(a Lad)	Conn	Killed	7-6-1779
Russell, Aron	Pvt 7 Md	Died	9-30-1778
Russell, Daniel	Pvt 5 Mass	"	1-1-1778
Russell, Elijah P	Pvt Conn	"	4-18-1778
Russell, Giles	Col Yale Conn	"	10-28-1779
Russell, Henry	Pvt 1 Md	"	2-1-1779
Russell, Jason	Mass	Killed	4-19-1775
Russell, Jason	N H	Died	6-17-1775
Russell, John	Pvt 5 NC	"	1-8-1778
Russell, Joseph	Pvt Mass	"	11-13-1776
Russell, Nathan	14 Mass	"	6-23-1777
Russell, Samuel	N H	Killed	6-17-1775
Russell, Solomon	Pvt R I	"	12-31-1775 Que
Russell, Urias	Pvt 10 NC	Died	10- 1781
Russell, Walter	Pvt Mass		1782
Russell, William	Pvt 9 Mass	"	10-20-1777
Russell, William	N C	"	1780
Rust, James	Pvt 1 Conn	"	6- 1777
Rusten, Will	Sgt SC	Killed	5- 1781
Ruth, Samuel	Pvt 1 Conn	Died	3-17-1777

Rutherford,	Maj SC	Killed	9-8-1781
Rutledge, Wm	R I	"	12-31-1775 Que
Rutter, Joseph	Pvt 1 NC	Died	5-28-1778
Rutter, Joseph	Pvt Mass	"	1781
Rutter, Thomas	Pvt 3 Md	"	12- 1778
Ryal, Stepna	Pvt 1 Conn	"	3-1-1778
Ryan, Hercules	Pvt 4 NC	"	11-24-1777
Ryan, Hugh	Pvt 6 Md	"	12-15-1779
Ryan, John	Pvt 5 Md	"	4-7-1777
Ryan, John	2 SC	Killed	6-28-1776
Ryan, Patrick	Cpl 4 NC	Died	9-6-1782
Ryder, James	Mass	"	5-9-1780
Ryley, James	Pvt 2 N J	Died	9-9-1780

S

Sabin, Abishai	Conn	Died	2-4-1782
Sabin, John	Conn	"	4-27-1777
Sabin, Lemuel	Pvt 7 Mass	"	1-11-1778
Sabin, Zebediah	Lt Conn	"	1776 Can
Sabins, Thomas	N Y	"	6-20-1778
Sacket, James	N Y	"	8-8-1781
Sacket, Samuel	N Y	"	4-15-1780
Sacketts, Sam'l	Capt 4 N Y	"	4-15-1780
Sackleford, William	Pvt Va	"	1777
Sadler, Humphy	Pvt 3 Md	"	8-30-1778
Saffray, Jean Louis	France	"	1781
Sage, Hosea	Pvt R I	"	9-21-1778
Sailer, Prosper	Pvt R I	"	7-8-1777
Sanky, John	Pvt 7 Md	"	5-13-1779
Sallemon, Antoine	France	"	1781
Salomon, Philibert-Antoine	France	"	1781
Salsbury, Philip	Pvt R I	"	10-21-1777
Salsbury, Thomas	Pvt 1 Md	"	2- 1779
Salter, Charles	Pvt 2 N J	"	1-1- 1778
Samson, Nathaniel	Mass	"	9-13-1778
Samson, Zabdiel	Mass	Killed	9-16-1776
Sampson, Benjamin	Mass	Died	12-1-1778
Sampson, George	Pvt Va	"	6- 1777
Sampson, Setto	Mass	"	1781
Sanborn, Daniel Tilton	N H	"	11-8-1777
Sanborn, John	Pvt N H	"	9-10-1778
Sanborn, John	Cpl N H	Killed	1783
Sanborn, Richard	Pvt Me	Died	1780
Sanders, Benj	Pvt 10 NC	"	9- 1778
Sanders, Isaac	Pvt 1 NC	"	5- 1778
Sanders, James	Pvt 1 N C	"	9-17-1778
Sanders, Jonathan	Sgt 14 Mass	Killed	7-7-1777
Sanders, Joshua	Sgt 4 Md	Died	1780
Sanderson, Caleb	Cpl 1 NC	"	12-2-1778
Sanderson, Oliver	Pvt 12 Mass	"	10-10-1777
Sandiford, Amoos	Pvt 10 N C	"	9-7- 1781
Sands, Joseph	Pvt 14 Mass	"	5-21-1778
Samford, Daniel	Ens Conn	"	1777
Sanford, Ebenezer	Pvt	Drowned	5-1-1778
Sanford, Joel	Pvt Conn	Died	2-8-1782

Sansfacon, Jean Louis	France	Died	1781
Sansimon, Joseph	Pvt Conn	"	1-30-1778
Sansimon, Nathaniel	Pvt Conn	"	7-35-1778
Santee, John	Capt Pa	"	1777
Sapavamken, John	Pvt 8 Mass	"	9-22-1778
Sarbetz, Barthelery	France	"	1781
Sargeant, Nathaniel	Mass	"	1781
Sargent, Phineas	Cpl Mass	"	1776
Satterlee, Benedict	Pvt Pa	"	7-14-1778
Saunders, Tobez	Del	"	11-5-1777
Saunders, Jno	Pvt 2 Md	"	2-15-1778
Savage, Samuel	Pvt 5 Mass	"	5-25-1777
Savage, Samuel	Conn	"	1779
Savequet, Dominique	France	"	1781
Savoix, Martial	France	"	1781
Savory, Isaac	Pvt 9 Mass	"	2-9-1778
Sawernian, Philip	Pvt Ger Reg	"	3-4-1777
Sawin, Silas	Pvt 15 Mass	"	3-24-1779
Sawyer, Abner	Lt Mass	"	9-4-1779
Sawyer, Abner	Pvt 15 Mass	"	11-7-1777
Sawyer, Ebenezer	Pvt 7 Mass	Killed	10-7-1777
Sawyer, Ezra	Ens Mass	Died	3-4-1776
Sawyer, Francis	Pvt 8 Mass	Killed	7-19-1777
Sawyer, Henry	Pvt 1 NC	Died	8- 1778
Sawyer, James	Maj N Y	"	1782
Sawyer, Jonathan	Lt 14 Mass	"	9-19-1777
Sawyer, Jonathan	Pvt 7 Mass	"	10-26-1777
Sawyer, Joshua	Pvt 5 Mass	"	2-3-1780
Sawyer, Nathaniel	Pvt 10 Mass	"	1-19-1778
Sawyer, Lemuel	Sgt 10 Mass	"	2-2-1778
Sawyer, Willis	Pvt 1 N C	"	5-7-1778
Sax, Richard	Pvt 6 Md	Killed	10-4-1777
Saxbury, Wm.	Pvt 1 NY	Died	12-19-1777
Saxton, Jeremiah	Pvt 1 NC	"	4-25-1779
Sayer, William	Pvt 11 Mass	"	7-1-1778
Saylor, Jacob	Pvt 2 NY	"	4-30-1777
Sayre, John	N J	"	1779
Scales, Samuel	Pvt N H	"	1778
Scamman, James	Pvt 9 Mass	"	3-13-1778
Scammell, Alexandor	Col N J	"	10-6-1781
Scammell, Alexander	Adj Gen Mass	"	1C-6-1781
Scantling, Jeremiah	Pvt 5 Mass	"	7-22-1777
Scantling, Willm	Del	"	11-3-1778
Scarff, William	Lt Md	"	1778
Scarf (Scharf) William	Lt Md	"	1778
Scarl, Davies	Pvt 12 Mass	"	9-17-1780
Scarlet, James	Pvt 10 NC	"	9-20-1782
Schaeffer, Jacob	N Y	Killed	6- 1778
Schegell, Jacob	Pvt N H	Died	1783
Schell, John Christian	N Y	"	1782
Schenck, John	Capt N J	"	1783
Schott, Sebastien	France	"	1781
Scholder, Francois	France	"	1781
Schoolfield, Benjamin	Pvt 7 N C	"	1-27-1778
Schoonhoven, Hendrick Van	Pvt N Y	"	1781

Name	Rank/Unit	Fate	Date
Schoonmaker, Edward	Pvt N Y	Died	7-1-1776
Schumacher, Johann Gottfried	N Y	"	1782
Schunnard, Thomas	N J	"	1781
Schwaner, Peter	Pvt Ger Reg	"	12-16-1776
Scisco, Francis	Pvt 4 Mass	"	6-11-1778
Scoby, John	Sgt 4 N J	"	10-17-1778
Scofield, Gershom	Conn	"	1- 1782
Scofield, Jacob	Conn	"	1781
Scofield, Silas	Pvt Conn	"	4-2-1778
Scollar, Isaac '	Pvt 1 NC	Killed	12-4-1777
Scondrick, Charles	Cpl Md	Died	7-1-1781
Scoonover, Wm	Pvt Pa	"	1777
Scott, Benjam	Pvt 9 Mass	"	10-5-1778
Scott, Ceasar	Pvt 7 Mass	"	11-26-1777
Scott, David	N H	Killed	6-17-1775
Scott, Gershom	Conn	Died	1-19-1778
Scott, James	N C	Killed	In War
Scott, James	Pvt N H	"	1776
Scott, James	Capt Va	Died	1779
Scott, James	Pvt Md	"	6-13-1776
Scott, James		Killed	1776
Scott, James	Del	"	1-20-1781
Scott, John	Sgt SC	Died	1779
Scott, John	Capt Va	"	1778
Scott, John	N Y	"	1781
Scott, John B	Capt N J	"	12-9-1775
Scott, Johnny	Capt Va	"	1778
Scott, Jonathan	Pvt 8 Mass	"	1-19-1779
Scott, Joseph	Pvt 12 Mass	Killed	7-31-1777
Scott, Patrick	Pvt 7 Md	"	8-16-1780
Scott, Robert S	Md	"	1776
Scott, Sylvanus	Mass	Died	1777
Scott, Timothy	Pvt 2 NY	"	6-27-1777
Scott, William	Pvt Conn	"	6-26-1777
Scudder, John	N J	"	2-26-1777
Scudder, Nathaniel	Col N J	Killed	10-15-1781
Scudder, William	Lt Col N J	"	In War
Scull, Daniel	Pvt 2 N J	Died	6-7-1780
Scull, Peter	Maj	"	1779 At Sea
Screven, James	Brig Gen Ga	Killed	11-24-1778
Scriables, Jeremh	Pvt 3 Md	Died	10-14-1778
Scribner, Robert	Sgt Md	"	2-15-1783
Scriggins, Samuel	Navy	"	6-7-1777
Scriven, James	Brig Gen Ga	"	1778
Scrivener, Robert	Sgt Md	"	2-15-1783
Scudder, Nathnial	Col N J	Killed	1781
Seals, John	Pvt 7 NC	Died	10- 1777
Seaman, William	Pvt Va	"	7-8-1777 Prison
Searle, Constant	Pa	Killed	7-3-1778
Searls, John	Pvt 15 Mass	Died	5-3-1778
Searls, Thomas	Pvt N C	"	9-7-1779
Sears, Joshua	Pvt Mass	"	11-1-1779
Sears, Judah	Lt Mass	"	1782
Sears, Noah	Pvt Md	"	4-3-1783

Name	Rank/Unit	Status	Date	
Sears, Noah	Pvt 1 Md	Died	1780	
Sears, Silas	Pvt 14 Mass	"	1-22-1778	
Sears, Silas	Pvt Mass	"	1780	
Sears, Zebedee	Pvt 14 Mass	"	12-10-1778	
Seaver, Joseph	Pvt 3 Mass	"	12-10-1779	
Seayers, John	Col 9 Va	Killed	10-4-1777	
Sebree, John	Va	Died	1781	
Sebring, Roelof	Capt N J	"	1782	
Sedger, Edmund	Pvt 9 Mass	"	10-10-1777	
Seeber, William	Maj N Y	"	1777	
Segins, Aaron	Pvt 11 Mass	"	11-10-1777	
Seeber, William Sr	Maj N Y	"	9-1-1777	
Seed, Benjamin	Pvt 4 N J	"	7- 1777	
Seeds, George	Pvt 4 N Y	"	4-9- 1781	
Seeley, Abel	Pa	"	7-3-1778	
Seeley, Mich'l	Pvt 5 NY	"	5-11-1778	
Seers, Nathaniel	Pvt 3 N J	"	2-18-1777	
Seixes, Isaac Mendes	N Y	"	11-11-1780	
Selden, Samuel	Col Conn	"	10-11-1776	
Selden, Samuel	Col Md	"	1776	
Selden, Samuel	N Y	"	1776	Prisoner
Seliquet, Jean	France	"	1781	
Sellinger, Absalom	Pvt 1 NC	"	5-3- 1778	
Sells, John	Pvt Pa	Killed	1781	
Senner, John	Pvt 2 Md	Died	12-25-1778	
Sepedre, Antoine	France	"	1781	
Sergeant, Thomas	Pvt 2 Md	"	11-20-1778	
Serjant, Benjamin	Pvt 9 Mass	"	5-5-1778	
Serjeant, Levi	Pvt 8 Mass	"	8-5-1777	
Serry, Luke	Pvt N C	"	9-7-1779	
Sersy, Luke	Pvt 10 NC	"	5- 1779	
Serve, Antoine	France	"	1781	
Servine, William	Pvt Can	"	10-4-1781	
Sessons, Abel	Pvt 10 N C	"	8-21-1782	
Sevalls, Daniel	Pvt 1 N C	"	4-14-1778	
Sever, Peter	Pvt W Va	"	1781	
Severance, Epham	Pvt N H	"	10-7-1777	
Severance, Thomas	Pvt N H	"	3-21-1780	
Severy, Jacob	Pvt 14 Mass	"	10-1-1780	
Sevier, Capt	SC	"	10-7-1780	
Sevier, Robt	Capt N C	"	10-15-1780	
Sevier, Robert	Col	Killed	10-7-1783	
Sevier, Robert B	N C	Died	10-16-1780	
Sevier, Robert	Va	"	1780	
Sewalls, Dan'l	Pvt 2 N C	"	4-14-1778	
Seward, Francis	Pvt Conn	"	6-25-1778	
Seymour, Elisha	N Y	"	1776	
Seymour, Zachariah	Pvt N Y	"	1777	
Shabshaw, Peter	Pvt 1 N C	"	9- 1779	
Shackleford, William	Lt Va	"	1777	
Shaffer, Jacob	Pvt R I	"	6-13-1778	
Shaffer, John	1 Lt Pa	"	11-3-1780	
Shaffter, Simon	Pvt 5 Mass	"	4-3-1778	

Shall, John	Pvt 2 NY	Died	8-8-1778
Shaltuck, Joseph	Mass	"	4-9-1778
Shanlee, Daniel	Matross Pa	"	7-6-1776
Shannon, George	N H	Killed	6-17-1775
Shannon, John	Sgt. Pa	Died	1780
Shannon, John	Pvt 11 Mass	Killed	7-7-1777
Shark, John	Pvt 7 Md	Died	In War
Sharon, Silas	Pvt 11 Mass	"	7-14-1778
Sharp, Jacob	Pvt Mass	"	9-4-1775
Shatluck, Daniel	Pvt 8 Mass	"	7-31-1777
Shattuck, Jeremiah	N H	Killed	6-17-1775
Shattuck, Joseph	Pvt Mass	Died	1778
Shattuck, William	Pvt N H	"	6-30-1777
Shaw, Abraham	Pa	"	7-3-1778
Shaw, Ebenezer	Pvt	"	1781 Prison Ship
Shaw, James 2d		"	1783 At Sea
Shaw, James	Pa	"	7-3-1778
Shaw, John	Pvt Conn	"	12-15-1778
Shaw, Jonathan P	Pvt Conn	"	1- 1778
Shaw, Joseph	Pa	"	7-3-1778
Shaw, Noah	Pvt 11 Mass	"	7-30-1777
Shaw, Oliver	Pvt N J	"	2-24-1777
Shaw, Samuel	Pvt 11 Mass	"	1-9-1778
Shaw, Silvanus	Capt R I	Killed	10-22-1777
Shaw, Thomas		Died	1778
Shaw, Thomas	Pvt 14 Mass	"	6-6-1778
Shedd, Reuben	Pvt Mass	"	1781
Shearman, Noah	Pvt Mass	"	10-6-1778
Shears, Joseph	Pvt 4 N J	"	5-10-1778
Shee, Murphy	Pvt Md	"	1-28-1783
Sheeley, John	Pvt 1 NY	"	7-9- 1778
Shelby, Moses	Pvt N C	"	1780
Shelding, Ceasar	Pvt R I	"	12-9-1780
Sheldon, Amasa	Capt	"	1780
Sheldon, A masa	Pvt Mass	"	1780
Sheldon, Asher, Jr.	Pvt Conn	"	1780
Sheldon, Ebenezer	Mass	"	In War
Sheldon, Elisha	Com Conn	"	9-1-1779
Shelly, Lemuel	Pvt Conn	"	5-3-1778
Shelton, Jno	Pvt 5 Md	"	4-10-1777
Shem, George	14 Mass	"	7-14-1777
Shepard, A bram	Lt N Y	Killed	1779
Shepard, Michael	Navy	Died	7-21-1781
Shepard, Timothy	Lt Conn	"	1776
Shephard, Abraham	Lt N Y	"	1779
Shepherd, Abram	Lt Del	Killed	7-22-1779
Shepherd, Thomas	Capt Conn	Died	1782
Shepherd, Thomas	R I	Killed	12-31-1775
Shepherd, True	Pvt 1 NY	Died	6-1-1777
Shepler, Henry	Capt Pa	"	1781
Sheppard, Peter	Pvt N J	"	1-25-1777
Sheppard, Phillip	N J	"	5-1-1777
Sheppard, Capt	SC	Killed	10-9-1779
Sherman, Benjamin	R I	Died	1783
Sherman, Joseph Jr	Pvt Mass	"	1777

Sherburne, Ephraim	N H	Died	10-7-1781
Sherburne, Henry	Maj N Y	"	1783
Shermon, David	Pvt Conn	"	3-29-1778
Sherrin, Joseph	Pvt 1 NC	"	5-20-1778
Sherry, William	Pvt 3 Md	"	10-4-1778
Sherwood, Isaac	Lt 2 NY	"	10-10-1777
Sherwood, John	Conn	"	1779
Sherwood, Micajah		"	12-1-1780
Sherwood, Seym	Pvt 2 NY	"	2-10- 1779
Shields, John	Capt Va	"	1779
Shile, Peter	Lt Pa	Killed	11-5-1777
Shink, Joseph	Pvt 3 Md	Died	2-24-1779
Shinn, George	Pvt Va	"	1782
Shinn, George	N J	"	1782
Shipey, Solomon	Pvt R I	"	4-8-1778
Shipley, Robert	Pvt Md	"	7-20-1782
Shipman, Israel	Pvt Conn	"	10-31-1778
Shipman, William P	Pvt Conn	"	4- 1777
Shippen, Edward	Pvt Mass	"	9-25-1781
Shippen, William	Capt	Killed	1-3-1777
Shirk, John	Pvt R I	Died	1779
Shirley, George	Pvt 3 Md	"	8-24-1778
Shirley, William	Pvt Md	"	6-12-1783
Shirtley, Joseph	Pvt Md	"	10-4-1777
Shirvin, Charles	Pvt 1 Md	"	9-29-1778
Shockley, Isaac	Pvt 1 NC	"	11-5-1777
Shoemaker, Elijah	Pa	"	7-3-1778
Shoemaker, Jacob R	Md	"	11-14-1782
Shoemaker, Jacob	Lt 4 Md	"	1780
Shoemaker, Peter	Pvt 7 Md	Killed	8-16- 1780
Shores, Peleg	Pvt N J	Died	8-4-1776
Short, Abraham	Pvt SC	Drowned	9- 1781
Short, Henry	Pvt 10 NC	Died	11-27-1778
Short, Jonathan	Sgt Md	"	3-26-1782
Short, Jonathan	Pvt Md	"	10-26-1782
Shortridge, Benjamin	Capt NH	Killed	7-8- 1776
Shortridge, Richard	N Y	Died	1776
Shreve, Samuel	Lt Col Va	"	1778
Shrouder, Thomas	Pvt N H	"	3-1-1778
Shubrick, Jacob	Lt 2 SC	"	4-27-1778
Shubrick, Richard	Capt 2 SC	Killed	11-8-1777
Shumer, Benjamin	Pvt 3 N J	Died	3-30-1778
Shute, William	Lt Pa	"	1783
Shutter, Volentine	Pvt R I	"	1-23-1777
Sibley, David	Pvt 9 Mass	"	8-26-1777
Sidon, Joshua	Pvt N J	"	11-20-1778
Sight, Henry	Pvt N J	"	1-10-1777
Sikes, Benjamin	Mass	"	8-2-1781
Sill, Richard	Maj Yale Conn	Died	1-14-1783
Sills, Chris	Pvt 1 NY	"	10-9-1778
Sillsbury, Jacob	Pvt 2 NY	"	9-20- 1777
Silsby, Henry Jr	N H	"	4-10-1779
Silvester, Luke	Pvt 10 NC	"	12-7- 1778
Silvester, Thomas	Pvt 5 MH	"	8-21- 1778
Silvey, Jacob	Pvt Md	"	8-4- 1777

Simeon, Lute	Conn	Died	1781
Simmons	Lt SC	"	In War
Simmons, Ephm	Pvt 5 NY	"	4-15- 1778
Simmons, Joseph	N H	Killed	6-17-1775
Simmons, Malachi	Music 1 NC	Died	5-1-1778
Simmons, Noble	Pvt 6 Md	"	7-2-1778
Simmons, Peter	Pvt 1 N C	"	8-15-1777
Simmons, Robert	Lt	Killed	1781
Simms, Ignatius	Pvt 1 Md	Died	7-17-1779
Simms, James	Sgt 3 Md	"	9-21-1779
Sims, William	Pvt 9 Mass	"	1-1-1777
Simons,	Lt SC	Killed	9-9-1781
Simons, John	Capt SC	Killed	7-7-1781
Simpon, William	N H	Died	5-14-1782
Simpson, Charles	Cpl 2 Md	"	2- 1780
Simpson, Salathiel	Va	"	7- 1777
Simson, Moses	Pvt 1 N C	"	9-7-1778
Sinclair, Brod	Pvt N H	"	3-5-1778
Sinemon, Tho	Pvt Conn	"	1-27-1778
Sinkins, George	R I	Killed	1777
Sinclair, Ebenezer	Pvt N H	Died	10-7-1777
Sisco, William	N H	Died	1783
Siske, Daniel	SC	Killed	10-7-1780
Sitzer, Barond	4 NY	Died	3-24-1780
Sinles, Anthony	Pvt NC	"	8-7-1782
Skipper, John	Pvt 1 Md	"	8- 1777
Skiff, James	W I	"	1783
Skiff, Joseph	Pvt Mass	"	11-7-1778
Skillings, John	Capt Mass	Killed	4-2-1777
Skinner, Benjamin	Mass	Died	1782
Skinner, Calvin	Cpl Conn	"	1777
Skinner, John	Capt	Killed	8-3-1778
Skinner, Richard	Capt NJ	"	7-1-1779
Skinner, Solomon	Mass	Died	1782
Skinner, Timothy	Pvt Conn	Killed	12-7-1777
Skinner, Truman	Lt Col Md	Died	1781
Skipper, Joseph	Pvt 1 NC	"	12-19-1777
Skirving, James	Capt SC	"	1778
Slack, Henry	Sgt Md	"	1783
Slade, John	Pvt 3 Md	"	2-3-1778
Slapp, Edward	Pvt N H	"	12-31-1777
Slaughter, John	Capt Va	"	1783
Slaughter, Lawronce	Lt Va	"	1779
Slaven, Samuel	Music 1 NC	"	4-15-1778
Sleeper, David	Pvt N H	"	1780
Slingerlant, Peter	Pvt 1 NY	"	7-17-1777
Sloan, James	Pvt 1 NJ	"	12-1-1778
Sloan, John	N Y	"	1778
Slocum, Jonathan	Mass	Killed	1778
Sloop, John	Pvt 6 Md	Died	8-3-1778
Slowman, John	Pvt 8 Mass	"	2-3-1780
Slyhoff, Godfrey	Pvt Ger Reg	"	5-12-1777
Small, Nathaniel	Pvt 9 Mass	"	7-13-1778
Smart, James	Pvt 12 Mass	"	7-8-1778

Smart, Jeremiah	Pvt N H	Died	10-7-1777
Smart, John	SC	"	10-7-1780
Smeel, Nogion	Pvt N Y	"	6-2-1777
Smelledge, Saml	Drum 8 Mass	"	11- 1779
Smith	Pa	"	1781
Smith	Capt N C	Killed	In War
Smith, Alex	Sgt 8 Pa	Died	6-25-1777
Smith, Alvin	Pvt 1 Md	"	3-5-1777
Smith, Andrew	Pvt Ger Reg	"	12-16-1776
Smith, Aaron	Capt Va	"	1776
Smith, Aaron	Mass	"	4-15-1776
Smith, Asa	Conn	"	8-19-1775
Smith, Benjamin	Pvt N C	"	11-20-1778
Smith, Benjamin	Mass	Killed	6-17-1775
Smith, Burrell	Sgt 10 NC	Died	1-26-1783
Smith, Daniel	Col Va	"	1781
Smith, David	Pvt N H	"	8-4-1778
Smith, Ebenezer	Mass	"	9-3-1780
Smith, Ebenezer	Mass	"	1781
Smith, Edward	N Y	"	10-18-1777
Smith, Egbert	N Y	"	1781
Smith, Eliakim	Mass	"	1775
Smith, George	Pvt Ger Reg	"	7-15-1778
Smith, Gershom	Conn	Killed	6-17-1775
Smith, Ignatius	Pvt Md	Died	4-20-1782
Smith, Isaac	Pvt N H	Killed	4-10-1780
Smith, Jabez Jr	Mass	Died	6-28-1780
Smith, Jacob	Pvt Mass	"	4-8-1776
Smith, Jer k	Pvt 2 N Y	"	6-11-1778
Smith, Jeremiah	Pvt 12 Mass	"	10-23-1780
Smith, Jeremiah	Pvt N C	"	9-14-1782
Smith, Jesse	Pvt N J	Died	4- 1778
Smith, Jno Sr	Pvt 2 N C	"	2-27-1778
Smith, Jno	Pvt 7 N C	"	2-24-1778
Smith, Jno	Pvt 10 N C	"	9-19-1782
Smith, Job	Sgt 14 Mass	"	8-30-1780
Smith, Joel	Conn	"	1- 1777
Smith, Joel	Pvt Mass	"	6-11-1781
Smith, John	Pvt Mass	"	11-14-1777
Smith, John	Pvt 1 N C	"	9-19-1782
Smith, John	N C	"	2-27-1778
Smith, John	Sgt 2 NY	"	1-29-1781
Smith, John	Mus N C	"	4-24-1778
Smith, John	Pvt 4 N J	"	7- 1777
Smith, John	Pvt 12 Mass	"	12-30-1778
Smith, John	Mass	"	1776
Smith, John	N H	"	1783
Smith, John	N Y	"	3-20-1777
Smith, John	N C	"	2-27-1778
Smith, John	Pvt N C	"	9-19-1782
Smith, John	Fife 2 NY	"	6-13-1780
Smith, John	Pvt 5 NY	"	11- 1777
Smith, John	Pvt Md	"	7-15-1781
Smith, Jonathan	Conn	Killed	1777

Smith, Joseph	Pvt 1 Conn	Died	4-26-1782
Smith, Josiah	Sgt Md	"	7-15-1781
Smith, Levin	Pvt 3 Md	"	10-20-1778
Smith, Martin	Mass	"	1780
Smith, Nathaniel	Cpl Conn	"	12-7- 1777
Smith, Nathaniel	Ens N Y	"	1- 1783
Smith, Nathan	Lt Mass	"	1780
Smith, Nathl	Pvt 1 Md	"	7- 1779
Smith, Nicholas	Pvt N Y	"	1778
Smith, Owen	Pvt 1 N C	"	8-17-1777
Smith, Patrick	Pvt 4 N J	"	9-11-1777
Smith, Philander	Pvt 11 Mass	"	10-20-1777
Smith, Reuben	Pvt Md	"	5-9-1783
Smith, Reubens	Pvt 5 N Y	"	2-12-1780
Smith, Reubin	Pvt Md	"	5-9-1783
Smith, Richard	Pvt 1 N C	"	9-16-1781
Smith, Richard	Pvt 10 N C	"	9-10-1782
Smith, Richard	Pvt 1 N C	"	9-10-1783
Smith, Robert E	N Y	"	1781
Smith, Robert	Pvt Can	Killed	10-2-1781
Smith, Robert	Capt Va	Died	1780
Smith, Russell	N H	"	8-24-1777
Smith, Samuel	Lt Pa	"	10-4-1777
Smith, Samuel	Sgt N Y	"	10-18-1777
Smith, Samuel	Lt Pa	Killed	5-27-1777
Smith, Sephaniah	Pvt 14 Mass	Died	2-4-1778
Smith, Simeon	Lt Mass	"	3-23-1777
Smith, Sivel	Pvt 15 Mass	"	2-7-1778
Smith, Solomon	Lt Mass	"	3-31-1780
Smith, Stephen	Pvt 10 N C	"	6-3-1783
Smith, Tho	Pvt R I	"	7-19-1777
Smith, Thomas	Pvt 4 N J	"	4-17-1778
Smith, Thomas	Sgt Can	"	6-20-1777
Smith, Timothy	Mass	"	1-10-1779
Smith, William	Pvt 12 Mass	"	1-7-1780
Smith, William	Lt Va	Killed	10-4-1777
Smith, William	Mass	Died	8-22-1779
Smith, William	Pvt Md	Killed	6-3-1783
Smith, William	Pvt 4 Md	Died	2- 1779
Smith, William	Pvt Ger Reg	"	12-16-1776
Smith, William	Sgt N C	"	4-9-1778
Smith, William	Pvt 1 N C	"	2-28-1778
Smith, William	N C	"	11-10-1780
Smith, William	Pvt 1 N C	"	3-31-1778
Smith, William	Lt Va	"	5-7-1777
Smith, Wm	Pvt 2 N C	"	3-31-1778
Smith, Wm	Pvt N C	"	2-28-1778
Smith, Williams P	Pvt Conn	"	12-4-1781
Smith, Zebediah	Pvt 8 Mass	"	3-31-1778
Smithy, John	Pvt 2 Md	Killed	8-16-1780
Smyser, Matthias	Pvt Pa	Died	1778
Smyth, John	Pvt 5 Md	"	7-17-1777
Smyth, Joseph	Pvt Md	"	8-25-1777
Snedeker, Johannes	N Y	"	1779 Prisoner

Name	Rank/Unit	Status	Date
Snell, George	N Y	Killed	1777
Smiles, Anthony	Pvt 1 NC	Died	8-7-1782
Snow, Charles	Pvt 2 Md	"	10- 1780
Snow, Edward	Mass	"	9-1-1781
Snow, Henry	Pvt N H	"	10-25-1779
Snow, James	Mass	"	1781
Snow, John	N H	"	5-12-1777
Snow, Jonathan	Pvt 4 Mass	"	8-19-1777
Snow, Samuel	Pvt 3 Mass	"	3-23-1778
Snow, Samuel	Mass	"	6-22-1781
Snow, Thomas	Pvt Conn	"	7-6-1781
Snow, Thomas	Pvt 14 Mass	"	7-19-1777
Snyder, Peter	Pvt Va	"	2-15-1777
Snyder, William	Pvt Ger Reg	"	12-16-1776
Sollers, Thomas	Maj Md	"	1783
Solomon, Amos	Pvt Conn	"	7-1-1778
Solomon, John	Pvt R I	"	9-5-1778
Somers, James	Capt N J	"	1779
Somers, John	Pvt N J	"	1783
Somerville, Alexander	Lt Col Md	"	1783
Somes, Isaac	Lt Mass	"	1782
Somers, James	Lt N J	"	1779
Somers, John	N J	"	1783
Somerwell, Alexander	Lt Col Md	"	1783
Somes, Isaac	Capt Mass	"	1782
Soper, Edmund	Maj Mass	"	9-27-1776
Sorrel, Thomas	Pvt 10 NC	"	9-16-1778
Sourson, Jean	France	"	1781
Southmayed, William	Conn	"	7-31-1778
Southwick, George	Mass	Killed	4-19-1775
Sowas, Richard	Pvt Conn	"	11-15-1777
Spafford, Darius	Pa	Died	7-3-1778
Spalding, Curtis	Conn	"	1777
Spalding, Ezekiel	Sgt Mass	"	1777
Spalding, Joseph	Lt Conn	Killed	6-17-1775
Spalding, Wm	Pvt 1 Md	Died	11-26-1778
Spark, Nicholas	Pvt 10 Mass	"	7-7- 1777
Sparks, James	Pvt Ger Reg	"	9- 1777
Spaulding, Leonard	Capt Va	"	6-17-1778
Spaulding, Robert	Mass	"	1776
Speake, Nathan	Pvt Md	"	10-6-1782
Spear, John	Me	"	3-13-1776
Spear, F. Henry	Del	"	11-16-1778
Spear, William	Mass	"	7-13-1782
Speary, Elisha	Pvt 4 Mass	"	5-23-1778
Speer, James	Pvt 4 N J	"	3-30-1777
Speer, Capt	13 Pa	"	2-8-1778
Spencer, Abner	Pvt	"	10-9-1777
Spencer, Benj	Pvt Md	"	6-18-1776
Spencer, James	Ens Va	"	1783
Spencer, Joseph	Pvt Conn	"	4-20-1778
Spencer, Josiah	Pa	"	7-3-1778
Spencer, Levi	Pa	"	7-3-1778
Sperry, Ambrose	Pvt Conn	"	10-10-1778

Sperry, Joel	Pvt Conn	Died	3-13-1778
Spicer, Samuel	Pvt Conn	"	7-1-1778
Spink, Ishmael	Pvt 12 Mass	"	4-27-1778
Spofford, Eliphalet	Pvt Mass	"	1776
Spooner, Charles	Lt R I	"	1779
Spooner, Ward	Me	"	1777
Spoor, Isaac	Pvt Mass	"	5-28-1780
Spoor, John	Pvt 12 Mass	"	6-26-1778
Sport, William	Pvt 1 N C	"	4-29-1783
Spraggs, John	Pvt 1 Md	"	3-6-1779
Sprague, Caffe	Pvt 15 Mass	"	2-24-1778
Sprague, Eleazer	Pa	"	7-3-1778
Sprague, Elkanah	Capt Vt	"	1781
Sprague, Jacob	Mass	"	1778 Prison
Sprague, John	Conn	"	2-5-1777
Sprague, Phineas	Mass	"	1775
Sprague, Samuel	Capt Mass	"	1783
Sprague, Sandy	Pvt 7 Mass	"	1-1-1778
Sprague, Terah	Me	"	1782
Sprague, William	Mass	"	1782
Spreewood, Nehemiah	Pvt 12 Mass	"	9-20-1777
Spring, Amos	Pvt 15 Mass	Killed	9-19-1777
Springer, Gabriel	Del	Died	1781
Springer, John	Mass	"	1783
Springer, John	Me	"	1783
Springer, Nathaniel	Capt Md	"	1780
Springsteen, John	Pvt 5 NY	"	12-27-1779
Sproul, James	Ens 4 NJ	"	6-26-1777
Sprowls, James	Ens N J	"	6-26-1777
Spyker, Benjamin	Capt Md	"	1780
Squier, Thomas	Pvt N J	"	1780
Squires, Benjamin	Pvt 7 Mass	"	10-23-1777
Squires, Ebenezer	Pvt Conn	"	8- 1778
Squires, James	Pvt Can	"	12-1-1777
Stagg, John	Pvt 4 NY	"	6-24-1778
Stalker, Eli	Pvt Conn	"	In War
Stanford, Robert	Pvt 10 Mass	"	11-3-1777
Standish, Moses	Pvt 14 Mass	"	3-22-1778
Standish, Zachariah	R I	"	1780
Standley, Bishop	R I	Killed	12-31-1775 Que
Standley, George	Cpl 6 Pa	Died	10- 1776
Standley, Hezekiah	Pvt Conn	"	2-7- 1778
Standley, Jonathan	Pvt Conn	"	12-1- 1778
Standley, Roger	Pvt 2 Md	"	10-10-1778
Standup, William	6 Pa	"	9-20-1776
Stanley, Thomas	Cadet Md	"	8-6-1781
Stanley, Timothy	Pvt Conn	"	1776
Stannard, Peter	Pvt Conn	"	1778
Stanton, Amos	Lt Conn	Killed	1781
Stanton, Enoch	Lt Conn	"	9-6- 1781
Stanton, Lester	Conn	Died	In War
Stanton, Phineas	Lt Conn	Killed	1781
Stanton, William	Pvt N H	Died	2-10-1777
Staples, Hezekiah	Pvt N H	"	1777

Staples, Joseph	Pa	Died	7-3-1778
Staples, Titus	Pvt 14 Mass	"	7-20-1778
Stark, Aaron	Pa	Killed	7-3-1778
Stark, Daniel	Pa	Died	7-3-1778
Stark, James	Pvt Pa	"	1777
Stark, James	Pvt Conn	"	1777
Stark, James	Pvt Pa	"	1777
Stark, John	Capt Vt	"	1781
Stark, Joseph	Pvt Conn	"	11-19-1778
Starr, Nicholas	Sgt Conn	Killed	9-6-1781
Starr, Daniel	Maj Conn	"	1777
Starr, Daniel	3 Lt Conn	Died	6-5-1780
Starr, David	Maj Conn	Killed	1777
Starr, Thomas	Conn	Died	9-6-1781
Starrs, Abijah	Pvt 8 Mass	"	2-15-1778
Statler, Jacob	Va	"	1778
Stautzer, Jacob	France	"	1781
Starbird, Elias	Pvt 12 Mass	Killed	7-7-1777
Stanley, Noah	Conn	Died	5-6-1778
Starkweather, Woodbury	Cpl Conn	"	In War
Steadman, James	Lt Ga	"	7- 1780
Stedman, Amos	Pvt 3 Mass	"	9-20-1777
Stedman, Amos	Pvt R I	"	6-13-1778
Stedman, John	Pvt 3 Mass	"	8-18-1777
Stearns, Daniel	Pvt N H	"	4-30-1780
Stearns, Isaac	Pvt N H	"	1-7-1778
Stearns, John	Pvt Mass	"	1775
Stearns, Solomon	Mass	"	1775
Stearns, William	Pvt 9 Mass	"	8- 1777
Steel, Aaron	Lt Mass	"	11-24-1777
Steel, Alexander	Del	"	1783
Steel, John	Chap Pa	"	1779
Steel, John	Pvt SC	Killed	10-9-1779
Steel, Joseph	Pvt 3 Md	Died	11-16-1778
Steele, Aaron	Lt 7 Mass	Killed	11-27-1777
Steele, Thomas	Pvt 5 Mass	Died	2-9-1779
Steele, Solomon	Pvt 7 Mass	"	7-13-1779
Steele, William	SC	"	10-7-1780
Steelman, Frederick	N J	"	1782
Steelman, John	Pvt N C	"	1778
Steelman,	Seaman N J	Drowned	2-7-1781
Stelle, Isaac	Pvt N J	Died	1781
Stephen, Crosby	Capt N Y	Killed	1776
Stephen, John	R I	"	12-31-1775 Que
Stephen, Stephen	Pvt 2 N J	Died	1-1-1779
Stephens, Benjamin	Pvt 1 N C	"	2- 1779
Stephenson,	Col Va	"	8- 1776
Stephenson, Hugh	Col	"	1776
Stephenson, James	Sgt N C	"	2-12-1778
Stepney, Senah	Pvt 10 Mass	"	12-17-1779
Sterling, Isaac	Pvt 1 N C	"	4-5-1778
Sterling, Wm Alexander	Lord Maj Gen NY	"	1-15-1783
Sternberg, John Jacob	Pvt N Y	"	1777
Sterno, Benjamin	Pvt Conn	"	5-10-1777

Stetson, Amos	Mass	Died	1777
Stetson, Amos	N Y	"	9-6-1779
Stetson, John	Mass	"	1-4-1776
Stetterson, Robert	Pvt N H	"	1783
Stevens, Asa	Lt Pa	Killed	7-3-1778
Stevens, Amosa	Cpl N Y	"	5-21-1780
Stevens, Darius	Conn	"	6-17-1775
Stevens, David Jr	N H	Died	9-7-1778
Stevens, Ephraim	Pvt N H	"	3-20-1780
Stevens, Gabriel	Pvt Va	"	3-1-1777
Stevens, George	Pvt 5 Mass	"	1-5-1778
Stevens, George	N C	"	11- 1783
Stevens, James	N Y	"	4-8-1780
Stevens, Jonathan	Mass	"	1777
Stevens, Jonathan	Pvt N H	"	5-25-1778
Stevens, Joseph	Pvt Conn	"	2-1-1778
Stevens, Oliver	N H	Killed	6-17-1775
Stevens, Peter	Pvt Conn	Died	1779
Stevens, Rufus	Pa	"	7-3-1778
Stevens, Samuel	Conn	"	9-24-1776
Stevens, Thomas	Pvt 10 Mass	"	11-30-1777
Stevenson, Benj.	Pvt 5 N C	"	2- 1779
Stevenson, James	Pa	"	7-3-1778
Stevenson, Jas.	Sgt N C	"	2-12-1778
Stevenson, Thomas	Conn	"	10-8-1776
Stevenson, Thomas	Pvt Ky	Killed	1782
Stevenson, William	Lt Va	"	1781
Stevenson, William	Pvt N C	Died	1780
Steward	Lt SC	Killed	9-9-1781
Steward, James	Pvt Md	Died	6-3-1783
Steward, John	Lt Col Md	"	1782
Stewart, Benjamin	Mass	"	1775
Stewart, Caesar	Pvt Conn	"	7-31-1778
Stewart, Charles	Pvt 5 Md	"	12-6-1777
Stewart, Daniel	Pvt Can	"	10-10-1782
Stewart, Daniel	Pvt 2 N J	"	5-10-1777
Stewart, Dan'l	Pvt 10 N C	"	10-4-1782
Stewart, Ebenezer	Pvt 10 Mass	"	7-12-1777
Stewart, James	Pvt 2 N J	"	2-21-1777
Stewart, James	Pvt Md	"	12-1-1782
Stewart, James 2	Pvt Md	"	6-7-1783
Stewart, John	Pvt Del	Killed	9-8-1781
Stewart, Lazarus Jr	Pa	Died	7-3-1778
Stewart, Lazarus	Lt Col Pa	Killed	1778
Stewart, Robert	Pvt	"	10-4-1777
Stewart, Robert	Pvt 4 N J	Died	12- 1777
Stewart, Seth	Pvt 14 Mass	"	2-13-1778
Stewart, Thomas	Pvt 7 Md	Killed	10-4-1777
Stewart, William	Pvt 15 Mass	"	6-28-1778
St. Houge, Joseph	Pvt Can	Died	3- 1779
Stidham, Joseph	Capt Del	"	1781
Stile, John	Pvt 7 Mass	"	2-3-1778
Stiles, Gideon	Lt Mass	"	1781
Stiles, John	N J	"	5-17-1777

Name	Rank/Unit	Status	Date
Stiles, Joseph	Pvt Conn	Killed	12-7-1777
Stiles, Richard	N J	Died	9-16-1776
Stiles, William	Pvt N J	"	1778
Stille, Ebenezer	Pvt Pa	"	1777
Stillwell, Abediah	Pvt N J	"	4-13-1777
Stiller, John	Pvt 1 N Y	"	2-16-1777
Stillman, Robert	Pvt Conn	"	12-22-1777
Stillman, Stephen	Pvt Conn	"	1-24-1778
Stimson, Abel	Pvt Conn	"	5-16-1782
Stineman, John	Pvt 3 N J	"	5-17-1778
Stirling, Lord	Maj Gen N J	"	1-15-1783
Stocking, George 2	Sgt Conn	"	1777
Stocking, George 3	Pvt Conn	"	1777
Stockwell, Jacob	Pvt Vt	"	1777
Stoddard, Aaron	N Y	"	1777 Prison
Stoddard, Benjamin	Pvt Conn	"	12-27-1781
Stoddard, David	Sgt N H	"	1777
Stoddard, Israel	Mass	"	6-27-1782
Stoddard, Josiah	Capt Conn	"	8-24-1779
Stoddard, Nathan	Capt Conn	"	5-15-1777
Stoddard, Nath	Sgt R I	Killed	10-22-1777
Stoddard, Nathan	Capt Conn	"	5-27-1777
Stoddard, Abed	Pvt Conn	Died	1777
Stockee, Abraham	Pvt Md	"	11-1-1782
Stocker, Eli	Pvt 5 N Y	"	2-26-1778
Stockhouse, Henry	Cpl 4 N J	"	7-26-1777
Stockton, Richard	N J	"	2-28-1781
Stoddart, Josiah	Capt Can	"	8-24-1779
Stoke, Balthazar	France	"	1781
Stokes, Thomas	Pvt Md	Killed	9-8-1781
Stoudert, Claude	Sgt Maj France	Died	1781
Stone, Benjamin	Pvt Mass	"	10-15-1781
Stone, John	Pvt 11 Mass	"	5-10-1777
Stone, John	Pvt N H	"	9-6-1777
Stone, Josiah	Pvt Conn	"	11-12-1777
Stone, Nathaniel	Pvt Mass	"	1783
Stone, Nathaniel Jr	Mass	"	1776
Stone, Samuel	Pvt N H	"	1-20-1778
Stone, Silas	N Y	"	1777
Stone, William	Pvt 8 Mass	"	7-18-1779
Storer, Joseph	Cpl Me	"	1777
Stores, F William	Pvt Conn	"	11-15-1777
Stoffee, Frederic	Pvt Md	"	1-16-1782
Stoffel, Fredk.	Pvt Md	"	1-16-1782
Stowits, Philip	Pvt N Y	"	1777
Story, Caleb	Pvt 10 N C	"	6-16-1778
Story, Jesse	N H	Killed	6-17-1775
Stout, Emanuel	Del	Died	1781
Stout, John	Pvt N J	Killed	In War
Stout, Joseph	Capt N J	"	9-11-1777
Stout, Uoseph	Capt N Y	"	8-1-1776
Stout, Joshua	Pvt 15 Mass	Died	4-1-1778
Stow, Stephen	Pvt	"	1777
Stow, Stephen	Pvt Conn	"	2-8-1777

Stowe, Stephen		Died	1782 Prison
Stowe, Elijah	Pvt 6 Mass	"	11-8-1777
Stowell, Bela	Pvt Mass	"	8-11-1775
Stowell, Daniel	Pvt Conn	"	1778
Strain, David	Pvt Pa	"	1780
Strait, Frederick	N J	"	5-21-1781
Stratton, Antho	Pvt R I	"	5-15-1778
Stratton, Cobb	Va	"	3-31-1778
Straw, John	Pvt 12 Mass	"	6-21-1778
Street, John	N Y	Killed	1776
Streeter, Joseph	Pvt R I	Died	1777
Streter, Joseph	Pvt R I	"	8-8-1777
Stribe, David	Pvt R I	"	6-1-1778
Stroman, John Jacob	Pvt SC	"	1781
Stroud, Jonathan	Pvt 10 Mass	"	3- 1778
Strough, John	Pvt Mass	"	4-4-1778
Strong, Aaron	Mass	"	10-16-1777
Strong, Aaron	N Y	Killed	1777
Strong, Daniel	Pvt Conn	Died	1-1-1778
Strong, John	Pvt 14 Mass	"	2-10-1778
Strong, Nathaniel	Maj N Y	"	1778
Strong, Return	Conn	"	1776
Stryker, Abraham Sr	N J	"	1777
Stryker, John	Pvt N J	"	1776
Stuart, Alexander	1 Lt Del	Killed	8-27-1776
Stuart, David	SC	Died	1783
Stuart, Ebenezer	Mass	"	1778
Stuart, Elisha	Pvt 7 Mass	"	8-14-1777
Stuart, Wentworth	Me	"	1776
Stuart, Wentworth	Capt Mass	"	4-17-1776
Stuayby, Wentle	Pvt Ger Reg	"	1-15-1777
Stubert, Adam	France	"	1781
Stubs, David	Pvt 2 N J	"	4-15-1777
Studson, Joshua	Col N J	Killed	12- 1780
Sturdevant, Moses	Pvt 14 Mass	Died	9-3-1777
Sturdevant, Nathan	Pvt Conn	"	10-27-1777
Sturdivant, Joel	Pvt Conn	"	5-30-1781
Sturges, Joseph	Pvt Conn	"	1779 Prison
Sturges, Joseph	N Y	"	1778 Prison
Sturges, Solomon	Conn	"	1779
Stutson, Amos	Pvt 7 Mass	"	9-6-1777
Stutson, Stephen	Pvt R I	"	12-22-1777
Styren., George	Navy	"	7-21-1781 Prison
Suber, William	Maj N Y	Killed	1777
Suginas, Joseph	Pvt 1 N C	Died	9- 1779
Suit, Edward	Cpl Md	"	7-24-1782
Sulliwan, Dan	Pvt SC	Killed	9- 1781
Sulliwan, Daniel	Capt Me	Died	1781
Sulliwan, Daniel		"	1781 Prison
Sulliwan, Darby	Pvt 5 Md	"	9-15-1779
Sulliwan, John	Pvt 2 N Y	"	1-22-1781
Sulliwan, John	Pvt 1 N C	"	4-3-1783
Summer, George	Conn	"	1778

Summer, Jothro	Col N C	Died	3- 1785
Summers, John	Pvt Va	"	1778
Summers, Loven	Pvt 10 N C	"	5-20-1779
Suplee, Peter	Pvt Pa	"	1778
Surton, Robert	Pvt 5 Md	"	10-30-1780
Sutherland, John	Matross Pa	"	9-24-1776
Sutor, David	Pvt Pa	"	1777
Sutphen, John	Pvt N J	"	In War
Sutton, Robert	Pvt N J	Killed	5-10-1778
Sutton, William	Pvt Del	Killed	1778
Sutton, William	Pa	"	1778
Sutton, Abner	Pvt 11 Mass	Died	5-8-1778
Swain, Reuben	Pvt N H	"	7-28-1780
Swain, Andrew	Pvt Can	"	3-17-1777
Swan, Edward	Pvt 14 Mass	"	10-21-1779
Swam, William	Lt Md	"	1782
Swann, Barton	Pvt 1 Md	"	9-20-1778
Swann, Basil	Pvt 3 Md	"	8-10-1777
Swaney, James	Pvt 2 Md	"	6-2-1779
Swasey, Joseph	Pvt 14 Mass	"	3-21-1778
Sweed, Naler	Pa	"	7-3-1778
Sweeney, Richd	Pvt 2 Md	Killed	8-16-1780
Sweet, Roger	Pvt 5 N Y	Died	12-20-1778
Sweeting, Perry	Pvt R I	"	8-31-1778
Swetman, Stephen	Pvt SC	Killed	5- 1781
Swift, Benjamin	Pvt 14 Mass	Died	10-10-1778
Swift, John	Mass	"	1775
Swift, Jeriah	Conn	"	7-28-1776
Swift, Jirah	Capt Mass	Killed	1776
Swift, Samuel		Died	8-3-1775 Prison
Swiles, Gideon	Pvt Conn	"	3-16-1778
Swink, John Little	Pvt N C	Killed	1781
Swink, John Lewis		"	1781
Sylvester, Arthur	Pvt 8 Mass	Died	5-20-1778
Sylvester, William	N Y	"	1778
Sylvester, William Jr	Pvt Mass	"	1779
Sylvester, William	Mass	"	1778
Symms, John	Pvt 7 Mass	"	4-29-1779
Syphax, Carey	Pvt 11 Mass	"	12-15-1777

T

Taaffe, Lt	R I	Killed	1779
Tabb, Robert	Va	Died	1775
Tabey, Samuel Rev	Mass	"	1781
Tabar, John	Pvt R I	"	4-21-1778
Taft, William	Conn	"	1781
Taft, Nathan	Mass	"	1781
Taggart	Capt R I	"	In War
Taggart, John	Lt N H	"	7-7-1777
Talbot, Coxon	Pvt 1 Md	"	5-23-1777
Talbot, Samuel	Cpl Mass	"	9-25-1779
Talboth, William	Pvt 4 Md	"	8-2-1778
Taliaferro, William	Col 1 Va	"	2-1-1778

Talliaferro, Richard	N C	Killed	3-15-1781
Talmage, Daniel	Pvt	"	7-22-1779
Talor, Jesse	Pvt N C	Died	3-20-1778
Talpy, Richard	Pvt R I	"	4- 1778
Tanner, Benjamin	N Y	"	1780
Tanner, Benjamin	R I	"	1777
Tanner, Christopher	Sgt Va	"	1781
Tanner, John	Pvt 5 Md	"	11- 1778
Tanner, Mattocks	Del	"	12-10-1781
Tanner, Phineas	Pvt 6 Mass	"	1-15-1778
Tanner, Thomas	Pvt Md	"	1-3-1782
Tanner, William	N Y	"	6-30-1778
Tanner, William	R I	"	1780
Tantlinger, Henry	Pvt Pa	"	6-3-1781
Tapley, Mansfield	Mass	"	1779
Tarbox, Solomon	Lt Mass	"	1778
Tarbox, Solomon	Lt Conn	"	12-20- 1777
Targee, John	Pyt R I	"	1-20- 1772
Tarr, John	Pvt Mass	"	1776
Tarr, Samuel	Pvt 7 Mass	"	3-15-1778
Tate, James	Capt	Killed	3-15-1781
Tate, James	Cpl Va	"	1777
Tate, James	Capt Va	Died	1781
Tate, Joseph	Capt 2 N C	"	6-2- 1777
Tate, William	Mass	"	1781 At Sea
Tatman, Ebenezer	Mass	"	1780
Tatson, Solomon P	Pvt Conn	"	5-22-1778
Taylor, Benjamin	Pvt Mass	"	1776
Taylor, Benjamin	Pvt 2 Mass	Killed	9-19-1777
Taylor, Bradstreet	N Y	"	1777
Taylor, Chase Jr	N H	Died	8-1-1776
Taylor, Eldad	Mass	"	1777
Taylor, Elias	Mass	"	1777
Taylor, Elias	Pvt Conn	"	5-31-1777
Taylor, George	Del	"	1789
Taylor, Henry	Pvt 9 Mass	"	9-30-1778
Taylor, Isaiah	7 Mass	"	2-9-1782
Taylor, Israel	Pvt Mass	"	9-2-1779
Taylor, John	Pvt 7 Md	"	11-23-1778
Taylor, John	Sgt 3 Mass	"	10-3-1777
Taylor, A John	Pvt 4 N J	"	3-20-1777
Taylor, John	N H	"	1777
Taylor, John	Pvt 2 Mass	"	9-5-1777
Taylor, John	Pvt Can	"	5-22-1777
Taylor, John	Pvt 9 Mass	"	5-18-1778
Taylor, H John	Pvt R I	"	8-1-1778
Taylor, Joseph	N H	Killed	6-17-1775
Taylor, Joseph	Pvt Mass	Died	1775
Taylor, Josiah	Pvt Conn	"	1781
Taylor, Noah	Pvt 12 Mass	"	12-1-1780
Taylor, Quila	Pvt 1 Md	"	1-1-1778
Taylor, Robert	Pvt 1 N J	"	5-20-1778
Taylor, Samuel	Pvt 14 Mass	"	1-29-1778
Taylor, Samuel	Pvt 1 Md	"	6-15-1781

Taylor, Thomas	Capt N H	Died	3-25-1778
Taylor, Thomas	Cpl Mass	"	1780
Taylor, Thomas	N H	"	8-25-1777
Taylor, Thomas	Col Pa	"	1782
Taylor, William	Pvt SC	"	1779
Taylor, William P	Pvt Conn	Killed	4-26-1777
Taylor, Willm	Del	Died	6-10-1777
Taymon, Benja	Pvt 6 Md	"	In War
Teal, Jacob	Pvt Conn	"	7-19-1777
Teas, Alexander	2 Lt Can	"	9-15-1777
Tebbens, Jennings	N H	Killed	6-17-1775
Tede, Abraham	Pvt R I	Died	1-20-1777
Teel, Titus	Pvt Conn	"	2-2-1778
Teffingwell, Daniel	Conn	"	1778
Templar, Thomas	Pvt 2 NY	"	5- 1778
Temple, Joseph	Mass	"	4-19-1775
Templeman, Andrew	Capt Ga	Killed	5-12-1780
Templeton, Andrew	Capt	Died	5-15-1780
Tench, Wm.	Del	"	5-7-1777
Ten Eyck, Cornelius	N J	"	11-21-1778
Ten Eyck, John	Lt N J	Killed	6-17-1777
Ten Eyck, John	Pvt 2 N Y	Died	6-3-1779
Tennant, Joshua	Pvt 7 Mass	"	10-9-1777
Tennant, Robert	Pvt 5 Mass	"	1-25-1777
Tennent, William	Chap SC	"	1777
Tenney, E Elisha	Pvt 7 Mass	"	1-10-1778
Tenney, John	Pvt 15 Mass	"	4-10-1778
Terrell, Nathan	Pvt Conn	"	6-30-1778
Terry, Ephraim	Maj	"	1783
Terry, Josiah	Pvt N J	Killed	4- 1782
Terry, Josiah	Pvt N J	"	12-15-1783
Terry, Levi	Pvt Conn	Died	3-16-1778
Terry, Nathaniel	Va	"	1778
Terry, Sam'l	Pvt 4 NY	"	2-1-1779
Terry, Thomas	Col Conn	"	1776
Terry, William	Va	"	1776
Terville, Andre-Philippe	Cpl France	"	1781
Terzer, John	Pvt 1 N J	"	In War
Tesler, Simon	Pvt Conn	Killed	12-8-1777
Tesley, John	Pvt N C	Died	10-24-1778
Tew, Henry	Capt	"	1783 Prison
Tewksbury, John	Mass	"	1775
Thacher, Rowland Rev	Mass	"	1779
Thackerel, Rezin	Pvt 1 Md	Killed	8-16-1780
Thaddeus	Conn	Died	1- 1782
Tharp, Jacob	Pvt 2 Md	"	5-31-1780
Thayer, Ephraim	Mass	"	6-13-1781
Thayer, Joseph	Mass	"	5-21-1777
Thayer, Moses	Mass	"	1783
Thayer, Stephen	Pvt 5 Mass	"	10-31-1777
Thayer, Stephen	Pvt Mass	"	1781
Thayer, William	Lt Mass	"	1779
Thessill, John	N H	Killed	6-17-1775
Thevenin, Louis	France	Died	1781

Thomas, Anthony	Mass	Died	7-14-1781
Thomas, Anthony	Col Mass	"	1781
Thomas, Daniel	Conn	"	1781
Thomas, Daniel	Mass	"	1781
Thomas, Davis	Pa	"	1781
Thomas, Edward	Mass	"	5-7-1778
Thomas, George	Pvt 1 Md	"	3-7-1777
Thomas, Hart Jr	Pvt Conn	"	9-7-1777
Thomas, Helen	Lt N C	Killed	1781
Thomas, Henry	Pvt Can	Died	2-20-1777
Thomas, Isaac	Del	"	1780
Thomas, Israel	Mass	"	6-29-1778
Thomas, James	Pvt 5 Mass	"	3-20-1778
Thomas, James	Va	Killed	1779
Thomas, John	Pvt 6 Md	Died	2- 1779
Thomas, John	Maj Gen Mass	"	5-30-1776
Thomas, John	Brig Gen Pa	"	1776
Thomas, John	Brig Gen Mass	"	6-3-1776
Thomas, John	Ens R I	Killed	8-7-1776
Thomas, John	Pvt Pa	Died	6-3-1781
Thomas, John	Pvt 4 NY	"	9-19-1777
Thomas, Joseph	Lt Col NH	Killed	9-19-1777
Thomas, Lemuel	Mass	Died	1-26-1776
Thomas, Mayo	Mass	"	1778 At Sea
Thomas, Michael	Pvt 5 Md	"	8-24-1777
Thomas, Richard	Pvt 14 Mass	"	1-4-1778
Thomas, Stephen	Pvt 10 Mass	"	4-8-1778
Thomas, Thomas	Del	"	4-9-1781
Thomas, Titus	Pvt 4 Mass	"	7-25-1778
Thomas, Willm	Del	"	10-28-1778
Thomas, Willowby	Pvt N C	"	1-12-1779
Thompson, Archd	Pvt 5 NY	"	7-27-1777
Thompson, Archibald	Pa	"	1779
Thompson, Bennitt	Pvt 2 Md	"	7-1-1778
Thompson, Carmon	N J	"	5-12-1782
Thompson, Daniel	Mass	Killed	4-19-1775
Thompson, David	Pvt 11 Mass	"	7-7-1777
Thompson, David	Pvt 1 N J	Died	5-15-1777
Thompson, Edwd	Pvt 7 N C	"	2-3-1778
Thompson, George	Capt NY	"	1782
Thompson, Goodin	Pvt 5 NC	"	8-22-1777
Thompson, Isaac	Pvt R I	"	1782
Thompson, Jabez	Lt Col Conn	Killed	9-15-1776
Thompson, James	Lt N Y	Died	6-7-1780
Thompson, James	Capt NC	"	1-28-1781
Thompson, Jeduthan	Pvt Conn	Killed	7-6-1779
Thompson, John	Pvt 2 NY	Died	2-26-1777
Thompson, Joshua Jr	R I	"	1775
Thompson, Joshua	Pvt 4 NJ	"	12- 1777
Thompson, Nathl	Pvt 4 NJ	"	5-4-1778
Thompson, Robert	Del	"	1-25-1781
Thompson, Saml	Pvt 1 Md	"	4-10-1777
Thompson, Thomas	Lt NY	"	1781

Thompson, William	Pvt 2 Md	Died	7- 1780
Thompson, William	Lt Conn	Killed	2-7- 1777
Thompson, William	Brig.Gen.Pa	Died	9-4- 1781
Thompson, William	Pvt 2 NY	"	11-29-1778
Thomson, Andrew	N C	"	1778
Thomson, Barth W	Pvt 7 Mass	"	6-17-1778
Thomson, Edward	Pvt N C	"	2-3-1778
Thomson, Isaiah	Conn	"	1781
Thomson, John	Pvt Pa	"	1779
Thomson, John	N C	"	1781
Thomson, Moses	Pvt SC	Killed	1781
Thomson, Richard	Pvt 1 Md	Died	10-21-1778
Thomson, William	Lt Va	"	1778
Thomson, Willis	Pvt NC	"	10-7- 1778
Thornkill, John	Pvt Va	"	1778
Thornson, Benjamin	Pvt Pa	"	10-1-1776
Thornton, Hugh	Pvt N H	"	3-1-1778
Thrift, Miles	Pvt 1 N C	"	5- 1779
Thrift, Solomon	Pvt N C	"	6-15-1778
Throp, Abel	Pvt N J	"	9-1-1780
Throp, Jacob	Conn	"	7-5-1779
Throp, Reuben	Pvt R I	"	4-7-1778
Thorpe, Adam	Pvt Conn	Killed	7-6-1779
Thorpe, Jacob	Pvt Conn	"	7-5-1779
Thoupe, Richard	Pvt 7 Md	Died	10-4-1777
Thow, Thomas	Pvt NC	"	7-20-1778
Thow, Thos	Pvt 2 NC	"	7-20-1778
Thrall, William	Conn	"	4-1-1783
Thunell, Abraham	Pvt NC	"	1- 1779
Thurrell, Abm	Pvt 8 NC	"	1- 1779
Thurnell, Jno	Pvt 6 NC	"	11- 1778
Thurstin, Jonathan	Pvt 3 Mass	"	11-7-1777
Thurston, Elihu	Cpl Mass	"	12-26-1777
Thurston, Walter	N Y	"	12-10-1777
Tibbets, James	Pvt 13 Mass	"	11-2-1777
Tibbets, Nathaniel	Pvt 4 Mass	"	2-23-1780
Tidd, Nathan	Cpl 3 Mass	"	10-28-1778
Tiffany, Samuel	Mass	"	1- 9-1781
Tiffts, Francis	Pvt R I	"	6-1-1778
Tift, Joshua	Pvt Conn	"	9-23-1778
Tilden, Cuff	Pvt 2 Mass	"	1-18-1779
Tillinghast, Charles	R I	"	1776
Tillinghast, Cuff	Pvt R I	"	9-1-1778
Tilton, Elisha	Pvt Mass	"	8-20-1781 Prison
Tilton, Jacob	N H	"	11-7-1776 Prison
Tilton, Joseph	Mass	"	1779
Tilton, Joseph	N Y	"	10-24-1777
Tim, Absalom	Pvt 2 N J	"	5-26-1777
Timothy, Nokes	Pvt 13 Mass	"	6-18-1778
Tinker, John	Pvt N C	"	10- 1781
Tinker, Nehemiah	Capt Conn	"	1783
Tinkham, Amasa	Mass	"	9-27-1778
Tinkham, Isaac	Mass	"	10-28-1779

Tinkham, Isaiah	3 Mass	Killed	9-11-1777
Tippet, Peter	Pvt Md	Died	12-15-1781
Tirrell, Jesse	N H	"	In War
Tisdale (Tisdel) Reed	Mass	"	1777
Tissier, Jacques	France	"	1781
Tite, James	Pvt Md	"	10-1-1782
Tob, Moses	Pvt 14 Mass	"	12-20-1777
Tobey, Elisha	Dr. Mass	"	1781
Tobias, Jacob	Pvt 5 N Y	"	1- 1779
Tobias, Jonathan	Pvt Conn	"	9-13-1781
Toby, Vernon	Pvt 14 Mass	"	5-14-1777
Todd, Asa	Pvt Conn	Killed	7-5-1779
Todd, James	Pvt 7 NC	Died	9-29-1777
Todd, Jonah	Dr Conn	"	3-17-1783
Todd, Justis	Pvt Conn	"	11-6-1779
Todd, Samuel	Pvt 12 Mass	"	10-7-1777
Tode, Thomas	Pvt 7 N C	"	9- 1777
Toker, Jonas	Pvt Mass	Killed	1775
Toland, Benjamin	Del	Died	1-7-1779
Toland, Hugh	Del	"	11-7-1778
Toland, John	Del	Killed	3-15-1781
Toland, William	Pvt Pa	Died	9-26-1776
Tolin, Hugh	Pvt 1 N J	"	4-10-1778
Tolley, Walter	Md	"	1783
Tolman, Ebenezer	Pvt 11 Mass	"	3-14-1780
Tolman, Elijah	Pvt 13 Mass	"	8-1-1777
Tolman, John	Pvt Mass	"	1779
Tomey, Charles	Pvt R I	"	12-16-1776
Tomkins, Benjamin	Pvt Conn	"	9-23-1782
Tomkins, Isaac	Pvt N J	"	4-3-1778
Tomlinson, Aaron	Pvt Ga	"	1780
Tonn, Asa	Pvt Conn	"	1781
Tongue, Geo	Pvt 5 NY	"	10-6-1777
Tool, John	Pvt 4 NY	"	3-20-1779
Tooley, John	Pvt Conn	"	8-26-1778
Toothaker, Timothy	N H	"	6-17-1775
Topley, Mansfield	Mass	"	1779
Topping, Paul	Pvt Conn	Killed	6-26-1777
Torrey, William	Mass	Died	3-1-1779
Touchstone, Christopher	Pvt Md	"	9-8-1781
Tourtellotte, Abraham	Conn	"	5-6-1779
Tousset, Jean	France	"	1781
Tower, Adam	Pvt R I	"	9- 1777
Town, Asa	Mass	"	1781
Town, Ebenezer	Ens 4 Mass	"	2-11-1778
Towne, Amos	Lt Mass	"	1779
Towner, Moses	Pvt Conn	"	8-14-1777
Townsend, Benjamin	Lt Mass	"	1783
Townsend, Caffey	Pvt 11 Mass	"	6-25-1778
Townsend, Daniel	Pvt 13 Mass	"	3-6-1778
Townsend, Daniel	Mass	Killed	4-19-1775
Townsend, Daniel	Mass	Died	1777

Townsend, Hendrick	Pvt 1 Conn	Killed	4-26-1777
Townsend, John	Pvt 13 Mass	Died	3-16-1778
Townshend, Aaron	Pvt 7 Md	"	10-9-1778
Townshend, Joseph	Pvt 7 Md	"	4-1-1780
Towson, Isaac	Mass	"	12-6-1782
Tracy, Patrick	R I	Killed	12-31-1775 Que
Tracy, Thomas	Pvt Mass	Died	1777
Trafford, Diah	Mass	"	1778
Trask, Benjamin	Pvt Mass	"	1776
Trask, Ebenezer	Mass	"	1779
Traves, Jacob	Pvt 2 NY	"	5-6-1778
Traysa, Patrick	Pvt R I	Killed	12-31-1775 Que
Treadwell, Hammond	Pvt 10 Mass	"	7-2-1777
Treasure, Richard	Del	Died	1781
Tredwell, James	Pvt R I	"	11-22-1777
Trego, James	Pvt 2 Md	"	1-7-1778
Trenchard, George	Capt N J	"	1780
Trentlen, John Adam	SC	Killed	1780
Trigg, Stephen	Col Va	Died	1782
Triplet, Charles	Ens 1 NC	"	12- 1776
Tripp, Isaac Sr	Pvt Pa	Killed	1778
Tripp, James 2d	Mass	Died	1781
Tripp, Stephen	Pvt 10 Mass	"	2-1- 1778
Trippe, Samuel		"	1778 At Sea
Troop, Geo.	Pvt 5 NY	"	10-7-1777
Trowbridge, Daniel	Sgt 11 Conn	"	9-20-1776
Trowbridge, Shubel	Pvt NY	"	1782
Troy,de Charles	Capt	"	12- 1779
Truck, Abraham	Pvt R I	"	In War
Truesdell, Gamaliel	Pvt NY	Killed	1778
Trumball, Isaac	Pvt 3 Mass	Died	9-18-1779
Trumbull, Joseph	Conn	"	4-23-1778
Truner, Edward	Lt Mass	"	1777
Trunk, Peter	Pvt R I	"	3-9-1778
Trusdale, Ebenezer	Pvt Can	"	5-30-1782
Trusler, William	SC	Killed	7-15-1781
Trusty, John	Pvt Md	Died	7-17-1781
Tubbs, John	Pvt Pa	"	1778
Tuck, John	Chap NY	"	1777
Tuck, Samuel	N Y	"	11-12-1777
Tucke, John	Chap NH	"	1777
Tucker, Anthony	Pvt Md	"	9-8-1781
Tucker, Joseph	Pvt 9 Mass	"	7-1-1778
Tucker, Manasseh	Mass	"	1778
Tucker, Samuel	Sgt Mass		1776
Tucker, Silas	N Y	"	1777
Tucker, William	Pvt Pa	"	6-3- 1781
Tucker, William	Sgt 1 Md	"	1780
Tucker, William	Pvt Md	"	2-18-1780
Tuel, Wm	Pvt Md	Killed	10-4-1777
Tuff, John	Pvt 6 Md	Died	5-10-1779
Tufts, Aaron		"	9-18-1781 Prison
Tufts, Adam	Pvt 10 Mass	"	4-16-1778
Tufts, William	Pvt 9 Mass	Killed	8-16-1777
Tufts, William	Lt Mass	Died	1783

Tugby, John	Pvt 6 Md	Died	10-28-1777
Tuggle, Henry	Pvt Va	"	1781
Tumand, Peter	Pvt 4 NY	"	5-20-1778
Tumelin, Nicholas	France	"	1781
Tumpum, Gideon	Pvt 2 Mass	"	2-5- 1778
Tunnell, William	Capt Del	"	1776
Turner, Capt	N C	Killed	10- 1777
Turner, Amos	Fifer Mass	Died	1780
Turner, Abram	Pvt 2 Md	"	9-30-1778
Turner, Benjamin	Pvt 2 NC	"	12-1-1777
Turner, David	Pvt Mass	"	1775
Turner, Danl	Pvt 8 NC	"	1- 1778
Turner, Edward	Sgt Mass	"	1777
Turner, Edward	Lt 5 Mass	"	12-26-1777
Turner, Ezekiel	Pvt 2 Mass	"	12-15-1778
Turner, Jacob	Capt 3 N C	Killed	10-4-1777
Turner, John	Pvt 1 Conn	Died	1-16-1778
Turner, Joseph	Pvt R I	"	In War
Turner, Mattocks	Del	"	In War
Turner, Nathan P	Pvt Conn	"	7-1-1778
Turner, Nicholas	Pvt Can	"	5-3-1778
Turner, Thomas		Killed	9-23-1779 At Sea
Turner, William			7-27-1781 Prison
Turner, Wm	Pvt 1 NC	Died	5-24-1778
Turney, Michael	Pvt 18 Cont	"	11-2-1776
Turnal, William	Va	"	2-25-1777
Turpin, William	Capt Md	"	1782
Turrill, Job	Pvt Conn	"	5-4-1778
Tussey, John	Pvt 4 N J	"	3-20-1777
Tusten, Benjamin Jr	Lt	Killed	1779
Tutkill, Barnabas	Maj NY	Died	1782
Tutkill, James	Pvt 4 NY	"	5-29-1778
Tuttle, Elisha	Pvt Conn	Killed	7-5-1779
Tuttle, Ichabod	Pa	"	7-3-1778
Tuttle, Jabez	Pa	Died	1777
Tuttle, John	Pvt Mass	"	1781
Tuttle, John Sen	Pvt 4 N J	"	9-30-1778
Tuttle, Levi	Pvt Conn	"	4-20-1780
Tuttle, Samuel	Lt Mass	"	12-11-1780
Tuttle, Thomas	Pvt N H	"	2-17-1778
Tuttle, Thomas	Pvt N H	"	1783
Twitchell, Moses	Pvt Mass	"	1777
Tyler, Abner	Lt Mass	"	1777
Tyler, Bezaleel	Capt NY	Killed	1779
Tyler, Boaz	Pvt Conn	Died	4-19- 1778
Tyler, John A	Pvt N J	"	3-20- 1777
Tyler, John Jr	Ens Va	"	1-7- 1777
Tyler, Jonathan	Pvt 12 Mass	"	1-8-1778
Tyler, Levy	Pvt Conn	"	7-22-1777
Tyler, Moses	R I	"	1782
Tyler, Robert	Col Md	"	1777
Tylor, Nathan	P Pvt 1 Conn	"	1778
Tyrell, Lawrence	Pvt Can	"	6-1- 1777
Twing, Aaron	Pvt 1 Conn	"	2-1-1778

Twining, John	Pvt 1 N J	Died	3-18-1778
Twist, Tho	Pvt Conn	"	4- 1780
Twitchell, Moses	Pvt Mass	"	1777
Twyford, William	Pvt 3 Md	"	12-22-1777

U

Ubel, Georges	France	Died	1781
Ubrich, Nicholas	Pvt R I	"	5-3-1777
Uinal, Benjamin	Pvt 11 Mass	"	8-25-1777
Underwood, Joseph	Pvt 5 Mass	"	10- 1778
Upaub, Dappo	Pvt Conn	"	9- 1777
Upton, Willis	Pvt N C	"	7-1- 1778
Usher, John	Pvt 5 Md	"	3-15-1777
Usurp, Joseph	Pvt Conn	"	3-22-1778

V

Vachel, Capt	Pa	Died	1778
Vachel, Howard D	Capt Va	"	1778
Vachere, Andre	Sgt France	"	1781
Vadeford, Noah	Pvt N C	"	3-5-1778
Vail, Benjamin	Capt N Y	"	1779
Vail, Benjamin	N Y	Killed	1779
Vail, Gilbert	N Y	Died	1779
Vail, Micah	Capt Vt	Killed	1777
Vail, Gilbert T	Pvt N Y	"	7-22-1779
Valentine, Elvin	Q M N Y	Died	1779
Valentine, Leonard	N C	"	11-18-1781
Valentine, Simon	Pvt 12 Mass	"	6-12-1778
Vallance, William	N Y	"	1781
Vallean, David	Sgt Pa	Killed	6-8-1776
Van Arsdale, Isaac	N J	Died	7-20-1776
Van Brunne, John De La	Lt Md	Killed	9-12-1781
Van Buren, Moas	Pvt N Y	Died	1783
Vance, James	Pvt 10 NC	"	11-15-1778
Vandemark, Gibert	Pvt 4 NY	"	10- 1779
Vanderhull, Gershon	Pvt N J	"	3-28-1778
Vanderpool, John	Pvt N J	"	2-27-1781
Van Derveer, Elias	N J	"	11-29-1778
Van Der Veer, Peter	Pvt N J	"	1778
Vander Voort, John	Pvt 4 NY	"	10-15-1777
Vandous, Henry	Pvt N J	"	10-14-1777
Vandyke, Charles	Pvt NC	"	4-3-1778
Van Dyke, John	Pvt N J	"	1778
Van Etten, Anthony	N Y	"	1778
Vangorder, Abraham	Pvt Pa	"	7-3-1778 Prison
Vangover, Darrick	Pvt R I	"	9-1-1778
Vangilder, James	Pvt 13 Mass	"	2-5-1778
Van Horn, Bernard	Lt Pa	"	1778
Van Horn, Henry	Pa	"	1777
Van Kenren, Abraham	Capt NY	"	1776
Van Liew, Denice	N J	"	10-17-1777
Van Metre, Abraham	N J	"	1783
Van Ness, Abraham	N J	"	8-12-1777
Van Ness, John	Col N Y	"	1776

Vanpelt, Daniel	Pvt N J	Died	1776
Vn Odle, Peter	Pvt N J	"	4-1-1778
Van Rensselaer, Killian	Col N Y	"	1781
Van Sant, Garret	Lt Pa	"	1779
Van Tassell, Corn	Pvt 1 N Y	"	1-3-1780
Van Vechten, Derrick	Maj N Y	Killed	1777
Van Veghten, Tobias	Pvt 1 NY	Died	7-26-1777
Van Vleiland, Cornelius 2	Lt SC	Killed	10-9-1779
Van Voorhees, Daniel	Lt N J	Died	1782
Van Vost, Christian	N Y	"	1781
Van Wee, John	Pa	"	7-3-1778
Van Winkle, Jacob	Lt N J	"	12-17-1778
Van Woerst, Christian	Pvt 1 NY	"	10-16-1781
Van Wyck, Cornelius	Capt N Y	Killed	10-31-1776
Vardell, Sgt	SC	Died	In War
Varennes, Jean	France	"	1781
Varner, Henry	Pvt 3 Ky	"	3-19-1778
Varnum, Stephen	Pvt 8 Mass	"	5-30-1777
Vaugh, Richard	Pvt N C	"	6-2-1778
Vaughan, Danl	Cpl 10 N C	"	9-26-1781
Vaughan, West	Pvt N C	"	2-20-1778
Vaughan, William	Lt Del	Killed	3-22-1777
Veasey	Capt N Y	"	8-27-1776
Veazey	Capt 1 Md	Killed	In War
Vedder, Aaron	Pvt 1 NY	Died	1-6-1778
Vellentine, Thomas	Capt Mass	"	1779
Verdavoir, Oger-Joseph	France	"	1781
Vernon, George	Pvt Md	Killed	3-3-1781
Vernier, Jos	Maj France	"	10-9-1779
Verrier, Joseph	France	Died	1781
Vial, Pierre	France	Died	1781
Viall, Samuel	Lt Mass	Killed	1777
Vibett, Isaac	Pvt R I	Died	2-23-1778
Vicory, Henry	Pvt N C	"	6-18-1777
Vicory, Marmaduke	Pvt N C	"	12-10-1782
Vickery, Marma	Pvt 10 NC	"	12-14-1782
Vickory, Eli		"	1777
Viets, John	Conn	"	1777 Prison Master
Villaret, Joseph	France	"	1781
Vincen, David	Pvt 10 N C	"	10- 1781
Vincent, John	Pvt Md	"	4-25-1781
Vinestreet, Jno	Pvt 5 Md	"	12-9-1777
Vinson, David	Pvt N C	"	10-7-1781
Vinton, Thomas		"	7-21-1781 Prison
Vitre, Jean Louis	France	"	1781
Vochel	Capt Pa	"	1778
Vollintine, Thomas	Capt Mass	"	1779
Vollume, Leonard	Pvt N Y	"	1777
Von Rayalin, Carl Frederick	Lt	"	1780
Vorhees, Peter	Capt N J	Killed	10-26-1779
Vorhies, Peter V	Capt N J	Died	10-26-1779
Vose, William	Pvt Mass	"	1778
Voss, Joseph	Pvt N C	"	7-10-1783
Vose, Joseph	Pvt 10 N C	"	7-10-1783

Name	Unit	Status	Date
Vose, Joshua	Mass	Died	1775
Vose, Seth	Pvt 5 Mass	"	2-26-1778
Vose, William	Sgt Mass	"	1776
Vose, William	Mass	"	1778
Vaughn, Jesse	Ens Mass	"	7-14-1782
Vrooman, Ephraim	Lt N Y	Killed	1780
Vrooman, Tennis	Capt N Y	Died	1780
Vrooman, Tunis	Capt N Y	Killed	8- 1780
Vulva, Thos	Pvt 1 N Y	Died	2-10-1777

W

Name	Unit	Status	Date
Wade, Edward	Lt Va	Died	1778
Wade, Joseph	Va	"	1778
Wade, Nathan	Pvt N J	Killed	7-2-1779
Wade, Nehemiah	N J	Died	1776
Wade, Stephen	Conn	"	1781
Wade, William	Pvt Can	"	5-15-1777
Wade, Zebulon	Pvt 8 Mass	"	9-23-1777
Wadleigh, Joseph	Mass	"	2-8-1779
Wadsworth, Amos	Mass	"	10-19-1775
Wadsworth, Benjamin	Mass	"	2-23-1782
Wadsworth, Jonathan	Capt Conn	"	1777
Waeger, Frederick	Pvt R I	"	7- 1777
Wogan, Jacob	Fifer Pa	"	1783
Waggoner, Jas.	Pvt 10 NC	"	2-25-1782
Wainright, Fisk	N H	Killed	6-17-1775
Wainright, James	Del	Died	1-25-1781
Wainright, Obediah	Pvt 10 N C	"	6-13-1783
Wait, John	Conn	"	1776
Wait, John	Pvt Mass	"	1776
Wait, Joseph	Lt Col N H	"	9-28-1776
Wait, Josiah	N Y	Killed	1776
Waite, Elias	Cpl 10 Mass	"	6-28-1778
Waite, Samuel Jr	Mass	Died	1783
Wake, Samuel	Pvt Conn	"	1-23-1778
Wakefield, Jonathan	Mass	Killed	1776
Walborn, May	Lt Pa	Died	9-21-1777
Walcott, Christopher	Ens Mass	Killed	7-7-1777
Walcott, Jabez	Mass	Died	1781
Wales, Ebenezer	Sgt Mass	"	1781
Wales, Jonathan	Mass	"	1780
Wales, Moses	Mass	"	5-3-1778
Wales, Thomas	Mass	"	10-23-1778
Wales, Timothy	Mass	"	1777
Walke, Anthony	Va	"	1782
Walker, Aaron	Lt Mass	"	10-19-1775
Walker, Alex	Pvt R I	"	1-13-1780
Walker, Asa	Mass	"	5-9-1782
Walker, Benjamin	Capt Conn	Killed	6-17-1775
Walker, Dyer	Pvt Conn	Died	12-15-1777
Walker, Elnathan	Pvt N Y	"	6-6-1775
Walker, Enos	Pvt Md	"	1782
Walker, Enos	Pvt Mass	"	1782

Walker, Isaac	Ga	Died	1781
Walker, Jacob	Lt Pa	"	1780
Walker, John	Mass	"	1782
Walker, John	Pvt 5 NY	"	9- 1778
Walker, Jonathan	Pvt N H	"	6-6-1778
Walker, Joseph	Pvt Ky	"	2-2-1776
Walker, Levi	Pvt 5 Mass	"	4-30-1778
Walker, Micah	Pvt 7 Mass	"	9-10-1777
Walker, Richard	Lt 5 Mass	Killed	8-29-1778
Walker, Zephaniah	Pvt Mass	Died	1775
Walklet, John	Pvt 8 Mass	"	6-9-1778
Wall, Pat	Pvt 1 N Y	"	1780
Wallace, Andrew	Capt Va	Killed	3-15-1781
Wallace, James	Ens Va	Died	8- 1777
Wallace, Robert	Capt N H	"	10-10-1782
Wallace, Samuel	N H	"	7-29-1778
Wallace, Thos	Pvt 10 N C	"	10- 1781
Waller, Allen	Ens Va	"	1- 1777
Waller, William	Pvt Va	"	2-15-1777
Wallis, Colley	Conn	"	1781
Wallis, Francis 2	Lt Md	"	1779
Wallis, Josiah	Pvt	"	1780 At Sea
Wallis, Richard	Pvt 3 Md	"	9-11-1777
Walls, Sutton	Pvt Md	"	1-6-1778
Walston, William	Pvt N C	"	1778
Walters, Walters	Pvt 10 N C	"	8-30-1779
Walton, George	Pvt Va	"	1780
Walton, Joshua	Pvt Mass	"	1783
Walworth, Charles	Capt Mass	"	1782
Walworth, Hugh	Mass	"	3-1-1780
Wand, James	Sgt Can	"	1-31-1782
Wannaker, B	Pvt 4 Md	"	4-8-1778
Waples, John	Del	"	11-14-1782
Ward, Benjamin	Pvt 10 N C	"	11- 1781
Ward, Charles	N C	Killed	1780
Ward, Daniel	Pvt Conn	Died	3-30-1778
Ward, Isaiah	Pvt 3 Mass	"	9-25-1780
Ward, Jack	Pvt R I	"	2-20-1778
Ward, John	Pa	"	7-3-1778
Ward, Kerley	Cpl Mass	"	6-17-1775
Ward, Nahum	Capt 9 Mass	"	3-6-1778
Ward, Patric	Conn	"	9-6-1781
Ward, Peter	Pvt 2 Md	Killed	6-28-1778
Ward, Rufus	Pvt R I	Died	6-30-1777
Ward, Samuel	Gov R I	"	3-25-1776
Ward, Samuel	Capt Mass	"	1778
Ward, Stephen	Pvt N J	"	In War
Ward, Thaddeus	Pvt 15 Mass	"	6-9-1778
Ware, John	Pvt Mass	"	9-18-1779
Ware, Nathaniel Sr	Mass	"	3-4-1781
Warner, Andrew	Cpl Conn	"	7-20-1778
Warner, Arbuckle	Pvt 5 Md	"	9-2-1780
Warner, Bristor	Pvt Conn	"	1-11-1778

Warner, Daniel	Pvt Conn	Died	1778
Warner, Daniel	Conn	"	1777
Warner, Ichabod	Pvt 9 Mass	"	7-19-1777
Warner, John	Cpl 7 Md	"	10-20-1777
Warner, Thomas	Pvt Conn	"	1778
Warner, William	Pvt N Y	"	1776
Warren, Elijah	Pvt 12 Mass	"	10-13-1778
Warren, Gideon		"	6-1777 Prison
Warren, Isaac	Capt 13 Mass	"	6-13-1778
Warren, John	Pvt 18 Cont	"	5-23-1776
Warren, John	Mass	"	4-25-1777
Warren, Joseph	Dr Mass	"	6-17-1775
Warren, Joseph	Maj Gen	Killed	6-17-1775
Warren, Mathew	Pvt 6 N C	Died	2-9-1778
Warren, Samuel P	Pvt Conn	"	8-8-1777
Warren, Samuel	Mass	"	1-26-1775
Warren, Zebu	Pvt 5 N C	"	2-15-1778
Warrener, Daniel	Pvt 10 Mass	"	8-27-1777
Warrin, William	N H	Killed	6-17-1775
Warring, James	2 Reg	Died	10-17-1780
Warring, Samuel	Pvt Conn	"	7-4-1778
Worsham, John	Capt Va	"	1779
Wortendyke, Frederick	N J	"	4-10-1780
Worthen, Ezekiel	Maj Mass	"	1783
Warwick, James	Del	"	10-20-1782
Washburn, Abiezer	Pvt 13 Mass	"	11-17-1777
Washburn, Benjam	Pvt Conn	Killed	12-7-1777
Washburn, Edward	Pvt 3 Mass	Died	2-1-1780
Washburn, Oliver	Pvt R I	"	3-20-1778
Washington, Augustine	Col Va	"	1781
Washington, John	Capt Va	"	3-14-1777
Washington, Samuel	Col Va	"	1781
Washington, Samuel Walter	Col Va	"	1781
Wasson, James	Conn	"	1781
Waterman, Flavins	Pa	"	7-3-1778
Waterman,	Hg Sgt 2 NY	"	7-20-1777
Waterman, John	Lt R I	Killed	4-20-1778
Waterman, Luther P	Pvt Conn	"	11-14-1777
Waterman, Samuel	Mass	Died	9-10-1778
Waterman, Saml	Pvt 2 NY	"	7- 1778
Waterman, William	Pvt 2 Mass	"	2-15-1777
Waters, Abiather	Pvt 6 Mass	"	11-20-1777
Waters, Elisha	Pa	"	7-3-1778
Waters, John	Pvt 6 Md	"	8-23-1778
Watkins, Benjamin	Md	"	1779
Watkins, John	Pvt Md	"	4-26-1783
Watkins, Peter	Pvt 3 Md	"	2-10-1778
Watkins, Peter	Pvt Del	"	1778
Watkinson, Benj	Del	"	11-2-1778

Name	Rank/Unit	Status	Date
Watrous, Samuel	Pvt Conn	Died	1775
Watson, Douglass	Pvt Va	"	1777
Watson, George	Pvt Md	"	7-4-1781
Watson, Isaac	Pvt Mass	"	11-8-1778
Watson, John	R I	"	1782
Watson, Jonathan	Pvt 9 Mass	"	1-28-1777
Watson, Marston	Mass	"	1783
Watson, Michael	Capt SC	Killed	5- 1782
Watson, Miles	Pvt 10 NC	Died	9-12-1778
Watson, Patrick	Pa	Killed	1780
Watson, Prince	Pvt R I	Died	3-1-1781
Watson, Richard	Pvt 3 NY	"	4-18-1779
Watson, Samuel	Lt SC	Killed	1781
Watson, William	Pvt Conn	Died	3-14-1777
Watts, Andrew	Pvt 4 N C	"	2-19-1778
Watts, James	Pvt 4 Md	Killed	7-15-1779
Watts, James	Sgt Pa	"	1779
Watts, John	Pvt N H	Died	9-19-1777
Watts, Wm	Pvt 9 N C	"	9-9-1777
Watts, W. William	Pvt	"	9-9-1774
Wattson, Edward	Pvt 3 Md	Killed	10-4-1777
Waugh, Robert	Mass	Died	12-8-1778
Way, Herman	Pvt Conn	"	9-6-1778
Wayne, Nicl.	Pvt Can	"	10-29-1781
Wear, Richard	Capt N H	"	8-2-1777
Weat, Nathan	Pvt 5 N C	"	11-30-1777
Weatherbee, Jacob	Pvt N H	"	1783
Weatherell, Jacob	Pvt 13 Mass	"	3-22-1778
Weaver, Christian	Drummer Pa	"	1783
Weaver, Jacob	Pvt R I	"	1-10-1777
Weaver, John	Pa	"	2- 9-1781
Weaver, Stephen	Pvt R I	Died	5-1-1778
Webb, Charles	Col Conn	"	1780
Webb, James	Md	"	In War
Webb, Jos.	Sgt 4 Md	"	2-11- 1778
Webb, Jotham	Mass	Killed	4-19-1775
Webber, John	Pvt Mass	Died	3-1-1778
Webley, Samuel	Pvt 6 N C	"	12-8-1777
Webster, Abel	Conn	"	3-27-1777
Webster, Amos	Lt N H	"	10-7-1777
Webster, Benjamin	Conn	"	1782
Webster, Eddy P	Pvt Conn	"	9- 1777
Webster, George	Mass	"	1781
Webster, George	Conn	"	1781
Webster, Jacob	Mass	"	1776
Webster, Joseph	Pvt 8 Mass	"	10-23-1778
Webster, Nathanl	Pvt 3 Mass	"	9-21-1780
Webster, Robert	Capt Mass		7-30-1778
Webster, Samuel	Rev N H	"	8-4-1777
Webster, Stephen	Pvt Mass	"	1782
Webster, Thomas	Pvt 2 Md	Killed	8-16-1780
Wedding, John	Pvt 3 Md	Died	9-23-1778

Weed, Benjamin	Mass	Died	6-25-1781
Weed, David J	N H	"	9-1-1778
Weed, John Jr	Pvt Conn	"	11-29-1777
Weed, Joseph	Pvt Conn	"	4-10-1778
Weedon, Jonathan	Pvt Md	"	2-13-1783
Weeks, Bartholomew	Pa	"	7-3-1778
Weeks, Jonathan	Pa	"	7-3-1778
Weeks, Nathan	Lt R I	"	1-26-1778
Weeks, Philip	Pa	"	7-3-1778
Weeks, Silas	Pvt 6 N C	"	5-22-1778
Weeks, Sylvanus	Pvt 1 N C	"	3-15-1778
Weems, William Loch	Md	"	1782
Weid, Elijah	Pvt Conn	"	5-9-1779
Weigh, Baltus	Pvt Pa	"	1777
Weir, Thomas	Capt N J	"	1-26-1777
Welch, Ephm	Sgt 4 N J	"	8-26-1777
Welch, Mort	Pvt Mass	"	8-18-1777
Welch, C Noah	Pvt 10 N C	"	4-21-1783
Welch, Philip	Pvt Md	"	12-1-1781
Welch, Whitman	Conn	"	3- 1776
Weld, John	Conn	"	1777
Weld, Solomon	Pvt 6 Mass	"	11-21- 1777
Weldon, Benjamin	Pvt 10 Mass	"	7-7- 1777
Welldon, James	Pvt Conn	Killed	9-4-1777
Weller, Henry	Pvt Can	Died	12-31-1779
Welles, James	Lt Pa	Killed	1778
Welles, Noah	Chap Md	Died	1776
Welles, Noah	Chap Yale Conn	"	12-31- 1776
Welles, William	Conn	"	1778
Wells, Abel	N Y	"	12-12-1777
Wells, Barker	Capt R I	"	1780
Wells, Ceaser	Pvt R I	"	12-15-1779
Wells, David	Pvt Conn	"	10-7-1777
Wells, James	Lt Conn	Killed	1778
Wells, James Sr	Pa	"	1778
Wells, Josiah	Pvt N H	Died	7-31- 1778
Wells, Moses	Pvt Mass	"	1778
Wells, Willis	4 N C	"	11-16-1778
Welsh, James	Pvt 2 Md	Killed	6-28-1778
Welsh, James	Pvt Can	Died	2-3-1777
Welsh, Patk	Pvt 5 Md	"	3-30-1777
Welsh, Silas	Sgt Mass	"	9-8-1776
Welton, Samuel	Cpl Conn	"	1777
Wenchel, Joseph	Pvt Conn	"	6-16-1777
Wendall, Thomas	N J	"	1777 Prison
Wendam, Charles	Pvt R I	"	4-6-1778
Wentworth, John	Capt Me	"	1781
Wentworth, Paul	Pvt Me	"	1783
Wentworth, Stuart	Mass	"	1776
Wesson, Richard	Pvt 15 Mass	Killed	8-20-1779
West, Alexander	Pvt Md	Died	11-1-1782
West, Benjamin	Lt Conn	Killed	6-17-1775
West, Charles	2 Reg	Died	8-16-1777

West, Fredk	Pvt 3 Md	Died	2- 1778
West, Josiah	Lt Conn	"	11-5- 1783
West, Samuel	Pvt Mass	"	7-15- 1778
West, Thomas	Mass	"	10-6-1782
Westbrook, Cornelius	Pvt Pa	"	1777
Westbrook, Peter	Capt N J	"	4-19-1780
Westervelt, David	N J	"	3-23-1777
Westervelt, David	Lt N Y	"	10-23-1777 Prison
Westervelt, Daniel	Ens N J	"	10-23-1777
Westervelt, Jacob	N J	"	12-22-1777
Weston, Geo.	Del	"	5-4-1777
Weston, Job	Lt Mass	"	7-15-1783
Weston, Jonathn	Pvt 6 Mass	"	10-19-1777
Weston, Joseph	Pvt Conn	"	10-16-1775
Weston, Joseph Sr	Me	"	10-16-1775
Weston, Nathaniel	Pvt 15 Mass	"	9-12-1777
Wetherall, Ebenezer	Pvt Mass	"	8-10-1778
Wetherbee, James	Conn	"	1781
Weymouth, Archd	7 Mass	"	8-31-1777
Wharf, James	Capt Conn	"	6-18-1778
Wharton, Revel	Capt Va	"	1776
Wharton, Revil	Master	"	1776 At Sea
Wharton, Thomas Jr	Pa	"	1778
Whatley, William	Pvt Ga	"	1780
Wheat, Thomas Jr	N H	Killed	6-17-1775
Wheatley, Luther	Pvt N H	Died	9-30-1777
Wheatley, William	Cpl 1 Md	Killed	6-28-1778
Wheaton, Aaron	Pvt 15 Mass	Died	5-9-1778
Wheaton, Ceaser	Pvt R I	"	12-15-1779
Wheaton, Joseph	Pvt 7 Mass	"	10-1-1778
Wheeler, Thomas	Pvt 7 Md	"	10- 1778
Wheeler, Abraham	Capt Mass	"	1778
Wheeler, Amos	Sgt N H	Killed	6-17-1775
Wheeler, David	Cpl 10 NC	Died	5-29-1783
Wheeler, Ephraim	Pvt 7 Mass	"	10-30-1778
Wheeler, Francis	Pvt Mass	"	1778
Wheeler, Hezekiah	Mass	"	1780
Wheeler, Libens	Pvt N H	"	7-10-1778
Wheeler, Peter	Pa	"	7-3-1778
Wheeler, Philip Jr.	Capt Mass	"	12-3-1774
Wheeler, Timothy	Mass	"	1782
Wheeler, William	Pvt 5 N Y	"	7-19-1778
Wheeler, William	Pvt Conn	Killed	2-20-1778
Wheeler, William	Pvt 10 Mass	Died	4-11-1778
Wheelwright, David	Pvt Mass	"	5-28-1778
Whelin, Luke	Pvt 9 Mass	"	2-23-1778
Whilton, Moses	18 Cont	"	10-8-1776
Whimble, John	Pvt Cont	"	8-3-1776
Whipple, Daniel	Ens R I	"	1783
Whipple, Eleazer	N Y	"	1776
Whipple, Eleazer	Pvt Mass	Died	1776
Whipple, Elisia	N Y	"	1783
Whipple, Joseph	Capt Mass	"	1777
Whipple, Nathan	Pvt 2 NY	"	6-24-1779

Whitaker, John	Pvt SC	Killed	6-	1781
Whitaker, John	N J	Died		1781
Whitcomb, David	Pvt 10 Mass	"	4-28-1778	
Whitcomb, Isaac	N H	Killed	6-17-1775	
Whitcomb, Joshua	Mass	"	6-17-1775	
Whitcomb, Peter	N H	"	6-17-1775	
White	Cpl N C	Died	9-10-1782	
White, Abijah	Pvt Mass	"	4-2-1778	
White, Alex	Pvt Pa	"	4-26-1780	
White, Benjamin Jr	Mass	"	1783	
White, Ebenezer	Mass	"	1776	
White, Carpus	Pvt Mass	"	1777	
White, Elisha	Mass	"	1777	
White, Isaac	Pa	"	1781	
White, James	Pvt	"	1-27-1778	
White, James H	Pvt Conn	"	11-25-1778	
White, Jeremiah	Pvt 8 Mass	"	5-15-1777	
White, Jeremiah	Sgt Mass	"	1778	
White, Jno	Pvt 7 N C	"	8-	1778
White, Jno	Pvt 2 N C	"	5-16-1778	
White, Jno	Pvt 3 N C	"	4-12-1778	
White, Jno	Sgt 6 N C	"	1-6-1778	
White, Job	Mass	"	1781	
White, John	Pvt 5 Mass	"	3-5-1777	
White, John	Lt Mass	"	In War	
White, John	Maj NC	"	10-	1779
White, John	Pvt Pa	"	7-15-1776	
White, John	Pvt Can	Killed	1-2-1777	
White, John	Pvt N C	Died	4-12-1778	
White, John	Pvt N C	"	8-	1778
White, John	Pvt N C	"	5-16-1778	
White, Joseph	Capt Mass	"	1780	
White, Joseph	Conn	"	1776 Prison	
White, Lemuel	Conn	"	5-4-1780	
White, Moses	Pvt 10 Mass	"	9-13-1777	
White, Moses Jr	Conn	"	1783	
White, Nehemiah	Mass	"	1776	
White, Robert	Pvt 3 Mass	"	9-23-1780	
White, Samuel	Conn	Killed	7-6-1781	
White, Stephen	Pvt 4 N Y	Died	4-13-1777	
White, Stephen	Pvt SC	"	1781	
White, Stephen	Sgt 1 N C	"	6-28-1778	
White, Thomas	Mass	"	3-18-1778	
White, William	Pa	"	7-3-1778	
White, William	Pvt N C	"	5-26-1783	
White, William	Pvt N C	"	3-31-1778	
White, William	Capt Mass	"	10-	1781
White, William	Pvt N H	"	7-28-1778	
White, William	Lt Va	"	9-16-1777	
White, William	Lt Md	"	1780	
White, Wm	Pvt 10 N C	"	5-26-1783	
White, Wm	Pvt 1 N C	"	3-31-1778	
Whitehead, Gershom	Pvt Conn	"	7-28-1778	
Whitehead, John	Lt Mass	"	1783	

Whitely, John	1 Va	Killed	1779
Whitemore, Jonas	Pvt N J	Died	3-25-1777
Whithed, Daniel	Pvt Can	"	6-22-1777
Whithed, Elishna	Pvt Can	"	7-17-1777
Whiting, Charles	Capt Conn	"	5-15-1777
Whiting, Charles	Capt Conn	Killed	7-10-1779
Whiting, Gershon	Pvt 4 Mass	Died	11-20-1777
Whiting, James	Mass	"	1781
Whiting, James	Conn	"	1781
Whiting, Nathaniel	Pvt Mass	"	9-4-1779
Whiting, Stephen	Sgt 3 Mass	Killed	7-22-1777
Whiting, Thomas	Lt Col Va	Died	1781
Whitington, Elijah	Pvt 9 Mass	Killed	9-19-1777
Whitley, William	5 N C	Died	11-2-1777
Whitlock	N J	"	In War
Whitlock, John	Lt N J	Killed	2-13-1777
Whitman, Seth	Pvt Mass	Died	1783
Whitman, Welch	Que	"	4-8-1776
Whitmore, James	N H	Killed	6-17-1775
Whitmore, Nathaniel	Pvt 15 Mass	Died	12-1-1777
Whitman, Enoch (Enos)	Pvt Mass	"	10-1-1778
Whitman, John	Pvt 4 N Y	"	6- 1778
Whitman, Josiah	Pvt Mass	"	3-30-1778
Whitman, Seth	Pvt Mass	"	10-17-1783
Whitney, Abram	Pvt 8 Mass	"	7-8-1777
Whitney, Andrew	Pvt Mass	"	1778
Whitney, Caleb	Pvt 15 Mass	"	2-1-1778
Whitney, Daniel	Mass	"	1782
Whitney, Eliasaph	Conn	"	1- 1782
Whitney, Hezekiah	Pvt Mass	"	6-15-1778
Whitney, Israel	Pvt Mass	"	7- 1778
Whitney, John	Pvt 18 Cont	"	5-5-1776
Whitney, Jonas	Pvt Mass	"	1781
Whitney, Silas	Mass	"	1781
Whiton, Elias	Capt Mass	"	1778
Whiton, Enoch	Capt Mass	"	1777
Whiton, Stephen	Pa	"	7-3-1778
Whittlesey, Asaph	Col Pa	Killed	1778
Whittlesey, John	Conn	"	1781
Whittlesey, Joseph	Pa	Died	7-3-1778
Whittlesey, Stephen	Conn	"	1781
Whitton, Moses	Pvt 18 Cont	"	10-8-1776
Wibberham, Peter	Pvt 15 Mass	"	11-15-1779
Wickes, Richard	Navy	Killed	6-29-1776
Wickom, John	Ens 2 SC	"	10-9-1779
Wicks, Nathan	Lt R I	"	6-28-1778
Widger, Davis	Pvt Conn	Died	9-17-1777
Wier, John	SC	"	1780
Wiggins, Thomas	Pvt 5 N C	"	4-27-1778
Wigglesworth, Toppan	Pvt Mass	"	2-2-1781
Wight, Jonathan	Pvt Mass	"	3-13-1782
Wight, Simeon	Surg Mass	Killed	1777
Wigton, James	Pa	Died	7-3-1778

Wikoff, Garet W	Pvt N J	Died	4-10-1777	
Wikoff, William	N J	"	1782	
Wilborn, Esan	Pvt 3 NY	"	8-7-1780	
Wilbur, Uriel	Pvt R I	"	2-30-1778	
Wilcocks, Shumar	Pvt Conn	"	10-19-1778	
Wilcox, Esen	Pa	"	7-3-1778	
Wilcox, Geo	Cpl 5 N C	"	11-4-1777	
Wilcox, James	Pvt 3 Md	"	3-10-1780	
Wilcox, John Sr	N J	"	9-22-1776	
Wilcox, John	N Y	"	1781	
Wilcox, Obadiah	N H	"	1780	
Wilcox, William	Lt Conn	"	1775	
Wilder, Asa	Lt Mass	"	1780	
Wildey, Thomas	Pvt N Y	Killed	1776	
Wildman, James	Pvt Conn	Died	1-15-1782	
Wiley, Aldrich	Lt 7 Mass	Killed	10-7-1777	
Wiley, Edward	Pvt Conn	Died	5-14-1778	
Wiley, John	Sgt 8 Mass	Killed	7-7-1777	
Wiley, Reuben	Pvt Pa	Died	9-21-1776	
Wilham, Thomas	Pvt 11 Mass	Killed	7-7-1777	
Wilkerson, Geo	Pvt 5 Md	"	9-11-1777	
Wilkeson, John	Pvt Md	Died	1-15-1781	
Wilkins, Bray	Sgt Mass	"	1775	
Wilkins, Burrel	Pvt 10 N C	"	11- 1781	
Wilkins, Daniel	Lt Mass	"	1776	
Wilkins, Sylvester	Pvt N H	"	11-7-1777	
Wilkins, William H	Pvt N H	"	6-22-1778	
Wilkinson, James	Del	"	4-1-1781	
Wilkinson, John	Lt Col Pa	"	1782	
Wilkinson, John	N J	"	2-17-1777	
Wilkinson, Thos	Pvt SC	"	4- 1781	
Wilkinson, William	Pvt 3 N J	"	1-28-1777	
Willagan, David	Pvt 1 NY	"	2-10-1777	
Willard, Benjamin	Sgt 15 Mass	"	1-22-1778	
Willard, Joseph	Lt Mass	"	3-17-1777	
Willard, Maxamillian	Pvt 15 Mass	"	10-23-1777	
Willard, Nathanl	Pvt 10 Mass	"	6-4-1778	
Willard, Simeon	Sgt Mass	"	4-9-1777	
Willcox, Daniel Jr	Mass	"	4-10-1776	
Willcutt, Joseph	Mass	"	1782	
Willet, Charles	Pvt Md	"	9-19-1782	
Willet, Joseph	Pvt Mass	"	11-7-1777	
Willet, Nathaniel	Pvt 10 Mass	"	2-10-1778	
William, Alexander	Maj Gen NY	"	1-15-1783	
William, Anibel	Mass	"	1781	
William, Chas	Pvt 1 NY	"	9-29-1778	
William, Cochrane	Lt Mass	"	1778	At Sea
William, Edward Pyson	Maj Mass	"	5-29-1777	
William, James	Col Va	"	1780	
William, Reuben	Pvt R I	"	12-1-1777	
William, Roach	Lt N C	"	1780	
William, William	SC	"	10-6-1776	
William, Wilmot	Capt Md	Killed	11-14-1782	
Williams, Abraham	Pvt N Y	Died	1780	Prisoner

Williams	Col SC	Died	10-7-1780
Williams, Capt	Capt 6 Md	Killed	8-18-1780
Williams, Abijah Sr	Conn	Died	3-3-1781
Williams, Abraham	Mass	"	7-10-1781
Williams, Azibah	Pa	"	7-3-1778
Williams, Benjamin	Capt Mass	"	1776
Williams, Charles	Pvt N C	"	5-15-1778
Williams, David	Pvt 15 Mass	"	1-15-1778
Williams, Dudley	Pvt 10 N C	"	1- 1778
Williams, Ebenezer	Conn	"	8-22-1780
Williams, Ebenezer	Mass	"	1775
Williams, Edward	Conn	"	8-4-1777 Prison
Williams, P Edward	Maj 3 Mass	"	5-27-1777
Williams, Eleazer	Conn	"	9-4-1778
Williams, Elihu Jr	Pa	"	7-3-1778
Williams, Francis	Pvt 2 NY	"	4-3-1779
Williams, Henry	Lt Conn	Killed	9-6-1781
Williams, Isaac	Del	Died	9-10-1781
Williams, James	Sgt Mass	"	1781
Williams, James	Col SC	Killed	1780
Williams, James	Capt N C	Died	5-2-1778
Williams, James	Capt 4 NC	Killed	10-7-1780
Williams, Jas	Sgt 10 NC	Died	9- 1778
Williams, Jas	2 N Y	"	8-10-1778
Williams, Job	Pvt 15 Mass	"	8-10-1778
Williams, John	Pa	"	7-3-1778
Williams, John P	Capt N C	"	1776
Williams, John	Pvt Mass	"	1-12-1778
Williams, John	Pvt Conn	"	2-19-1778
Williams, John	Mass	"	1783
Williams, John	Capt Conn	"	9-6-1781
Williams, John	Capt Conn	Killed	In War
Williams, John	Pvt 4 NY	Died	3-18-1778
Williams, John P	Del	"	9-3-1782
Williams, John	Va	"	In War
Williams, John	Capt NY	"	1780
Williams, John Pugh	Capt N C	"	1776
Williams, Jonas	Pvt NY	"	1780
Williams, Joseph	Md	Killed	11- 1781
Williams, Joseph	Pvt Mass	Died	7-13-1778
Williams, Joshua	Pvt Mass	"	7-2-1778
Williams, Nathan	Lt 7 Md	Killed	8-16-1780
Williams, Rufus	Pa	Died	7-3-1778
Williams, Samuel	Lt Conn	"	4-6-1782
Williams, Solomon	Rev Conn	"	2-28-1776
Williams, Thomas	Pvt 5 NC	"	7-20-1777
Williams, Thomas	Mass	"	1776
Williams, Thomas	Conn	Killed	9-6-1781
Williams, Thomas	Pvt Mass	Died	9-22-1779
Williams, Thophis	Pvt 7 N C	"	3-21-1778
Williams, William	Mass	"	1775
Williams, William	Pvt N J	"	10-4-1777
Williams, William	Pvt Conn	"	4-23-1778
Williams, Zepha	Pvt 3 Md	Killed	8-16-1780

Williamson, Jesse	Pvt Mass	Died	4-30-1777
Williamson, Richard	Pvt 3 N J	"	9-11-1777
Williamson, William	N J	"	1-18-1780
Willing, John	Pvt Md	"	12-15-1781
Willis, Ebenezer		"	5- 1777 Prison
Willis, Elijah	Sgt Mass	"	1775
Willis, John	Pvt Mass	"	4-29-1777
Willis, Wm	Del	Killed	5-1-1781
Williston, John	Mass	Died	1776
Williston, John	Mass	"	1783
Willmarth, Nehemiah	Mass	"	1780
Willmot, William	Capt Md	"	11-14-1782
Willowly, Jno	Pvt 8 N C	"	2-14-1778
Wills, John	Pvt 5 N Y	"	12- 1779
Willson, John	Pvt 8 Mass	"	3-26-1778
Willson, Jonathan	Capt Mass	Killed	4-19-1775
Willson, Moses	Pvt 18 Cont	Died	4-8-1776
Wilmarth, Thomas	Cpl Mass	"	1779
Wilmore, John	Pvt Va	"	1779
Wilmot	Capt Md	Killed	In War
Wilson	Lt Va	"	9-9-1781
Wilson, Barney		Died	7-21-1781 Prison
Wilson, David	R I	Killed	12-31-1775 Que
Wilson, George	Lt Col Pa	Died	1779
Wilson, George	Lt Col N J	"	1777
Wilson, Henry Wright	Surg Va	"	1778
Wilson, James	N H	"	4-15-1777
Wilson, James	Pvt Va	"	2-15-1777 Prison
Wilson, Jno	Pvt 1 N C	"	2-21-1778
Wilson, John	Pvt SC	"	1781
Wilson, John	Lt Va	"	9-8-1781
Wilson, John	Pa	"	7-3-1778
Wilson, John	N C	"	1779
Wilson, John	Pvt N J	"	1-18-1777
Wilson, John	Pvt N H	"	1783
Wilson, John	Lt 4 Va	Killed	9-8-1781
Wilson, Jonathan	Capt Mass	"	4-19-1775
Wilson, Joseph	Pvt N H	Died	1783
Wilson, Joseph	Pvt 1 Conn	"	3-8-1782
Wilson, Nathaniel	Lt Mass	"	1778
Wilson, Nicholas	Pvt R I	"	In War
Wilson, Parker	Pa	Killed	7-3-1778
Wilson, Robert	Surg 6 N C	Died	10-28-1777
Wilson, Robert	Pa	"	1781
Wilson, Thomas	Del	"	1783
Wilson, Thomas	Del	"	1778
Wilson, Titus	Pvt N H	"	7-7-1777
Wilson, William	Pvt 6 Mass	"	2-28-1778
Wilson, William	Capt Va	"	1780
Wilson, William	Pvt Va	"	2-15-1777
Wilson, William	Pvt 2 Md	Killed	8-16-1780
Wilson, William	Pvt Mass	Died	1778
Wilton, William	Pvt Mass	"	12-13- 1777
Willson, Alexander	Lt Can	"	4-26-1780

Willson, Ambrose	Pvt Can	Killed	9-4-1777	
Willson, Henry	Pvt Mass	Died	4-29-1777	
Willson, John	Pvt N C	"	2-21-1778	
Willson, John	Pvt 3 N J	"	1-13-1777	
Willson, John	Pvt 7 Mass	"	5-30-1778	
Willson, Moses	Mass	"	10-31-1776	
Willson, Robt	Surg N C	"	10-28-1777	
Willson, Samuel	Pvt Mass	"	10-19-1777	
Willowby, John	Pvt N C	"	2- 1778	
Willoughby, Jones	Mass	"	1783	
Wilmarth, Moses	Capt Mass	"	11-16-1779	
Wilmarth, Thomas Jr	Pvt Mass	"	11-26-1779	
Wilmott, William	Capt Md	Killed	11-14-1782	Last Killed in Rev.
Wiltshire, William	Sgt Mass	Died	1-1- 1780	
Wimble, Samuel	Pvt 13 Mass	"	5-20-1777	
Winans, John	N J	"	1783	
Winburn, Jno	Lt 7 N C	"	11- 1777	
Winchel, Ira	Pvt Conn	"	8-16-1777	
Winchell, Azariah	Sgt Mass	"	6-9-1776	
Winchell, David	Pvt 13 Mass	"	4-27-1778	
Windsor, John	Del	"	10-18-1778	
Wine, Jacob	Pvt Va	"	2-15-1777	
Wineler, H. John	Pvt Pa	"	10-27-1779	
Wing, Joseph	Pvt Conn	"	6-5-1778	
Wing, Samuel	Mass	"	1777	
Wing, Sylvanus	Mass	"	1778	
Winn, Abiather	N H	"	8-24-1783	
Winship, Isaac Sr	Mass	"	1783	
Winship, Jason	Mass	Killed	4-19-1775	
Winship, Samuel Sr	Mass	Died	1780	
Winship, Simon	Pvt Mass	"	1780	
Winslow, Benjamin	Sgt Mass	"	1776	
Winslow, Edward	Pvt Conn	"	11-7-1778	
Winslow, John	Mass	"	1777	
Winslow, John	Capt Mass	"	1778	
Winslow, Kenelm	Mass	"	8-13-1780	
Winslow, Thomas	Mass	"	1782	
Winslow, William	Pvt 7 Mass	"	3-22-1778	
Wise, Adam	Pvt Pa	"	1781	
Wise, Jno	Pvt 8 N C	"	3-6-1777	
Wise, Samuel	Maj 3 SC	Killed	10-9-1779	
Wisner, Gabriel	Ens Del	"	7-22-1779	
Wisner, John	Capt N Y	Died	1778	
Witham, Asa		"	6-7-1777	Prison
Witham, Jedediah	Pvt 15 Mass	Killed	6-28-1778	
Witham, Joseph	Pvt 2 N Y	Died	6-20-1778	
Witham, William	N Y	"	1781	
Withers, James	Pvt 6 Md	"	2-21-1778	
Witherspoon, James	Maj N J	"	10-4-1777	
Witherspoon, John	N C	"	11-7-1778	
Withington, Elijah Sr	Mass	"	3-17-1778	
Withington, Peter	Capt Md	"	1777	

Withington, Samuel	Sgt Mass	Died	1781
Witt, Ebenezer	Capt Mass	"	7-5-1781
Wobben, Isaac	Pvt 5 Mass	"	8-1-1777
Woedtke, Baron de	Brig Gen Ger	"	7-28-1776
Wogen, Jacob	Fifer Pa	"	1783
Wolcott, John	N H	"	1783
Wolcott, John	Pvt N H	"	1783
Wolcot, Garshom	Pvt Conn	"	11-28-1782
Wolfarth, Martin	N J	"	1780
Wood, Benjamin	N H	Killed	6-17-1775
Wood, Cornelius	Pvt 6 Mass	Died	7-18-1777
Wood, Ephraim	Mass	"	11-8-1783
Wood, Ephraim	Mass	"	12-4-1781
Wood, Ezekiel	N Y	"	1781
Wood, Ezekiel	Surg Mass	"	1782
Wood, Jonathan	Capt Pa	"	1777
Wood, Jonathan	Conn	"	12-13-1781
Wood, Jonathan	Mass	"	6-19-1781
Wood, Joseph	N H	"	6-11-1779
Wood, Joseph	Mass	"	7-21-1775
Wood, Judah	Lt Mass	"	3-22-1783
Wood, Nathan	Mass	"	1777
Wood, Nicholas	Md	"	3-22-1778
Wood, Oliver	N H	Killed	6-17-1775
Wood, Primus	Pvt Mass	Died	9-13-1778
Wood, Robt	Lt 2 N Y	"	3-10-1777
Wood, Samuel	Pvt 15 Mass	"	3-16-1778
Wood, Samuel	Pvt Conn	"	8-17-1777
Wood, Silas	Pvt 5 Mass	"	11-29-1778
Wood, Thomas	Pvt 3 Md	"	4-3-1778
Wood, Toplet	7 Mass	"	8-24-1781
Wood, William	Pvt 1 Md	"	8-19-1777
Woodall, William	Pvt Md	"	1780
Woodam, Robert	Pvt 7 Md	Killed	8-16-1780
Woodberry, John	Pvt 5 Mass	Died	3-2-1778
Woodbridge, Christopher	Conn	"	9-6-1781
Woodbridge, Henry	Conn	"	9-6-1781
Woodbridge, John	Maj Mass	"	1782
Woodbridge, Russell	Capt Conn	"	11-5-1783
Woodbury, Benjamin	Pvt Mass	"	1781
Woodbury, Jonathan	Pvt N H	"	1776
Woodbury, Peter	Sgt Mass	"	1775
Woodford, William	Brig Gen Va	"	11-13-1780
Woodford, William	Col N Y	"	1780
Woodhouse, William	Capt Va	"	1783
Woodhull, Nathaniel	Gen N Y	"	9-20-1776
Woodin, Samuel	Pvt Conn	Killed	7-5-1779
Woodin, Silas	Pvt Conn	"	7-5-1779
Woodman, Benjamin	Pvt 5 Mass	Died	3-25-1778
Woodman, Moses	Pvt 10 Mass	"	3-12-1777
Woodringer, William	Pa	"	7-3-1778
Woodruff, Aaron	N J	"	8-29-1780
Woodruff, Jno	Pvt 10 N C	"	9-8-1781
Woods, Andrew	Va	"	1781
Woods, David	Pvt 7 Md	Killed	8-16-1780
Woods, Elisha	Pvt Conn	Died	8-23-1781

Woods, Henry	Pvt 15 Mass	Killed	7-19-1777
Woods, Joseph	Pvt 7 Md	"	8-16-1780
Woods, Nathaniel	Pvt 7 Mass	Died	1776
Woods, Solomon	Conn	Killed	In War
Woods, Solomon	Mass	Died	5-1-1783
Woods, William	Pvt Va	"	1782
Woodson, David	Pvt 10 Mass	"	3-1-1778
Woodthey, John	Pvt 3 Md	"	2-12-1778
Woodward, Caleb	Pvt 10 N C	"	9- 1778
Woodward, Elijah	Pvt Mass	"	11-1-1777
Woodward, John	Pvt 9 Mass	"	10-17-1778
Woodward, Joseph	Lt Mass	"	2-2-1778
Woodward, Joshua	Pvt Mass	"	11-21-1776
Woodward, Lee	Pvt Conn	"	2-20-1777
Woodward, Richard	Pvt 6 Md	"	1-26-1778
Woodward, Samuel	Mass	"	1782
Woodward, Thomas	Capt SC	Killed	5-12-1779
Woodward, Thomas P	Pvt Conn	Died	8-31-1777
Woodworth, Simeon	Pvt	"	6-10-1778
Wooldrick, Fritz	N C	"	11-2-1781
Wooling, Mason	Pvt 6 Md	"	10-23-1778
Woolsey, Josiah	Pvt N Y	"	1778
Wooster, David	Brig Gen Conn	"	5-3- 1777
Wooton, William	Pvt 2 N C	"	4-21-1778
Wooton, Wm	Sgt 8 N C	"	5-1-1778
Wolcutt, Asabel	Pvt 1 Conn	"	8-24-1782
Wolf, Peter	R I	Killed	12-31-1775
Word, Charles	Pvt Va	"	1780
Work, James	Mass	Died	1783
Work, James	Sgt. N Y	"	1783
Worsley, Benjamin	Pvt 7 Mass	Killed	11-11-1778
Worth, Joseph	Lt 2 N C	Died	4-6-1777
Worthen, Ezekiel	Maj N H	"	10-16-1783
Worthington, Matthew	Pvt N H	"	1783
Worthington, Robert	Va	"	1775
Wotton, William	Sgt N C	"	5-1-1778
Wright	Mass	"	1775
Wright, Adam	Mass	"	1776
Wright, Cuff	Pvt Conn	"	8-4-1778
Wright, Edward	Pvt Md	"	3-4-1783
Wright, Elisha	Pvt Conn	"	3-5-1778
Wright, Elizur	Conn	"	1781
Wright, Ephriam	Mass	"	9-14- 1775
Wright, Jacob	Capt N Y	Killed	1778
Wright, James	Del	Died	10-8-1777
Wright, James	Pvt 4 N J	"	5-22-1778
Wright, John	Pvt N C	"	1779
Wright, John	Mass	"	1775
Wright, John	Pvt Pa	"	1777
Wright, John	Pvt 4 N J	"	3- 1778
Wright, Jonathan	Pvt Mass	"	3-25-1778
Wright, Joseph Jr	Pvt Mass	"	2-11-1777
Wright, Josiah	Mass	"	1783

Wright, Obadiah	Pvt Pa	Died	7-31-1776	
Wright, Richard	Cpl 3 Md	"	9-24-1779	
Wright, Samuel	Pvt Md	"	1-20-1782	
Wright, Thomas	Pvt 15 Mass	"	1-25-1778	
Wright, William	Pvt 3 Md	"	11-20-1777	
Wrist, Thomas	Pvt Mass	"	3-14-1778	
Wyan, Jabez	Pvt Mass	Killed	4-19-1775	
Wyampy, Charles	Pvt Conn	Died	8-14-1777	
Wyatt, John	Sgt 1 N C	"	4-29-1777	
Wyath, Ebenezer	Pvt Pa	"	1779	
Wyley, Mason	Pvt Mass	"	9-8-1778	
Wylie, Samuel	Sgt	"	1777	At Sea
Wylie, Samuel	Pvt Va	Killed	1781	
Wylie, Samuel	Sgt Me	Died	1777	
Wyllis, Samuel	Maj Gen	Killed	1777	
Wyman, Amaziah	Pvt 6 Mass	Died	7-27-1779	
Wyman, Jabez	Mass	Killed	4-19-1775	
Wyman, Jesse	Sgt Mass	Died	1782	
Wyman, Nathaniel	Mass	Killed	4-19-1775	
Wyman, Silas	Pvt 15 Mass	"	8-5-1779	
Wyman, Thomas	Pvt Mass	Died	11-21-1776	
Wynn, Thomas	Pa	"	1782	
Wynns, Benjamin	Col N C	"	1777	

Y

Yale, Ozias	Pa	Died	7-3-1778	
Yarbarough, Jas	Pvt 6 N C	"	1779	
Yates, Richard	Pvt 2 Md	"	9-15-1778	
Yepler, Henry	Pvt Pa	"	1777	
Yohant, John	Pvt Can	"	7-20-1777	
Yonkins, Geo	Pvt 1 N Y	"	9-4-1777	
York, Amos	Pvt Conn	"	1777	
York, William	Pvt 7 Md	"	9-14-1778	
Yorke, Edward	Capt Pa	"	1781	At Sea
Yost, Casper	Maj Pa	"	1782	
Young, Daniel	Pvt 6 Md	"	11-21-1778	
Young, Isaac	Pvt 10 NC	"	2-13-1778	
Young, Henry	Pvt SC	Killed	5- 1781	
Young, James	N J	Died	9-20-1783	
Young, John	Pvt Mass	"	4-2-1778	
Young, Martin	Pvt Pa	"	1777	
Young, Thomas	Pvt Pa	"	1780	
Young, William	Pvt 6 NC	"	2-28-1778	
Youngman, Ebenezer	N H	Killed	6-17-1775	
Yves, David	France	Died	1781	

Z

Zabdiel, Sampson	Mass	Killed	1776
Zeager, Thos	Pvt 1 NY	Died	10-13-1778
Zell, John	Pa	"	1781
Zimmer, Jacob	N Y	Killed	1782
Zimmerman, Christopher	Pvt Pa	Died	1782

CPSIA information can be obtained at www.ICGtesting.com
Printed in the USA
LVOW12s1125220714

395369LV00014B/311/P

9 780806 302751